LUTHER'S *HELIAND*

BERKELEY INSIGHTS IN LINGUISTICS AND SEMIOTICS

Irmengard Rauch
General Editor

Vol. 80

PETER LANG
New York • Washington, D.C./Baltimore • Bern
Frankfurt • Berlin • Brussels • Vienna • Oxford

Timothy Blaine Price

Luther's *Heliand*

Resurrection of the Old Saxon Epic in Leipzig

PETER LANG
New York • Washington, D.C./Baltimore • Bern
Frankfurt • Berlin • Brussels • Vienna • Oxford

Library of Congress Cataloging-in-Publication Data

Price, Timothy Blaine,
 Luther's Heliand: resurrection of the Old Saxon
 epic in Leipzig / Timothy Blaine Price.
 p. cm. — (Berkeley insights in linguistics and semiotics; vol. 80)
 Includes bibliographical references and index.
 1. Heliand—Influence. 2. Old Saxon language. 3. Universitätsbibliothek
 Leipzig. 4. Luther, Martin, 1483–1546. I. Title.
 PF4000.P75   839'.411—dc23   2011026754
 ISBN 978-1-4331-1394-9
 ISSN 0893-6935

Bibliographic information published by **Die Deutsche Nationalbibliothek**.
Die Deutsche Nationalbibliothek lists this publication in the "Deutsche
Nationalbibliografie"; detailed bibliographic data is available
on the Internet at http://dnb.d-nb.de/.

The paper in this book meets the guidelines for permanence and durability
of the Committee on Production Guidelines for Book Longevity
of the Council of Library Resources.

© 2011 Peter Lang Publishing, Inc., New York
29 Broadway, 18th floor, New York, NY 10006
www.peterlang.com

All rights reserved.
Reprint or reproduction, even partially, in all forms such as microfilm,
xerography, microfiche, microcard, and offset strictly prohibited.

Printed in Germany

Contents

Acknowledgments xi
Symbols, Abbreviations, and Terminology xiii

Part I: Materials and Modern Theories

1. Issues and Solutions

1.1 Project Background 3
1.2 Scope and Direction 4
1.3 Considerations 5
1.4 Methodology 6

2. Manuscripts and Fragments

2.1 Discovery of the Manuscript Fragment 13
2.1.1 The Six Extant Manuscripts 15
2.1.2 Relevance of the Discovery 18
2.2 *Stammbaum* Theories 19
2.2.1 Taeger's Manuscript Tree 20
2.2.2 Baesecke's Manuscript Tree 23
2.2.3 Manuscript *Stammbaum* Revised in Light of MS L 26
2.3 Additional Evidence Linking MSS P and L 29

3. Question of Authorship

3.1 Significance of Identifying the *Heliand* Poet 33
3.1.1 Parameters and Considerations 33
3.2 Evidence at Hand 34
3.2.1 Historical Clues 34
3.2.2 Description of the Poet from the *Prefaces* 40
3.3 Current Theories: If not "Who?", then "Where?" 41
3.3.1 Fulda and Werden 42
3.3.2 Westphalia 47
3.3.3 Beyond the Elbe 53
3.3.4 Verden and others 57

4. Novel Tools vs. Standardized Error

4.1 Overview of Standard Works 63
4.1.1 Otto Behaghel 65
4.1.2 Eduard Sievers 69
4.1.3 Johann Andreas Schmeller 76
4.2 New Transcriptions to Overcome Old Errors 82
4.2.1 Presentations: Overlapping Texts 83
4.2.1.1 Parallel MSS C and M 83
4.2.1.2 Parallel MSS M, C, and P 87
4.2.1.3 Comparison of *Heliand* and Luther's Bible translations 92

Part II: Historical Accounts of an Old Saxon Codex in Leipzig

5. A Short History of Leipzig

5.1 From Monastery to University 105
5.1.1 The Paulinerkirche 105
5.1.2 Early Protestant Movement in Prague 106
5.1.3 University of Leipzig Established 107
5.1.4 University Expansion 108
5.2 Library Holdings in the *Paulinum* 110

6. Latin *Prefaces* to an Ancient Germanic Gospel

6.1 The Latin *Prefaces* 113
6.1.1 Johann Georg von Eccard 113
6.1.2 Linking the Latin *Prefaces* to the Old Saxon *Heliand* 116
6.1.3 *Prefaces*' Proof of Authenticity 117
6.2 Georg Fabricius: Scholar, Educator, Linchpin 118
6.2.1 Matthias Flacius Illyricus, Protestant Firebrand and Printer ... 119
6.2.2 Fabricius' Earliest Reference 124
6.2.3 Brotherhood of Knowledge 127
6.2.4 Overlooked Fabricius Reference 131
6.3 Conclusions from Fabricius' Letters 136

Part III: Reformation Rumors of an Old Saxon Bible

7. Prologue: the Rumors Recorded 141

7.1 Introduction to the Rumors 141
7.1.1 The Reformers' Interest 141

7.1.2 From Fabricius to Eccard 143
7.2 Joachim Feller: Bridge between Periods 143
7.2.1 Pierre le Gallois, Rumor Intermediary 145
7.2.2 Polycarp Leyser, Rumor Publisher but not Author 147
7.2.3 Rumor Resources Revealed 148
7.3 Organizational Note 149
7.4 Terminology 151

8. The Education of Martin Chemnitz

8.1 Biography of Martin Chemnitz 153
8.1.1 First Studies under Melanchthon 153
8.1.2 Königsberg Work and Studies 154
8.1.3 Second Studies under Melanchthon 156
8.2 Circumstances of Chemnitz' Report 156
8.2.1 Dates to Consider 156
8.3 Chemnitz' Contact with Melanchthon 157
8.3.1 First Period in Wittenberg 158
8.3.2 Second Period in Wittenberg 158
8.3.3 Third Period at Wittenberg 159
8.4 Dating via Parallel Historical Evidence 160
8.4.1 Chemnitz' Reliability 161
8.4.2 Devil's Advocate: Arguing Hearsay Evidence 161
8.4.3 Motivation for Reward 162
8.4.3.1 Greater Risk than Reward 162
8.4.3.2 Possibility of Charitable Selfishness 164
8.4.3.3 Easier Means to Reward 165
8.4.4 Chemnitz' Knowledge of Latin 166

9. The Enigmatic Ioannes Manlius

9.1 Rumor of a Luther Codex 167
9.1.1 Source of the Rumor 169
9.2 Identifying *Ioannes Manlius* 169
9.2.1 Similar Names in Biographical Resources 170
9.2.1.1 Hans Mandl 170
9.2.1.2 Jakob Mennel 171
9.2.1.3 Johannes Jacobus Manlius de Bosco 171
9.2.1.4 Einer aus Ansbach, einer aus Auerbach 172
9.2.2 Establishing working dates 173
9.2.2.1 Wittenberg Matriculation 174

9.2.2.2 Basel Matriculation 177
9.2.2.3 Return to Mittelfranken 178
9.2.2.4 A New Life in Slovenia 180
9.2.2.5 Banishment from Hapsburg Lands 183
9.3 Implications of Manlius-Menlin-Mandl 184

Part IV: Dating and Verifying the Rumor Reports

10. Chemnitz' Report Dissected

10.1 Significance for Dating the Rumors 189
10.2 Published Report 189
10.2.1 *Clusivity*: Chemnitz as an 'Eyewitness' 190
10.2.2 Finite Equivalents to Latin Infinitives 191
10.2.3 The Extended Modifier 193
10.2.4 Triangulating the *monotessaron*, Melanchthon, and Leipzig 193
10.3 Conclusions about Chemnitz' Report 195

11. Clues from Manlius

11.1 Differential between Two Rumor Reports 197
11.1.1 Assertions about Luther 199
11.1.2 Anonymous source(s) 200
11.2 Historical Hints at Manlius' Source 203
11.2.1 Concurrent reigns of an emperor and a king 205
11.2.2 Private information about the Emperor 206
11.2.3 The Emperor's counselor Granvelle 209
11.2.4 Manlius' link to Camerarius 212
11.3 Conclusions about Manlius' report 215

Part V: Religious Politics of a Secular Empire

12. An 'Ace Up the Sleeve' in a Religious War

12.1 Imperial Reaction to the Reformation 221
12.2 Threats from Worms 221
12.2.1 Breaking the Revolt of Ghent 224
12.3 Lead-up to the Schmalkaldic War 226
12.3.1 The Division of Leipzig 226
12.3.2 Ernestine Saxony 227
12.3.3 Albertine Saxony 227

12.4 Battle of Mühlberg 228
12.4.1 Power Swap in Wittenberg 229
12.4.2 Continuing Wettin Influence 231
12.5 So-Called 'Peace' in Augsburg 232
12.5.1 Ferdinand I's New Approach 233
12.5.2 Revival of Tactics by Philip II of Spain 234
12.6 The *Heliand* as Response to Anti-Protestant Policies 235

13. The Codex from Naumburg

13.1 Hypothesizing **Codex L* 237
13.1.1 Links between Leipzig and Naumburg 239
13.1.2 Previous Search for Evidence in Naumburg 241
13.1.3 Alternative Hypothesis 242
13.2 Saxony's *Fürstenschulen* 243
13.2.1 The Library at Pforta 245
13.3 The Cistercians at Pforta 247
13.3.1 Legacy of the Cistercians 248
13.3.2 Instruments of *Ostkolonisation* 250
13.3.3 Cistercian Proselytism: an Example 252
13.4 Before Pforta 254
13.4.1 Ottonian Homeland 254
13.4.2 Quedlinburg, Gandersheim, Magdeburg 257
13.4.3 Ottonian Links to the *Heliand* and Old Saxon Genesis 259

14. A More Easterly Provenance?

14.1 Great Contribution from a Small Fragment 267
14.2 Luther and the Leipzig *Heliand* Codex 268
14.3 Ottonian Connection to the *Heliand* Provenance 269
14.3.1 MS M via Matilda of Ringelheim 270
14.3.2 MS C via Mathilde II of Essen and Matilda of Ringelheim 270
14.3.3 MS C via Mathilde II of Essen and Bernward of Hildesheim 272
14.4 The *Heliand*'s Eastern Genesis 273
14.5 Poet's Use of Something besides Tatian 273
14.5 Remaining Questions 274

Bibliography 277

Appendix A

A.1: Letter to Meurer: 7 January 1545 (17–18) 287
A.2: Letter to Meurer: 16 September 1545 (21–22) 288
A.3: Letter to Meurer: 24 November 1545 (22–24) 289
A.4: Letter to Meurer: 18 December 1545 (23–24) 290
A.5: Letter to Andreas Fabricius: 24 March 1561 (16–17) 291
A.6: Letter from Christoph von Carlowitz to Georg Fabricius: 19 October 1556 (418) 292

Appendix B

B.1: Extract from Feller's *Catalogus codicum manuscriptorum Bibliothecae Paulinae, Dedicatio* 295
B.2: Extract from Feller's *Catalogus codicum manuscriptorum Bibliothecae Paulinae, Praefatio* 297

Appendix C

C.1: Extract from Chemnitz' *Harmoniae evangelicae* (Part I, Prolegomenon, Caput 2, 4–8) 299

Appendix D

D.1: Deutsches Biographisches Archiv entry for Ioannes Manlius 301
D.2: Excerpt from Manlius' *Locorum communium collectanea* (Tomus III, 99–102) 303
D.3: Excerpt from Manlius' *Locorum communium collectanea* (Tomus II, 283–285) 306
D.4: Names resembling 'Manlius' in *Album Academicae Vitebergensis* 308
D.5: 'Johannes Manlius' in *Die Matrikel der Universität Basel* (II. Bd., pp. 130–135, 623–625) 312

Index 313

Acknowledgments

I would like to thank Prof. Irmengard Rauch for her direction in conducting and publishing this research. I am also grateful to Prof. Thomas F. Shannon and Prof. John Lindow for correcting and commenting on the dissertation that served as the basis of this book. Furthermore, I would like to express my gratitude to Universität Leipzig for the opportunity to pursue my research topic there, and in particular to Drs. Ulrich Johannes Schneider and Christof Mackert of the Universitätsbibliothek Leipzig for providing me with a digitization of MS L, thereby allowing me to discover a small (but hardly insignificant) and heretofore overlooked detail. I am grateful also for the funding provided by the Fulbright Program, whose mission to build bridges between cultures I find of greatest importance. Similarly, I thank the German Department and the Graduate Division at the University of California, Berkeley for their support.

Most of all, I am indebted my wife, Kimberly, for accompanying me on an adventure halfway around the world (twice!), as well as for her skills in editing, organizing, advising, encouraging, and motivating—all while working full-time and pursuing her own education. I am indeed grateful for her.

Symbols, Abbreviations, and Terminology

AAV	*Album Academiae Vitebergensis*
ADB	*Allgemeine deutsche Biographie*
BBKL	*Biographisch-Bibliographisches Kirchenlexikon*
BSB	Bayerische Staatsbibliothek
DBA	*Deutsches biographisches Archiv*
DNB	Deutsche Nationalbibliothek
Gk.	Greek
Gmc.	Germanic
Goth.	Gothic
IE	(Proto-)Indo-European
Lat.	Latin
MHG	Middle High German (German: *mhd.*)
ModE	Modern English
MS(S)	manuscript(s)
NDB	*Neue deutsche Biographie*
NHG	New High German (German: *nhd.*)
OE	Old English (German: *ags.*)
OHG	Old High German (German: *ahd.*)
OS	Old Saxon (German: *as.*, *asächs.*)
PND	Personennamendatei
PPN	PND-Indentifikations-Nummer
Prefaces	*Praefatio* + *Versus*, as printed by Illyricus
RE	Recording Event, i.e. when y recorded the TE
TE	Transfer Event, i.e. when x spoke about the document
terminus ante quem	date before which an event must have occurred
terminus post quem	date after which an event must have occurred
UBL	Universitätsbibliothek Leipzig
WBIS	*World Biographical Information System*
WGerm.	Common West Germanic
/x/	phonemic representation
<x>	graphemic representation
x, y, z	notation variables (used only in front matter lists)

Extant manuscripts and manuscript fragments

C	London *Heliand* manuscript (Cottonianus)
L	Leipzig *Heliand* manuscript fragment (Lipsiensis)
M	Munich *Heliand* manuscript (Monacensis)
P	Prague *Heliand* manuscript fragment (Pragensis)
S	Straubing *Heliand* manuscript fragment (Straubingensis)
V	Vatican *Heliand* manuscript fragment (Vaticani)

Hypothetical manuscript stages

**O	original *Heliand* composition, i.e. poet's product
*A	hypothetical archetype from which all extant MSS stem
*C	hypothetical ancestor of MS C
*Ch	Document referenced by Chemnitz
*Codex L	hypothetical full *Heliand* codex once present in Leipzig
*Essen	hypothetical ancestor of *C
*F	Baesecke's notation; split here into *F_f and *I for discussion
*F_f	document referenced by Fabricius
*I	document from which Flacius Illyricus copied his *Prefaces*
*L	hypothetical matrix of MS L
*L_m	document referenced by Manlius
*M/S, etc.	hypothetical ancestor of the two listed MSS
*PL, etc.	hypothetical immediate source of the two listed MSS
*V	hypothetical ancestor of MS V
G	OS version of *Genesis*
g	extant fragment of OS *Genesis*
g_b	fragment of OS *Genesis*, extant in the OE *Genesis B*
$h_{1,2}$	hypothetical redaction(s) of the *Heliand* original
I	*Prefaces* as printed by Illyricus, replaces Baesecke's F notation
$p_{A, B, C}$	hypothetical redaction(s) of the Latin *Praefatio* and *Versus*
x (y + z)	document x with subparts y and z

Part I:

Materials and Modern Theories

1. Issues and Solutions

1.1 Project Background

This book began as a project to investigate the linguistic and paleographic evidence found on MS L with the goal of determining what could be said about that manuscript's age and authorship. In particular, it was the claims of the manuscript's identifier that MS L represents the oldest *Heliand* manuscript fragment found to date that inspired my research. Along the way, I became aware also of the possible connections between MS L and a rumor about Luther having possessed an ancient Germanic biblical codex. During my investigations, the focus of my project, by this point financed by a Fulbright fellowship at the University of Leipzig, turned ever more toward the discovery and verification of the Luther rumor and of evidence that might link MS L to the codex purportedly possessed by the Reformer. Not knowing fully what would come of this historical expedition, I continued with the original research design by visiting the location of each *Heliand* manuscript (i.e. Leipzig, Berlin, Munich, and London—leaving only the Vatican out of my visits due to the three-year closure of the Vatican library during my year-long stay in Germany)[1] to see the manuscripts first-hand and to collect digitized images of them for further investigation.

I came upon the idea of using digitized versions simply out of necessity. The University of Leipzig Library was hesitant to allow me access to the actual manuscript fragment (it having just come from being displayed to the public, which display I had missed by several months by virtue of not having been in Europe at the time). Instead, I was offered a high-resolution digital image of both sides of the manuscript. Thanks to several years of experience as a web designer, I have acquired enough skill with the program Adobe Photoshop to be able to control and enhance the color depth of images in order to bring out detail otherwise obscured by darkness and muddiness of hue, both results of either (1) the digitization process (i.e. digital photography), and (2) aging of the manuscript itself. Since the inks used to write on the parchment by their very nature differ from the chemical make-up of the sheep skin, even those areas that appear at first sight to have been lost to age often retain enough of a chemical trace or at least

---

[1] Nevertheless, I was able to obtain a copied version of MS V by mail.

impression or quill scratch to be identifiable. This process is not perfect, but it acts in a way as a poor man's version of the expensive and highly involved process used to discover the original text of the Archimedes Palimpsest ("The Imaging of the Archimedes Palimpsest," *The Archimedes Palimpsest Project*). Having been given less than personal access to MS L, I was in not able to propose such a drastic study of the parchment and inks. Furthermore, the cost of an involved materials study was not in my budget. For now, I hope to do nothing more than to stoke the fire of interest in MS L, so that some day performing more detailed and expensive processes on the manuscript will become justified, if they are indeed needed at all. That is, though my Photoshop process is imperfect in certain ways, it does stand up to scientific critique. All the more important, it has revealed several small but important elements heretofore overlooked and/or missed by those who published the first transcriptions of the MS L text (cf. 2.3).

As I explain in Ch. 11, much of the current bottleneck in *Heliand* research—and for that matter in Old Saxon studies—stems from problematic transcriptions of the *Heliand* texts. These problems stem from there having been different transcribers for each manuscript, transcriptions having been performed during different eras between which the emphasis on academic rigor varied, the improper standardization and leveling out of important variation between the manuscripts, and altogether false reading of the characters actually present on the parchment. Initially, my design was to make my own transcriptions of all the texts—something I am still working on and plan to publish in the future. In my being the sole transcriber of all six manuscripts, I hope to avoid the four problems presented above. In this way, future research into the spelling and therefore dialect variation in each of the manuscripts will be less susceptible to transcription differences, hopefully yielding more accurate results and better conclusions about the origin of the *Heliand* epic.

1.2 Scope and Direction

Although the scope of my research changed, I still find it necessary to provide background for each of the manuscripts involved (cf. Ch. 2). Similarly, I highlight the errors in the standard transcriptions later (cf. Ch. 4) in order to introduce a set of my own transcriptions, which I then use in a textual comparison with Luther's translation of the New Testament Gospels. The future publication of my transcriptions of all six *Heliand* manuscripts will include a side-by-side comparison not only with one another where these overlap, but also with Luther's translations. The purpose of this will be to bring the body of evidence brought to light in this book full-circle. Unfortunately, this question is too large in scope to fit into a single book. Thus, the following thesis sets the stage for further research into linguistic clues that speak for or against what can be presumed as Luther's purpose in possessing a *Heliand* codex—namely, as a reference for his own translation.

Yet this proposition, whether proved by linguistic comparison or not, is not the only possible conclusion. If the Luther rumor is indeed true—i.e., that he possessed a *Heliand* codex—there are still a variety of reasons beyond that cited above for why Luther might have been interested in an ancient retelling of the Gospels. Suffice it to say that until the surfacing of MS L in 2006 no amount of hypothesizing about Luther's reasons admitted too much, because nothing in the way of evidence was even remotely available to verify that he had such a document. In fact, the rumor had long become considered just that—a piece of folklore like many others that are perpetuated about the controversial figure that was Martin Luther.

1.3 Considerations

The discovery of MS L in Leipzig—a mere 60 km away from Luther's Wittenberg (within a day's travel in his time)—brings the veracity of the rumor back into question. Is MS L the long missing evidence that will shed light on this rumor and link Luther to the Heliand? Only time and scientific inquiry will tell. Outside of a quotation directly from Luther himself proclaiming his use of the *Heliand*,[2] the realms from which any evidence for or against the rumor will come will be either the historical record (i.e. secondary claims, rumors, historical timing, etc.) or a linguistic analysis attempting to find evidence in Luther's writing that exposes his use of *Heliand* material. While one might think first to turn to chemistry and physics to gain some

---

[2] The *Heliand* has only been called such since Schmeller in 1830 (cf. 4.1.3). Luther would have therefore likely used some periphrastic description when referring to the *Heliand*, as was done by the several other men in Early Modern history who record knowledge of it. As has been done with these men's references, any mention by Luther of an ancient Germanic Gospel harmony would likely only spur debate about which medieval documents he really meant.

answers, the fact is that any material analysis of MS L would not yield any answers about Luther: (1) as a medieval document assumed to be from the ninth century, any chemical evidence from the parchment and/or ink would not be of any value in linking the manuscript to sixteenth-century Luther (that is, a materials analysis would only verify or debunk the beliefs about the age of the document as a ninth-century product); (2) even if a materials analysis were to promise answers to our questions, current interest in MS L is nowhere near the level that is needed to justify the cost of such an analysis nor the intrusion into the document. Until interest in MS L grows, analysis of the material of MS L is not realistic. Ultimately, a material analysis would be useful in determining the veracity of the Luther rumor only if the results were to show MS L to be a forgery. Then the Luther link would likely be a moot question (although, depending on the age determined for a forgery, new questions might arise). In short, a materials analysis seems unnecessarily tangential to any progress that can be made.

While some have questioned the authenticity of MS L (Judasson 2007), the general consensus among scholars, gleaned from the appearance of the document and the language of the text on it, is that it is authentic ninth-century work. In any case, until proven otherwise, it is at least necessary to assume MS L is authentic in order to drive investigations of it forward. Thus, it is a beneficial assumption.

1.4 Methodology

As stated, I came upon several problems in the field of Old Saxon Studies. The multitude of transcriptions available for the growing body of manuscripts is the largest problem. The variations that exist between transcriptions that purport to reflect the same manuscript impacts dialect-based studies of the Old Saxon language. This is no small problem, since any question about the *Heliand* poet—his identity, his location, his native dialect, etc.—are not answered by any obvious means; rather, these characteristics about the anonymous author can only be gleaned from the linguistic information made available by the manuscripts. For example, researchers have often interpreted variations in the spelling of words as they occur on the manuscripts—with those from MS M often receiving the most favor for being 'correct'—as reflecting pronunciation differences in the dialects of each particular manuscript's scribe. Thus, various proposals about the nationality of the poet have been proposed. These range from a native Old Saxon speaker to a complete foreigner, i.e. a western Frankish Latinate speaker. In between, there is a range of proposals that suggest he was possibly Frisian, Anglo-Saxon, Frankish, and High German dialect speaker. Strangely, these proposals about the nationality of the poet are based upon the dialect information of the manuscripts' scribes. It should be noted that these two characters—the poet and the scribe—are not necessarily played by the same person. In fact, given the dating of the manuscripts widely assumed (cf. 2.1.1), it is most likely that not one of the extant manuscripts is the poet's original. Nevertheless, studies regularly take the linguistic and paleographic evidence as relevant to the discussion about the poet, and most proposals accepted today suspect a northerner of some nationality who later moved southward to a scriptorium where certain reference materials would have been on hand. Proposals for the location of the scriptorium vary, as well: Fulda, Essen, Werden, Verden, Vreden, Mainz, Magdeburg, to name just a few.

Given that the spelling differs between manuscripts in mostly minimal ways, the difference of a single letter carries immense weight in the decisions of modern scholars about the nature of the scribes and poet. Thus, errors in modern transcriptions are immensely problematic. Take, for example, Old Saxon *hêrron* (gen. sg. of *hêrro*) 'Lord': is Behaghel's rendering <hêrren>, Sievers' spelling <heren>, or Schmeller's form <heren> the original (cf. 4.1)? The form in question is the rendering of exactly the same word from the same place in the text (line 5830). Here, two modern transcribers admit that they are deviating from what they found on the manuscript: the italicized characters are suppositions—either because the transcriber could not read the character (Schmeller) or because he is trying to level out variation in order to offer a 'perfectly systematic' version of the text (Behaghel). Thus, it is apparent that different motivations lie behind each transcription. As more manuscripts have been discovered, transcriptions of each have been undertaken separately from one another. Consequently, the body of transcriptions that exist for all the manuscripts is vast and highly varied. No one individual has yet undertaken a transcription of all six extant manuscripts so as to provide a full library of original text variations as they truly occur in their original form, performed according to the same standards and motivated by one single scholarly goal: accurate representation of the characters as they occur ink-on-parchment. Thus, my first goal was to make six parallel transcriptions—one for each manuscript. It should be noted that the six manuscripts do not all overlap with one another. Where overlapping of the text does occur, it does so with only two or three (cf. 2.1.1).

The aforementioned example—OS *hêrran*—reflects a second, related problem. As evidenced in Schmeller's spelling, the text on some of the manuscripts has been made difficult to read by wear and age. However, that is not the case with the occurrence of this particular word (cf. 4.1). Yet, where this does occur on the manuscripts, modern transcribers have dealt with the issue differently. Some resort to representing the form as it occurs on another manuscript—thus mixing the data. Others skip it altogether. Others still add in what they assume the form to have been—thus introducing data that is unverifiable. This makes the standard modern transcriptions extremely problematic for linguistic analysis: it is impossible to tell whether variation between modern transcriptions is the result of transcriber error, transcriber edition, transcriber emendation, text mixture, or true variation between manuscripts. It is one thing when transcribers note their interventions into the text in footnotes; however, I found that such revelations were inconsistent. For this reason, I again found it necessary to return to the manuscripts in order to obtain the text. In the cases of two manuscript fragments in particular (MS P and L), entire pages are worn and difficult to read. By approaching these with digital imaging software, I have been able to lift much of this text out, making it more legible. I have therefore been able to make accurate transcriptions of these and other similar problematic areas on the other manuscripts. That is, in many cases, guesswork and assumption are no longer the only means: when a particular character is not legible by the naked eye, digital imaging software can be used to differentiate the ink from the leather—a naturally occurring phenomenon since light reflects differently off of different materials due to their different molecular make-up. Application of computer technology simply intensifies these variations in color, which the eye then translates as a character on a page. In one case, I have discovered a single character on MS L that is of vast importance to investigations of the provenance of this manuscript fragment and potentially to all the rest as well (cf. 2.3).

Returning to the aforementioned example (OS *hêrron*): what appears to be nitpicky analysis is indeed highly valuable. As demonstrated by Georg Baesecke (cf. 2.2.2), the appearance of <rr> vs. <r> in this word reveals much about the history of the *Heliand*. That is, the six extant manuscripts stand in some kind of relationship to one another: by necessity, one must have been created before the others. By analyzing the linguistic and paleographic features on all six manuscripts, it is possible to rank each by its relative age. The result is a manuscript *Stammbaum*, i.e. a family tree (cf. 2.2). Similarly, the single character I have discovered and discuss in Ch. 2 verifies the positioning of the extant manuscript on this relationship tree.

Beyond this, there is additional evidence about the provenance of the *Heliand* that comes from a preface found separately from the six manuscripts and later re-connected (cf. 6.1.2) to the *Heliand*—the *Praefatio* and *Versus* (cf. 3.2.2). This preface work offers evidence about the circumstances under which the *Heliand* was written. Already clear from the storyline of the *Heliand*, it is clear that this retelling of the biblical Gospels was done in the spirit of an ancient Germanic epic. The preface material reveals hints about why it was written: it states that this poet was under the commission of Charlemagne's heir (cf. 3.2). Thus, it can be determined that the poet worked during the first half of the ninth century. Comparing this evidence to known historical events, a fuller, nonetheless incomplete story begins to emerge about the treatment of a conquered people who refused to be converted to Christianity by the sword (cf. 3.2.1). Thus, the *Heliand* appears to be an attempt at deliberate religious adaptation, of mixing Christianity with elements of Germanic paganism in order to make it more palatable (read: "understandable") to the ancient populace of northern Germany. At very least, the Christian hegemony sought to present the Gospel through a medium readily accessible and acceptable to newly subjugated non-believers.

Interestingly, the discovery of MS L has had an impact on what is known about the heritage of the *Heliand*. In particular, this is evident in two time periods: the Medieval Period and the Early Modern Period. Regarding the former, a small detail present in MS L (cf. 4.2.1) has potential relevance for the assumptions that have come to be largely accepted about where and when the *Heliand* was written (cf. 14.5). These assumptions place great importance on what is known of Fulda Abbey: when it was founded; the presence of men like Rabanus Maurus; and literary works known to have been located there, namely the Old High German version of Tatian's *Monotessaron*, a gospel harmony that represented the first translation of the Bible into a Western Germanic dialect. It has been proposed that the *Heliand* follows Tatian closely (cf. 4.2.1.3). This trifecta—The Old High German translation of Tatian, Rabanus Maurus, and Fulda—is commonly used in studies of the *Heliand* and the *Praefatio-*and*-Versus*, the conclusion of which favors placing the poet in Fulda when composing the epic. Yet, the small detail hinted at here calls the veracity of this assumption into question. That is, apparently the *Heliand* poet had something more than just Tatian at his disposal, since his epic contains information that can not be traced back to the Old High German Tatian *Monotessaron*, its Latin version, or to Rabanus Maurus' *Matthäuskommentar* (14.5).

While investigating another intriguing historical connection of the Old Saxon epic, I came upon this piece of evidence regarding the resources the *Heliand* poet must have had at hand. As already stated, MS L was discovered in a location with historical ties to Martin Luther (cf. 5.1.4; Ch. 13). Rumors about Luther once making use of an ancient *monotessaron* commissioned by Charlemagne's son, Louis the Pious, have been known since as late as the late seventeenth century (cf. 5.2; 7.1.2–7.2.3). In light of this, I sought to compare the language of Luther's bible translations with that of the *Heliand*, assuming that the Reformer would have been interested in an ancient Germanic Bible because he was attempting to imbue his own translations with a sense of the German Spirit. This led me to wonder whether Luther might have turned to the *Heliand* for aid in converting non-German(ic) idioms and analogies into Germanic equivalents. Certainly, appealing to a text that at his time was already seven centuries old would yield potentially deeply ingrained cultural expressions.

During the process of comparing the *Heliand* text with Luther's translations of the Bible, I began to realize the vastness of such a study, and so I have left any conclusions about such a hypothesis for a later publication (cf. 4.2.1.3). I continue to make slow progress on this comparative linguistic work toward fulfilling my initial goal—indeed, it will be included as an integral part of my *Habilitationsschrift*, which I plan to complete in association with my postdoctoral research with the LOEWE Project "Digital Humanities" at the Johann Wolfgang Goethe-Universität Frankfurt am Main.

As far as the present book is concerned, it is in researching the historical angle of this relationship between Luther and the *Heliand* that I have made the greatest progress. I present this historical data starting with Ch. 5, where I begin with a historical synopsis on the city of Leipzig, a city which played an important role in the Reformation movement. This analysis shows that it is not completely surprising that a *Heliand* document was found in that city. Furthermore, I investigate the provenance of the aforementioned rumor linking Luther with the *Heliand*. This analysis stretches from Chs. 6 to 10, in which I reveal the original sources of the rumors, including new information about the personality of one of the original recorders of this rumor, a man named Ioannes Manlius.

This man was apparently long lost to history. Consequently, very little could be said previously about him. However, new research reveals his activity as a student and inflammatory anti-Catholic publisher throughout the Holy Roman Empire and on its frontier (cf. 9.2–9.3). In Ch. 11, I offer an analysis of Manlius' published rumor.

Similarly, I offer the resource and an analysis of another rumor source, namely Martin Chemnitz, in Chs. 8 and 10, respectively.

Furthermore, I publish herein the first mention of the Leipzig *Heliand* manuscript dating to early 1545 (cf. 6.2), i.e. well within the Luther's lifetime. This source, Georg Fabricius, provides interesting details about how the *Heliand* manuscript came to be at Leipzig and, moreover, the nature of the interest in it by contemporaries of Luther (cf. 6.2.3).

Altogether, what can be gleaned from these three men is that three important characters in the Reformation movement—Ph. Melanchthon, C. Borner, and J. Camerarius, all men very close to Luther—were not only aware of the Leipzig *Heliand* codex, but in fact responsible for its presence there and for its use during the early-to-mid-sixteenth century.

In Ch. 12 I provide historical context of the events that took place during the heat of the Reformation. From this I conclude the purpose behind the *Heliand* codex's Leipzig location. Furthermore, in Ch. 13 I verify that the various rumors and mentions of *Heliand*-like document indeed refer to actual versions of the *Heliand*, and that these historical mentions refer to manuscript(s) that still exist in fragments today. Herein I continue with a hypothesis proposed by the discoverers of MS L (cf. 2.1.2) that MS L and MS P represent two pages separated from the same original codex, whence I turn to show that this unitary codex was in fact the codex located at Leipzig and mentioned variously by the aforementioned men in letters and publications. I call this hypothetical document *Codex L*.

From there I return to Georg Fabricius' epistolary descriptions of the Leipzig *Heliand*, in particular a hint he provides about the codex's location prior to Leipzig. This small detail provides evidence that allows this copy of the *Heliand* to be traced back to the ninth-century Ottonian Dynasty. This family of Holy Roman Emperors ironically descended from the very Saxon peoples that had been subjugated by Emperor Charlemagne. I discuss this family's many ties to the extant *Heliand* documents (13.4), with which I include the Old Saxon Genesis (cf. 2.2). Ultimately, that which can be linked very nearly directly to the relatives and descendants of Otto the Great includes all but one of the extant *Heliand* manuscripts, the Old Saxon Genesis, Caedmon's Old English Genesis B fragment and still further historical works of importance to Old Saxon Studies (cf. 14.3).

2. Manuscripts and Fragments

2.1 Discovery of the Manuscript Fragment

On April 20, 2006 Thomas Döring, a librarian at the 'Bibliotheca Albertina', the Special Collections division of the Leipzig University Library, made a startling discovery (Schulte 2006). Döring, a specialist in early printed works—i.e. late fifteenth century onwards—was at work waiting for a repository colleague to finish a task. While waiting, Döring let his eyes wander around a shelf containing the donated holdings from Leipzig's Thomaskirche, a collection of early Reformation-era printed works in Latin. Focusing shortly on a vigesimo-size volume (12.8 × 7.5 cm, spine: 3 cm), on the outer binding of which there appeared a faint, recurrent scrawl. Upon closer observation Döring discovered the binding was a manuscript parchment recycled as a book cover. Quite unexpectedly,[1] the handwritten text on the binding was clearly not Latin. Döring consulted with his colleague, Dr. Falk Eisermann, and together they deduced a Germanic nature in the language.

The duo then informed Prof. Dr. Hans Ulrich Schmid, Chair of Historical Linguistics at the University of Leipzig, of the find. Schmid relates that upon first glance several details revealed to him the nature of the document that had been found: (1) a Carolingian minuscule hand, (2) alliterative language, (3) keywords such as *sten, idise, giungarom, ik uuet* (Schmid 2006). The book around which the parchment had been wrapped is a combination of two early seventeenth-century student handbooks (St. Thomas 1490); however, its cover is obviously older: the Carolingian minuscule hand alone reveals it to have been written between ca. 800 and ca. 1200. This indication of the parchment's age would have been sufficient justification to remove it from an otherwise invaluable Reformation-age artifact.

The language of the text reveals more still. Alliteration was a commonly-employed literary device used by medieval Germanic poet-authors. Its presence would lend credence to Döring and Eisermann's suspicion that the language on the parchment is vernacular. Characteristics of the keywords noted by Schmid further indicate a Germanic dialect, more specifi-

---

[1] The holdings of the former St. Thomas Church library have been described as "vielleicht die wertvollste handschriftliche Sammlung *lateinischer* Kirchenmusik von evangelisch-deutschem Boden" (Johannes Wolf 1913, emphasis mine).

cally an early form of a Low German dialect: *ik* and *uuet* both have final consonants that are unaffected[2] by the Second or Old High German Sound Shift.[3]

The semantics of *sten* 'stone', *idise* 'women', and *giungarom* '(to the) disciples' (cf. Germ. *Jüngern*) reminded Schmid of the Gospel tale recounting the women weeping at Christ's empty sepulchre (cf. Luke 24). Schmid's three noted details intersect to describe a Carolingian-era Christian text in an early Low German dialect. Very few documents are known to fit these criteria; thus, Schmid admits an easy conclusion: "Es konnte folglich kaum noch etwas anderes sein als ein Stück aus dem 'Heliand'" (2006: 309). Comparing the legible areas of the well-worn manuscript text to the corresponding story section in the standard reproduction of the *Heliand* epic, Eduard Sievers' *Heliand*, proves Schmid's hunch: the manuscript text corresponds to lines 5823–5846,[4] midway through story of the empty grave in fitt LXIX. In fact, the differences between the text on the newly found Leipzig fragment and the version printed by Sievers' are minimal (cf. 4.1.2). These minimal differences, however, ultimately prompt further research.

With the value of the fragment text verified, attention turned to the reverse side, where it was hoped that the text continued. This required separation of the binding from its book host, for which the researchers received the permission of the University Library Director, Prof. Dr. Ulrich Johannes Schneider. Removal of the fragment revealed a relatively unworn surface containing a clearly legible textual continuation, providing lines 5846–5870. Within this span occurs the transition to fitt LXX.

The newly-found fragment carries the shelfmark "Leipzig, Universitätsbibliothek, St. Thomas 4073 (Ms)" and has been designated 'fragment L'

---

[2] Cf. NHG *ich* : Goth. *ik* and NHG *weiß* : Goth. *wáit*. Both New High German forms have shifted final consonants.

[3] The first Germanic consonant shift refers to a series of variations that affected the Germanic languages, differentiating them from their sister languages—the other Indo-European languages. An example of this variation is visible when comparing initial consonants of ModE *ten* and Lat. *decem*. Later, a sub-group of Germanic dialects underwent a second series of consonant shifts, further distinguishing the ancestor of the High German dialects from the ancestors of Low German, Dutch, and English. This distinction is visible when comparing ModE *ten* and NHG *zehn* (<z> represents /ts/).

[4] Schmid (2006: 309–310) erroneously announces this as lines 5823–5845 and the lines of the verso as 5845–5869. More accurately, the recto begins partway through 5823a (*andan* of *astandan*) and ends with all but the last word of 5846b (after *te*). The verso begins completing 5846b (*strang*) and ends midway through line 5870 (after *forahta*).

("MS L") in keeping with the pattern of using the initial of the city in which the manuscript was first discovered.

2.1.1 The Six Extant Manuscripts

The discovery of MS L has brought the total number of *Heliand* exemplars to six. With such a small number of data sources, the addition of a single fragmentary document is substantial for research. The significance of the MS L find lies in this fragment's potential relationships with the other extant manuscripts. Before discussing their apparent relationships to one another, I will present a short description of each document.

The six manuscripts are generally divided into two groups: the major ones and the fragments. The major manuscripts comprise two documents: (1) MS C, a nearly complete version of the Gospel epic, and (2) the MS M, which contains roughly half of the complete story—a text that can be compared to and correlated with nearly half of that contained on MS C.

The second grouping, i.e. the fragments, comprises the four remaining documents, MSS P, V, S, and the newly-discovered MS L. All of these manuscript fragments consist of one- or two-page sections of what can be presumed to have been larger codices. In the case of three of the four—viz. MSS P, S, and L—the single sheets had been reused as coverings for other books that were published much later. The expanded chart on the following page gives relevant data for each manuscript (information compiled from Taeger 1996 unless otherwise indicated: *Sahm 2007; †Zangemeister 1894).

A closer look at the details from that chart produces statistics that provide a point of comparison. One should note that the circumstances of MSS P and L are nearly identical:

MS	C	M	P	V	S	L
Leaves	165	74.5	**1**	2	2.667	**1**
Total poetic lines	5969	4880.5	**49**	80	157	**47**
Ave. poetic lines/leaf	36.1758	65.51	**49**	40	58.8676	**47**
Ave. poetic lines/side (leaf/2)	18.0879	32.755	**24.5**	20	29.4338	**23.5**

MS.	C	M	P	V	S	L
Location (formerly)	London	Munich (Bamberg)	Berlin (Prague)	Vatican	Munich (Straubing)	Leipzig
Holder	British Library	Bayerische Staatsbibliothek	Deutshces Historisches Museum	Biblioteca Apostolica Vaticana	Bayerische Staatsbibliothek	Bibliotheca Albertina
Call number	Cotton Caligula A. VII sign. 3–11	cgm. 25	R 56/2537 (PA)	Palatini Latini 1447	cgm. 8840	Thomas 4073 (Ms)
Discovered	1587	1: 1720; 2: 1794	1880	1894	1979	2006
By	F. Junius d. J.	1: Siegler, Eccard; 2: Gerard Gley	H. Lambel	K. Zangemeister	B. Bischoff	T. Döring, H. U. Schmid
Est. date	Second half of 10th century	Around 850, 850–875*	Around or after 850; 840–850*	early- to mid-9th c.	Around or after 850	840–850*
Leaf size	222 × 140 mm	272 × 202 mm	241 × 170 mm*	210 × 326 mm†	200 × 120 mm	240 × 165 mm*
Equiv. leaves	165	74.5	1	2	2.667	1
Leaf numbers	5–169 (11–175)	2–75	—	27r, 32v	—	—
Constitutes poetic lines	1–5968	85–2198a, 2256–2514a, 2576–3414a, 3491–3950, 4017–4674, 4740b–5275a, (5968–5983)	958–1006	1279–1358	351–360, 368–384, 393–400, 492–582, 675–683, 693–706, 715–722	5823b–5870a
Poetic lines	5969	4882	49	80	157	47
Rows / leaf	24	24	23	18†	25	23

2. MANUSCRIPTS AND FRAGMENTS

Furthermore, the sizes of the parchment which make up the physical material of the manuscripts are remarkably similar, i.e., MSS P and L are roughly the same size:

MS	C	M	P	V	S	L
Leaf size	222 × 140	272 × 202	**241 × 170**	326 × 210	200 × 120	**240 × 165**
Text box (mm)	194 × 101	210 × 147	**190 × 122**	(164)[5]× 195	163 × 103	**190 × 121**
Rows/side	24	24	**23**	18	25	**23**
Chars./row[6]	34.71	56.79	**47.33**	94.56	34.36	**45.10**
x-height[7] (mm)	2.4	2.0	**2.3**	1.4	2.0	**2.3**
Baseline (mm)	8.6	9.0	**9.0**	7.2	7.0	**9.0**

These sizes are for the parchment leaves themselves, which in the case of MSS P, S, and L have been cut down from larger sheets to make covers for other books. Therefore, any discrepancy between the height and width of these two fragments is negligible.

More important are the measurements the text box areas, which are physical evidence from the scribes own hand. In particular, it is the height measurements that are most indicative, as the width measurements of the lines are affected by what one would now call left-hand justification of the text, i.e., the line lengths are inconsistent. The average line length is skewed slightly by overlong lines breaking into the right-hand margin in all MSS.[8]

---

[5] Because the Old Saxon text covers neither side completely (ca. bottom 2/3 on 27r, ca. bottom 1/3 on 32v), the height of the text box is irrelevant. Given here is the text box height on 27r for the Old Saxon text only.

[6] Taken as an average from randomly selected leaves: ~~16~~/22r (C); 20v (M); 1v (P); 27r (V); 2v (S); 1v (L) – all but line 1, which is cut off at the end, and 18 & 19, which have an inset roman majuscule that displaces the left-hand side of the text box for these two lines. Includes spaces where they are clear (cf. 4.1.3).

[7] The x-height measurements are an average of the heights of the instances of character i on the page cited above for each manuscript. Similarly, the baseline spacing measurement averages the spacing between rows from the same pages.

[8] My measurements were taken as such: vertically, from the median line (i.e. top of character x-height) of the topmost text line to the baseline of the bottommost text line; horizontally, from the left margin (thus not including any offset majuscules) to the rightmost point of the final character on the right of the same text row, the longest on the page.

Also relevant are the average number of characters per row, the x-height,[9] and the baseline spacing measurements. The first measurement bespeaks the average width of a character, though this is merely illustrative as the actual number of characters in any given row varies by how far the text breaks into the right-hand margin of the text box and by the variety of characters present. That is, the script is not fixed-width, e.g. an *m* is much wider than an *i* and an *l*. Thus, any row containing a greater number of thin characters vs. wide characters will potentially have more characters overall. Thus, the measurement of the average number of characters per row is merely indicative in its purpose.

The second is much more reliable, as the x-height is the measurement of the main body of all characters regardless of their ascenders and/or descenders. Thus, this measurement gives an indication of how tall writing is. As noted, this measurement is based on the average height of the dot-less minuscule *i*, which as the simplest character in form represents the basic vertical stroke upon which all other characters are based.

Similar to the x-height measurement, the baseline spacing is a reliable indicator of the similarity of the manuscripts, as it both informally accounts for ascenders and descenders so long as these do not overlap with the text of surrounding rows (this does not occur in any of the manuscripts), and formally correlates with the vertical text box measurement—only a certain number of rows will fit within the confines of the text box height.

Together, these measurements give an overall sense of the penmanship of the scribes who drafted the manuscripts. These penmanship indicators show a rough correspondence between MSS P and L that further supports the conclusion that the two fragments are closely related—perhaps separated from the same codex or, at least, written by the same scribe.

2.1.2 Relevance of the Discovery

In his presentation of the newly discovered fragment to the public, Schmid similarly describes the appearance of MS L as being reminiscent of MS P (2006, p. 310):

---

[9] I.e., the average height of a miniscule glyph between midline and baseline, therefore excluding any ascenders and/or descenders.

> Größe, Einrichtung und Schrift könnten darauf hindeuten, daß L zu Makulaturzwecken demselben Codex entnommen worden ist wie das einst Prager, jetzt Berliner Blatt P, das bis in Einzelheiten der Ausstattung (und Verstümmelung!) mit L übereinstimmt.

The MS L parchment nearly matches that of MS P in both size and shape. More convincing still, the script hands on both are virtually identical. Even more, both manuscripts were discovered in similar reused functions as book bindings. Due to these similarities it has been speculated that the two separate manuscript fragments initially belonged to the same medieval codex. If true, MS L would automatically inherit speculation surrounding P, specifically its assumed privileged position amongst the Heliand manuscripts. Sahm notes: "Das Fragment P [...] hat innerhalb der frühen Textzeugen eine Sonderstellung inne, weil es als der Überlieferungszeuge gilt, der dem Archetypus am nächsten steht" (2007: 81-82). This view of MS P as the oldest extant representation of the Heliand epic is based on linguistic evidence presented by Taeger, namely the relationship between the Old Saxon phoneme and its graphemic representation in the manuscripts. Yet Taeger warns that the advantages of MS P are counterbalanced by its material paucity (Behaghel/Taeger 1984, 9th ed., xxviii, footnote 44):

> [Es] scheint die ursprüngliche graphematisch-sprachliche Erscheinungsform unseres Denkmals am getreusten in P bewahrt zu sein. Gemäß dem geringfügigen Umfang und der Lückenhaftigkeit dieser Textzeugen schlägt seine Sprachform für die Textgestaltung nicht durch. Das gleiche gilt wie für die ebenfalls dem Archetyp recht nahestehende Textform von Heliand V für die besonders archetypferne, nordseegermanisch geprägte Textgestalt des Fragments S.

Like the Leipzig fragment, MS P consists of a single parchment leaf with text on both sides. Compared to MS C's 165 folios and MS M's 75 folios, MS P provides less data for comparison with other manuscripts by virtue of its being only a single leaf. But if MS L is indeed as closely related to MS P as has been surmised, its discovery is monumental: it doubles what is regarded as the version closest to that of the Heliand poet's original.

2.2 *Stammbaum* Theories

Beyond MSS P and L, one can use the features present in all the manuscripts to create a genetic tree that reveals the relationships between all six extant manuscripts. I find two such *Stammbäume* particularly illustrative and noteworthy: Taeger (1996) and Baesecke (1948).

2.2.1 Taeger's Manuscript Tree

To begin, Burkhard Taeger is quite obviously influenced by the proposal put forth by Rooth in 1956 (Eichhoff & Rauch, 208):

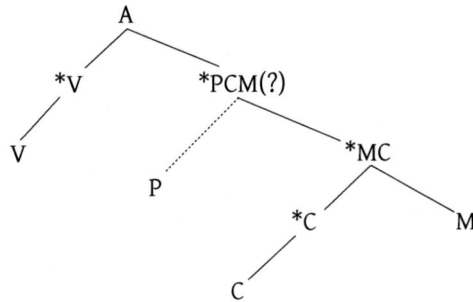

Rooth justifies the construction of the *Stammbaum* as such for the following reasons (207):

> Die größte Sicherheit wird natürlich verbürgt, wo alle Versionen im Gebrauch übereinstimmen, dann besonders auch beim Zusammengehen eines der beiden Fragmente P und V an gleicher Stelle mit den beiden Versionen M und C. Etwas geringere Sicherheit gewähren die Konstellationen V+C, V+M und P+C, P+M. Man muß immer mit der Möglichkeit rechnen, daß die Schreiber ihre eigene Mundart einschwärzen. Ein fester Punkt in der Rekonstruktion ist die Version *MC, die schon Schlüter auf Grund der von der Vorlage abweichenden, besonders im 3. bis 5. Tausend der Verse klar zum Vorschein kommenden mundartlichen Züge des Schreibers von M in den Hauptpunkten herausgearbeitet hat. Da M, wie P, meistens um 850 datiert wird [...], ist die Version *MC für die Beurteilung des Archetypus von großem Gewicht.

Rooth continues to reconstruct various characteristics of his hypothesized *MC node based on the variances in MSS V, P, C, and M, including vowel quality (e.g. treatment of West Germanic long vowels and diphthongs), nominal declensions (e.g. *a*-stem vs. *ja*-stem, weak masc.), adjectival declensions, *r*-less pronouns, use of reflexives, unitary verbal conjugation in the pl., etc.

Taeger reconstructs Rooth's proposal to include MS S, which by virtue of its being first discovered in 1979 was not available to Rooth. To do so,

Taeger adopts Rooth's notion of a textual archetype—a hypothetical manuscript from which all of the extant manuscripts are thought to have been copied. The text of Archetype corresponds more or less to the linguistic reconstructions developed by Rooth. Regarding the relationship of MS S to the other then-extant manuscripts, Taeger remarks (xxii-xxiii):

> Dem Archetyp am fernsten steht das Fragment S. Es ist vom Einband einer zuerst für Stift Millstadt/Kärnten nachweisbaren Schedelschen Weltchronik (Nürnberg 1493) abgelöst, aus dem Besitz der Staatl. Bibliothek am Joh.-Turmai-Gymnasium Straubing. [...] S steht [...] zu M nicht nur der graphematisch-sprachlichen Umsetzung des Textes in M am nächsten – und übertrifft sie noch bei weitem in der Durchführung nordseegermanischer Eigentümlichkeiten –, sondern erweist sich auch durch Bindefehler in v. 508 bzw. v. 566 mit M am nächsten verwandt.

Thus, the addition of MS S to the *Stammbaum* proposed by Rooth does not cause any major disruptions to the branch structure, rather adds an additional node below MS M.

Taeger himself finds particular importance in MS M (xix):

> [Es] sind in M außer durch die Lagen- und Blattverluste noch an mehreren Stellen kleinere Lücken vorhanden, die ebenfalls nach C ergänzt werden müssen. M ist für die Textherstellung dennoch der wertvollste Zeuge, da C eine große Zahl von Flüchtigkeiten aufweist.

Furthermore, he describes the problems present in MS C (xx):

> C [...] is nach R. Priebsch in der 2. Hälfte des 10 Jahrhunderts in Südengland[10] geschrieben, nach Priebsch, N. Ker und U. Schwab von einem Angelsachsen. [...] Ein Hinweis auf die ags. Abkunft des Schreibers sind die gelegenlichen ags. Sprachformen in der Handschrift; besonders auffallend ist die Häufung von ags. Substantiv- und Verbformen in der kurzen Strecke C (215.) 255-265.

Consequently, MS M becomes the central point around which Taeger furthers the goal of his publication (notably, the continuation of Behaghel's rendition of the *Heliand*, for which Mitzka served as editor prior to Taeger). In short, Taeger continues the century-old habit of leveling out variation between the manuscripts in order to offer a single, 'corrected' version of the text. Though this serves the purposes of the Old Saxon student first

---

[10] Cf. 13.4.3.

approaching the *Heliand*, it unfortunately raises problems for research. These problems and a solution will be discussed in the Chapter 4.

In further support of the branching structure posited in Rooth's *Stammbaum*, Taeger offers his own evidence of the relationship between MSS M and C (xx-xxi):

> *CM: M und C sind durch Bindefehler als miteinander enger verwandt erwiesen; Behaghel hat in den früheren Auflagen dieser Ausgbe eine große Anzahl zusammengestellt, von denen jedoch nur ein Teil beweiskräftig ist. Als hinreichend gesicherte Bindefehler erweisen eine gemeinsame Vorlage *CM die Stellen vv. 483. 641. 1081. 1121. (C1M). 1308. 1600. 1977. 2426. 2434. 2476. 2730. 3166. 3918. 4097. 4136. 4170. 4238. 4264. 4467. 4980. 5061. 5071. 5132. 5202.

Note that Taeger's *CM corresponds with Rooth's *MC.

Also echoing Rooth's proposal, Taeger finds MS V to be unique, and therefore deserving of its own branch from the Archetype (xxi):

> Von d[er] Vorstufe *CM ist das Fragment V, das, zusammen mit den Exzerpten aus der ‚As. Genesis' [...], in [eine] vatikanische komputistische Sammelhandschrift [...] eingetragen ist. Die im frühen 9. Jahrhundert geschriebene Handschrift stammt aus Mainz; die as. Exzerpte sind etwa im 3. Viertel des Jahrhunderts eingetragen, jedoch nicht in lokalisierbarer Buchschrift, sondern mit Einflüssen aus der Urkundenschrift; der Eintragungsort selbst, unbeschadet der Beziehung zu Mainz, bleibt damit unbekannt. V überliefert die vv. 1279–1538 (Anfang); dadurch, daß V allein die ursprüngliche Leseart des in M und C verkürzt bzw. verändert überlieferten Verses 1308 bietet, erweist es sich als unabhängig von *CM.

The true issue with Rooth's *Stammbaum*, as noted by Rooth himself, is the placement of MS P, whose branch he indicated with a dashed line to imply his uncertainty regarding whether to consider MS P an offshoot of his *MC or that of an even earlier hypothetical stage *PCM. Taeger takes up this very issue, finding evidence to support the branching for MS P from a hypothesized intermediary *CP stage, which itself branches off of the *CM node (xxi-xxii):

> [...] P hingegen läßt sich wegen einer Fehlgemeinschaft mit C als ebenfalls von *CM abhängig ansehen. P [...] ist [...] vom Einband eines 1598 in Rostock gedruckten Buches abgelöst [...]. Es steht graphematisch-sprachlich dem Archetypus besonders nahe, andererseits teilt es in v. 980 einen eindeutigen Fehler mit der Hs. C, führt also auf den Ansatz einer Vorstufe *CP.

Thus, Taeger's revised *Stammbaum* appears so (xxiv):

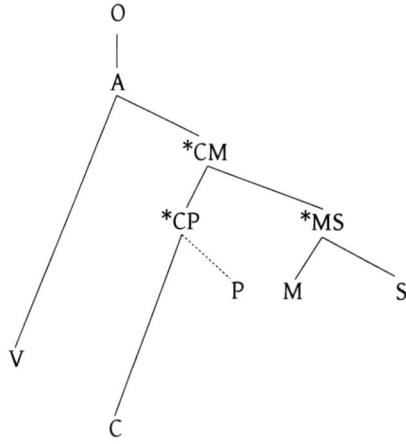

Here Taeger also introduces another stage, Original (O), which reflects the Heliand poet's original composition that was later edited as the Archetype (A), at which point the first set of linguistic and paleographic contaminations entered the text. Taeger remarks:

> Die Aufstellung eines Stammbaums ist bei der Beteiligung von drei Fragmenten, die sich nirgends überlappen, natürlich ein Wagnis; aber die Überlieferungsverhältnisse des ‚Heliand' scheinen doch trotz der Komplikationen, die sich im einzelnen mehrfach ergeben, nicht so undurchsichtig und verwickelt zu sein, daß man mit Mehrfachredaktion, lagenweise wechselnder Schreibereigentümlichkeit im Original bzw. Archetyp und mit Kontamination rechnen muß, wie dies geschehen ist.

2.2.2 Baesecke's Manuscript Tree

A similar conclusion regarding the placement of MS P was posited by its discoverer, Hans Lambel, in 1881. Baesecke (1948) mentions first that two manuscripts share a commonality of missing lines in nearly the same place (Fitt 12)—MS P (lines 969b–970) and MS M (lines 961–962). This, he suggests, might not be an indication of a relationship between these two manuscripts at all, for it is impossible to tell whether the missing lines were coincidentally similar mistakes on the part of the scribes. Rather, he argues, a more reliable relationship can be seen in what Lambel demonstrated as common spelling errors (57):

Auslassen konnte P einen Vers von *C wie von *M, aber auch von *MC und etwa sonstigen Vorlagen. So wenden wir denn zur Bestimmung einen Fehler an, den P mit C gegen M gemeinsam hat: *herran* PC gegen *heran* M 980, nämlich *hebancuning*. Das ergäbe für das Eintreten von *rr* für *r* in *heran* diese Anordnung, die dann etliche Fehler auf M oder C verschiebt (Lambel S. 619):

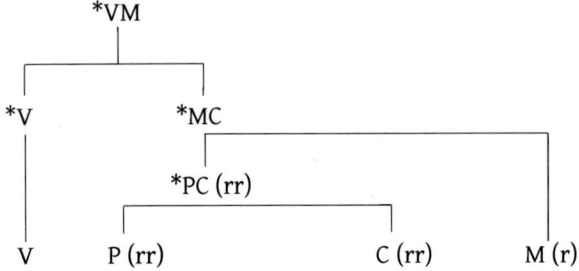

Georg Baesecke's tree structure of the presence of *rr* for *r* in *heran* 'lord (cf. Germ. *Herr*) is remarkably identical to Taeger's Stammbaum structure.

Gleichwohl läßt sich die Abneigung gegen Herkunft von P aus *MC, wenn wir nicht ins Jenseits steuern wollen, nicht mit der Auslassung eines *MC-Verses (970) in P vereinen. Und die macht es uns nun leicht, den mundartlichen Fehler *herran* 980 sogar erst aus einem *C=*PC herzuleiten, das ja wie P aus der Mitte des 9. Jahrhunderts stammen könnte.

Thus, Baesecke builds his own *Stammbaum* (presented on the following page)—by far the most detailed yet offered—taking into account not only manuscript relationships, but also the dates of their inscription and events that might be more than coincidental thereto (79):

I und II [repräsentieren] die Vorreden, I/II ihre Zusammenziehung und Bearbeitung, h1 und h2 die beiden Ausgaben des Heliand, g die Genesis und, neben V, ihre Bruchstücke; links die Zeitgaben[.]

Furthermore, the unusual identifier 'A' in the following chart stands not for Archetype as in Taeger's *Stammbaum*, rather for a hypothesized division of the Old Saxon Genesis text as proposed by Baesecke (74):

Es fragt sich noch, wie jenes Stück der as. Genesis etwa in das Stemma einzubauen sein, das in England übersetzt und im letzten Viertel des 10. Jahrhunderts in die ags. Genesis B eingeschoben wurde (=A), und aber vom Cottonianus [i.e. MS C] unabhängig schien.

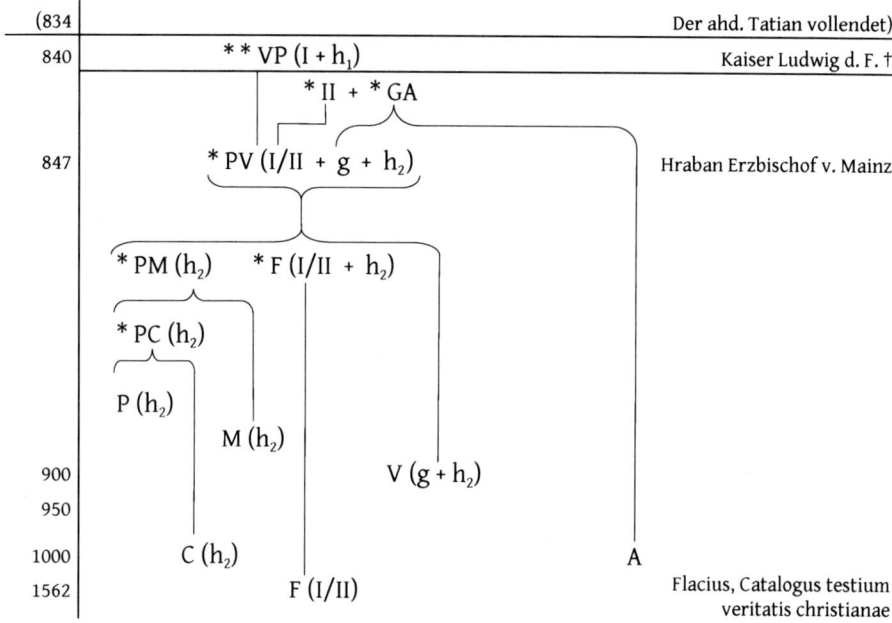

Baesecke's division of the Old Saxon Genesis into multiple parts itself refers to the remarkable discovery made by Sievers (1875), who regarded several lines of the Anglo-Saxon Genesis (MS Junius 11, a.k.a. the 'Caedmon manuscript'), namely those in Genesis B, to be oddly similar to Old Saxon. His resulting hypothesis was that a copy of the Old Saxon Genesis had somehow made it to Britain. Regarding the veracity of this theory, Philip Krapp writes in his introduction to *The Junius Manuscript* (1931, xxvi):

> The Anglo-Saxon translation [in Genesis B] follows the Old Saxon [discovered as part of MS V in 1894] so closely that all thought of accidental similarity or mere imitation is excluded. [...] Intercourse between the Saxons of the Continent and the Anglo-Saxons was not uncommon at this time, and no special knowledge of Old Saxon would be needed to enable an Anglo-Saxon to translate from that language into his own. It is quite possible, indeed, that the translation was one of the many effects of the cosmopolitan activities at Alfred's court in the second half of the ninth century.[11]

---

[11] Cf. 13.4.3.

2.2.3 Manuscript *Stammbaum* Revised in Light of MS L

The chart below is a revision of Baesecke's *Stammbaum*-timeline, to which I have made several updates and notable changes as described below:

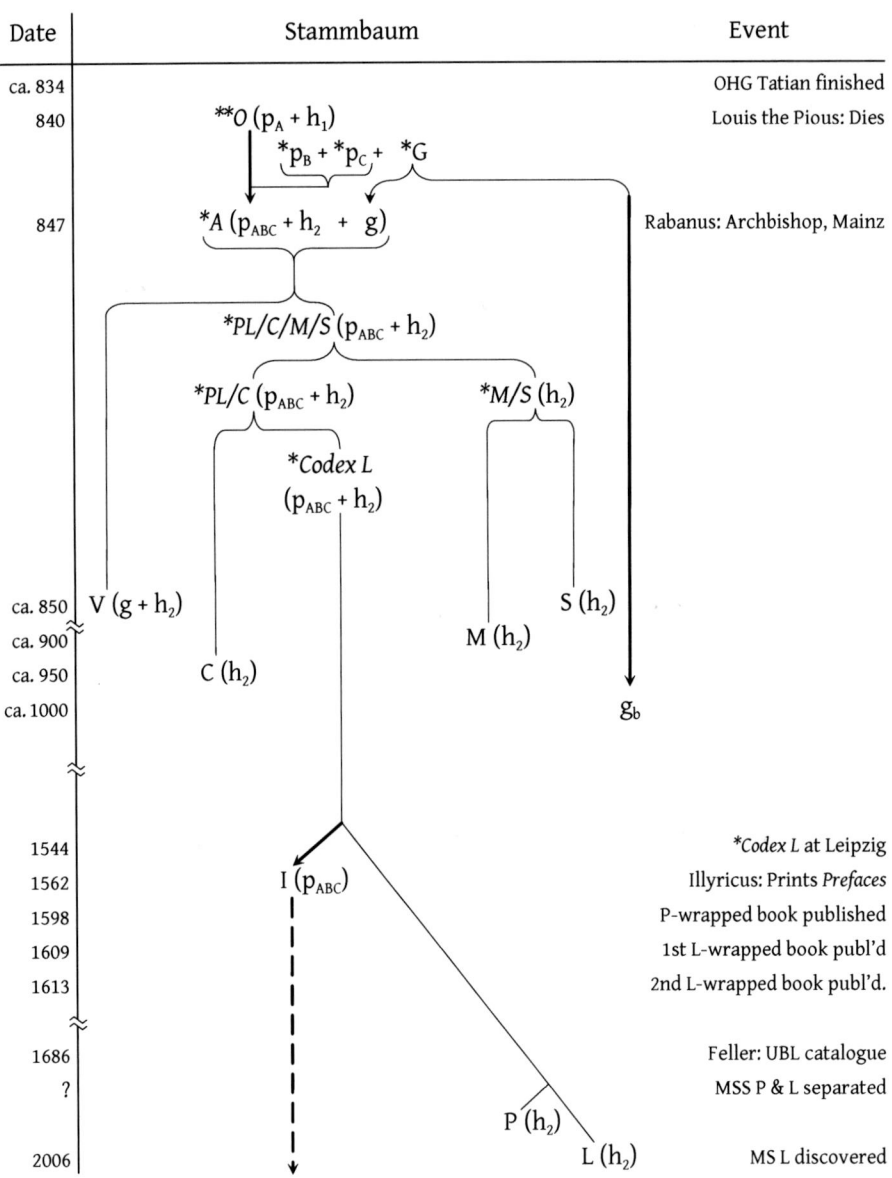

1. The addition of a node for the MS S, discovered 1979 and dated to "around or after 850" (B. Bischoff in Taeger 1996, xxii).
2. The addition of a node for MS S, discovered 2006 and dated to 840–850 (Sahm, 96).
3. The use of Taeger's indicators <O> for 'Original' (in place of VP) and <A> for 'Archetype' (in place of PV). Similarly, Baesecke's indicator for the Old Saxon Genesis, namely <GA>, has been replaced by <G>, so as to avoid confusion with the new use of <A> for 'Archetype'. Furthermore, the fragments of the Old Saxon Genesis are marked with a lowercase <g>. The matrix text thought to be the inspiration of the MS Junius' Genesis B is marked with a subscript B, i.e. <g_b>.
4. The use of lowercase <p> to indicate the various *Praefatio*-and-*Versus* parts, namely <p_A> and <p_B> replace Baesecke's Roman numeral I and <p_C> for his Roman numeral II. The subscript indicators are combined on a single indicator <p> to reflect their combination into a single text. The use of lowercase <h> mirrors Baesecke's use, i.e., with subscript qualifiers to indicate editions of the *Heliand* text. Together, the indicators <p>, <g>, and <h> stand in parentheses following the document they comprise.
5. A re-ordering of the lower branches from left to right. Here I have adopted the order of the manuscripts as they appear in the *Stammbäume* of Taeger, Rooth, and Lambel, i.e. (V – C – P – M – [S]). I feel that this aids one in comparing the various charts.
6. Similar to point 3., I have renamed the hypothetical stages to reflect the extant manuscripts that have been derived from them separated by a slash. This includes the addition of *M/S, which stands in place of Baesecke's M and corresponds with Taeger's *MS, from which MSS M and S have descended.
7. A new indicator I (for 'Illyricus') to replace Baesecke's F, since his indicator can be confused (Fabricius or Flacius?). I prefer to elucidate this distinction throughout the book by referring to Matthias Flacius by his cognomen 'Illyricus'. A dashed line extends from node I to indicate that the *Prefaces* (i.e. *Praefatio* + *Versus*) have been reproduced from Illyricus' publication many times.
8. Following the argument that I make in this and following chapters, MSS P and L are shown descended from a single codex that I call *Codex L* (cf. 13.1). This hypothetical document is more or less

equivalent to the combination *PL*, which is not divided by a slash to indicate that the two descendent manuscripts represent unitary leaves removed from a common source codex.

9. I introduce a distinction between hypothetical textual elements (indicated by *) and hypothetical manuscripts (indicated by *italics*), e.g. **A* is hypothetically both (1) a unique manuscript, and (2) a text that can be reconstructed partially from various overlapping parts from extant manuscript texts. ***O* is marked with two asterisks after Baesecke's usage. This reflects its nature as being hypothesized from a separate hypothetical stage, namely **A*.
10. Extant manuscripts are in bold.
11. Arrows represent a split or merger of pieces.

Consistent with Baesecke's proposal, I have indicated dates in the left-hand column. These mark approximate positions within the tree structure. For several of these I have indicated an associated event, also after Baesecke's habit. For example, 1609 and 1613 are the publication dates of the two volumes for which MS L was reused as a book cover; both were printed in Wittenberg. Similarly, 1598 is the publication date of the volume for which MS P was reused as a book cover; this book was printed in Rostock.

It is uncertain when MSS P and L were (1) removed from their matrix, and (2) recycled as book covers; nevertheless, the latter applications could not have occurred until the publication dates of the (later) book around which it was found (i.e. 1598 for MS P; 1613 for MS L). Whether the two MSS were removed early and simultaneously, after which MS L was then reserved for 15+ years (the difference between 1598 and 1613), is unknown. Another explanation might have the two MSS separated simultaneously at a date after 1613 and applied roughly simultaneously to the books. A third explanation might have the MSS cut out of the matrix at separate times, e.g. MS P just after 1598 and MS L just after 1613.

An apparent wrinkle in any of these possibilities is Joachim Feller's mention of **Codex L* in his 1686 *Catalogus codicum manuscriptorum Bibliothecae Paulinae in Academia Lipsensis* ('List of the manuscript books of the Paulinum Library at the University of Leipzig'), the first catalogue of the holdings of the University of Leipzig Library (cf. 7.2). This mention occurs in the foreword of the catalogue (Praefatio, v), yet no explicit mention of the same codex exists in the catalogue listings. Whether this is an indication of the codex having been lost is unknown. On the other hand, many instances of New Testament codices occur in the listings, the vast majority without any qualification to indicate the language of the text or any other description information. Perhaps one of these is the *Heliand* codex. All the same, Feller's mention of **Codex L* in the catalogue's foreword has implications for when MSS P and L were separated from their matrix: if the full codex was present in Leipzig as late as 1686, then neither could have been recycled to their new functions until after that date. This means that the Leipzig *Heliand* codex might well have survived in its full form in Leipzig into the eighteenth century.

2.3 Additional Evidence Linking MSS P and L

Besides having been recycled in similar fashions as coverings for books that were printed within 15 years of one another, and in addition to having been found at locations with historical links to one another, the texts of MSS P and L show many commonalities to suggest they once belonged to the same matrix. Several paleographic features have been presented (cf. 2.1.1) in support of this hypothesis. Schmid (2006) presents more paleographic similarities, including shared use of the small majuscule <N> in non-word-final positions and the second-hand addition of neumes (medieval musical notation for chanting purposes). Much of the scholarly literature published since the discovery of MS L discusses the relationship—as well as the relationship of MS L to the other four documents—based on linguistics evidence in the texts, notably the presence of words and spelling differences (cf. Sahm 2007, Rauch 2007 for more details).

In my analysis of the high-resolution digital scan of MS L, I discovered an overlooked character that further supports the P-L theory. I believe this character has been overlooked by other researchers because it lies within a fold that formed when the parchment was re-used as a book cover. The fold in question is the upper-left crease on the recto side, i.e. the outward-facing side of the book cover and therefore the more worn of the two sides, meaning that the hidden character is further obscured by wear. The first word of the second row is cited by Schmid (2006) as *thit*, (2007) *thit* and by Sahm (2007) as *T hit*. I provide an image of the row in question below:[12]

Fig. 2.1: MS L, row 2

ᴛ hιᴛᴛ graf aɴᴛhefuɴ grιoᴛa ɴ u m u g u ɴ gι g aɴgaɴ

This corresponds to Taeger (1996, 205):

5824 thit graf an theson griote.   Nu mugun gi gangan [...]

The overlooked character occurs in the first word, which is clearly spelled <T hitt>, i.e. with two final <t> characters. This seemingly minor detail has major implications, since only one other occurrence of this spelling exists in the entire *Heliand* and Old Saxon Genesis library (Sehrt, 588 and 597), namely in MS P, version, row 15, fifth word:

Fig. 2.2: MS P, row 15

ᴛhar ma hᴛιgna · herroɴ   habdu ɴ ᴛhιᴛᴛ ιſ quad hιe

---

[12] The top image is a desaturated version of the original image thus creating a black-and-white; no other alteration has been performed. The middle image has had the grey of the parchment reduced so as to make the ink appear darker in contrast with its environment, though no alteration to the ink image has been performed; the full image was then desaturated to create a black-and-white image. The bottom image has had the parchment background reduced nearly to white, while the ink color has been darkened; this has been achieved by maximizing the value of the black channel in all color ranges and minimizing the value of the black channel in the grey color range within the 'Selective Color' dialog. To show the effectiveness of this technique, consider the second word, *graf*, which appears slightly more legible in the bottom image than in either of the other two.

This corresponds to Taeger (1996, 41):

> [...] thar mahtigna
> 997 hêrron habdun: '*thit* is', quað he, [...]

Both appearances of *thitt* involve the neut. sg. nom. declension of the demonstrative pronoun. Ideally, one should want an instance of *heran* (cf. 2.3.2) in order to complete Lambel's analysis comparing <rr> vs. <r> in the spelling of this word throughout the manuscripts. Unfortunately, no form of *heran* occurs in MS L. In lieu of this, the similarity of MS L to MS P strongly suggests that the former is closely related to the latter, allowing one to assume that whatever assumption about the placement of MS P in the *Stammbaum* can be applied equally to MS L.

3. Question of Authorship

3.1 Significance of Identifying the *Heliand* Poet

Due to this proposal that MSS P and L represent the oldest extant version of the *Heliand*, the discovery of the new fragment has reignited the debate about who authored the *Heliand* epic, as well as when and where this took place. The importance of these questions is summarized by Eichhoff & Rauch (1973, VIII):

> Die Fragen nach der Person, der Herkunft und Erzeihung des Dichters sind in letzter Zeit etwas in den Hintergrund des wissenschaftlichen Interesses gerückt, würden aber, wenn sie sich beantworten ließen, auf andere ungelöste Heliandprobleme ein neues Licht werfen.

Discovering the *Heliand* poet could be considered the proverbial Holy Grail of Old Saxon studies: by unlocking this key mystery, many other currently inexplicable elements would become self-evident. The author's identity would shed light on questions regarding the linguistic variation seen in the manuscripts, as well as the purpose of the epic and related circumstances surrounding its creation. Unfortunately, with only little in the way of clues to the identity of the author, research follows the opposite course to the ideal: we are left to infer an entire back-story by first seeking to secure evidence from the smallest of elements. Many scholars have put their hands to the task in this manner. In fact, the relative lack of concrete evidence seems not to be a limiting factor for the number of hypotheses that promise to pinpoint the home of the *Heliand*.

3.1.1 Parameters and Considerations

In approaching the question of origin, individual scholars interpret 'home' differently; viz., one methodology may focus on the chronology and geography of the epic's intended audience, while another may center on a facet of the author's identity. Certainly, both are relevant, as author and audience are tightly tied, and thus discovering one will aid in revealing the other. Similar difficulty arises when trying to link history and geography with the potential suspects for author. Furthermore, it is uncertain what the purpose behind the epic's creation was—e.g., whether it was primarily a religious tract or a political tool—and how it's audience received the work.

Invariably, arguments for the heroic epic's origin are built on data gleaned from the *Heliand* text itself. Other research explanations—e.g., folk movements, cultural studies, comparative dialectological analyses, history of Christianization, etc.—may well be employed then to bolster and/or verify these origin claims. Whatever the account, a study of the European mainland's northern-most non-Scandinavian Germanic peoples customarily begins with a dissection of the *Heliand* text. This reliance on a single text arises because little else in the way of endemic narrative monuments was left by the Old Saxon culture—if indeed a single, unified society had managed to coalesce before its constituent groups were forcibly fused into the Frankish nation. Thus, the accuracy of any academic claim about the mainland Saxons, whether individually or as a group, depends heavily on the accuracy of the modern *Heliand* transcriptions. Thus, the accuracy of the transcription is of utmost importance (cf. 4.1).

3.2 Evidence at Hand

Of the many hypotheses dealing with the identity of *Heliand* author, none has been able to provide much definitive external, i.e. historical, evidence. While it is tempting to add to the pot of speculation, in the end I feel I have little substance toward this end. Therefore, it is not my purpose to unmask the anonymous poet. Furthermore, the various theories exist in their published forms and are therefore readily accessible to the research. I will therefore not go into the details behind every proposed theory of the identity of the *Heliand* poet. Instead, I will discuss a few of the more notable features associated with that person, which have been discerned from the generations of close analysis of the language in the manuscripts as well as an ever broadening understanding of the monastic institutions that existed in Saxony during the Medieval Period.

3.2.1 Historical Clues

To determine the timing of the epic's composition one need only to look at the language and the nature of the story being told. As has been discussed, linguistic characteristics have allowed researchers to determine both the

Germanic and furthermore the Old Saxon nature of the text. This allows one to shrink the possibilities in time and place to a relatively narrow window of time of ca. 200 years in length, i.e. 800–1000. Much of what we know about the history of the continental Saxons comes from the historical writings of a monk-scribe by the name of Widukind of Corvey, who as his epithet shows was active at Corvey Abbey, founded in 815 by two of Charlemagne's cousins, Wala and Adelard (Catholic Encyclopedia). The abbey was populated by monks from the older abbey Corbie in Picardy, after which the new location was named.[1]

Widukind (ca 925–973) penned *Res gestae Saxonicae* ('The Deeds of the Saxons') in the years prior to his death to record what was until then an oral history of the Saxon people's conquering and conversion to Christianity at the hands of Charlemagne. He thus also gives us a round-about explanation for the timing of the *Heliand*, as this Christian-themed text in Old Saxon must have come about during or after the Christianization period.

Though attempts to convert the heathen Saxons had begun with St. Boniface (680–754) around 723, the Saxons met these with great resistance. Boniface had begun preaching to the Saxons' neighbors, the Frisians, in 716 after noting a similarity of their language with his native Anglo-Saxon. In 723, Boniface felled the Saxons' holiest pagan relic, Thor's Oak, probably located near modern-day Fritzlar in Hesse. His success in cutting down this tree without being struck down by Thor likely prompted the conversion of the first Saxon Christians. Nevertheless, it seems that proselytizing efforts made little headway during the eighth century, since several attempts by Charlemagne to baptize the reticent heathens at the tip of his sword failed. The final blow to the Saxons came through Charlemagne's success at quashing a rebellion led by the Saxon duke Widukind[2] that had lasted from ca. 777 to 785. Upon losing, Widukind accepted baptism. Another Saxon revolt against the Carolingian Empire would not take place until half a century later, when the grandchildren of Widukind's generation rose during the *Stellinga* ('comrades') revolt (841–842). This revolt was brought about by the *frilingi* ('freeman') and the *lazzi* ('semi-free serfs'), who together represented the two lowest castes in Saxon society, not including slaves. The aim of the revolt—nominally, the reinstatement of the right of the people to

---

[1] Corvey Abbey is also called New Corbie.
[2] A different man from Widukind of Corvey.

practice their ancestral religion freely—was countered by the *edhilingui* ('nobility'). Though this class had resisted in 782 when Charlemagne outlawed public meetings—e.g. the yearly Marklo council—by 785 the Saxon nobles had come to realize the potential for gain: by allying themselves to Charlemagne, the *edhilingui* could wrest for themselves the decision-making power that had traditionally been decided upon democratically. This tradition had originally given the nobility more votes than the other two voting groups, but the latter had become more populous over the generations and thus threatened the old balance of power. To the Saxon nobles, Charlemagne's conquest meant re-ensuring their influence over their own people, but did so at a cost (Goldberg, 110):

> [...] Saxon society was somewhat less hierarchic and oppressive than that in Francia. Although the *edhilingui* were the most wealthy and powerful group, the *frilingi* and *lazzi* had a say in local assemblies, and they apparently owed only dues, but not services, to their *edhilingui* landlords. However, Charlemagne's conquest worsened the condition of the *frilingi* and *lazzi*, since the Saxon peasants on estates confiscated by the king, Church, and Frankish nobles now were compelled to render services as well as dues to the lord. [...] Moreover, the newly erected Church compelled all Saxons to pay the tithe—one-tenth of their annual income—to support the local bishop and parish priests.

The *edhilingui*'s acceptance of Charlemagne as their lord and Christianity as their religion was blatant political treachery. Yet it worked. A Christian Saxon noble had a better chance at becoming a vassal to the Frankish king, and thereby being placed back in power over his people. The only real cost: conversion.

The Saxon peasantry had little motivation to convert except for perhaps fear. On the other hand, their reticence toward the state religion was the only true means of rebellion left to them (110–112):

> As a sign of their resentment of Frankish domination, the Saxon peasants clung to their ancestral polytheistic beliefs throughout the ninth century.
> Despite what must have been widespread resentment of noble lords among the agricultural laborers, large-scale popular revolts were unusual in early medieval Europe. This is because a mob of angry, half-starved peasants wielding pitchforks was no match for a small, disciplined troop of heavily armed nobles on horseback. Peasant resistance to aristocratic domination therefore usually took less spectacular forms, such as refusal to render dues and services, appeals to the king and his representatives, or flight. However, the political chaos caused by the Carolingian civil war and the infighting among the Saxon nobles gave the *frilingi* and *lazzi* a rare opportunity to unite against them and revolt in 841.

Thus, the survivors of the battle lost by Widukind in 785 continued to subvert the system in the only way possible to them. The children and grandchildren who grew up in this environment of social resistance must have been told stories about how their forefathers had been wronged. Like any ethnic myth, this Saxon heritage would have been linked to specific habits and traditions that were propagated as cultural ideals to the following generations. Similarly, given the right set of environmental circumstances, this cultural myth would provide justification for 'freedom fighters' who were, after all, merely returning to the ways of their fathers. Such environmental circumstances did develop some 56 years following Widukind's lost rebellion.

When Louis the Pious died, he left his vast territory to his sons: Lothar I (795–855), Pepin I of Aquitaine (797–839), Louis the German (806–876), and Charles the Bald (823–877). Having originally divided his realms among the three eldest, in 823 Louis the Pious attempted to rewrite his will to include Charles, whom he had produced from his second marriage. In the subsequent years until their father's death, the sons resisted his will and fought among themselves, resulting in Lothar's 829 dethroning and banishment to Italy. The hectic situation was lightened by Pepin's death in 838, after which his territories were eventually given to Charles the Bald, but only after Pepin's son Pepin II died in 860. Finally, Lothar's son Lothar II died without an heir, and so his kingdom was divided amongst Charles the Bald and Louis the German in 870 (Treaty of Meerssen). Thus, the period between 823 and 870 is referred to as the Carolingian civil war, which presented the descendants of Widukind's Saxon rebellions with the perfect opportunity to try their hand again at succession (112):

> "That year [841] throughout all Saxony" Gerward wrote, "the serfs rose up violently against their lords. They called themselves Stellinga [...] and committed much madness. The serfs violently persecuted and humiliated the nobles of that land." As part of their rebellion, the Saxon peasants openly renounced Christianity and reverted to polytheism.

These nobles whom the *Stellinga* "persecuted and humiliated" no doubt included Saxon lords and their descendants who had gained advantage by siding with Charlemagne. This uprising obviously had the potential for serious change, since Lothar attempted to use the *Stellinga* revolt to propel himself over his brother, Louis the German, the Saxon's new king by inheritance:

> As a sign of his desperation after Fontenoy, Lothar even appealed to the Stellinga, promising them their traditional rights and customs in return for support against Louis. Lothar's appeal ultimately backfired, because the nobles saw it as an unholy alliance against themselves and the Church. For the moment, however, Louis feared the Stellinga would unite with the neighboring polytheistic Danes and Slavs and drive the Franks and Christianity out of Saxony altogether.

Considering this fate the worst of all options, Louis the German instead sought to reconcile the issue with Lothar.

> [...T]he Stellinga uprising illustrates one of the main reasons why the nobles wanted an end to the civil war as quickly as possible. Such prolonged warfare and social upheaval threatened to open the floodgates to peasant resistance and thereby undermine the very foundations of Frankish aristocratic power.

In 842, the two swore the Oaths of Strasbourg, essentially creating the infancies of France and Germany as nations. Yet, as Goldberg notes, the long-lasting effects of the Treaty of Verdun were likely not foreseeable to anyone at the time (113–114):

> Like the Strasbourg Oaths [...] the 843 division [through the Treaty of Verdun] must be viewed in its ninth-century context. First, extreme distrust still dominated relations among Louis the Pious's heirs and their followers. Thousands, if not tens of thousands, had died during the civil war, and nobles on every side had unresolved grievances and scores to settle. Everyone must have viewed the 843 division as a temporary respite in the hostilities, and it would therefore be more accurate to speak of the Truce of Verdun. Realpolitik would continue and the 843 truce would be broken as soon as the opportunity presented itself. Moreover, Lothar and Louis already had multiple sons, meaning that the empire would have to be divided once again within a generation. Everyone at Verdun would have been shocked to learn that the 843 division cast such a long shadow on the political map of Europe.

The treaty struck was merely a concession by the rulers, who saw that neither had a chance at victory over the other as long as their feud continued to promote anarchy in the population, for this threatened their very positions as kings. Indeed, at least in the case of Louis the German, the division of the Empire was not intended to be long lasting (Haubrichs, 414–415):

> Nach Verlust des *imperium* [durch den Vertrag von Verdun] hatte sich - in Grenzen des alten fränkischen Gesamtstaates - eine fiktiv die Gesamtstaatsidee weitertragende Regierung der drei Söhne Ludwigs des Frommen eingerichtet. Innerhalb dieser Periode der gegenseitigen Konsultationen wiederum sind es die Jahre 847 bis 851, während derer Ludwig der Deutsche bestrebt war, aufgetretene

Spannungen zwischen seinem Stiefbruder Karl dem Kahlen und dem nominell das *imperium* ausübenden Lothar, dem Regenten des Mittelreichs, auszuräumen. In jenen Jahren diplomatischer Aktivität war es ganz deutlich unter den Brüdern Ludwig, dem die politische Initiative zukam. Er war *ordinator rei publicae*, der mit staatsmännlicher Weisheit die Geschicke des fränkischen Staates in die rechten Bahnen lenkte – und in dieser Rolle wollte er auch gesehen werden.

Nevertheless, the concessions of the Treaty of Verdun had granted Louis the German a respite from his concerns with his brothers, freeing him to turn his attention to the threat within his own domain (Goldberg, 112):

> Thus, as soon as Louis struck the armistice with Lothar in the summer of 842, he headed east to make an example out of the Stellinga: "Louis traveled throughout Saxony, where by force and terror he crushed all those still opposing him. He captured all the leaders of that unholy scheme, men who had abandoned the Christian faith and resisted him and his faithful men with such determination. He punished 140 of them with beheading, hung fourteen on the gallows, maimed innumerable others by amputating their limbs, and left no one able to oppose him further." While Louis's actions seem horrific today, contemporary chroniclers (who of course came from the nobility) praised him for acting "bravely" and "nobly" and subjecting the Saxon peasants to "their proper and natural state." When the bold Saxon peasants rebelled once again several months later, the now united Saxon nobility easily slaughtered them in a great bloodbath. In the words of Nithard, "the rebels were crushed by the very legitimate authority without which they had dared to rise up."

This social environment, "[eine] Verbindung von staatlicher Tätigkeit und religiöser Intensivierung" (Haubrichs, 416), continually produced ill effects for the Saxon peasantry. Much like his father and grandfather, Louis the German had reason to mix these two spheres, after all "[d]er Herrscher gilt als der von Gott eingesetzten Leiter und Beschirmer der Kirche". Practically speaking, a Christian vassal was much easier for him to understand and trust than a heathen one. He also had a ready audience of Saxon nobles who were willing to support Christianity in order to maintain their power. The same logic works for the peasantry: a homogenous populace is easier to govern than a heterogeneous one. Thus, the post-civil war climate accords well with a renewed effort to convert the remaining heathen Saxons, whether by the sword or by education. From this historical evidence alone, I envision the *Heliand* poet creating his epic during the early reign of Louis the German and see its creation as an effort to aid in convincing the hard-nosed peasantry by accommodating elements of the autochthonous Saxon culture into the Gospel message.

3.2.2 Description of the Poet from the *Prefaces*

In addition to the six extant manuscripts containing the *Heliand*, another text offers clues into the timing and purpose of the epic's creation. Nevertheless, the history of this document, too, is shrouded in historical fog. First printed in a Protestant tract in 1562 (cf. 6.1), the *Prefaces*—called such after the Latin title of the first of two parts, the *Praefatio* and the *Versus*—stood from that point on as a unitary text. Only in 1720 was this material re-linked to the *Heliand* after Johann Georg von Eccard, a nobleman librarian from Würzburg, stumbled upon what is now called MS M and later read the 1562 publication in which the *Prefaces* had been printed (cf. 6.1.1). Due to what seemed to him a similarity between the two documents—namely, the overall theme of the two documents, the language of MS M and the language described in the *Prefaces*, and what he surmised to be the purpose behind the text of MS M vis-à-vis the explanation in the *Prefaces*—Eccard hypothesized that the two texts once belonged to the same book—or at least to different copies of the same book. This is a piece of what he read from the *Prefaces* (Hellgardt 2004, p. 177–178; German translation, p. 181):

> [...] Ludouicus pijssimus Augustus [...] [p]ræcepit namq; cuidam uiro de gente Saxonum, qui apud suos non ignobilis Vates habebatur, ut uetus ac nouum Testamentum in Germanicam linguam poetice transferre studeret, quatenus non solum literatis, uerum etiam illiterates sacra diuinorum præceptorum lectio panderetur.

> [...] Ludwig, der sehr fromme Augustus [...] befahl nämlich einem gewissen Mann aus dem Stamm der Sachsen, der bei den Seinen als ein sehr angesehener seherischer Dichter galt, dass er sich anstrengen sollte, das Alte und das Neue Testament poetisch in die germanische Sprache zu übertragen, damit nicht nur den Schriftkundigen, sondern auch den Schriftunkundigen die heilige Lesung der göttlichen Gebote sich erschließe.

Since Eccard first proposed the link between the *Prefaces* and the *Heliand*, researchers have sought to discover the Old Saxon author's identity. These proposals invariably consist of a laundry list of personal characteristics, mostly taken from the *Prefaces* and typically including the following:

1. The poet lived during the reign of Emperor Louis, i.e., either
   a. Louis the Pious, or
   b. Louis the German
2. The poet was a man

3. The poet's people were the Saxons
4. The poet was at least somewhat famous among his own people
5. The poet translated at least parts of the Bible into the "Germanic" language

Scholars disagree on the reliability of various parts of the *Prefaces* (cf. Taeger 1996, pp. xxxiii-xxxviii). Consequently, proposals toward the identity of the poet, his homeland, his native dialect, his location while composing the epic, and the precise timing of his work, all vary in specificity. On aggregate, this offers an awkward mix: historical personalities—both named and unnamed—and invented characters are linked to historical events, allied with likely colleagues and cohorts, and tracked down to geography—both narrow and broad—based on speculations about the original poet's mother tongue, his training, and his resources. One seemingly obvious solution would be to average these characteristics: assuming the most specific characteristics might yield a clearer picture of the poet. Yet many of the authorial characteristics that the hypotheses propose are mutually exclusive. At best, the proposals agree on vague (and therefore not very useful) points: the poet was a male with very good, if not native command of some variety of a Continental West Germanic language that was unaffected by the High German consonant shift (Second Sound Shift), i.e. some variety that would now be classified as Old Frisian or Old Low German.[3]

3.3 Current Theories: If not "Who?", then "Where?"

If taken as factual, the history provided by the *Prefaces* allows one to narrow the window of time during which the *Heliand* must have been written from ca. 200 years to two periods of ca. 30 years each, namely those encompassing the various reigns of two men named Louis, i.e. Louis the Pious (Holy Roman Emperor: 813-840) and Louis the German (King of East Francia: 843-876). An argument for the authenticity of the *Prefaces* material is provided in 6.1.3. More crucial to any investigation of the *Heliand* is whether the *Prefaces* text presents a factual history. Yet, despite any potential arguments against its veracity, the only real clues about the timing of the

---

[3] I.e., *Altniederdeutsch*, a term used in German scholarly literature which generally includes Old Low Franconian and Old Saxon.

Heliand's creation are provided in the *Prefaces*. Consequently, for the sake of discussion alone, there is hardly a choice but to assume that the history provided in the *Prefaces* is—at least to some degree—factual.

Outside of the *Prefaces* the only source of information about who composed the *Heliand* exists in the details of the manuscripts themselves. So, while the precise identity of the author remains unknown, certain details of his life have been pursued in previous scholarly studies. These attempts always refer to some degree back to the assumptions that can be drawn from the *Prefaces*. For example, linguistic features ostensibly revealed from spelling choices might well indicate a particular region from which the author might have stemmed, assuming that a scriptorium and a dialect existed in the same region at a certain time. Similarly, spelling conventions might suggest that the author was educated, or at least influenced in some way, at what was a limited number of scriptoria in existence at the time of the proposed date of authorship. In all, much of the evidence coming from such questions requires one to suppress his doubt slightly, since each proposition rests upon presumptions that may or may not be true. For example, if the *Prefaces* material tells the truth about the circumstances of the epic's creation (and furthermore, if the researcher intuits correctly that the emperor mentioned therein was Louis the Pious), then certain conclusions may be made about the timing of authorship. If, however, the research has erred in this guess, and the "emperor" suggested by the *Prefaces* was Louis the German, a new set of criteria develop for the timing and, therefore, for the presumptions made about the location of authorship. Suffice it to say that outside of the paltry information provided by the *Prefaces*, little exists on which to hang one's hat. Therefore, for the sake of discussion, the *Prefaces* must be taken at face value, i.e. as being historically truthful and not myth. From this point, only a few possible circumstances exist from which to hypothesize the provenance of the *Heliand*.

3.3.1 Fulda and Werden

Concerning the five characteristics taken from the *Praefatio* of the *Prefaces* (3.2.2), Wolfgang Haubrichs makes a stand both as to poet's time and location: "Mit ziemlicher Sicherheit darf man nun die Identität des Inspirators der as. Evangeliendichtung mit Ludwig des Deutschen behaupten" (422). He makes his conclusion after first discussing the timing of when the *Praefatio* was written and appended to the *Heliand*. Haubrichs thus begins with an argument regarding the identity of the emperor cited in the Praefatio. The identification of this person is generally assumed to limit the timing of the *Heliand*'s creation to a 26-year period in the early ninth century (400):

> Aus dem Wechsel der Tempora im Text der Praefatio konnte man schließen, daß die Vorrede erst nach Abschluß des Werkes, aber noch während der Regierungszeit des betreffenden Fürsten geschrieben wurde. Die imperiale Titular schien diesen eindeutig als Ludwig der Frommen auszuweisen; der ›Heliand‹ mußte somit in den Jahren zwischen 814 und 840 entstanden sein.

However, Haubrichs warns that identifying "Augustus Ludouuicus piisimus" with Louis the Pious may be too immediate a conclusion (400–401):

> Drögereit hat denn auch den Widerspruch [...], daß der angeblich so unverwechselbar mit Ludwig dem Frommen zu identifizierende *Augustus Ludouuicus* der Praefatio durchaus auch auf den ostfränkischen König Ludwig den Deutschen (843–876) bezogen werden kann – wurde doch auch er zuweilen durch den Kaisertitel geehrt.

Thus, as one of the successors of Louis the Pious, one must also take Louis the German as a viable candidate. Moreover, though now considered strange, the imperial title was variously used by and applied to Louis the German (432):

> Seit 833 urkundete Ludwig der Deutsche nicht mehr als König der Bayern, sondern als ostfränkischer Souverän. Ehrgeiz und Macht wachsen mit seinen Ansprüchen. die sich auf das gesamte *regnum orientalis Franciae* erstrecken, welches er 833/34 konstituieren kann.

As noted above, the Carolingian civil war broke out in response to Louis the Pious rewriting his will to include his fourth son—the first and only by his second wife, and one a full generation younger than his three elder brothers. Thus, with Lothar's banishment to Italy, Louis the German began making aspirations to succeed his father as emperor over the whole of Francia. These aspirations were put on pause after the Treaty of Verdun in 842, when Louis the German's claim was officially delimited to the territory of Germania. Nevertheless, the claims coming from Louis the German's subjects remained equally pretentious in regard to his role. One particular location is noted for continuing to refer to him by the imperial title (401):

> Es ist immerhin bemerkenswert, daß der Gebrauch der imperialen Titulatur für Person und Herrschaft des ostfränkischen Königs in der überwiegend Mehrzahl der Belege auf Fulda weist – also auf ein Kloster, das mit gewichtigen Gründen von einem Teil der Forschung als Heimat des ›Heliand‹ betrachtet wird. Zatschek hält es für möglich, daß der Imperatortitel in Urkunden eines eng mit der Reichspolitik jener Jahre verknüpften Klosters wie Fulda politischen Motiven entspringt, vielleicht „eine Stimmung am Hofe Ludwigs des Deutschen widerspiegelt". Die meisten Belege sind in das Jahrzehnt zwischen 840 und 850 zu datieren.

Haubrichs thus shifts his time window to Louis the German's early reign and reduces it to the decade between 840 and 850. Yet, given Louis the German's activity as ruler of Bavaria even during his father's lifetime, Haubrichs sees the possibility that the *Heliand* project was begun earlier than the decade noted above (432):

> Ludwig der Deutsche veranlaßt eine as. Evangeliendichtung vor 840 (*imperii tempore*), die Bestandteil eines über das speziell altsächsische Sprachgebiet ausgreifenden Übersetzungsprogramms in die Volksprache ist. Da er dazu erst in der Zeit seiner Herrschaft über das gesamte rechtsrheinische Gebiet (vgl. *cunctus populus suae ditioni subditus, Theudisca loquens lingua*) zwischen 833 und 838 Anlaß hatte, datieren wir in diese Periode.

Thus, Louis the German's leadership in Bavaria actually spread beyond this region to the north, encompassing all territory east of the Rhine. Moreover, the use of the term *Germanicum* in the *Praefatio* points to a particular part of the territory over which Louis the German ruled prior to Louis the Pious' death in 840 (426–427):

> Den Hintergrund des Gebrauchs von *germania lingua* – so dürfen wir abschließend feststellen – bildet dabei die regionale Gliederung des ostfränkischen Reichs in *Noricum, Raetia* und jenen im Gefolge der bonifatianischen Missionsterminologie bestehenden Bereich der *Germania* auf den Hraban bewußt anspielt, wenn er auf der Synode von Mainz 852 diese Stadt als *metropolis Germaniae* bezeichnet. Tatsächlich lag ein Großteil der Mainzer Suffraganbistümer in Sachsen. Wollte man sich daher von der Sprachbildung allein führen lassen, so würde sie auf jene fuldischen Kreise verweisen, die in der Mainzer Kirchen- und Reichspolitik seit 847 eine Rolle spielen.

Haubrichs points both to the Mainz archdiocese's role in the missionary efforts in Saxony, but more so to the leadership at Mainz—a circle of clerics that had been schooled at Fulda in the 820s and 830s. So while Mainz may have been the *Heliand*'s gateway to the Saxons, he argues that it was at

Fulda that the epic germinated. This leads him to a conclusion about the personality behind the *Heliand*'s creation (423):

> Bisher hat man zwei wesentliche Vermutungen über die Person des Autors geäußert: Hraban und Lupus von Ferrières wurden mit ihm identifiziert. Interessant genug ist, daß beide Autoren der Schule von Fulda entstammen.

That neither of these men was a native Saxon does not concern Haubrichs, since he finds linguistic evidence to assume that the author belonged to a different nationality:

> [... G]ewinnt die Aussage, daß der sächsische Dichter *apud suos* als *vates* galt, „erst außerhalb Sachsens im Munde eines N i c h t s a c h s e n ... gedanklich und stilistische Natürlichkeit".

Furthermore, he argues that "Eigentümlichkeit[en] Hrabans" (428) in the Praefatio point distinctly to that abbot. Moreover, he cites historical connections between Rabanus Maurus (780–856) and Louis the German that might underlie the composition of the *Heliand* (430):

> In dem Bemühen um Ordnung im Staat und Bewahrung der *rectitudo* der Religion dürfen wir das entscheidende sachliche Moment sehen, das ihn [i.e. Hraban] zu einer Zusammenarbeit mit Ludwig dem Deutschen nötigte. In diesen Jahren - seit 847 - auf den mit Ludwig gemeinsam abgehaltenen Synoden tut er im Auftrag des Königs das, was die Heliand-Praefatio als vornehmste Aufgabe des Herrschers hinstellt - sich um das Seelenheil seiner Untertanen zu bemühen, sie zu unterrichten und den *populus christianus* zu Besseren zu führen, das 'Schädliche' und die 'Häresie' aber auszurotten.

As to the composition of the *Heliand*, Haubrichs divides this role into two parts potentially performed by two different men: (1) the poet-author, and (2) the editor-compiler. Moreover, he triangulates a relationship between the unnamed author, Rabanus (editor), and Louis the German (commissioner) (433):

> Wie immer sich auch das Verhältnis des Dichters der Evangelienharmonie zu Hraban und Ludwig gestaltet haben mag, da in der Praefatio von einem ausdrücklichen Beschluß (*praecepit*) des Herrschers die Rede ist, so werden wir am ehesten mit dem Zusammentreffen des Abts und des Königs in Fulda 835 oder 836 als der Keimzelle der Dichtung zu rechnen haben.

To wit, Louis the German and Rabanus shared goals that, as per the *Prefaces*, were the inspiration and purpose behind the *Heliand*. In his role, Rabanus was responsible for acquiring a poet to rework the Bible into a Germanic epic, the completion of which goal is otherwise unattested. Still, the *Heliand* certainly encompasses the Gospels, and fragments of the Old Testament written in Old Saxon were discovered in the Vatican along with MS V. So, one might conclude that the *Prefaces*' references to both New and Old Testament are fulfilled in extant examples. However, according to Haubrichs and Krogmann, the Praefatio was intended only as an introduction to the *Heliand*, i.e. only to the New Testament translation (408):

> Krogmanns Ansicht, daß die echte Praefatio von Anfang an nur für den ›Heliand‹, nicht auch für die altsächsische ›Genesis‹ bestimmt war, kann man auch [...] nur unterstützen.

In response to anyone who would wish to counter him by pointing out the obvious, i.e., that the *Praefatio* mentions both Old and New Testaments ("vetus ac novum Testamentum"), Haubrichs explains that such language applies to an end goal that had not yet been reached:

> Wenn schließlich mit denselben Argumenten auch gegen die beiden Worten *vetus ac* (Z. 18) Bedenken vorgetragen werden, so ist ausgelassen, daß in diesem Satz noch nicht von der Endgestalt der Dichtung die Rede ist, sondern von dem Auftrag des Fürsten an den Dichter, sich um die poetische Übertragung beider Testamente zu bemühen *(studere!)*. [...] So sind denn auch diese beiden Worte nicht von vornherein aus dem genuinen Text auszuzeichnen, sondern die mit ihnen gegebene Einheit der Aussage muß zunächst auf ihren möglichen Sinn hin betrachtet werden.

What had been finished, according to Haubrichs, was the *Heliand*-rendition of the Gospels, which thus required an introductory comment by Rabanus. Haubrichs finds a date and place for the penning of this introduction, finding also therein the date by which the *Heliand* must have been finished (433):

> Um 850 – die Gottschalksynode als Anhaltspunkt der Datierung fand 848 statt – schreibt Hraban eine Praefatio zum Heliand, der um eben diese Zeit beendet war, denn um 850 setzt auch Drögereit die handschriftliche Überlieferung für Werden an.

Here, Haubrichs mentions Werden Abbey, a scriptorium in Saxony founded in 799 by Ludger, containing substantial holdings including a history of producing vernacular manuscripts. Also often discussed among Germanists as a possible home of the *Heliand*, Werden has historical links to Fulda that to Haubrichs may clarify why some evidence from the extant manuscripts and fragments seems to point to the one location, while other data from the same documents points to the other (434):

> Ist vielleicht zu diesem Zeitpunkt der Dichter des Heliand nach Werden übergesiedelt, in dessen Mauern noch bis 840 die Anhänger Ludwigs des Deutschen die Oberhand hatten, vielleicht weil er dem König näher stand als Hraban? *Werden* hatte sich aus den Tagen seine Gründers Liudgers, dessen Sippe noch lange die Geschicke des Klosters lenkte, eine gewisse Tradition volksprachlicher Tendenzen bewahrt. Dort, in einem Skriptorium mit altsächsicher Schreibtraditionen, wie sie Fulda nicht besaß, ließ sich ein repräsantives Werk, wie es der Heliand zweifellos war, wohl vervielfältigen. Werden hatte überdies, wie seine Kaisertitulatur für Ludwig den Deutschen 847/48 und 855 beweist, auch zur fraglichen Zeit der paläographischen Datierung gute Beziehungen zum König. Der Kontakt zwischen Fulda und Werden ließ sich in den dreißiger Jahren durch den mit Hraban befreundeten Abt des westfälischen Klosters Gerfrid (auch Bischof von Münster 809–839) herstellen.

Thus, the still unknown poet-author's education at Fulda under Rabanus might explain literary influences apparent in the *Heliand* and in the *Praefatio* that can be tied back to that monastery, while spelling tendencies and western linguistic elements can be explained as the result of the author's move to a safer climate on the Ruhr. In short, the character Rabanus provides links to three locations previously posited as the home of the *Heliand*.

3.3.2 Westphalia

Haubrichs echoes much of what Willy Krogmann had proposed 18 years earlier; however, minor differences of opinion lead to varying conclusions. For example, Krogmann sees not Rabanus Maurus, but Lupus Servatus (805–862; German 'Lupus von Ferrières') as the composer of the *Praefatio*. Nevertheless, Krogmann also favors Fulda as the location at which at least the *Praefatio* was written. For this he turns to particular items in the language of the Praefatio.

Krogmann first cites Sievers in considering the *Praefatio* and *Versus* as the product of multiple writers. In fact, according to Sievers, the *Praefatio* itself was written in two parts: A and B. Moreover, Sievers proposed that the author of *Praefatio* B coincides with the author of the *Versus*. Krogmann counters Sievers' assumption about the background of the *Praefatio* B/*Versus* author (Krogmann, 23):

> Sievers' Annahme, daß die Versus vom Verfasser des zweiten Teils der Praefatio (B) herrührten, weil in beiden Bedas Caedmonerzählung benutzt sei, und daß beide aus diesem Grunde von einem Angelsachsen geschrieben seien, durfte man seiner Meinung nach nur hinnehmen, wenn man beide Stücke in derselben Handschrift von Anfang an zusammengehören ließ. Sie wird ihm aber hinfällig, wenn man den Heliand in Fulda entstanden läßt, wo Bedas Historia ecclesiastica mindestens von Würzburg her zugänglich war.

Thus, Krogmann lights upon the idea that the *Praefatio* and *Versus* were attached to the completed *Heliand* after the latter's completion. This realization drives his argument further; however, first he rids himself of the burden of explaining the timing of the addition of *Praefatio* B and the *Versus* to the full codex, since such must have been after the *Praefatio* (A) was written (46):

> Wer der Interpolator [i.e., whoever combined *Praefatio* A, *Praefatio* B, and *Versus*] war, läßt sich kaum feststellen. Günstiger scheinen mir die Verhältnisse beim Verfasser der ursprünglichen Praefatio zu liegen. Hier glaube ich in der Tat eine bestimmte Persönlichkeit nahmhaft machen zu können.

Originally, Krogmann concluded *against* Fulda due to semantic peculiarities in the *Heliand*. He took as evidence certain words that, to him, reveal defining characteristics of the author's homeland (25):

> Daß der Dichter nach Ausweis des von ihm zweimal verwendeten Wortes *leia* 'Stein, Fels' dem Gebiet des Rheinischen Schiefergebirges entstammt, also im Sauerland beheimatet war, würde freilich noch nicht ausschließen, daß er sein Werk in Fulda verfaßt habe.

Assuming the etymological source of OS *leia* to be Lat. *lapidem*, Krogmann initially argues that the poet's homeland was in one of the Westphalian district closest to the former Roman border. Presumably, because of their proximity to historical Latin speakers, the Saxons of this region borrowed and nativized the Latin word for 'stone'. Furthermore, Krogmann argued against Fulda (25–26):

> Dagegen spricht jedoch die ausschließliche Verwendung der Festbezeichnung *pāscha* 'Ostern'. Im Anschluß an Frings/Niessen habe ich diese als einen Ausdruck der Kölner Kirchenprovinz erwiesen können. Wenigstens für die altsächsische Zeit ist neben dem *pāscha*-Gebiet ein *ōstara-/ōstarun*-Gebiet anzunehmen. Im Bereich der Erzdiözese Mainz, also in den Bistümern Paderborn, Hildesheim, Verden und Halberstadt hat zunächst *ōstara*, *ōstarun* gegolten, das durch die angelsächsische Mission eingebürgert worden war. Erst später ist *pāschen* über die Grenzen der

Kölner Kirchenprovinz hinausgedrungen. Das Kloster Fulda gehörte nun zur Erzdiözese Mainz und damit zum ōster-Gebiet. Hätte der Heliandichter eine nähere Beziehung zu ihm gehabt, wäre er, wie man gemeint hat, in ihm gebildet worden, so hätte er aller Wahrscheinlichkeit nach auch den Ausdruck ōstara, ōstarun mit aufgenommen. Er hätte ihn zum Zwecke der Variation ebenso neben pāscha gebraucht [...]. Daß er es nur durch tīdi und hēlaga tīdi variieren konnte, bietet nicht nur die Gewähr, daß er dem pāschen-Gebiet entstammte, sondern sicher zugleich die Auffassung, daß er in ihm seine Ausbildung erfuhr und tätig war. Ich habe deshalb auf die ältere Anschauung zurückgegriffen, daß der Dichter sein Werk in Werden an der Ruhr verfaßt habe.

Thus, Krogmann originally used Frings & Niessen's (1927) work to assume that the scriptorium at which the *Heliand* was written must have been subordinate to the Archdiocese of Cologne—namely Werden Abbey. This evidence also seemed to speak against other proposals other than Fulda (26):

Außer Fulda scheiden daher auch Klöster wie Corvey aus, das ebenfalls von verschiedenen Forschern als Entstehungsort des Heliand betrachtet wurde. Es unterstand dem Bistum Paderborn und damit der Erzdiözese Mainz.

Furthermore, paleographic evidence seemed to favor Werden due to spelling habits[4] long since associated with that location:

Gestützt zu werden scheint sie mir durch die [...] Tatsache, daß das in allen Heliandhss. und der Genesishs. gebrauchte Zeichen *b* für den labialen Reibelaut, das erst auf sächsischem Boden nach dem Vorbild von ags. *d* geschaffen wurde, ein Kennzeichen der Werdener Schreibschule war.

Yet in 1948 Krogmann realizes this paleographic evidence is not conclusive:

Da wir auf jeden Fall mehrere Vorstufen anzusetzen haben, erscheint es durchaus als möglich, daß das Zeichen *b* auf einer Stufe der Überlieferung von einem Werdener Schreiber eingeführt wurde. Allerdings könnte es auch andernorts ein Schreiber unter dem Eindruck einer Heliandhs. aufgegriffen haben. Wie gebräuchlich wenigstens in Werden der Buchstabe *b* war, geht daraus hervor, daß selbst in dem aus zwei Doppelblättern und zwei auseinandergeschnittenen Blättern bestehenden Werdener Glossar B aus dem 9./10. Jh., das Teile eines lateinischen Glossars umfaßt, für lat. *v* neben *b* in *colobiem* einmal *b* begegnet.

So, the direction of the borrowing of *b* might have been the opposite of the earlier proposal. That is, given the date of the Werden documents from

---

[4] For a discussion of vocalic evidence from MS C interpreted to be a further indication of a Westphalian origin of the *Heliand*, see Basler (1923); also, Collitz (1901).

which Krogmann made his first assumption, it would appear that the authors had in fact borrowed this character from an even earlier document, e.g. the *Heliand*. As such, the possibility exists that the *Heliand* did not originate from Werden, rather migrated to that abbey. The writers at that scriptorium then would have then used the *Heliand* as a paleographic model for the ƀ character, not vice-versa.

Concerning the reliability of Krogmann's semantic arguments for assuming the Heliand poet was from Sauerland, the evidence from the cases of *pāscha* is not as clear cut as Krogmann might suggest. Following the five instances of *pāscha* as noted by Sehrt (428), only one ought to be used by Krogmann as supporting evidence (text given after Taeger 1996; italics his, bolding [mine] indicates alliterating staves):

    4562 gômono neoton,   Iudeonon pascha

    4202 that sie scoldun **h**aldan   the **h**êlagon tîdi,
        Iudeono **p**ascha.   **B**êd the godes sunu

    4459 'that nu o**b**ar **t**uâ naht sind   **t**îdi kumana,
        Giudeono pascha,   that sie sculun iro **g**ode thionon,

    5141 ac quâðun that sie *im* sô **h**luttro   **h**êlaga tîdi,
        uueldin iro **p**ascha halden.   **P**ilatus antfeng

    5258 that sie that *thia* **h**êlagun tîd   **h**aldan scoldun
        pascha Iudeono.   **P**ilatus gibôd thô,

From these cases, it is clear that the word choice in lines 4202–4203, 5414–5415, and 5258–5259 is required in order to maintain the pattern of alliteration. Only in line 4460 does the alliteration pattern not fall on the chosen word for 'Easter', thereby leaving a choice for the poet to make between *pāscha* and *ōstara*. Line 4562 breaks with alliteration altogether; however, since replacing *pāscha* with *ōstara* would hardly provide any better alliterative result, and since this occurrence of the 'Easter' word is not a variation of *(hêlaga) tîdi*, it is impossible to know why the poet decided to use this word in this environment. The opposite argument would work equally as well, had the poet used *ōstara* in 4562; however, with a lack of comparative data, I would argue that this occurrence should be thrown out as evidence for either side. Therefore, only one case truly stands as proof of Krogmann's theory that the *Heliand* poet must have been native to the region governed by the Archdiocese of Cologne. In other words, his usage of *pāscha* might not be native at all, rather acquired. The circumstances of its usage are simply too ambiguous (i.e., only one poetically unrestricted occurrence of *pāscha*) to allow for jumping to the conclusion that the *Heliand* author was a westerner.

As for the claim echoed by Haubrichs that the *Heliand* poet was not a native Saxon, Krogmann states (27):

> [D]ieser Umstand hat gar nichts mit der Frage nach dem Entstehungsort des Heliand selbst zu tun [...]. [... D]iese Beschreibung [gehört] nicht zur Urhs., sondern zu einer späteren Abschrift [...]. Ihr Verfasser weiß so wenig über den Dichter zu berichten, daß die Annahme eines räumlichen Abstandes unerläßlich ist. Mit vollem Recht erklärt schon Windisch: „Augenscheinlich stand der Schreiber der eigentlichen Praefatio den Kreisen fern, in welchen das Gedicht entstanden ist. Er weiß uns ja nicht einmal den Namen des Dichters zu nennen." Sollte die Praefatio wirklich in Fulda geschrieben worden sein, so wäre der Heliand keinesfalls dort entstanden.

Ultimately, this is all the further Krogmann goes with the question of the poet's identity. From here he turns to identifying the composer of *Praefatio A*—the *Verfasser*—whom he assumes knew nothing about the *Heliand* author.

Krogmann explains his hypothesis regarding the identity of the *Praefatio A* composer by citing the occurrence of the word *Germanicus* in the Praefatio. He quotes Hennig Brinkmann's discussion of the historical difference between *theodiscus* vs. *germanicus* (47):

> Die von Hraban selbst verfaßte Praefatio A soll zunächst, als sie den Umkreis des Volkes, zu dem gesprochen werden sollte, bestimmte, *theodiscus*, nachher bei der Schilderung des geschichtlichen Vorgangs statt des erwarteten *theodiscus* aber *germanicus* gebraucht haben. „Aber gerade die Verwendung von *germanicus* im Anschluß an die Antike", meinte er, „verweist uns sicher nach Fulda. Hier schreibt 836 Lupus von Ferrieres, der unter einem Schüler Alchvines im Kloster Ferrieres aufgewachsen und dann gegen 828 nach Fulda zu Hraban gesandt worden war, eine Vita Wigberts, in der die Wendung *gentili Germanorum lingua* begegnet. *gentilis* hat an dieser Stelle die taciteische Bedeutung; auch *lingua Germanorum* geht auf Tacitus zurück. In der Völkerwanderung verschwindet die Bezeichnung *Germani*, die schon Gregor von Tours nicht mehr kennt. Bonifatius spricht nur von *gentes Germaniae*, Alchvine verwendet nur zweimal *Germania*, aber nicht *Germani*. Für den Gebrauch von *Germanorum* oder *Germanica lingua* kann also diesmal nicht Alchvine verantwortlich sein, sondern nur Tacitus selbst, den Lupus wohl in Fulda kennen lernte, wo Rudolf, der unter Hraban eine bedeutsame Rolle spielte, in der Translatio S. Alexandri die Germania ausschrieb. Von Fulda aus feiert Lupus die Karlsvita Einharts, die Vertrautheit mit Tacitus verrät. Dieser Tatbestand zeigt, daß in Fulda alle Voraussetzungen fpr den Gebrauch der Wendung *Germanica*

> lingua gegeben waren. Hier kann *theodiscus* durch *germanicus* ersetzt werden, um so mehr als *theodiscus* ausschließlich Sprachname ist."

Yet, as Krogmann notes, Brinkmann overlooked the fact that the composer of *Praefatio* A had used both terms in reference to the Saxon language (49):

> Brinkmann hat mit Recht die Sonderstellung der Bezeichnung *Germanica lingua* hervorgehoben, die dem Verfasser der Praefatio eignet. Zu erwarten wäre in der Tat *lingua Theodisca*, das gegen Brinkmann, der hierin auch von Sievers abweicht, der Interpolator zweimal gebraucht. *Theodiscus* ist im Frankenreich in jener Zeit die übliche lateinische Bezeichnung der germanischen Sprachen.

Krogmann continues by explaining that the use of *Germanica lingua* is not something common among Rabanus' writings; rather, that *lingua Theodisca* is that monk's trademark. "Germanicus statt theodiscus finde ich überhaupt nur bei Lupus von Ferrieres [...]" (50). He notes that Lupus Servatus was educated in Fulda (830–836), from where he sent several letters using *Germanicus* and related forms to monks and other abbeys. The mixed usage of Latin style prevents Krogmann from concluding completely that Lupus Servatus was the composer of *Praefatio* A (51):

> Ebenso wie die schon von Brinkmann gewürdigte Verwendung des Wortes *Germani* ist der Gebrauch des sprachlich gewandten *germanicus* der Ausdruck eines so bewußten Strebens nach einem reinen lateinischen Stil, daß ich nicht anstehe, Lupus von Ferrieres als den Verfasser der Praefatio zu erklären.

This is due to the fact that Krogmann considers Lupus' "reiner lateinischer Stil [...] in jener Zeit einzigartig" (52). Moreover, "[i]n seine Tätigkeit in Fulda fügt sich eine Abschrift des Heliand und die Beifügung der Praefatio reibungslos ein." Consequently, Krogmann favors Lupus enough to conclude that Lupus likely provides some evidence of the timing of the *Heliand* epic's creation (53):

> Konnten wir auf Grund der Praefatio bisher nur das Jahr 840, das Todesjahr Ludwigs des Frommen, als spätesten Zeitpunkt angeben, so schiebt der Umstand, daß Lupus von Ferrieres die Praefatio verfaßte, diesen Terminus um wenigsten vier Jahre zurück[: s]pätestens im Jahre 836 [...].

3.3.3 Beyond the Elbe

The conclusion that Fulda was somehow in the mix is everywhere in the literature. All the same, the relationship of the *Heliand* poet to the scriptorium at Fulda differs as much as the theories about who the poet was and from where he stemmed. Haubrichs forwards a view of a Fulda-educated monk who later transferred to Werden. Krogmann forwards a view of a Westphalian-born man who grew up among the slate crags of Sauerland, and who later moved to Fulda. Notably, neither of these excludes the other necessarily. Georg Baesecke, on the other hand, contests Westphalia as the poet's patria. Appealing to the imagery of the *Heliand*, Baesecke finds a more northerly region that served as the poet's muse (80–81):

> Bei Tatian steht also nach palästinischem Gegensatz ein Haus irgendwo im Lande auf Sand statt auf Fels, im Heliand auf dem „Sand und Grieß" des Strandes oder auf „fester Erde" (nicht auf Fels!), und so werden aus den *pluvia* und *flumina*, die es bedrohen, *uuago strom* und *sees udeon*, und es ist die Westflut der Gezeiten, die es „zerschlägt" und „zerwirft": „Sand und Grieß" können es nicht stützen, wie die „feste Erde" täte. Alles ist umgedacht, umgesehen, und zwar in den Weststrum hinein, der die Hochflut bringt, dorthin wo heute nur noch Inseln, Halligen und Meerbusen oder Watten sind. Hat der Dichter nicht solche Sturmfluten erlebt? Die furthbare des Jahres 819, von der die Kunde bis zu uns gelangt ist?

Baesecke's argument implies that the changes to the Gospel story made by the poet in describing the Holy Land belie too strong an emotional connection to the landscape described to be simply an academic description—"Ich wüßte im Heliand nichts, was kraftvoll-eigner wäre" (81). Indeed, raw is the description of a storm-swept coastline, where the threat of the westerly wind brings with it dangers of deadly floods. While in both the traditional telling and in the *Heliand* the foolish man built his house upon the sand, the distinction of the wise man was not that he built his house upon the rock, rather here upon the steadfast land. Even then, the description of the sand differs. This is not a desert landscape, rather a seascape. Furthermore, Baesecke finds evidence of the poet's acquaintance of northern rivers in the description of the Nile (Taeger 1996, 33: lines 757–760, translation mine):

> [...] an thana grôneon uuang,
> an erðono beztun, thar ên aha fliutid,
> Nîlstrom mikil norð te sêuua,
> flôdo fagorosta [...]

> [...] at the green meadow, the best on earth, there flows a water, the Great River Nile north to the see, the most graceful of rivers [...]

Furthermore, the poet's exceeds a passive knowledge learned from Anglo-Saxon manuscripts at Fulda, as posited by Krogmann, Wrede, Jostes, Metzenthin, and others (82):

> [E]s lohnt, den in einem besonderen Kapitel dargebotenen Stoff neu zu betrachten, z. B. Salz [...], Süßes Wasser [...], Grab und Galgen *an griote* [...] (vgl. die Hinrichtung des Tempelschänders am Meeresstrange nach der christlichen *Lex Frisionum: ducitur ad mare et in sabulo, quod accessus maris operire solet, ... immolatur diis quorum templa violavit.* [...]), -*sand* in Inselnamen [...], -*wurd* [...], Westwind [...], -*holm* [...] usw.

Especially significant here is the mention of the fact that the *Heliand* description of the judgment of the temple money changers (cf. Matt. 21:12, etc.) echoes the practice adjudicated by the *Lex Frisionum*, the special set of laws extended to the Frisians by Charlemagne after he had conquered these North Sea people in 785. This arrangement allowed the Frisians to maintain many of their legal habits, including e.g. *wergeld* and trials by ordeal. Notably, the clergy was exempted from the *Lex Frisionum*. Perhaps then, if the *Praefatio* can be interpreted as Krogmann has, the non-Saxon poet was at home among the Frisians.

Furthermore, Baesecke argues against the interpretation that of Krogmann that "'[w]ir sind nicht berechtigt anzunehmen, daß jener (dichter) gerade die Wirkung des Westwindes am Meeresstrande aus eigner Erfahrung kannte.'" To this he reponds (81):

> Was sollte also der Unglückliche tun, wenn er eines Tagen sagen wollte oder mußte, daß der Westwind wehte, aber selbst noch nicht an eine binnenländischen Heimat wie Halberstadt oder Werden gebunden war und als Kenner der Küste die Namen der Winde und sogar die Windrose kannte? Und den Formelschatz der Seestimmungen seiner ags. Vorbilder hatte doch der liebe Gott nicht eines Tages zum Verbrauch geschenkt, sondern er war durch Beobachtung angewachsen, und so kam der *uuestoni uuint*, und zwar noch mit dem natürlichen noch nicht substantivischen *uuestroni*, aus der Windrose in die Poesie.

Although Baesecke differs in his opinion of the *Heliand* poet, he ultimately agrees with the majority view that Fulda was the location of the epic's creation, finding in its essence the signature of that scriptorium (64):

> [i]n die Sprache der nachmals deutschen Osthintersasses der römischen Rheinprovinzen. Und in diesem Germanisch dichtet der auserkorene Sachse. Das ist die fuldische Hausmarke.

Still more relevant for him is the information that can be gleaned from the history of MS V (55–56):

> Weit erkenntnisträchtiger [...] sind die Bruchstücke in einer Vatikanischen Handschritf des 9. Jahrhunders (V), die ein Mainzer Kalendarium (mit Magdeburgischen Nachträgen [...]) enthält und noch 1479 im Besitze des Mainzer Domkapitels war. [...] Sie ist dann nach Heidelberg in die Palatina gekommen und 1623 mit ihr in den Vatikan entführt. Auf leergelassenen Seiten und Seitenteilen aber hatten dann nach Sprach- und Schreibeigentümlichkeiten drei Schreiber noch des 9. Jahrhundets Bruchstücke unsrer Bibeldichtung eingetragen [...].

From this relationship of MS V to the Cathedral in Mainz, Baesecke concludes the following (56):

> Hier haben wir endlich auch einmal eine Festlegung der Heimat, wenigstens eines Textes: der Amtssitz des Erzbischofs Hrabanus Maurus von Mainz. Und in seiner Umwelt gab es Leute, die Magdeburger Einträge in den Kalendar schoben und andre, die sächsische Dichtungen auszogen, dabei aber mancherlei rheinfränkische Sprachspuren durchließen [...], sie sie auch in Mainz geläufig sein mußten.

Baesecke thus sees not signs of Werden or Cologne in the Frankish features, rather further evidence of Mainz and therewith the influence of Rabanus Maurus.

As for the timing of the Heliand's creation, Baesecke states: "Die erhaltene Fassung der ›Praefatio‹ gehört also in die Zeit nach dem Tode des Kaisers [Ludwigs des Frommen] und nicht zur ersten Ausgabe der Dichtung" (66). Herewith he implies that the *Heliand* itself must have been completed earlier than the Praefatio, and therefore within the lifetime of Louis the Pious, i.e. well before 840.

Finally, Baesecke comes close to putting a name to the poet, offering instead his homeland and an intensive explanation of how this man from the North could have come to be at Fulda. He provides the latter first by an appeal to history, citing Louis the Pious' attempts at converting the heathen Danes (84–85):

> Als Kaiser Ludwig [der Fromme] den vertriebenen Dänenkönig Heriod [... und] das Vold der Dänen dem seinigen durch Einheit des Glaubens verbinden wollte, also einen frommen Mann Gottes suchte, [...] da fand sich Anskar, und ihm schloß sich Autbertus an. Beide waren Mönche von Corvey. Ludwig versorgte sie [...] dazu[,] Ermahnungen für den Glaubensdienst an Heriold und die Bekehrung der Dänen [zu schaffen].

Concerning Anskar and Autbertus' imperial mission to the land north of the Elbe, Baesecke points to evidence in the historical record suggesting that that they not only preached to the heathen, but also concerned themselves with the local Christians (86):

> Immerhin hören wir, daß die beiden Missionare ihre Arbeit auch auf Christen richteten, und das müßten wohl von [Erzbischof] Ebo [von Reims] gewonnene Dänen oder aber Sachsen der Nachbarschaft des [Dänenw]alls von Itzehoe sein, in der wir auch den nachmaligen Helianddichter dachten: empfing er hier fortwirkende Eindrücke aus christlichen Predigten oder Gesprächen? Die ihn dann nach Fulda führten?

So herein Baesecke finds the homeland of the *Heliand* poet—a northerner, perhaps Frisian, perhaps Danish, perhaps Saxon; though in this region the populace was likely heavily mixed all the same—and provides for him a motivation: the poet was already a Christian and a layman.

Baesecke then finds more reason to believe his hypothesis, finding a thread of commonality between the Emperor, the Danish king, the missionaries, and ultimately Rabanus Maurus:

> Auch Heriod betätigte sich mit, und so haben wir wieder den Faden in der Hand, der schon seit seinem ersten deutschen Aufenthalt (814) von und zu Hraban geführt haben muß. Dieser Faden wird noch dadurch verstärkt, daß Gauzbert, Ebos Nachfolger in Münsterdorf und Anskars Geschenke an kirchlichen Gegenständen, namentlich Büchern erhält [...].

Furthermore, he offers an explanation for Krogmann's *pāscha*-vs.-*ōstara* evidence that supports a more northerly interpretation for the poet's dialect: "Er bezeichnete das Osterfest nicht wie Fulda und die Tatianübersetzung mit *ostrun*, sondern wie Hamburg und seine Mission *pascha*. [...] So aber auch die Dänen." Furthermore, he gives a more specific location and, given the known timing of Emperor Louis' Danish mission trips, a set of times during which the poet might have moved south to Fulda:

3. QUESTION OF AUTHORSHIP

Wollen wir indessen seine Übersiedlung nach Fulda an eine Gemeinschaft zwischen Heriold und Hraban knüpfen, so könnte sie schon 814, bei der ersten Fahrt des Königs nach Franken geschehen sein, aber auch noch im Jahre 826, als er mit Anskar zur Dänenmission auszieht und etwa in Münsterdorf den Sänger findet. Der hätte dann in Fulda, und zwar noch während Walahfrids Fuldaer Zeit (bis 829), die Schule genossen und wäre für den Heliand ausersehen.

As for the poet's nationality, Baesecke's places his homeland beyond the Elbe, meaning that the interpretation presented by Haubrichs, Krogmann, and Baesecke that *apud suos* 'among his own (i.e. not our) [people]' implies that the author was not Saxon. On the contrary, at least according to Baesecke, the poet very well might have been a Saxon after all. This, argues Baesecke in line with Krogmann, is because the use of *gentiles Germanorum lingua* reflects Tacitus' style (Krogmann, 47)—i.e., that *gens* had a political meaning—so that, according to Krogmann, the poet must have been an imperial citizen but not a Saxon. Given Baesecke's interpretation, it is possible that the semantics of *gens* was being confused, because not all of the Saxon-controlled territory had been annexed by Charlemagne or his successor—namely, the territory beyond the Elbe remained free. There, Saxons mixed with Danes, Frisians, and even Slavs to some degree. Thus, both requirements provided in the *Praefatio* are potentially fulfilled in Baesecke's localization of the poet's patria somewhere north of the Elbe: the poet was famous among his own people (*apud suos*) who did not belong to the Empire, yet as an immigrant Saxon to Fulda he would have nevertheless been seen as a member of the *gens Germanicus*. Baesecke gets to have his cake and eat it, too.

3.3.4 Verden and others

A plethora of other proposals have been offered by generations of scholars. These could quite obviously fill several books; I find it beyond the scope of this book to entertain them all. Nevertheless, I find it responsible to mention one of the more recent hypotheses, namely that of Clemens Burchhardt.

Burchhardt describes his discovery in 2001, which he takes to be the fruit of his nearly 30-year search for the identity and locality of the *Heliand* poet (10, emphasis mine):

Wer war der Verfasser? Wo ist es geschrieben? [...] Es wurden Fulda und die Abtei Werden/Ruhr genant. Auch dass es ein friesischer mönch gewesen sein könnte[...]. In den Acta Sanctorum, abgekürzt ASS, von Patres der Gesellschaft Jesu in Antwerpen 1658 gesammelt und gedruckt, gewöhnlich Bollandisten genannt, suchte ich in der Reihe der Namen der zehn ersten Verdener Bischöfe nach einem brauchvraen Hinweis. Vergebens, so schien es. Bis ich im Februar Band 2 De Sancto Tancone Episc. *Verdensi in Saxonia Inferiore* [Verden in Lower Saxony], Seite 889 unter Nr. 5 die Worte fand: „eum scripsisse in omnia evangelia librum unum", dass er (?) alle Evangelien in einem Buch geschrieben hätte, „sed quo id auctore probat". [...] – Da aber alle mir bekannten Forscher die zeitliche einordnung mit Kaiser Ludwig dem Frommen und der Jahreszahl 830 vornahmen, zögerte ich nicht mehr länger, hierfür den Autor *Heligand* in Betracht zu ziehen. Einer Eingebung folgend konnte ich das Bild und den Text aus der Spangenberg-Chronik hier als unübersehbaren Hinweis deuten.

Burchhardt finds his answer in the *Acta Sanctorum*—a series of annals printed by the Bollandists in 1658 and based on manuscripts penned in the fourteenth century Sure enough, he provides the promised page of the "Spangenbergische Chronik" (12–13; Spangenberg. pp. 24–25):

HELIGANDUS IX.
Bischoff.

Episcopus IX. Verdensis.

HELIGANDUS, IX. Episcopus Verdensis, eligitur
Anno 833.

ISte Diœcesi Verdensi præfuit illo
Tempore. Gambrivia Præsul quô Ansgarus in urbe
Dicitur à sancto Ludvico Cæsare factus,
Cujus erat dicta facti spectator in urbe.

Zur Zeit als *S. Ansgarius*
Zu *Hamburg* war ohn all Verdruß
Von Kayser *Ludowig* gesetzt/
Ward dieser hier Bischoff geschätzt.

Der IX. Bischoff zu Vehrden Hilligandus ist um das Jahr 833. ein Seel-Sorger der kirchen zu Vehrden gewesen zu den Zeiten / da der Heil. Anscharius Bischoff zu Hamburg im Leben gewesen / und dem Erz-Stifft Brehmen / so der Zeit den Sitz zu Hamburg gehabt / vorgestanden / und haben diese zwo Bischöffe gute *fraternität* mit einander gehalten / hat das Stifft Vehrden 27. Jahr lang regiert / GOttes Wort fleissig gelehrt und gepredigt / und *Anno* 860 gestorben / ıc.

3. QUESTION OF AUTHORSHIP 59

The image of Heligandus shows him in priestly dress with a crook in his left hand and a scroll in his right. Burchhardt comments on this reproduced page:

> Heligand, 9. Bischof von Verden. Das spätmittelalterliche Bild aus der Spangenbergischen Chronik zeigt ihn als einzigen mit einem Konvolut in der Hand. Der Text hebt die Liebe zum Wort Gottes besonders hervor und Heligands Freundschaft mit Ansgar.

It seems the following evidence serves as the crux of Burchhardt's argument: (1) a bishop of Verden in roughly 830, and (2) the name of this bishop is Heligandus, roughly similar to the name of the Old Saxon poem itself (8):

> Da ich über Spangenbergische Chronik im Archiv verfügte, versuchte ich, aus der Reihe der dort abgebildeten Inhaber des Bischöflichen Stuhles eine herauszufinden, der mit Text und Symbolik sich in die These [...] einfügen ließ. Das konnt nur Heligand sein, auch Helmgaud genannt.

This last point is inconclusive, however, because the name *Heliand* was first bequeathed upon the poem by Schmeller in 1830. Is this just coincidence? Or did Burchhardt's man actually take as his nickname the title of his creation—a title first bequeathed by Schmeller a full millennium later? This all seems anachronistic and, thus, highly unlikely.

In fact, as seen in Vogtherr's translation (1998), the name 'Heligandus' is only one of many readings of the name originally penned on the manuscript from which the *Chronicon episcorum Verdensium* was reproduced in print. Vogtherr has as the tenth bishop of Verden one Helmgaud (62-63)—a name that also appears in the Latin text as 'Hellingandus'. Thus, we see that the interpretation of the name's spelling might render an *m* for *in* and a *u* for *and n*, turning 'Helmgaud' into 'Heligand'—both quite common misinterpretations when medieval inscriptions were transcribed for later (early modern) prints. All the same, the strangeness of this bishop's name is highlighted in the *Chronicon episcorum Verdensium* (Vogtherr's translation, bolded emphasis mine):

> [10] Helmgaud (829/31 – 838/39)
>
> Hellingandus (*Hellingaudus; Hellingadus) huius ecclesie episcopus X. Istos bonos viros nullus **propter raritatem nominum parvipendat**, quia omnia cum tempore mores nomina simul et loquela mutantur, quod evidentissimis indiciis iam

apparet. Iste que et quanta fecerit in introitu et tempore ponitifactus suir, in scriptis minime invenitur, qui tamen credendus est ecclesie Verdensi prefuisse doctrina, humilitate, constancia, qui tun temporis locum tenuit in ecclesia dei ut pastor pervigil et fidelis, fositan morte preventus vel aliis impedimentis vel deficiente notario, qui conscriberet, gesta sua memoria sunt elapsa. Circa hec tempora, prout colligi potest, crescenta religione christiana et pace reddita ecclesia Verdensis creditur denuo possessa s suis pontificibus, qui du dispersi sedem suam repetentes verbum dei predicantes, arguentes, obsecrantes oportune et inportune et involas terre ad viam veritatis et ad anitionem fidei revocantes sederunt ut viri simplices et devoti, quia semper presumendum est de bono quamdiu contrarium non apparet.

[...]
Helmgaud, der zehnte Bischof dieser Kirche. Diese guten Männer soll niemand **wegen der Seltenheit ihrer Namen** geringschätzen, weil sich mit der Zeit alles ändert, Sitten Namen und auch die Sprache, was schon aus den augenfälligsten Anzeichen zu sehen ist. Was jener und wieviel er beim Eintritt in sein Amt und während seines Pontifikats tat, findet sich in Schriften überhaupt nicht. Dennoch muß man annehmen, daß er der Verdener Kirche in Gelehrsamkeit, Demut, Beständigkeit vorgestanden habe, der er seinerzeit die Stelle als ein sehr aufmerksamer und treuer Hirte in der Kirche Gottes versah. Vermutlich wurde von unzeitigem Tod überrascht oder seine Taten sind wegen anderer Hindernisse oder weil kein Schreiber vorhanden war, der sie aufgeschrieben hätte, aus der Erinnerung geschwunden. Um diese Zeit is, wie man in Erfahrung bringen kann, durch das Anwachsen der christlichen Religion und nachdem er Erfahrung bringen kann, durch das Anwachsen der christlichen Religion und nachdem der Frieden zurückgewonnen war, die Verdener Kirche wieder von ihren Bischöfen in Besitz genommt worden, die lange verstreut waren und versuchten, ihren Sitz dadurch zurückzugewinnen, daß sie das Wort Gottes predigten, daß sie tadelten und ermahnten, willkommen und unwillkomment, daß sie die Einwohner des Landes auf den Weg der Wahrheit und zur Erkenntnis des Glaubens zurückriefen und daß sie nun als einfache und ergebene Männer amtierten, weil ja immer das Gute zu vermuten ist, solange das Gegenteil nicht augenscheinlich wird.

Nevertheless, Buchhardt's claim seems to overreach logic.

Still more, Burchhardt shows a leap in logic regarding his source, *Acta Sanctorum*. These fourteenth-century annals were not printed until the seventeenth century, and thus are hardly primary source literature about a ninth-century bishop. Furthermore, Burchhardt oversells the text from this reproduced "Spangenbergische Chronik" page by claiming it highlights a "Love of the Word of God" in Helingandus and by implying the scroll in Heligandus' hand is the *Heliand* itself. Note, the reproduced page is not from the *Acta Sanctorum* rather from a different listing of the historical bishops of Verden—Andreas Mendelsloh's (1590–1666) "Spangenbergische Chronik" which, due to Eilard von der Hude's[5] (1541–1606) participation in writing the German verses, can be dated to between 1590 and 1606.

Thus, there is folly in Burchhardt's view that either book presents accurate signs that can be inferred to represent the *Heliand* and thus reveal its author's identity. That is, while Burchhardt is completely willing to accept the *Acta Sanctorum* reference to the "omnia evangelia librum unum" and the "Spangenbergische Chronik" image of Heligandus holding a scroll as evidence of the *Heliand* text, I am unable to accept either as such. Both accounts can only be recognized as exactly what they are—namely, assumptions. These are, of course, interesting historical inferences to take into account; however, I see no reason to whole-heartedly assume that the writers of the *Acta Sactorum* had any clearer idea of who Heligandus was than we do in our day, since that bishop predated the writers by nearly five centuries. In all, it makes interesting speculation, but nothing more.

Still, Burchhardt's proposal provides an identity with a name and a home, and as such is more detailed than many others which, as Bernhard Sowinski shows, exist in plenty (Burchhardt, 283):

> Man hat den Verfasser des Heliand mit verschiedenen Persönlichkeiten des 9. Jahrhunderts zu identifizieren gesucht; weder HAIMO VON HALBERSTADT (nach R. Heinrichs) noch der Frise BERNLÊF (nach J. v. Weringha), weder ein im Kloster Werden (Ruhr) sächsisch lernender Angelsachse (wie W. Krogmann vermutete) noch ein ebenso unbekannter Friese (R. Drögereit) sind bisher als Autoren der as. Bibeldichtung bestätigt worden. Gleiches gilt für den von W. Haubrichs vermuteten Notar Ludwigs des Deutschen ADALLEOD (830–37 nachgewiesen) und für den im Laufe seines Lebens verfolgten sächsischen Theologen GOTTSCHALK (um 8000–870?), den H. Rupp für den *Heliand*-Dichter hält.

Not all of these proposals have merit; some come with a great deal of historical evidence. As stated previously, a full analysis of all of them would fill more than this book can handle. Consequently, it is here that I leave the question about the identity of the *Heliand* poet. For the meantime, simply pushing back our ignorance by a few steps will have to suffice.

---

[5] Eilard von der Hude was himself the author of *Historiam Episcoporum Verdensium*.

4. Novel Tools vs. Standardized Error

4.1 Overview of Standard Works

Over the past two centuries, the body of scholarship on the *Heliand* has grown multitudinously. Generally speaking, a few standard works serve as the foundation for the field of Old Saxon studies. Having been written at various points over a long period of time, these volumes retain interpretations of oft varying academic conventions. "We [...] stand[...] upon the shoulders of giants" (Bernard of Chartres in John of Salisbury, 1159) when it comes to the *Heliand* materials that exist today; nevertheless, it must be said that much of the standard Old Saxon library—of which some volumes are now in or nearing double-digit editions—was created in an academic climate much different from our current one. Written and published at a time when standardizing linguistic material was favored over relaying the text as it appears in manuscripts sources, the standard works generally misrepresent the *Heliand* language as it appears on the extant manuscripts. Consequently, using these works for any comparative study of the Old Saxon language soon becomes very frustrating, since the manuscripts and their texts might very well contain important variations that lead to insightful discoveries.

This book began as a dissertation project investigating possible paleographic and linguistic differences between the texts of the newly-found MS L and that of MS C. The hope was that by delineating such differences, some light may shed on the relationship of L to the other extant manuscripts. That project began with the gathering of recognized standard works on the *Heliand*: Otto Behaghel's (1996) *Heliand und Genesis*, Eduard Sievers' (1878) *Heliand*, and J. A. Schmeller's (1830) *Heliand*. An example of the various representations (i.e. "corrections") from these three editors is offered below with an image taken directly from a scan of the original manuscript (MS C) for comparison. The data is taken from *fitts* LXIX and LXX, both previously available only on MS C, but now also paralleled on MS L. I offer the three editors' transcriptions as they occur printed in their publications, i.e. the typography given here reflects the authors' own usage (e.g. diacritics and characters in italics represent, among other things [cf. 4.1.1–4.1.3], proposed corrections to match a hypothetical, "more original" form):

Fig. 4.1. Standard transcriptions compared with source

Line	Behaghel[1]	Sievers	Schmeller	MS C
5829	uuilitisconi	ulitisconi	ulitifconi	Ulitq fconi
	uuîf	nuib[2]	uuib	uuib
5830	hêrren	heren	heren	heren
5833	gisiðon	gisithon	gifithon	gifithon
	suoðon	suothon	fuothon	fuothon
5834	dôđe	dođe	dođe	dođe
5845	idison	idision	idifion	idifion
5847	lîchamen	lichamen	liclic hamen	lic lic ha men
5855	selƀo	selƀo	felƀo	felbo
5857	hettiandero	hetandero	hetandero	hetandero
5859	slôgin	slogin	flogin	flogun
5865	habit	habit	habit	habit

It should be noted that the given are purely examples; in reality many more tokens of these examples occur within lines 5824–5870, and yet more and still other incongruities occur throughout the standard transcriptions. What is noticeable is that all three editors find different words problematic: in some cases (e.g. 5865), one will correct what the other two do not; in other cases (e.g. 5855), all three list a spelling different from the manuscript, but not all make a note of the difference (e.g. in a footnote); and finally, some cases exhibit outright erroneous representations or (e.g. 5829: 'uuilitisconi', 'uuîf', 'nuib'). Why do these standard works not agree? The answer: each follows its own rules of transcription rooted in the academic philosophy that prevailed at the time of publication. A more useful, universal tool would present the manuscript texts as they are and would leave the

---

[1] 10th ed.
[2] Besides the <f> ~ <b> alternation, it seems that Sievers has a misprint of initial <u> as <n>; however, apparent misprints such as this only further aggravate the situation. It is often difficult to discern between one editor's misprint and another's re-interpretation or unique reading of the manuscript text.

interpretation of a spelling's correctness to the reader. The following subsections presents information on the editors toward understanding their motivations in offering inaccurate representations of the *Heliand* text.

4.1.1 Otto Behaghel

Now in its tenth edition, Behaghel's standard *Heliand* volume has been under the tutelage of three Old Saxon scholars. Behaghel himself maintained five editions until his death in 1936, a sixth being published posthumously. Walther Mitzka edited and published editions seven and eight before 1976, when he died. Since then, Burkhard Taeger has been at the editing helm, publishing the editions nine through ten, the last appearing in 1996.

In his introduction to the tenth edition, Taeger (1996: vii) clarifies the goal of the three editors over the previous century of publication: "Das Bestreben der Editoren war es bis dahin vordringlich gewesen, die immer lebhafte Forschung für die Textherstellung der Ausgabe nutzbar zu machen." Behaghel's objective in offering a "useful" redaction of the *Heliand* epic was to simplify for the sake of the reader the vast amount of variation that occurs both between and within the manuscripts available at a given time. At the time of the first edition only three manuscripts were known to exist: MS C in London; MS M in Munich; and MS P, which had only just been discovered in Prague in 1880. Since P is only a small fragment relative to the other two, the bulk of Behaghel's transcription comes from MSS M and C. Furthermore, despite MS C's offering almost 1½-times as much of the story as in MS M,[3] Behaghel greatly favored the Munich manuscript. Taeger (1996: xxxviii; quoting Behaghel, 1st ed., Vorwort) explains:

> Der vorliegenden Ausgabe hat Behaghel, in Übereinstimmung mit den Untersuchungen von E. Sievers, für den ‚Heliand' die Hs. M zugrundegelegt, „in dem Sinne, daß in jedem einzelnen Fall die Fassung der beiden Handschriften gegeneinander abgewogen, aber die Lesung von M aufgenommen wurde, wenn sich keine innere Entscheidung treffen ließ."

Behaghel's transcription preference for MS M over MS C is a bit surprising. According to Taeger, there is a close link between MSS C and P—the manuscript fragment which he considers the closest to the Archetype. This rela-

---

[3] MS C offers 5969 lines (of an assumed 6000) compared to MS M, which offers 3889 lines.

tionship between MSS C and P is significant enough that it disproves the earlier hypothesis that MSS C and M descended from the same immediate source (1984: xvii-xviii):

> Es steht graphematisch-sprachlich dem Archetypus besonders nahe, andererseits teilt es in v. 980 einen eindeutigen Fehler mit der Hs. C, führt also auf den Ansatz einer Vorstufe *CP. Die zweifel, ob dieser Befund mit der graphematisch-sprachlichen Nähe zum Archetyp vereinbar ist, haben sich durch eine entscheidende Verfeinerung der statistischen Auswertungsmethode zur Rekonstruktion vom *CM beheben lassen.

Despite this evidence, the Behaghel transcription's continued preference for MSS M over C is immediately apparent in its spelling choices. Yet Behaghel's desire to use the MS M as the primary version becomes complicated by the lack of material it provides relative to MS C. Taeger (1996: xxxix) continues:

> Auch die sprachlich-graphematische Erscheinungsform des Textes ist die des Monacensis, soweit er vorhanden ist; in den leider so zahlreichen Lücken tritt dafür die Textgestalt der Hs. C ein.

Thus, Behaghel needed to supplement the material missing in MSS M with that of C.[4] In doing so, the goal of offering a simple, approachable study transcription—one that avoids confusing variations in graphemic representations—is compromised. Thus, the Behaghel transcription standardizes certain Old Saxon spellings in order to overcome the graphemic differences between the manuscripts (1984: xxix):

> Normalisiert ist im ‚Heliand' wie in der ‚As. Genesis' regelmäßig nur insoweit, als für die dentale Spirans im Inlaut und Auslaut đ/ð gesetzt ist, für die labiale ƀ im Inlaut, f im Auslaut.

Yet, what seems a simple rule of usage for the two character sets <ð> vs. <đ> and <ƀ> vs. <f> is actually much more complex than Taeger leads one to believe.

The use of the grapheme <ƀ> presented a particular difficulty for Behaghel. Its occurrence is greater in MS C than in MS M, in which it is

---

[4] MS C's rendition is continuous: lines 1-5968. MS M contains many gaps: lines 85-2198a, 2256-2514a, 2576-3414a, 3491-3950, 4017-4674, 4740b-5275a, and 5968-5983. Notice that M overlaps with C in all but the final segment.

more likely to be realized as <b>, or only rarely <v>. In many cases, <ƀ> in one manuscript alternates with <f> in the other (line 288: Taeger has 'uuîf', MS M has 'uuif' [5r, row 6, sixth word], MS C has 'uuib' [12/18r, row 12, seventh word; line 297: Taeger has 'uuîf', MS M has 'uuif' [row 12, fifth word], MS C has 'uuib' [row 23, last word]). Of these two examples the first (line 288) is the nom. sg.; the second is the acc. sg. This lexeme descends from Gmc. *wība- (Kluge, 862; Gmc. *ƀ < IE *bh). The voiced fricative would be expected to remain word-internally. Indeed, in both MSS M ('uuibes' [row 1, fifth word]) and C ('uuibes' [row 4, third word]), the gen. sg. occurs with the voiced fricative. On the other hand, one would expect final devoicing (i.e. Gmc. *f < IE *bh) to occur in the nom. and acc. sg. examples, producing 'uuif'. This effect was equally efficient in Old English as in Old Saxon (Kluge: "asächs. afries. ags. 'wīf'"); notably however, MS C maintains the voiced fricative spelling -ƀ bucking not only Old Saxon but Old English convention therewith. This bit of dialectal variance present in manuscript texts is of potential use to the researcher, as it leads one to question why even Old English morphophonemic habit is being broken. The answer may well have import to dating and locating the different manuscripts' creation.

Behaghel sought to regularize this <f> ~ <b> ~ <ƀ> ~ <v/u> variation, preferring the <b> in word-initial positions (Taeger, line 1704 'brôðar', MS M: 'brodar' [26r, row 18, first word], MS C: 'bruother' [47/53v, row 14, fourth word]; cf. Gmc. *brōþar < IE *bhrā́ter-, *bhártor- [Kluge, 106]), in word-medial position <ƀ> (281 'uuîƀes'; cf. 5832 'graƀe', MS M 'graue' [Sehrt, 208], MS C 'grabe' [165/171r, row 21, fourth word] MS L 'graua' [1r, row 10, first word]), <f> and in word-final position (288 'uuîf'; 297 'uuîf'), and completely eliminating <v>. Thus, Behaghel's attempts to regularize the variation in spelling by appealing to the reconstructed morphophonology of Proto-(West-)Germanic.

Similarly, Behaghel levels the manuscript variation of <th> ~ <đ> ~ <d>. He also uses a character not found in the manuscripts, namely <ð>. Like the bilabial fricatives, the occurrence of these graphemes reflects in part the phonemic reflexes of Proto-Indo-European phonemes, some of which have been voiced/devoiced due to environmental triggers based on their syllabic position. Due to Verner's Law and final devoicing, a merger of phonemes occurred in the Proto-Germanic period, with the devoiced Germanic phonemes that evolved from Proto-Indo-European voiced phonemes being confused with those that had descended from Proto-Indo-European unvoiced phonemes.⁵ When in morpheme-initial position, Gmc. *þ is represented quite regularly in the *Heliand* as <th> (MS M 'thit' [17v, row 3, second word], MS C 'Thit' [~~33~~/39v, row 9, fifth word], MS P: 'thitt', MS L 'thitt', etc.); however, in all other positions both Gmc. *þ < IE *t and *ð < IE *dh are represented in one of four ways: <th>, <đ>, and <d>. The examples cited above for 'brother' illustrate this in part: Taeger line 1704 'brôðar', MS M 'brodar', MS C 'bruother'; cf. Taeger line 968 'blîði', MS M 'blidi' [15r, row 10, seventh word], MS C 'blidi' [~~29~~/35v, row 4, second word], MS P 'bliđi' [1r, roe 10, third word]). Behaghel levels these reflexes to <th> in initial position and <ð> everywhere else.⁶

While aiding his reader by limiting confusion due to grapheme variations, Behaghel's normalizations hinder comparative study of the manuscript texts. This is due to the fact that, once made, Behaghel's "corrections" remove their own traces: it is impossible to recognize which uses of <f>, <ƀ>, <b>, <th> and <ð> truly occur in the manuscripts. Moreover, by narrowing the eight occurring graphemes to five, Behaghel destroys any evidence of <v>, <đ>, <d>, thereby eliminating any chance for a detailed analysis of grapheme usage.

Besides destroying evidence, the Behaghel transcription complicates its own usefulness by applying normalizations in a way that is not readily discernible, even counter-intuitive. He writes (1984: xxix):

> Darüber hinaus hat Behaghel aber für das As. in einer ganzen Reihe von Einzelfällen ebenfalls Unregelmäßigkeiten der Schreibung normalisiert; da dies der Funktion der Edition als einer Studienausgabe entgegenkommt, wurde an diesem Gebrauch festgehalten und in solchen Einzelfällen auch weiterhin nach der Regel ausgeglichen, dabei aber stets die Lesung der Leithandschrift im Apparat verzeichnet. Ihre Grenze haben diese Eingriffe an zwei Punkten gefunden, nämlich einmal bei erkennbarer Unfestigkeit in ganzen grammatischen Kategorien (so wurde in den Präsens-Endungen des Verbums und denen des schwachen Part. Prät immer die handschriftliche Lesung belassen, so bunt dadurch das Bild auch wurde); und zum anderen z. T. offenbar dialektal geltenden Nebenformen, die

---

⁵ Thus, Gmc. *þ became voiced to *ð when not geminate in intervocalic position, and Gmc. *ð became devoiced to *þ when syllable-final. This resulted in another two-way merger: Gmc. *þ, *ð merged to *ð medially, but merging to *þ finally.

⁶ Unlike in the labial series, morpheme-initial position of Gmc. *þ, *ð did not result in occlusion to /d/; however, occlusion did occur to geminated Gmc. *ð. Just like the labial series, all the *Heliand* manuscripts use <đ>, <ð>, <d>, and—in certain circumstances—<th> interchangeably to a great degree (cf. Rauch 1992, 114–117).

dann ihrerseits Eingang in das Wortverzeichnis gefunden haben (dies haben auch Behaghel und Mitzka bereits so geregelt).

In addition to dental and bilabial fricatives, the leveling out of variation in unspecified "isolated cases" further confuses the transcription. Through this set of normalizations the editors again hope to simplify the text. Ironically, it only complicates the situation by promoting changes conditionally: normalizations are applied only as long as (1) the changes do not complicate the recognition of grammatical function, and/or (2) the unusual form is obviously dialectal. Yet, it is impossible for the reader to recognize whether a given word has been normalized, or whether it has been left unaltered because a change would have rendered the word more difficult to recognize or understand.

Despite the confusion brought about by normalization of the text, as long as the changes are noted and clarified in the apparatus (as is promised), the reader should be able to recognize where the transcription has altered the manuscript representations. But a footnote mention seems only to occur in the cases Taeger calls "isolated", and not where the bilabial and dental fricatives have been altered. Should the reader be expected to recognize these changes without a hint in a footnote? Ultimately, despite being regarded as the standard resource in Old Saxon studies, Behaghel's rendition of the *Heliand* is highly unreliable, making it virtually impossible to perform any research into whether graphemic variation within and between the manuscripts is significant.

Of course, this should come as no surprise, since Behaghel's stated goal was to produce as unified text that would be more accessible to the learner. The needs of the learner and those of the researcher are understandably different.

4.1.2 Eduard Sievers

Eduard Sievers' *Heliand* transcription serves as the standard work for other standard works. Taeger acknowledges Sievers to verify his continuation of the Behaghel transcription; he writes: "Alle sprachwissenschaftliche Arbeit am ‚Heliand' hat von der Ausgabe in Paralleldruck von M und C durch E. Sievers auszugehen, Titelauflage 1935, vermehrt um den Text der Fragmente P und V" (1984, xxvii). Here, Taeger refers to a 1935 reprint.

Sievers' transcription as printed in the original 1878 work is the basis of the following discussion.

In his transcription, Sievers balances his desire to relay the text from the manuscripts accurately with his wish to offer something more useful than previous transcriptions, namely Schmeller's 1830 publication; Sievers notes (1878: xx):

> Für den handgebrauch litt Schmeller's text an dem übelstande, dass er, bei zeilengetreuer wiedergabe der Münchener handschrift und dem mangel einer satzinterpunction den überblick über den zusammenhang wie über die metrische form erschwerte, sowie daran, dass der text des Cottonianus, soweit er dem des Monacensis parallel gien, nur mit einiger umständlichkeit aus den varianten ermittelt werden konnte.

Schmeller's transcription is true to the manuscript format: each manuscript page is imitated on its own printed page. The result is a printed page whose layout mimics the visual form of the manuscript page. Thus, on the printed page, each line contains the exact word count (however, not necessarily the same word divisions!) as the lines from each manuscript page.

For Sievers, it is folly to print the epic according to manuscript arrangement. In doing so, Schmeller overlooks the simplicity of the poetic line. Sievers hopes to remove the disparallelism between MSS M and C, which resulted when different sizes of script fit a disproportionate number of words into each manuscript line. In order to bring the manuscript texts into parallel with each other, Sievers follows MS M. Heyne's (1866) practice of dividing the texts into its poetic lines. Since both texts are formatted similarly, comparison of the texts from different sources is as easy as finding the analogous line numbers. As an added benefit, this format is beneficial for an investigation into Old Saxon metrical patterns, which Sievers (1893) later did with great success.

In reality, the presentation choice is a trade-off. By representing the visual form, much of the detail unique to each manuscript is preserved; by reformatting the text according to its poetic features, the poet's sound-play and linguistic artistry become clearer. The former method benefits an investigation into the scribes' linguistic comprehension; the latter benefits a study of patterns. In light of features present in MSS L and P, it is arguable that the early *Heliand* scribes understood the metrics of the *Heliand* and even attempted to represent it visually: an offset initial occurs at the con-

4. NOVEL TOOLS VS. STANDARDIZED ERROR 71

vergence of a poetic line and a handwritten line. Both methods are useful to different ends.

Other than his format alterations, Sievers considers his transcription cautious: "In der behandlung der texte bin ich möglichst conservativ verfahren" (1878: vii). Indeed, when compared to Behaghel's method of leveling out variation, Sievers' transcription is much more apt to represent the text true to the manuscripts. Certainly, the two transcriptions differ in scope: while Behaghel seeks to introduce a unified text that will benefit the student, Sievers' agenda is to aid the researcher in comparative investigation: "Die gegenwärtige ausgabe unterscheidet sich von [früheren] dadurch, dass sie zunächst eine grundlage für das wissenschaftliche studium bilden möchte" (xx). To further aid researchers, Sievers prints the two texts in a side-by-side format with parallel texts on facing pages. As only two manuscript texts were available in 1878, this parallel page format is effective. Since that time, however, four additional manuscript fragments (MSS P, V, S, L) have been discovered (cf. Ch. 2). These are obviously missing from Sievers' book. Other scholars have sought to fill this void by publishing editions that include the fragment transcriptions offered at the various times of discovery; however, most do so by relegating the fragment texts to footnotes or appendices. Such is the case with the aforementioned 1935 Sievers/Schröder reprint, described by its title: *Heliand Titelauflage vermehrt um das Prager Fragment des Heliand und die Vaticanischen Fragmente von Heliand und Genesis*. Still, notably missing from this reprint are the S and L—discovered in 1979 and 2006, respectively. Sievers' goal of providing an easy means of comparing the various manuscript versions of the *Heliand* presents a challenge when more exemplars are found. It is unfortunate when these new finds are simply not fully investigated in the standard works. Furthermore, since the transcriptions of MSS P and V were performed by other scholars (respectively, Zangemeister/Braune, 1894; and Bischoff, 1979), comparison is complicated by varying academic attitudes and styles.

Despite Sievers' conservative approach with what was available, there are inconsistencies in his work, as shown in Fig. 4.1. For example, it appears that Sievers' transcription suffers from typos. In any kind of transcription, the presence of misprints begins to raise suspicion about the accuracy of the rest of the text. The problem is simple: it is virtually impossible for a reader to distinguish a mistake from an unusual-but-otherwise-correct transliteration. Well aware that errors exist in his transcription, Sievers attempts to remedy them by addendum (1878: vii):

> Für die correctheit der gebotenen texte glaube ich einstehen zu können, da bei der correctur alle nur möglichen vorsichtsmassregeln angewant wurden, um das eindringen von fehlern zu vermeiden. Dass trotzdem eine so lange und unliebe fehlerliste des Cottonianus angehängt werden muste, hat seine besonderen gründe. Als ich im januar 1871 die ersten collation dieser hs. vornahm, konnte ich nur ein exemplar der Heyne'schen handausgabe als grundlage der vergleichung benutzen, da ich die möglichkeit einer vollständigen collation auch des Heliand nicht voraussehn konnte, als ich zur untersuchung der Oxforder bibliothek nach England gieng. In der tat konnte ich damals auch nur in aller eile die hs. einmal mit Heyne's text vergleicehn. Damit aber die hierbei unvermeidlichen fehler noch rechtzeitig berichtigt werden könnten, habe ich den gedruckten text im herbst 1876 nochmals mit der hs. verglichen, die letzten bogen sind nach der hs. selbst corrigiert worden.

Granted, errors are likely to occur when transcribing anything the size of the *Heliand* epic. Typos are also an almost inevitable by-product of print publication. This was especially true before personal computing enabled an author to be his own typesetter. It is laudable that Sievers attempts to remedy his errors by noting corrections in an appendix. Yet despite accounting for forgivable circumstances and Sievers' attempts to assuage the problems, the presence of errors in a 130 year old publication (one that scholars still rely upon as a major reference) only highlights the need for an updated review of the manuscripts towards a new, credible transcription.

Sievers' inadvertent gaffes are not the only source of confusion. He openly admits to inferring scribal error and substituting material from one manuscript for that in the other. Thus, Sievers effectively mixes the two sources into one—not unlike Behaghel, only to a lesser degree (ibid.):

> In der regel ergab sich die richtige lesung einer stelle die in der einen handschrift verderbt ist durch einen blick in die andere; ich habe daher im allgemeinen in solchen fällen den leser einfach durch einen stern im texte auf die andere hs. verwiesen. Doch habe ich es für unnötig gehalten, jede orthographische kleinigkeit, die man ohne weiteres beim lesen selbst berichtigt, auf diese weise auszuzeichnen oder die fehlerhafte lesart unter den text zu verweisen, da die ausgabe ihrer ganzen anlage nach doch nicht zur allerersten einführung in das studium des Heliand bestimmt ist. Nur wo bloss eine handschrift vorlag, bin ich entschiedener vorgegangen.

Obviously, when a clear reading is available, there should be no problems in transcribing; however, the *Heliand* manuscripts present occasional difficulties. Sievers notes that in some cases text is missing in the manuscripts, be it due to degeneration in the parchment or to scribal omission. For both cases, Sievers turns to MS M to fill in the (supposed) hole. For example, where it runs parallel to MSS P and L, Sievers finds in MS C five presumed omissions for which he offers a correction:

Fig. 4.2. Sievers' insertions in the MS C text

Line	Sievers	MS C	MS M
958	thena heland uuili	thena uuili	thena heleand uuili
964	uuilleon quam / thar	uuilleon thar	uuilleon quum thar
975	us so girisit	uf girisit	uf so girisid
5843	spracun im mid	spracun mid	—
5867	uuarth san after	uuarth after	—

Where Sievers infers scribal omissions in MS C, there are no indication that the scribe indeed was mistaken. There is no indication because there is no mark on the manuscript page. Sievers presumes an omission exists in MS C after comparing it to MS M. When MS M has additional words that do not appear in MS C, he concludes that the scribe of MS C erred. Sievers borrows the word from MS M and inserts ("re-inserts" in his interpretation) it into his transcription of MS C; e.g. in lines 958 (*heland*),[7] 964 (*quam*), and 975 (*so*). Though he marks these insertions in italics, Sievers action reveals a predisposition to assume primacy in MS M.

In the large span of MS C for which MS M offers no parallel material, Sievers approaches his transcription "more resolutely" (1878: vii: "entschiedener"), i.e. less conservatively. By this, Sievers means that he takes upon himself the authoritative right to interpret what *should* be in the text. This is even worse than supplementing the MS C text with materi-

---

[7] Sievers also alters borrowed *heleand* (MS M) to *heland* in the C transcription. Maybe this is to match a perceived tendency that umlaut triggers are missing from C. However, cf. Fig. 4.1. above, line 5857, where the same alteration is reversed: to *hetandero* he restores the umlaut trigger and accompanying intervocalic consonant germination. Neither occurs in the manuscript.

al from MS M, because Sievers deliberately invents material; e.g. lines 5843 (*im*) and 5867 (*san*). Here MS M does not provide material parallel to MS C at all. Sievers inserts monosyllabic words in order to make the poetic line match his model of Old Saxon metrical patterns and phonology. Instead of revising his theory to account for perceived abnormalities, he forces the textual data to suit his presuppositions.

Sievers' intervention into the MS C text contradicts with his stated motive of providing a transcription of the manuscripts that would aid comparison of their texts. A more useful tool would be truer to the actual conditions of the manuscript texts, leaving speculation about the scribal perceptions for an external discussion. Indeed, Sievers downplays the role of textual analysis in his transcription (1878: xxi):

> Den schwerpunkt bei der textbehandlung gab weniger die textkritik ab, für welche nur ein äusserst geringer spielraum übrig blieb (...), als vielmehr das bestreben nach einer sinn- und versgemässen interpunktion (namentlich genauerer gliederung der grösseren satzgebäude) und einer correcten versabteilung.

Sievers' aim to clarify the texts through formatting, in this case rather than through explication, is once again visible. It would seem that he would have his readers come to their own conclusions about the *Heliand* story. The main focus, then, is not an explication of the text, but rather a reorganization of it, such as to induce clarity. In the case of syntax, the distraction results from a lack of clear clausal separation and haphazard word division (1878: xii):

> Die interpunktion is vollkommen willkürlich; für die versabteilung ist aus ihr nichts zu gewinnen. Das gleiche gilt bezüglich der worttrennung. Im allgemeinen folgt auch unsere hs. der sitte, zusammengesetzte wörter in ihre einzelnen bestandteile aufzulösen.

To resolve this, Sievers introduces contemporary punctuation into the texts: "[I]n diesen punkten bin ich ohne rücksicht auf das verfahren der hs. ohne weiteres dem jetzt üblichen gebrauche gefolgt." This insertion of punctuation into the transcription is questionable in two ways: (1) it assumes that punctuation habits are linguistically universal; (2) it is superfluous.

Sievers applies late-nineteenth century New High German punctuation rules to ninth century Old Saxon. The age discrepancy is not the only problem: New High German and Old Saxon are obviously not the same language.

That both are West Germanic languages does not guarantee that a given punctuation rule will be equally applicable in both languages. Furthermore, even New High German punctuation tendencies have varied greatly over the past century. Sievers insertion of punctuation also seems superfluous in light of his division of the text into poetic lines. Moreover, his format further aids accessibility by dividing the poetic line into two half-lines. Even with the epic thus divided and despite Sievers' punctuation attempts, the language of the *Heliand* requires some getting used to. Eventually, one recognizes that the poet often uses the half-line in collaboration with clausal division. The chiasmatic structure of the *Heliand* also helps the reader identify important phrasal groups, as these are often repeated in the next poetic line. Once a reader recognizes these hints, Sievers' inserted punctuation is less imperative.

Given that Sievers applies punctuation rules to Old Saxon from a foreign language, and that the benefits of this added punctuation diminish over time, it becomes apparent that this is yet another of Sievers' unintended consequences into the *Heliand*. Taken as a whole, Sievers' transcription of MSS M and C is interspersed with distracting elements that, ironically, were intended by the editor as helpful.

While any change to the original manuscript texts ought to be avoided, several innovations to the *Heliand* that Sievers transmits are so beneficial, that their presence outweighs their absence. The first is Heyne's (1866) formatting of the epic into numbered poetic lines. This formatting provides immediate referencing possibilities between the various source texts. It does come with a small price, since it occasionally requires dividing the lines in places where the manuscripts do not have word divisions. However, such an occasion ought to be noted in a footnote; indeed, a footnote notation of a circumstance where the transcription is incongruent with its source manuscript on just such a word-division seems more acceptable than relegating an authentic manuscript spelling to the footnotes. The second innovation is the use of in-line markings for manuscript folio boundaries (i.e.,) and manuscript line conversions (i.e.,), in concert with the respective manuscript folio number and manuscript page line number. This notation is appreciably helpful when comparing the transcription to its source manuscript.

4.1.3 Johann Andreas Schmeller

Despite earlier knowledge of *Heliand* manuscripts,[8] the first full publication of the *Heliand* story in modern times did not occur until J. A. Schmeller's 1830 book. By this time, both major documents were known to academics, and the idea of conflating the two must have been popular, because Schmeller warns against taking such as evidence (1830: x):

> E texta unius alteriusque exemplaris tertium quondam conflare, qui, quamvis melior, neutrius tamen esset, veneranda monumenti vetuit antiquitas, vetuit ratio ipse hujus primae editionis, in qua, si quodammodo fieri posset, genuinus et unius et alterius exemplaris textus proprio peritorum judicio sujiciendus videbatur.

> Sometimes the two versions of the text can be melded into a third, if indeed an expert's judgment sees that it coincides with the original versions themselves. While the third version might seem better, it really is not: due both to its [lack of] age and to the existence of the manuscript originals, it can not be regarded as evidence.

Schmeller believes that, even if the merged text coincides with the original versions, it is nevertheless a theoretical work that will compete with original versions to some degree or another. Thus, early on in the modern reproduction of the *Heliand* it is recognized that, while it might be beneficial on some accounts, a re-writing of the *Heliand* text to include all the material in one unified transcription can not be taken seriously for academic research. With this as a fundamental principle, Schmeller's work immediately stands out from the philosophy behind Behaghel's unified transcription. Yet Schmeller's transcription does indeed suffer from problems similar to Behaghel's, for Schmeller merges the texts from MSS C and M into one by substituting material for MS C where it is lacking in MS M. He explains (1830: xi):

> Integras paginas, quarum textus deficiente Codive Monacensi ex uno Cottoniano depromptus est, lector primo obtuta distinguet, suntque: 1, 2, 67, 68, 77, 78, 105, 106, 121, 122, 143, 144, 161—175. Singulae vero lineae e Cod. Cotton. desumptae, quas textui Monacensi ipsi his locis mutilo insertas lector ex adnotationibus agnoscet ignoscetque, habentur in paginis 3, 4, 14, 26, 107, 157 et 158.

---

[8] MS C was found by Franciscus Junius Jr. in 1587; and noted in Thomas Smith's *Catalogus* (1696).

> At first look, the reader will discern that there are entire pages of text missing from the Monacensis Codex. Therefore, material from the Cottonianus substitutes for these missing areas. These are: 1, 2, 67, 68, 77, 78, 105, 106, 121, 122, 143, 144, 161–175. In fact, other than by the footnote indication of the lines taken from Cod. Cotton., the reader will not recognize and even overlook the fact that material has been introduced in place of the missing Monacensis text. This includes pages 3, 4, 14, 26, 107, 157 and 158.

Here Schmeller offers an explanation for his transcription's weakness: except for footnotes indicating what has been taken from MS C, the reader will not recognize and even overlook the fact that material has been introduced in place of text missing from MS M. Thus, it becomes the task of the reader to keep the two texts separate from each other. This only serves to tax one's patience during comparative study, since there is no clear division of where one source ends and the other begins. Schmeller himself regards this task as simple (ibid.):

> Frequentiores textus Cottoniani discrepantias, quamvis undique obliquis Monacensis nostri literis arguantur, omnibus in locis expresse apponere minime necessarium duxi, quippe quas lector ipse facile conjiciat, dummodo pauculis, quae subsequentur, regulis dirigi velit.

> Very often Cottonianus text differs wherever our Monacensis manifests straight characters. In all cases I have sought expressly to juxtapose the fewest cases necessary. In fact, they are so few in number, that the reader can easily guess them for himself, as they should seem to be arranged according to a pattern.

Schmeller attempts to mix the two manuscript texts (i.e. MSS M and C) as seldom as possible. Where he does mix the two, Schmeller considers the resulting leveled text to be self-evident, i.e. that his interventions are apparent because they follow some implicit pattern. Still, though Schmeller does not attempt to level out irregularity in spelling as Behaghel does, similar to the latter, Schmeller does assume that the reader is able to deduce where the transcription is conservative and where material has been introduced from elsewhere. This is highly problematic for any reader wishing to distinguish the original texts from one another.

Schmeller's solution to presenting those areas where the two manuscripts overlap is to assume that one manuscript has primacy over the other. This assumption succeeds him for generations; in fact, it is familiar to and practiced by all the editors presented above. Schmeller unabashedly admits a preference for following M over C; he writes (x):

> Cum textus Cottoniani in capita divisio variis incommodes laboret, Monacensis vero prorsus nulla sit, haec ad illius paginas et lines relatio ad locos in glossario et vocabula citanda commodissima erit.

> The Cottonianus text suffers from a number of errors in its chapter divisions where the Monacensis does not: the page and line divisions of the latter are far more favorable as references for citing text locations and vocabulary in the glossary.

Even though MS C has quite clear (and often decorative) *fitt* divisions, Schmeller claims these are too erroneous to be of use in referencing. Furthermore, he claims that MS M does not suffer from this same weakness, and that its structure is more favorable for reference purposes. Yet Schmeller (x–xi) feels that MS M offers better indications of line division than MS C; however, only slightly:

> Puncta versiculos vel, quod in antique hoc Germanicae poeseos genere idem forme est, sententias distinguentia in Cod. Cottoniano rarissima in Monacensi eo frequentiora sunt, sed tamen et pauciora et plura, quam quae ad versus sine ullo arbitrio propria quemque linea scribendos certam regulam praebuissent.

> Individual verses, i.e., what roughly corresponds to sentences in this ancient form of Germanic verse, are only rarely differentiated in the Cod. Cottonianus. In the Monacenisis the differentiation is more frequent; nevertheless, indications offering anything close to a clear rule are few and far between compared to the verses without any kind of line demarcation.

In the same sentence, he offers both a reason for using MS M as the primary source and an excuse for why it is, nevertheless, not useful for using it as such: line punctuation is more frequent in MS M than in MS C, but still it is too few and far between to offer any fast rule of line division. Moreover, only a few lines before this, he states a contradicting opinion about the divisions in MS M, i.e., that it contains no divisions at all (x, emphasis mine):

> Quod ut *sine divisionibus arbitrariis et sine numeris vel aliis signis textui immixtis fieri posset*, curavi, ut exemplaria impressa non solum quoad literam et verbum, sed etiam quoad lineam et paginam archetypum Monacense accuratissime referent, linearum inaequalitatem inde progredientem levissimae notae maculam ratus (emphasis mine).

> Because *the Munich manuscript does not feature many intervening divisions, verse numbers or any other structural indications*, I have been careful in printing the Monacensis text as accurately as possible—not only so far as the letter and the

word are concerned, but also the line and the page—from the faintest recognizable mark to the unevenness of the lines.

MS M does not offer reliable information in the way of structural divisions—the exact same reasoning he uses earlier to reject MS C as unreliable. Having rebutted his own logic, Schmeller seeks another justification for accepting MS M as the lead text, which he finds in its page layout. Schmeller sees herein an alternative referencing system, using the ordinal occurrence of a word in its particular line. Accordingly, Schmeller is all the more careful to present an accurate reproduction of MS M. To him, this means representing each manuscript page on its own printed page, and thereon each manuscript line as its own printed line. He is also careful to represent character sizes as they appear on the manuscript (xi):

> Ceterum literas majuscules atque minusculas non quas hodiernae orthographiae ratio, sed quas codices, praesertim Monacensis, praescribebant ponendas duxi, quin etiam manifesta librariorum sphalmata non in textu, sed in glossario et in grammatica corrigenda censui, ubi etiam quae melior quoque loco visa fuerit lectio indicabitur.
>
> Otherwise, I have conveyed both majuscules and minuscules—especially those found in the Monacensis—as they appear in the manuscripts, and not according to today's orthographic reasoning so to avoid committing bookish hypercorrections that do not appear in the originals. Rather, places have been designated where an otherwise better reading may be had, and an appraisement correcting such locations can be found in the glossary and in the grammar.

While Schmeller is clear to mention his desire to avoid making "bookish hypercorrections" to the text, he does allow himself to interpret where word divisions occur. This is not a minor task, as it is not always clear in any of the manuscripts whether or not there is a space present to divide words. Moreover, it is uncertain what concept the Old Saxon scribes had of word boundaries, since some lexical items appear joined together. This is especially typical with prepositions, e.g. MS M *aniromodspenit* (20v, row 23, third word: for 'an iro mod spenit'), MS C *angalileoland* (~~165~~/171v, row 4, last word: for 'an galileoland'), MS L *angalileoland* (1v, row 19, second word). To be sure, it is uncertain how meaningful the presence or lack of a space was to the Old Saxon scribes. As such information might provide evidence for meaningful research, it behooves a transcriber to alter word divisions as little as possible. With the excuse that he is aiding the reader in finding lexical tokens in the glossary,[9] Schmeller provides his own interpretation of word division, especially where it is not clear in one manuscript or the other. Later in the century, Sievers believed that Schmeller was unable to see past the visual presentation of the manuscript to the simplicity of the text's poetic structure. Sievers sought to remedy this in his transcription of the *Heliand* manuscripts. Ultimately, both presentations of the text offer valuable detail; luckily, the two are not mutually exclusive. In my transcription, I hope to account for both the information provided by the manuscript and the poetic structures.

Another point of contention is whether Schmeller had an accurate idea of what the MS C manuscript contained. Indeed, he admits not having the opportunity of seeing the London manuscript for himself (1830: x, emphasis mine).

> *Codicem Londinensem inspicere mihimet ipsi non contigit*: et quam in illius apographo supra memorato nonnulla minus certa et liquida viderentur, ut ex ejus quoque cum fragmentis ab Hickesio et Nyerupio editis comparatione perspicitur, lectioni exemplaris Monacensis quamvis pluribus locis mutili, quippe quod propriis oculis consulendum adesset, in locis, qui in uiroque habentur, partes praecipuas tribuendas duxi, ita quidem, ut lectio Cottoniana ubi non eadem esset, in adnotationibus perpetuis infra positis exhiberetur (emphasis mine).

> *I did not manage to inspect the London Codex for myself*: some less clear and less certain parts in this [the London] manuscript can be seen highlighted in the upper part [of the page]. In many places, the reading of the Cotton Ms. is not the same when compared to the published fragments of Hickes & Nyerup and to the text of the Munich manuscript (wherever it is not cut off). Thus, I have drawn attention to particular parts [in the text]—indeed that which should be present for consideration with one's own eyes (which are had by man)—to be presented in continuous annotations located at the bottom [of the page].

Schmeller never indicates his source for the MS C text. Whatever he used, he states that he compared it to earlier partial transcriptions[10] of MS C, as well as to a transcription of MS M. He found that that MS C differs from both resources. He concludes that MS C is the one in error, or at least "some less certain and less clear" content. He highlights these uncertain parts in the material he borrows from MS C to complete the Munich text.

---

[9] Not provided in the 1830 publication, rather first in his 1840 recension.
[10] George Hickes (1705); Rasmus Nyerup (1787).

He comments on these in the apparatus, presenting to the reader that which should be considered "with one's own eyes". The use of italics to highlight questionable areas of the text becomes a tradition followed by subsequent transcribers, albeit each has his own idea of what is and is not unclear. Examples of this variation among editors can be seen in Fig. 4.1., e.g. line 5829, where Schmeller has italicized the initial <u>, whereas neither Sievers nor Behaghel does. Similarly, all three editors differ in what they interpret as questionable (i.e. highlighted) and unremarkable material, e.g. lines 5830, 5834, 5855, 5857, and 5859.

Line 5859 is a noteworthy case, since it reveals that Schmeller himself is inconsistent in what he deems as "unclear and uncertain". In this example, Schmeller changes what quite obviously appears in MS C as a <u> (*flogun*) to an <i> in his transcription (*flogin*). This is a meaningful change, since OS *slogun* is the 3pp pret. indic. (i.e. "was slain"), while OS *slogin* is the 3pp pret. subj. (i.e. "should be slain"). The word appears in a string of conditional clauses that describe what would happen to Christ (my transcription, bolded emphasis):

```
5856         [...] huohie scoldigigeban uuer than
       gisald selbo     an sundigaroman no
       hetandero hand    helag drohtin
       Thatsiaina quelidin    endi ancruci slogun
5860   dodan gidadin    endithathie scoldi thuru drohtines craft
       anthrid dion dage    thiodateuuillion
       libbiandi astandan [...]
```

```
5856         [...] how he would be given,
       himself, ceded to the man of sins
       into the hand of the haters, the holy Lord.
       That they would smite and would slay him on the cross,
5860   would cause him to die; and that he would through Divinity's might
       on the third day, for the good of the throng,
       arise again living. [...]
```

It is plain that *slogun* stands out from the crowd of highlighted verbs. Schmeller changes it in his transcription to *slogin* presumably to make it parallel in mood to the other verbs. Since this fitt (LXIX) is transmitted only by MS C, Schmeller is unable to make recourse to MS M in order to make an interpretation. This is a perfect case for what Schmeller would describe as "unclear and uncertain". The spelling in MS C occurs without apparent reason—other than to invoke scribal error. Yet the form stands in the middle of a string of subjunctive forms; therefore, one might surmise that it would have been apparent to the scribe (or the owner of the second hand), and is perhaps not a mistake at all. Nevertheless, the true reason behind its occurrence is inexplicable. Similarly, Schmeller's change comes with no remark. By his own rule, Schmeller's change ought to be indicated in italics and a footnote clarification. Lack of these indications is an error on Schmeller's part. Indeed, it is one with long-lasting effects: using Schmeller as a primary resource, subsequent transcribers—including Sievers and Behaghel—continue printing the changed form, also without indication. In other words, they take Schmeller's transcription for granted.

Luckily, a fortunate development comes from the discovery of MS L, which provides the means for comparison with MS C on lines 5856–5862.

4.2 New Transcriptions to Overcome Old Errors

In light of the various weaknesses discussed, the standard transcriptions available to Old Saxon scholars hamper research requiring fine textual detail. The variations that exist between and within the manuscripts are on one hand an obstacle, yet on the other an important source of data. These variations provide unique linguistic information that may well reveal information about the epic's provenance. Transcriptions that misrepresent what the manuscript originals contain—whether by means of well-intended "corrections" or simply due to transcription error—only frustrate the research process, because this detail is either removed or obscured by emendations. Such is the case with the standard academic transcriptions of the *Heliand*. With these standard resources also showing their age, the discovery of a new manuscript underscores the need for an updated, reliable transcription—particularly of those areas shared by two or more manuscripts so that comparative Old Saxon research can be performed accurately. Due to my objections to previous transcriptions, I began making my own transcriptions of the *Heliand* manuscripts. Until now the full *Heliand* library has been transcribed piecemeal by multiple editors; the result has allowed for the introduction of errors, since different transcribers identify and interpret problem areas differently. As the sole transcriber, my hope is that some of the problems have been avoided, since I handle similar difficulties across the manuscript texts in a similar fashion with the goal of maintaining textual idiosyncrasies.

4.2.1 Presentations: Overlapping Texts

In the sections below, offset characters are denoted in a separate column to the left of the main text body. All manuscripts consistently use offset characters wherever poetic line divisions corresponded to the start of a new text row. This is proof that the scribes understood the division of the poem into alliterating poetic lines.

Throughout my transcriptions, bolding is used to mark oversize characters, e.g. line 5824 MS L 't hitt graf [...]'. More often than not, these oversized characters are larger versions of the minuscules found elsewhere. Occasionally, a Roman majuscule occurs. In such a case, I have provided the character in both its majuscule (i.e., 'capital') form and in bold.

My marking of the offset characters works universally except for the one occasion in MS M (line 959; cf. 4.2.1.2), where an offset capital occurs in the manuscript's left margin but in no way corresponds to a new poetic line. Similarly, both MSS M and C often demonstrate the use of capitals/oversize minuscules at the beginning of a second half-line (i.e., midway through a poetic line). This does not occur in fragments MSS P and L, rather overlarge minuscules that occur mid-poetic line in these two manuscripts are of an intermediate size between the regular script and the offset oversized minuscules. In the case of MS L, there is one occurrence of an extremely large Roman capital <H> (line 5865), which has the height of two-and-a-half rows and encroaches into the regular textbox, thus shifting the start of those rows (equivalent to poetic lines 5864 and 5865) by a distance roughly equal to the width of four normal-size script characters (e.g. four <N> letters). I have marked this in bold also.

The text left missing due to holes in MS P are marked with square brackets, i.e. In lines 959–960, the tails of <r> and <g> are visible beneath the holes. The corresponding spot on the verso side obscures part of line 985; however, the tail and hook of an oversized <s>, i.e. <ſ>, are still visible.

4.2.1.1 Parallel MSS C and M

C 5823	achie ist astandan iu	endi sind thesa stedi larea
L 5823	andaN iú	eNdi sind thesa stedi lárea

        thit graf antheson griote   nu mugun gi gan gan herod
        t hitt graf an thesuN griota   Nu muguN gi gangaN herod

C 5825	**N**ahor mikilu	ikuuet that isiu ist niud sehan
L 5825	**N**ahor mikilo	ik uuet that is iu is ᴎiod sehaᴎ

    antheson stene innan   hier sind noh thia stedi scina
    anthesaᴎ stéᴎ innaᴎ   hier sind ᴎoh thiu stedi skina

    Thar is lichamo lag   lungra fengun
    thar is líchamo lag   lungra fenguᴎ

    gibada an iro brioston   bleca idisi
    gibada an iro briostuᴎ   blecoᴎ idise

    uliti sconi uuib̃   uuas im uuil spell mikil
    uuulitesconion uuíf   uuas im that uuill spell m*i*kil

C 5830	tegihorianne	that im faniro heren sagda
L 5830	**t**eg*i* hóreanna	that im fan iro hérroᴎ sagda

    engil thes alo uualden   hiet sia eft thanan
    engil thas alouualdoᴎ   hiet sia eft thanaᴎ

    fan th́em grab̃e gangan   endi faran tethem iungron cristes
    faᴎthem graua gangan   endi faraᴎ te them giungarom xr*i*stas

    seggian them isgisithon   suothon uuordon
    seggiaᴎthem is gisiđoᴎ   suođon uuordoᴎ

    that iro drohtin uuas   fandođe astandan
    t ha iro drohtin uuas   fandođa astandaᴎ

C 5835	**h**iet oc ansundron	simon petruse
L 5835	**h**iet ok ansundroᴎ	symoᴎ petrusa

    uuill spell mikil   uuordon cuthian
    uuillspell mikil   uuorduᴎ kuđeaᴎ

    Cumi drohtines   gie that crist selb̃o
    kumi drohtinas   io that xrist selb̃o

4. NOVEL TOOLS VS. STANDARDIZED ERROR

        uuas angalileoland   that ina eft is iungron sculun
        uuas aɴgalileo la*nd*   thar *ina eft* is giungaroɴ sculuɴ

        gisehan isgifithos   sohie im er selƀo gisprac
        giseha**ɴ** is gesiɖos   so hie im er selƀo gisprak

C 5840   uuaron uuordon   **R**eht sothuo thiu uuiƀ thanan
L 5840   **u**uarom uuorduɴ   reht so thúo th*ia* uuif thanaɴ

        gangan uueldun   so stuodun im tegegnes thar
        gangaɴ uueldu**ɴ**   so stuoduɴ *im* te gegnas thar

        engilos tuena   an ala huiton
        engilos tueɴa   aɴalohuitoɴ

        uuanamon giuuadion   endi spracun midiro uuordon tuo
        u*u*anamoɴ giuuadeom   eɴdi sprakuɴ im mi*d* iro uuordoɴ tuo

        helag lico   hugi uarth giblothid
        hélaglico   hugi uuar*d* gibló*d*id

C 5845   **T**hen idision anegison   nemahtun an thia engilos godes
L 5845   them i*d*isoɴ an egisoɴ   ɴimahtuɴ aɴ thia engilos godas

        bi themo uulite scauuon   uuas im thiu uuanami te strang
        b i them uulite uulitaɴ (scauuoɴ)   uuasim thiu uuaname (scone) te strang

        tesuithi tesehanne   thuo spracun im san an gegin
        tesiúkle (t skir) tesehanna   thúo sprákuɴ aɴgegiɴ

        uualdandes bodun   endi thiu uuiƀ fragodun
        uualdandas bodoɴ   endi thea uuif fragoduɴ

        Tehui sia cristan tharod   quican mid dodon
        tehui sia crista tharod   quicaɴ mid dóduɴ

C 5850   suno drohtines   suokian quamin·
L 5850   **s**uno drohtinas   suókian quámiɴ

ferahes fullan   nugi ina ni findat hier
ferahas fullaɴ   ɴú gi ina ɴefiđat hier

antheson sten graƀe   achie ist astandan nu
aɴ thesuɴ steɴgraua   ac hie is astandaɴ giu

Anis lic lichamen   thesgi gilobian sculun
aɴ is líchamoɴ   thes gí giloƀeaɴ sculuɴ

endi gihuggian therouuordo   the hie iute uuaron oft
Eɴdi gehuggiat thero uuordo   the hie iu teuuaraɴ oft

C 5855   selbo sagda   thann hie an iuuuon gisithe uuas
L 5855   selƀo sagda   thann hie aɴ iuuuoɴ gesídea uuas

Angalilealande   huo hie scoldi gigeban uuerthan
aɴ galileo landa   hu hie scoldi gigeƀeɴ uuerđaɴ

gisald selbo   an sundigaro manno
gisald selbo   ansundigaro manno

hetandero hand   helag drohtin
hetteandero hand   helag drohtiɴ

That sia ina quelidin   endi ancruci slogun
that sea ina queledin   endi aɴ crucea slúogiɴ

C 5860   dodan gidadin   endi that hie scoldi thuru drohtines craft
L 5860   dóđaɴ gidádiɴ   endi that hie scoldi thuruh drohtinas craft

anthriddion dage   thioda teuuillion
aɴ thriddioɴ daga   thioda teuuilleaɴ

libbiandi astandan   nu habit hie all gilestid so
L ibbeaɴdi astandaɴ   ɴú habat hie all gilestid só

Gifrumid mid firihon   Iliat ginu forth hinan
g efrumid mid firihoɴ   íleat gí nú forđ hinaɴ

gangat gahlico   endi duot it them isiungron cuth·
gangat gahlico   eɴdi giduat it them is giungarom kúd

LXX ·
[LXX.]

C 5865 **h** ie habit sia iu fur farana   endi ist im forth hinan
L 5865 **H** ie habat sia giu farfarana   endi is im ford hinaɴ

angelileo land   thar ina eft is iungron sculun
aɴgalileoland   thar ina eft is giungaroɴ sculuɴ

gisehan is gisithos   Thuo uuarth after thiu
gisehan is gesídos   thuo uuard sáɴ aftar thiu

them uuibon an uuillon   that sia gihordun sulic uuord sprecan
thém uuiboɴ aɴ uuilleoɴ   that sia gihórduɴ sulic uuord sprekaɴ

Cuthian thia craft godes   uuarunim so acumana thuo noh
kudeaɴ thia craft godas   uuaruɴ im só akumaɴa thúo noh

C 5870 gie so forahta giefrumida   giuuitun im forth thanun
L 5870 **ia** forohta

4.2.1.2 Parallel MSS M, C, and P

M 958   éndi anthanaheleanduuili   hluttrogilobeaɴ.
C 958   **E**ndi anthena uuili   hluttro gilobean
P 958   uuili   hluttro giloboɴ ·

lefteanislera.   **T** ho niuuaslang tethiu
lestean is lera ·   **T**huo niuuas lang ti thiu
Lesteaɴ is lera   thuo ɴiuua lang afte[r

M 960   thatimfongalilea giuuet   godes egan barn
C 960   that him fan galilea giuuet   godes egan barn
P 960   ]at im fan [g   ]giuuet ·   godes egaɴ barn .

M		
C	**D**iurlic drohtines sunu	dopi suokean
P	**d**iorlic drohtinas suno	dope suokeaɴ .

M		
C	uuasim thuo anis uuastme	uualdandes barn
P	**u** uas im thuo in is uuastma	uuldandas barn ·

al so he midtherothiodu   thritig habdi
all so hie mid thero thiedo   thritig habdi
alla so hie mid thero thioɗo   thritig habdi

uintro anisuueroldi .   tho heanisuuilleon quam
uuintro anis uueroldi   Thuo hie anis uuilleon
uuintro aɴ is uueroldi   thuo hie an is uuilleaɴ qua ·

M 965	thar iohannes	aniordanes strome
C 965	thar iohannes	aniordana strome
P 965	**t**har giohannes	aɴ giordana stroma .

allan langandag   liudi manage
allan langan dag   liudi managa
allan langana dag   liodi managa .

dopte diurlico .   **R**ehtosohethoisdrohtin gisah
dopta diurlico .   **R**eht sohie thuo is drohtin gisah
dopta diorlico.   reht so hie thuo isdrohtiɴ gisah ·

holden herron .   souuardimishugi blidi
holdan herron   so uuarth im is hugo bliɗi
holdaɴ herraɴ   so uuarɗ im is hugi bliɗi ·

thesimthea uuilleo gistod .   endi spracimtho midisuuordunto
thes im thie uuillo gistuod   endi sprak im thuo mid is uuordon to
thes im thie uuilleo gistuod   eɴdi sprak miɗ is uuordoɴ tuo ·

M 970	suuido god gumo.	Iohannes tekriste .
C 970	suithuo . guod gumo	iohannes te criste
P 970		

Nucumis thuteminero dopi   drohtin fromin
Nu cumis thu teminero dopi   drohtin fromin
ɴu cumis thu te mi*n*ero dopi   drohtiɴ fromiɴ

thiodgumono bezto .   soscoldeic tethinero duaɴ .
thied gumo best   soscolda ik te thinero duan ·
thiod gumoɴo bezto   so scolda ik te thinaro doaɴ ·

huuandthubist allaro cuningo craftigost .   krist selbo gibod
huand thu bist allero cuningo craftigost.   crist selbo gibod
h*ua*nd thu bist allaro kuningo craftigost   crist selbo *gibod*

uualdanduuarlico   that henispraki thero uuordo than mer.
uualdand uuarlico   that hie nispraki thero uuordo than mer .
uualdand *uua*rlico   that *hie ni spraki thero* uuordo thanmer

M 975   **V**uest thu thatusso girisid quad he   allaro rehto gihuuilig
C 975   **u**uest thu that us girisit quat hie   allaro rehto gihuilik
P 975   **u** uest thu that us so gerisid quad hie .   allaro rehto gehuilic ·

tegifulleanne   forduuardes nu.
tigifullanne   for uuerdes nu
tegifulleanna   forduuardas ɴu ·

angodes uuilleon.   Iohannes stod
an godes uuillon ·   iohannes stuod
aɴ godas uuilleaɴ   giohannes stuod ·

dopteallandag   druhtfolc mikil.
dopta allan dag   druht folc mikil .
dopti allan dag   druht folc mikil ·

uuerod anuuatere .   endi og uualdand krist
uuerod an uuatere   endi oc ualdan crist
uuerodaɴ uuatara   eɴdiok uualdand crist .

M 980   heranhebeɴ cuning   handun sinun
C 980   herren heban cuning   handon sinon
P 980   **h**erraɴ hebaɴkuning   handuɴ sinum

	an allaro baðo them bezton.	endi imthar tebedu gihneg
	an allero bethuo them beston	endi im thar tebedu gihneg
	aɴ allaro baðo them beztom	eɴdi im thar tebeda gihneg .

	ancneo craftag	krist . up giuuet.	
	ankneo craftig	crist up giuuet	
	aɴ knio kraftag	crist *u*pp giuuet ·	

	fagar fonthem flode.	fridubarn godes.
	fagar gan them flode	friðu barn godes
	fagar fan them fluoda	friðubarn godas·

	liof liudio uuard.	**S**ohe tho thatland afstop.
	liof liudeo uuard	**S**o hie thro that land of stuop
	Liof liodo uuard	so hie thuo that land af stuop ·

M 985	so anthliduntho himilesdoru .	endi quam the helago gest.
C 985	so anthlidun thuo himiles duru	endi quam the helago gest
P 985	[s]duɴ thu[ ]las doru	eɴdiquã thie helago gest ·

	fonthem alouualdon	obane tekriste .
	fan them aluualdan	obona tecriste .
	fon them alouualdoɴ	obana te crista ·

	uuasiman gilicnissie	iungres fugles
	uuas im angilicnesse	lungras fugles
	uuasim aɴ gelicnessia	lungras (gitalas) fuglas·

	diurlicara dubuɴ.	endi sat imuppan uses drohtines a(h)slu .
	diurlicaro dufun	endi satim uppan usses drohtines ahsla .
	diurlicaro duboɴ	eɴdi sat im uppan usas drohtinasahslo(ɴ)·

	uuonoda imobar them uualdandes barne .	**A**ftar quamthar uuordfonhimile.
	uuonoda im obar them uualdandes barne	after quam thar uuor(d;) fanhimile
	Uuuɴoda im oborthem uualdan das barna	aftar quã thar uuord fan himila ·

M 990	hlud fonthemhohonradura.	en grottathane helean selbon
C 990	hlud fan them hohon radore	endi gruotta thena heland selbon·
P 990	**h**lud faɴ them hohom radura	eɴdi gruotta thana heland selbaɴ

	krist.allarcuningo bezton.	quad thathe ina gicoranan habdi.
	Crist allaro cuningo beston	quat that hie ina gicoranan habdi
	cristaallaro kuningo beztoɴ	quad that hie ina gicoranaɴ habdi ·
	selbo fon sinun rikea.	quad that im the sunulicodi
	selbo fan sinon rikea	quat that im thie suno licode
	selbo fan sinum rikea	quad that im thie suno licodi·
	bezt allaro giboranaro manno	quadthatheimuuari allarobarnoliobost.
	best allero giboranero manno	quat that hie im uuari allero barno leobost ·
	bezt allaro giboranaro manno	quad that he im uuari allaro barno liobost .
	That moste iohannes	tho alsoit goduuelde
	That muosta iohannes	all so it guod uuelda
	That muostagiohanns thuo	all so it god uuelda .
M 995	gisehan.endigihorean .	hegidedaitsan aftar thiu
C 995	gisahan endi gihorean	hie gideda it san after thiu
P 995	gisehaɴ eɴdi gihoriaɴ	hie gideda it saɴ aftar thiu ·
	maɴnun mari	thatsie thar mahtigna
	mannon mari	that sia thar mahtina
	mannom gimarid	that sia thar mahtigana ·
	herron habdun .	Thitisquad he hebencuningessunu .
	herron habdun ·	That is quat hie heban cuninges suno
	herroɴ habduɴ	thitt is quad hie hebakuningas suno ·
	enalouualdand .	thesas uuilleo ic urcundeo
	enalo uualdan	theses uuilleo ik urkundeo
	Eɴ·alouualdand	thesas uuilleo ik urkundeo ·
	uuesan an thesarouueroldi .	huuanditsagdamiuuorgodes.
	uuesan anthesaro uueroldi	huand it sagda mi uuord godes
	uuesaɴ an thesaro uueroldi	uuand it sagdami uuord godas·
M 1000	drohtinesstemne	thohemidopean het
C 1000	drohtines stemna	thuo hie mi dopean hiet
P 1000	drohtinas stemna	thuo hie mi dopeaɴ hiet ·

	uuerosanuuatare .	sohuuar soicgisahi uuarlico
	uueros an uua tere	sohuar so ik gisauui uuarlico
	uuerosaN uuatara	sohuar so ik gisauue uuarlico ·
	thanahelagon gest.	
	thena helagna gest	fan heban uange
	thana helagon gest	fan hebanuuanga·
M		
C	anthesan middil gard	enigan man uuaron
P	**a** N thesaro middilgard	enigaN maNN uuaroN ·
M		
C	**C**uman midcraftu	that quat scoldi crist uuesan
P	**c** umaN mid craftu	that quad that scoldi crist uuesaN ·
M 1005		
C 1005	diurlic drohtines suno	hie dopean scal
P 1005	**d** iorlic drohtinas suno	hie dopean scal ·
M		endihelean managa
C	anthana helagan gest	endi helean managa .
P	**a**N thana	

4.2.1.3 Comparison of *Heliand* and Luther's Bible translations

The linguistic comparison of the *Heliand* with the language of Luther's translations of the New Testament Gospels is an ongoing project that encompasses ca. 25,000 rows of data and spans over 300 letter-size pages. The scope of this project falls outside the confines of this book. Instead, I plan to publish this and my complete transcriptions from all the extant *Heliand* manuscripts (also in parallel where these overlap) as a reference volume some time in the near future.

As it stands, the project from which the current book is derived has required multiple stages of data mining, organization, and analysis. To give an idea of the scope of such a project, I offer the following description of the steps I undertook.

4. NOVEL TOOLS VS. STANDARDIZED ERROR 93

I completed my own transcription of the *Heliand* texts from all manuscripts where the minor manuscripts overlap with the major manuscripts.[11] Of the minor documents (MSS P, V, S, and L), all overlap with both MSS C and M with the exception of MS L, which overlaps only with MS C. Using the uninterrupted 5969 lines (1–5968) of MS C as the basis for comparison, the following statistics represent the amount of parallel text provided by each manuscript:[12]

1. MS M contains 3874 poetic lines (85–2198a, 2256–2514a, 2576–3414a, 3491–3950, 4017–4674, 4740b–5275a) worth of text,[13] which constitutes 64.90% of MS C.
2. MS P contains 46 poetic lines (958–1006) worth of text, which constitutes 0.77% of MS C.
3. MS V contains 81 poetic lines (1279–1358) worth of text, which constitutes 1.36% of MS C.
4. MS S contains 164 poetic lines (351–360, 368–384, 393–400, 492–582, 675–683, 693–706, 715–722) worth of text, which constitutes 2.75% of MS C.
5. MS L contains 46 poetic lines (5823b–5870a) worth of text, which constitutes 0.77% of MS C.

Thus, the minor manuscripts together act as a secondary and/or tertiary witness to 5.65% of the full *Heliand* library. For the discussion to follow, I will only take into account the textual material of MSS L and P, which in total accounts for 1.54% of MS C. The discussion seeks to find indications linking the *Heliand* language to the language in Luther's Bible translations. The previous chapters have introduced the hypothesis that MSS L and P once belonged to the same codex (cf. 2.1 ff.). The remainder of this book argues that this unitary codex, *Codex L*, was the same manuscript codex discussed variously as having been present at Leipzig by at least four historical figures (cf. Chs. 7–11, 13). Given historical information that places

---

[11] The minor manuscripts do not overlap with one another.
[12] These numbers are based on MS C as the most complete manuscript. Only one manuscript has material that MS C does not, namely MS M (see following footnote).
[13] MS M has an additional 15 poetic lines worth of the text (5968–5983) not contained elsewhere in the manuscripts. This makes the total number of poetic lines contained by MS M 3889.

Luther in close proximity to events important in the establishment of the University Library at Leipzig (cf. 5.1.4), the same institution at which MS L was discovered in 2006 (cf. 2.1), it can be concluded that Luther had access and, according to rumor, even made use of *Codex L. Following this argument and the information gleaned regarding when *Codex L was present at Leipzig (cf. 6.2 ff.), it appeared to me that Luther might have used information and even language from the *Heliand* to aid him in his translation of the Bible. It is for this reason that I consider only MSS L and P in the current discussion, since it can be argued that they were once directly in the hands of Luther.

To continue with my process of creating a parallel text that encompasses both the *Heliand* text and Luther's translations: following my transcription of the manuscripts, I created a parallel database (α) of the overlapping texts. I have provided these in 4.2.1.1 and 4.2.1.2. I then gathered digitized versions of Luther's translations made available at the digital text repository *Wikisource* (http://de.wikisource.org/). From these I created a second database (β), wherein I set the parallel storylines of the four Gospels side by side. I did this for two of Luther's translations, which I then turned into a third database (γ), in which I set the above side-by-side Gospel databases for the two Luther translations in a side-by-side layout. This produced a tool that aids comparing both the synoptic Gospel texts and Luther's translation changes. I chose to use only two of Luther's published translations, the 1522 'Septembertestament' and the 1546 'Letzter Hand', for two reasons: (1) these two texts were readily available in digital form, (2) being Luther's first and last Bible published translations, respectively, these two texts together serve as a gauge of any changes he made to the language of his translation. Regarding this very issue, Sebastian Seyfert, author of a dissertation comparing Luther's four published Bibles for linguistic variances in *Epistle to the Romans*, says (229):

> Für die Zeit von 1522 bis 1545 fällt allgemein eine unerwartet hohe Anzahl sprachlicher Veränderungen im Verhältnis zu einer relativ schmalen Textbasis auf. Dies bestätigt Luthers intensive Revisionsarbeit.

Furthermore, Seyfert dates when these changes in translation occurred:

> Es können insofern drei Revisionsstufen erschlossen werden (229–230): 1. 1522b wird zumeist geringfügig die Wortstellung modifiziert. 2. 1534 wird der bedeutendste lexikalisch-syntaktische Eingriff in die Textgestalt vorgenommen. 3. 1545

treten hauptsächlich lexikalische Ersetzungen, aber auch syntaktische Veränderungen auf. Die zweite Revisionsstufe dürfte größtenteils auf eine 1529 mit Melanchthon veranstaltete Überarbeitung zurückgehen.

Such changes in the translations might indicate a new way of conveying the language of Scripture—something that might have been inspired by Luther's finding the *Heliand*. The timing might also indicate Melanchthon's involvement in knowing about and/or using the *Heliand*—an interesting connection given the discussion in Ch. 10, where it becomes apparent that Melanchthon did indeed know about the Leipzig codex.

I am not the first to suspect that Luther had vernacular works as ready resources. Seyfert condenses G. Bruchmann's three theories of how Luther went about translating (28, emphasis mine):

> Die erste – auch ›Umbruch-Theorie‹ genannt – geht davon aus, daß zwischen den lutherschen und mittelalterlichen Übersetzungen so große Differenzen bestünden, daß beim Vergleich sie eine gewaltige sprachliche Überlegenheit des Reformators zu verzeichnen sei. Deshalb liege auch kein Abhängigkeitsverhältnis zu den mittelalterlichen Drucken vor. Somit bestehe also keine Verbindung zwischen der Lutherbibel und den mittelalterliche Vorlagen.
>
> Die zweite Theorie, die ›Benützungs-Theorie‹ besagt, *daß Luther bei seiner Übersetzung dt. Vorlagen benutzt habe*. So bekräftigt schon Freitag auf Grund phonologischer, flexivischer und lexikalischer Ähnlichkeiten, Luther habe die Zainerbibel verwendet.
>
> Die dritte, die ›Überlieferungs-Theorie‹, geht davon aus, der Reformator habe nicht nach einer bestimmten Vorlage gearbeitet. Ferner seien aber *bestimmte sprachliche Berührungen mit den mittelalterlichen Übersetzungen nicht zu negieren*. Es sei somit selbstverständlich, daß einige Wendungen Martin Luthers schon bei seinen mittelalterlichen Vorgängern zu beobachten gewesen seien, weil *längst vor der reformatorischen Zeit solche biblischen Wendungen dt. Gemeingut gewesen wären*. Dazu kommt der Umstand, daß die Sprache der Erbauungsliteratur der vorangehenden Zeit (Plenarien, *Evangelienharmonien*) dem Lutherdeutsch näher stehe, als die der vollständigen mittelalterlichen Bibel.

I am, however, so far as I can tell, the first to suggest that Luther used the *Heliand* as a linguistic resource.

A final explanation of how I created the parallel *Heliand*-Luther resource: I created the last database (δ) by combining Database 'α' (parallel-*Heliand* manuscript transcriptions) with Database 'γ' (synoptic Gospels in parallel 1522 and 1546 Luther translations). I find Database 'δ' to be a resource of infinite potential that will ultimately provide linguistic evidence for or against the argument of whether Luther used the *Heliand* *Codex L as a Bible translation resource. The statistics I provided above reveal the potential for reward and the reason to continue this research: for my dissertation project I considered only 1.54% of the total *Heliand* text available for comparison with Luther's translations.

That having been said, I wish to note one potentially informative detail that resulted from Database 'δ': simultaneously to building the comparison corpus containing the *Heliand* texts and the Luther translations, I also compared Database 'α' (parallel *Heliand* transcriptions) with the Old High German and Latin Tatian *Monotessaron*, i.e. the supposed source used by the *Heliand* poet in composing the Old Saxon epic. I have done this in part after reading Seyfert's argument regarding what Luther used as resources, which he gives immediately prior to introducing the three theories cited above (28, emphasis):

> Die vermehrt in der ersten Hälfte des 20. Jahrhunderts geführte Diskussion über die Vorlagendominanz des Griech. oder Lat. förderte erstaunlich uneinheitliche Ergebnisse zutage. Es entsteht der Eindruck, daß die Gegestandsbestimmung mehr von geistesgeschichtlichen Präjudizien und weniger von textimmanten Parametern aus erfolgte. So scheinen eine Reihe von Arbeiten a priori erzielte Auffassungen zu hypostasieren und im nachhinein Belege aufzugreifen, anstatt unvoreingenommen vom Gegenstand selbst – den Übersetzungstexten – auszugehen. Den gesamten Bereich der Vorlagenproblematik beurteilen ältere Forschungsarbeiten geradezu bedenkenlos apodiktisch. So wartet 1897 F. Sandvoß mit der ausgefallenen *These* auf, *die lutherische Bibel sei »im Großen und Ganzen schlankweg aus der Vulgata übertragen«*, [...] ohne auch nur im Ansatz linguistische Anhaltspunkte bezusteuern. Im entgegengesetzten Extrem bewertet 1929 O. Albrecht [...] das griech. NT als Luthers Haupttext und untermauert seine Hypothese hauptsächlich mit der nur schwer nachvollziehbaren Begründung, die neutestamentliche Schriftanordnung entspreche der Abfolge des griech. Testaments und nicht derjenigen der Vulgata. Ebenso unterstreicht E. Hanne (Hanne: Septemberbibel, 41–43) 1914 für die Septemberbibel die Vorlagendomninaz des griech. Erasmustextes von 1519. Er führt u.a. Beispiele an, bei denen die Vulgata vom Griech. abweicht – obschon er einräumt, daß die Vulgata häufig mit dem Griech. übereinstimmt. Daraus und aus der Nichtauffindung lat. Belegstellen resultiert auch seine *Vermutung, die Vulgata habe keinen Einfluß auf die Septemberbibel gehabt und der lat. Erasmustext sei allenfalls eine Nebenquelle gewesen*. Gerechtfertigt werden die Ergebniss mit dem Hinweis auf den humanistischen Leitsatz ›ad fontes‹. (Die immer wiederkehrende Affirmation vorurteilsbeladener Hypothesen bewirkt kaum automatisch deren Richtigkeit im wissenschaftlichen Tradierungsprozeß.)
>
> Dagegen entzaubert H. Dibbelt in seinem Aufsatz von 1941 – aus dem zeitgeschichtlich-biographischen Kontext heraus – den bis dahin gemeinhin theologisch-kultivierten Tabustatus des Griech. Seine Beweisführung stützt sich u.a. einerseits auf Selbstzeugnisse, (Luthers Briefe, dt. Schriften und exegetische Kommentare sind gemeint) anhand derer er Luther geringe Griechischkenntnisse zuspricht. anderseits verweist er auf *Beispiele in der Postillenübersetzung und im*

4. NOVEL TOOLS VS. STANDARDIZED ERROR

S[emptember]T[estament], die den prägenden Charakter lat. Vorlagentexte (V bzw. El) herausheben. [...]

[...]
Geht es um den Gebrauch spätmittelalterlicher Bibeln, entsteht ein recht heterogenes Bild. Hierbei wurde auf einen etwaigen Einfluß auf übersetzungstechnische Veränderungen in den Lutherbearbeitungen hingewiesen, ohne jedoch im Detail der Frage nachzugehen.

While researchers in the past were only willing to *hypothesize* about the resources Luther had, modern advancements in linguistic database studies actually provide data to prove or disprove such. Thus, we no longer have the excuse that comparative linguistic analysis is too difficult.

What does this have to do with the *Heliand*? Consider line 5835, Mark 16:7, given below in its context. Here, the women are approaching the sepulchre in which Jesus' body had been lain, where they find the angel and the rolled-back stone. For simplicity's sake and the lack of page space, here I offer Taeger's *Heliand* transcription (split into half-lines) and only Luther's 'Septembertestament' (1522) translation next to the Old High German Tatian:

Heliand (5180–5840)	Luther (Matt. 16:4–7)	Tatian (216,3–219,1)
5810 [...]		
Thuo sâuun sia ina sittian thar,	**[4]** vnd sie sahen da hyn, vnd wurden gewar,	
5811 thiu uuîf uppan them uuendidan stêne,	das der steyn abgeweltzet war, denn er war seer gros,	quuer aruuelzit úns then stéin fon then turon thés grabes? her uuas thrato michil.
		[217,1] Inti sinu tho erthbibunga uuaa giuortan michil:
	[5] vnnd sie giengen hyneyn, ynn das grab, vnd sahen eynen iungling zur rechten hand sitzen,	gotes engil steig fon hímile inti zuogangenti aruúalzta then stein **[2]** Inti scóuuuonto gisahun aruualztan then stein fon themo grabe inti engil sizzantan ubar ínan.
endi im fan them uulitie quâmun,	der hatte eyn lang weyß kleyd an,	**[3]** Uuas sín gisíuni samasa blekezunga inti sin giuuati samasa snío.

5812 them idison sulica egison *tegegnes:*	vnd entsatzten sich.	**[4]** Thuruh sina forohta erbruogite uuarun thie hirta inti uurdun uuortan samasa
all uuurðun fan them grurie		
5813 *thiu frî forahton mikilon*		
furðor ne gidorstun		
5814 *te them grabe gangan,*		
êr sia thie godes engil,		
5815 *uualdandes* bodo	**[6]** Er aber sprach zu yhnen,	**[5]** Tho antalengita ther engil, quad then uúibon:
uuordon gruotta,		
	Entsetzt euch nicht,	ni curet íu forohtan:
5816 quað that hie iro ârundi		
all bicunsti,		
5817 uuerc endi uuillion		
endi thero uuîbo hugi,		
5818 hiet that sia im ne andrêdin:		
'ik uuêt that gi iuuuan drohtin suokat,	yhr sucht	ih uueiz thaz ir
5819 neriondon Crist	Jhesum	then heilant
fan Nazarethburg,	von Nazareth	
5820 thena thi hier quelidun	den gecreutzigten,	ther dar arhangan ist suochet.
endi an crûci slôgun		
5821 Iudeo liudi		
endi an graf lagdun		
5822 *sundilôsian.*		
Nu nist hie selbo hier,		**[6]** Nist er hier:
5823 ac hie ist astandan iu,	Er ist aufferstanden, vnd ist nicht hie,	her arstúont,
		sosa her quad:
endi sind thesa stedi lârea,		
5824 thit graf an theson griote.		
Nu mugun gi gangan herod		quaemet
5825 nâhor mikilu		
— ik uuêt that is iu ist niud sehan	Sihe da,	inti gisehet
5826 an theson stêne innan —:		
hier sind noh thia stedi scîna,	die stete,	this stat
5827 thar is lîchamo lag.'	da sie yhn hyn legten,	uuar trohtin gilegit uuas.
Lungra fengun		
5828 gibada an iro brioston		**[218,1]** Inti uuard tho, mittiu sio in muote arforhte uuarun fon thisiu,
blêca idisi,		

5829 uulitiscôni uuîf :			
uuas im uuilspell mikil			
5830 te gihôrianne,			
that im fan iro *hêrren* sagda			
5831 engil thes alouualden.			

[2] Senu thó zuuene man stúontun nah ín in scinentemo giuúate. [3] Mittiu sio tho forohtun Inti helditun iro annuzi in erda, quadun zi ín: uuaz suochet ir lebentan mit toten? Nist er hier, oh her arstuont. Gihuget uuio her zi íu spráh, mittiu her noh nu in Galileu uúas, quaedenti uuanta gilinfit then mannes sun zi selenne in hant suntigero manno inti arhangan uuerdan inti thritten tages arstantan.

Hiet sia eft thanan		
5832 fan them grabe gangan		
endi faran te them iungron Cristes,	[7] gehet aber hyn,	Inti slíumo gangente
5833 seggian them is gisîðon	vnd saget seynen iungern,	quædet sinen iungoron
suoðon uuordon,		
5834 that iro drohtin uuas		
fan dôðe astandan.		uuanta her arstuont fon tode,
5835 Hiet ôc an sundron		
Sîmon Petruse	vnd **Petro**,	
5836 uuillspell mikil		
uuordon cûðian,		
5837 cumi drohtines,		
gie that Crist *selbo*	das er fur euch hyn	inti senu her forafuor íuuuih
5838 *uuas an* Galileo land,	ynn Gallilean gehen wirt,	in Galileam:
'thar ina eft is iungron sculun,		
5839 gisehan is *gisîðos*,	da werdet yhr yhn sehen,	thar gisehet ir inan:

	sô hie im êr selbo gisprac	wie er euch gesagt hat.	senu bifora sagata her iz íu.
5840	uuâron uuordon.'		Inti gihugitun thó sinero uuorto,
		[...]	

Consider line 5835, Mark 16:7. A small detail exists in the *Heliand* and Luther that does not occur in Tatian. When the angel calls upon the disciples to go to Galilee, he calls upon Peter by name (in bold). If the *Heliand* poet was following primarily a recently-finished Tatian, as Baeseck argues (76–78), where did this detail about Peter come from? It could not have come from either the Old High German or Latin Tatian—it's not there! This has unforseeable consequences for future studies, since many researchers (cf. Foerste, 93–95, including Baesecke, have based their dating of the poet's original (cf. **O in 2.2.3) on the assumption that he used the Old High German Tatian, which he dates to ca. 834. If this assumption is incorrect, then the dating of the *Heliand* can be decoupled from the finishing of the Old High German Tatian. Walther Henß also had doubts about the Tatian assumption (191):

> Die Quellenfrage in der abendländischen Tatian-Überlieferung ist keineswegs so bequem, wie es lange Zeit schien, ja nicht einmal der Umkreis möglicher Erforschung ist bis jetzt endgültig abgesteckt worden.

Furthermore, as the Tatian assumption is often used in tandem with Rabanus' *Matthäuskommentar* as evidence for the *Heliand* poet's presence at Fulda, it seems that the mention of Peter by name in line 5835 calls into question both the assumption that the *Heliand* poet had access to Rabanus' commentary and the likelihood that the poet was at Fulda. As Krogmann states (20):

> [...] Georg Baeseck [kommt] auch eingehend auf die ›Praefatio [...]‹ und die ›Versus [...]‹ zu sprechen. Dabei geht er von Eduard Sievers' Annahme aus, daß die ursprüngliche Praefatio von Hraban geschrieben worden sei. [...] Als Beweis kämen für ihn nur die aufgeführten Übereinstimmungen mit anderen Vorreden Hrabans in Betracht [...]. Anderseits wäre ihm eine Beteiligung Hrabans an der Enstehung des Heliand nicht wunderbar, sondern bei einem königlichen Auftrag das Natürliche, wenn die altsächsische Dichtung, was er annimmt, wirklich in Fulda verfaßt wurde. Daß nur dort der Matthäuskommentar Hrabans so bald nach seiner Niederschrift als Quellenwerk zu haben gewesen sei, ist ihm freilich kein Beweis, solange er nicht weiß, wie bald der Heliand nach 822, dem Jahr seiner Vollendung [i.e., of the *Matthäuskommentar*] gedichtet wurde. Zeit für ihn hat er bis zum Tode

> Ludwigs des Frommen im Jahre 840, und er glaubt kaum, daß innerhalb Fuldas die erst in die dreißiger Jahre des 9. Jahrhunderts fallende prosaische und mangelhafte Tatianverdeutschung jünger sei als er [i.e. the *Kommentar*].

Krogmann here shows how Baesecke's hypothesis—i.e., placing the *Heliand* composition in Fulda between 834 and 840—is based on the presence and completion of the Old High German Tatian, Rabanus' commentary on Matthew, and on the life of Louis the Pious. All these assumptions have their individual merits; however, evidence has been shown in 3.2 that speaks to Louis the German's involvement, not Louis the Pious. Moreover, the specification of Peter in line 5835 brings into question whether the *Heliand* poet indeed used the Old High German Tatian (or even Latin, for that matter). Still more, noting that the only of the four Gospels to specify Peter in this scene is Mark, it is necessary to conclude that the *Heliand* poet had something other or in addition to Rabanus' Matthew commentary. What this might have been, I have no idea.

It suffices to say that the issue of the timing and location of the *Heliand* poet remains as obscure as his identity. Despite this, it appears that people over many centuries who have come into contact with *Heliand* manuscripts have interpreted "Ludouuicus pijssimus Augustus" as Louis the Pious. In the following chapters, I make use of this assumption and its link to the *Heliand* to investigate a second fascinating mystery about the Old Saxon epic: Did Luther really have a copy of the *Heliand*?

Part II:

Historical Accounts of an Old Saxon Codex in Leipzig

5. A Short History of Leipzig

5.1 From Monastery to University

In Fall 2009, the University of Leipzig celebrated the 600th anniversary of its founding with the dedication of a newly-constructed Main Building on the historic site of the *Paulinerkirche*, one of the University's first buildings. The history of the University of Leipzig is tightly intertwined with that of the *Paulinerkirche*, a building first erected at the center of the Dominican monastery from which it earned its name. The location and existence of the *Paulinerkirche* and the surrounding buildings of the former monastery to which it belonged play a central role in discussions throughout this book. For this reason, it is appropriate to present a review of the history of the locale.

5.1.1 The Paulinerkirche

In 1231 a Dominican monastery dedicated to St. Paulus was established just inside the city wall on the eastern side of medieval Leipzig at *Grimmaische Tor* (near present-day *Augustusplatz*). The *Paulinerkirche*—center of monastery activity—was dedicated in 1240, and became Leipzig's third intramural religious edifice (after the *Nikolaikirche*, begun 1165 as a merchant church; and the *Marktkirche*, converted 1212 into the *Thomaskirche* by Augustinian monks).

Leipzig attracted settlers from both religious and mercantile realms for its location at the intersection of the *Via Regia* and *Via Imperii*—two highly productive medieval European trade routes. The tradition of Leipzig as a center of commerce has affected its development throughout history, and continues to do so today. Also important for consideration is that, prior to the Reformation, Leipzig belonged to the Bishopric of Merseburg (968–981, 1004–1565). Ultimately, the productivity of the St. Paulus monastery declined. As a result, it was dissolved in 1539, and its property was secularized shortly thereafter in 1541 ("Universitätsbibliothek Leipzig," *Leipzig-Lexikon*).

5.1.2 Early Protestant Movement in Prague

Well over a century prior to the demise of the St. Paulus monastery, the seeds of the founding of a university in Leipzig were sown as a result of the Jan Hus Controversy. In 1403, the doctrines of John Wycliffe stirred disagreement over what doctrine could be taught at the Charles University in Prague, the premiere educational institution in the Holy Roman Empire and the very institution that thanked its existence to the Holy Roman Emperor himself, i.e. to Charles IV, who a decade prior to his ascension to the Imperial throne requested a bull from his friend and ally Pope Clement VI. This papal decree called Prague's university into being in 1347. Half a century later, Hus, a Czech national, promoted inclusion of Wycliffe's controversial doctrine in the curriculum, and therein faced opposition from the Polish, Saxon and Bavarian faculty that comprised three of the four subdivisions of the University's legislative body. In 1408 these tensions along national lines reached a breaking point as a result of additional political stress stemming from the ongoing Papal Schism. These two conflicts met as one in the Bohemian (read 'Czech') King Wenceslas (King of Germany—i.e. 'King of the Romans': 1376–1400; King of Bohemia by inheritance—as Wenceslas IV: 1378—1419), who, having faced humiliation when he was deposed as King of Germany in 1400, feared also that he was being overlooked for the future position of Holy Roman Emperor. Fearing that papal claimant Gregory XII would consolidate the powers that sought to keep him from the title of Emperor, Wenceslas disavowed the Roman pope and stated his expectation of the University—the institution founded by his father, Charles IV—to remain absolutely neutral on the subject of the Papal Schism.

The division of the University faculty's voting power along national lines was a policy instated at the institution's founding by Charles IV himself. As a result, four nations (Polish, Bohemian, Saxon, and Bavarian) shared equal weight in deciding academic matters. This division of power according to national heritage reflected the climate of Prague at the time— a multicultural imperial capital in the middle of an otherwise homogeneously Bohemian territory. Wishing to maintain (nominal) neutrality on the subject of papal succession (in reality, his clear failure to support Gregory XII was an unmistakable line-in-the-sand), but also finding himself beholden to his father's idealistic measure of influencing national equality at the Academy, Wenceslas tweaked the University's bylaws to ensure that the faculty powers did not break his sworn neutrality by siding with any papal pretender. By signing the Decree of Kutná Hora (German: *Kuttenberger Dekret*), Wenceslas effectively redistributed the power of the faculty vote in the academic senate: three votes to the Bohemian nation compared to one vote each to the Polish, Bavarian and Saxon nations. As a result of the Bohemian nation's new power at the University, Jan Hus was elected University Rector and enforced his academic preferences. Being favorable to Wycliffe's controversial writings, Hus introduced changes to the curriculum that were subsequently protested by faculty from the Polish and the two German nations. Noticing that their protests fell on deaf ears and fearing that they were effectively excluded from management of the University, the non-Bohemian academics began to look for greener pastures.

5.1.3 University of Leipzig Established

In 1409 between 5,000 and 30,000 Polish, Bavarian and Saxon faculty and students fled Prague for other areas of the Empire. Around 1,000 congregated in Leipzig, at the time the leading commercial center of the Margraviate of Meissen, which bordered Bohemia to the north. For the scholars, Leipzig represented the first sizeable stopping point in their exodus from Prague. Once they had arrived in Leipzig for what was presumably an indefinite stay, the Faculty of Arts took to resuming instruction. The city responded immediately by offering a building on Petersstraße near the city's southern gate, the *Peterstor*. The co-rulers of the Margraviate of Meissen, brothers Friedrich IV ('der Streitbare') and Wilhelm II ('der Reiche') authorized a budget of 500 Guldens for the establishment of two colleges to be housed tax-free in two buildings on Ritterstraße just north of what would later become Augustusplatz. Soon after, antipope (Pisan line) Alexander V granted a *Studium Generale* to the new institution to garnish favor from the academics that had been deposed as a result of the Papal Schism. Despite the outcome of the fight for the papal throne, this decree lent the fledgling institution much needed academic credence and officially established it as the University of Leipzig. Following the decree, the University elected its first rector, after which the new university, in its search for learning materials, became closely associated with its neighbor to the south, the Dominican monastery.

5.1.4 University Expansion

The University of Leipzig maintained its cramped quarters on Ritterstraße for almost a century-and-a-half until 22 May 1543, when it was granted the Dominican monastery (dissolved in 1539) building complex ca. 200 meters away. The sudden expansion of University property was realized as part of widespread educational reforms throughout Saxony, led by Duke Maurice (Moritz; later also Elector) of Saxony. Among these reforms were the Duke's intentions for the University to be founded anew ("Neufundation," *Neue Deutsche Biographie* [NDB], 143), and entailed a restructuring of the institution ("Umstrukturierung," loc. cit.) under the leadership of Caspar Borner, Joachim Camerarius and Philipp Melanchthon. Furthermore, the University Library (*Universitätsbibliothek Leipzig*, henceforth UBL) was established officially on 28 June 1543 with automatic inheritance of all former Dominican monastery materials. Prior to this no central, independent library had been established for the University, although the individual colleges, nations, and the four faculties of the University had accrued academic materials of their own from its founding in 1409 (Manns, 9). Within the year, more materials were transferred to the UBL from Leipzig's Augustinian monastery and Franciscan monastery.

Accompanying the University's acquisition of former monastery property was the space necessary to facilitate Duke Maurice's objective of restructuring the entire academic institution. Former monastic dormitory space was converted to administrative offices and classrooms. Additionally, the University acquired the St. Paulus Chapel, i.e. the *Paulinerkirche*, which would serve as the University's icon until its controversial destruction in 1968 at the hands of the city's communist leadership. The chapel underwent renovation between 1543 and 1545, at the end of which it was rededicated as the Protestant *Universitätskirche St. Pauli*. The consecration ceremony was performed by Martin Luther and took place on 12 Aug 1545—just six months and one week before the Reformer's death.

The UBL was given its first home complex facing what would become Augustusplatz (built 1785–1794; renamed 1839), in a large arcaded space at the former St. Paulus monastery. It is from the Library's association with this building that the UBL became known as "Bibliotheca Paulina" or the *Paulinum* for short (cf. 4.2.2: Fabricius' 24 November 1545 letter).

The basis of the UBL's holdings (the "Gründungsbestand") consisted of 2000 volumes of manuscripts and printed books from the Dominican collection, plus an additional 375 from Leipzig's Augustinians (St. Thomas) and 300 from Leipzig's Franciscans (Zum Heiligen Geist) (Manns).[1] Yet the number of holdings grew more swiftly still. Wanting to ensure that the space recently appropriated for the Library would be filled completely, Duke Maurice enforced the secularization of small monasteries in Leipzig's immediate surroundings and throughout what today comprises the Federal States of Saxony, Saxony-Anhalt and Thuringia, thus effectuating the closure of many of these edifices. The collections of writings confiscated from these monasteries were subsequently awarded to the University of Leipzig as holdings of the new UBL.[2] Speaking to the effect of this move of written materials on modern scholarship, Heinrich Kramm wrote that Librarian C. Borner "[hat] mit mehr als 4000 Büchern und Hss. das Beste des mitteldeutschen Bildungsgutes aus dem Mittelalter gerettet" (170). That is, regardless of the means of their acquisition, the centralization of materials at the UBL ensured the survival of invaluable historical documentation that may have otherwise never made it into the hands of the public. In addition to these more-or-less documented transfers of materials from regional monasteries, there also existed other private channels (cf. 13.1.1) by which the UBL increased its early inventory (Hannemann, 11), e.g. via professors', students', and/or wealthy private citizens' personal collections (Manns), which were themselves acquired through still other connections. In short, to attempt to discern the means by which any given object made its way to the UBL would be a virtually impossible undertaking. Nevertheless, contemporary academics made mention of certain documents, leaving hints of a trail for future researchers to trace.

---

[1] Other sources put the total of the Gründungsbestand at 1500 manuscripts and 4000 printed books (Leipzig-Lexikon; cf. literature of Bähring and Rüddiger [2008], Loh [1987], and Horst [2005]).

[2] Manns states: "So erhielt die Universitätsbibliothek wertvolle Teilbestände oder sogar den gesamten Bestand von den Zisterzienserklöstern Altzelle (1543) und Buch (1547), den Benediktinern in Pegau (1543) und Chemnitz (1544), von den Augustinern vom Lauterberg (Petersberg) bei Halle (1543), von den Franziskanern aus Langensalza (1544) sowie von den Dominikanern aus Pirna (1545). Diese Schenkungen verdeutlichen auch das untergebrochene Interesse Moritz' von Sachsens an der Entwicklung der Leipziger Universität" (9, footnote 4).

5.2 Library Holdings in the *Paulinum*

Leipzig's situation on two important *Reichsstraßen* has given the city historic advantage in trade and commerce, which in turn has attracted populations in search of opportunity. It is hardly surprising that those scholars and professors who fled Prague at the height of the Great Schism looked for new prospects in nearby Leipzig. There they established modern-Germany's second oldest continually operating university. Thus, the University of Leipzig had been established a century prior to Luther's arrival on the world scene.

The Leipzig institution played a key role during the period of upheaval known as the Reformation, as the University was not only located geographically in the thick of the fight, but became a tool for the advancement of the Saxon royalty's political and religious aims. As a result of the educational reforms conceived by Duke Maurice of Saxony, the University became the center of liberal education in a resurgent Saxony. The power to carry out the Duke's reforms was granted to Reformation theologians Borner, Camerarius, and Melanchthon, who, as stated, centralized the 134-year-old University's bibliographic materials into the UBL. In a matter of three years, this cutting-edge institution became home to the largest collection of written materials in Saxony, even rivaling the libraries of more established institutions in prestige if not in number of holdings. Thus, Leipzig's historic reputation as the City of Books ("Bücherstadt Leipzig") was beginning to be recognized already in the mid-sixteenth century.

Ultimately, the needs of the growing University were met by the opportunity created by the decline of the St. Paulus Dominican monastery. Whether it was through the consolidation of regional materials to fill the *Paulinum*'s vaulted space, through the direct inheritance of manuscripts from the original Dominican monastery itself, or through private channels, it is in this period that antique manuscripts related to the *Heliand*—perhaps even an original codex—first appeared at the UBL.

Indeed, a number of published statements from the mid-to-late sixteenth century make mention of a *monotessaron* (i.e. a Gospel harmony) that told of its composition at the request of the Emperor Louis the Pious, Charlemagne's son. These sources invariably claim the UBL's *Paulinum* as the location of this *monotessaron*. Thus, when eighteenth-century Germanists rediscovered the *Heliand* epic, it became a goal to hunt down the Leipzig *monotessaron* there, and for multiple reasons. The interest in the *Heliand* epic was precipitated by the initial discovery of MS M in Bamberg ca. 1720 (it was subsequently lost and rediscovered later in Munich).

Eccard was the first to hypothesize a link between the Old Saxon *Heliand* epic (though he called the language "Franco-Danish") and the Latin *Prefaces*, known via multiple imprints tracing back to one Illyricus—a peer of the Reformation giants Luther and Melanchthon. Furthermore, a rumor stretching back at least to Joachim Feller, *Paulinum* librarian in ca. 1680, claimed that Luther himself had possessed a document that was likewise composed under Louis the Pious and was housed in Leipzig. Thus, the rediscovery of relatable documents not only presented an exciting mystery of its own stretching back many centuries, it also portended some unknown link to Luther, who was still a folk celebrity in von Eccard's time.

Despite the promise of finding answers to questions looming about the age and provenance of the Old Saxon text and its link to the Reformation, efforts to locate the *monotessaron* were fruitless. Nothing of the sort could be found in Leipzig. Consequently, over time the stories of the Leipzig *monotessaron* and its connection to Luther were disregarded as mere folklore.

The rumors were trotted out now and again during the nineteenth century, when the *Heliand* epic was printed for the first time, e.g. Schmeller (1830, 1840), etc. This publication followed the two manuscripts extant at the time (MSS C and M). Additional publications followed again at the turn of the twentieth century and thereafter, when the first three fragmentary manuscripts (MSS P, S, and V) were discovered. Still, the 1900s went by without much substantive to say about the rumored Leipzig-Luther connection to the *Heliand*.

Then in 2006, the discovery of the fourth manuscript fragment bearing the text of the *Heliand* was discovered among the holdings of the UBL. This physical evidence finally lends credibility to the rumors of yore, suggesting that these were never really just rumors at all, but that they contain some truthful detail. Nevertheless, the 2006 discovery does not affirm the rumors outright, rather the question still stands: Does the MS L corroborate the claims that Luther possessed a copy of the *Heliand*? Moreover, if it does, further questions necessarily follow, e.g., "How did he get it?", "Why did he have it?", and "What did he do with it?"

The subsequent chapters discuss the evidence behind the rumor linking Luther with a *Heliand* codex. Chapter 6 focuses on the history of the

Prefaces, knowledge of which can be documented to within Luther's lifetime. Following the discussion in that chapter, I divide the rumor according to two post-Luther publications: the chapters in Part III discuss the men responsible for these publications, while the chapters of Part IV discuss what these publications say.

6. Latin *Prefaces* to an Ancient Gmc. Gospel

6.1 The Latin *Prefaces*

The two Latin texts "Praefatio in librum antiquum lingua Saxonica conscriptum" ('Preface to an ancient book composed in the Saxon language') and "Versus de poeta et interprete huius codicis" ('Verse about the poet and translator of this book') are also known by the shortened labels *Praefatio* and *Versus*. For ease of discussion I will henceforth refer to the combination, i.e. *Praefatio* and *Versus* together, as the '*Prefaces*'.

The *Prefaces* survive in no original manuscript form (cf. 6.1). Rather, its first known instantiation comes from the second edition of *Catalogus testium veritatis* ('List of true witnesses'), a Protestant tract printed[1] by Matthias Flacius Illyricus[2] in 1562, where the *Prefaces* appear on p. 93 f. (Hellgardt 2004). Much of the history of the first printing of the *Prefaces* is unknown. For example, it is not known whether the full titles were taken directly from the original manuscript texts or assigned by either Illyricus or his printer (cf. Baesecke 1948). Moreover, for much of modern history it was unknown where these texts had come from; i.e., what served as Illyricus' source. In light of this obscurity, the *Prefaces*' ties to the *Heliand* have been debated since Johann Georg von Eccard[3] (1664-1730) first hypothesized the link between the two.

6.1.1 Johann Georg von Eccard

In the early eighteenth century, Eccard inherited Gottfried von Leibniz' position as librarian to the House of Hanover—a position which, with its

---

[1] The 1st ed. was print 1556. It does not contain the *Prefaces*.
[2] Matthias Flacius the Elder (1520-1575): born Vlačić in Albona, Istria (modern-day Labin, Croatia), hence "Illyricus" (i.e., referring to *Illyricum*, the Latin name for the Adriatic's eastern shore). He is not to be confused with Matthias Garbitius (1505-1559), also from Istria and thus sometimes also called "Illyricus": Garbitius matriculated at Wittenberg 6 May 1534 as "Matthias Illyricus" (AAV, vol. I pg. 153). Nonetheless, the two men were certainly separate persons: Grabitius had a laudable career as a professor at Tübingen, while Flacius was essentially banished from Jena, Antwerp, Frankfurt and Strasbourg, and forced to live his later life in hiding due his polemic nature.
[3] A.k.a. Eckhart, Eckhardt, i.e. the assistant of polymath Gottfried Wilhelm Leibniz.

association with two powerful libraries,[4] coincidentally gave him access to one of the largest collections of Reformation-period manuscripts. Eccard had attended university at Leipzig first to study Theology, but his interests soon turned to the subjects of History and Philology. It is primarily for his work in these fields that he is known today. In 1711, Eccard published *Historia studii etymologici linguae germanicae hactenus impensi* ('History of the etymological study of the Germanic language applied up to today'), an early philological investigation into the history of the constellation of Germanic languages known at the time. In 1723, he fled Hanover inexplicably, deserting his family there, and converted to Catholicism in Cologne. Soon after this, he took a position in Würzburg as librarian to the Bishop Franz Christoph von Hutten. It is during his time in Hanover and Würzburg that Eccard became important to Old Saxon studies.

In 1720 Eccard read an excerpt of the *Prefaces* in *Historiae Francorum Scriptores, vol. II* (1636) by Andreas Quercetanus[5] (Hellgardt, p. 175). That same year, Eccard reprinted the excerpt in *Veterum monumentorum Quaternio* ('On real memorials in four parts'). He would later reprint it again in *Commentarii de rebus Franciae Orientalis et episcopatus Wirceburgensis* ('Commentaries on the handlings of Eastern Francia and of the Bishopric of Würzburg', itself reprinted in 1929), in which Eccard presents noteworthy materials from the library in Würzburg. Strangely, despite occupying well-connected positions, it appears that Eccard did not know about Illyricus' printing of the *Prefaces* in *Catalogus testium veritatis* despite its having been in existence for nearly half a century. Rather, in the commentaries to his two publications of the *Prefaces*, Eccard credits Quercetanus (not Illyricus) as his ultimate source. Eccard is cited by Hellgardt (125, note 10, emphasis mine):

> habebatur ... Bibliorum Codex in nostrum idioma translatus. Poeta Saxo sub Ludovico Pio eum jam poetice transtulerat. Testis est Praefatio ejus ... apud Quercetanum ... Utinam autem, qui nobis Praefationem hanc dedêre, Galli integrum illum librum Saxonicum in lucis auras protulissent, aut saltem, ubi lateat (lateret 1729). Eckhart 1720, S. 41f.; so auch 1729, *wo es darüber hinaus heißt:* Prologus ... quem Andreas Quercetanus ...

---

[4] The *Königliche Öffentliche Bibliothek* in Hanover (now called *Gottfried Wilhelm Leibniz Bibliothek-Niedersächsische Landesbibliothek*) and *Bibliotheca Augusta* in Wolfenbüttel (*Herzog August Bibliothek*).

[5] A.k.a. Duchesne, also spelled *du Chesne*.

> In the holdings there was [...] a Codex of the Bible translated into our language. Moreover, a Saxon poet under Louis the Pious had conveyed it poetically. A witness to it is its preface [...] [printed] by Quercetanus [...] If only he who gave us this preface would have brought the entire Saxon book into the broad daylight of France,[6] or at least would (have 1729) stash(ed 1729) [it] away [somewhere!] [...] *additionally in 1729:* A prologue [...] that Andreas Quercetanus [...]

Von Eccard's evident frustration over the lost codex would remain with him for the rest of his life. Yet his disappointment was due not only to his failure to locate Quercetanus' source, rather also in part to his loss of what would later come to be known as MS M, which had been discovered originally at Würzburg, i.e. right under von Eccard's nose: G. C. Siegler discovered it there in 1720. When Siegler later returned to the location with Eccard to show him what he had found, the manuscript could not be located. MS M would not be rediscovered until well after von Eccard's death in 1730: it reappeared in 1794 in Bamberg, where it was found by Gérard Gley. How the manuscript moved from Würzburg to Bamberg remains a mystery to this day.

Despite the loss of the stashed-away document he had hoped for, von Eccard left a legacy of writing on the topic of what would later come to be known as the *Heliand*, including what he saw as the probable existence of an Old Saxon rendition of the Bible. It is ultimately from Eccard that we have the first hypothesis that the *Prefaces* described the *Heliand* and that both therefore stemmed from the same larger work. This comes from his postulations about the lost MS M (based on Siegler's descriptions of the lost Würzburg manuscript) and Quercetanus' excerpts of the *Prefaces*. Unbeknownst to Eccard, other literature about the *Heliand*[7] existed in the form of publications by Thomas Smith (1696) and George Hickes (1705), who wrote about the London-based MS C, which had been discovered in the sixteenth century, but nevertheless remained virtually unknown on the Continent until the following century.

---

[6] I.e. the Holy Roman Empire.

[7] The name of the epic was a perennial problem until J. A. Schmeller formalized the usage of *Heliand* through the title of his 1830 book. Prior to this, a variety of descriptors were used, including '*monotessaron*' (*a one-in-four* [cf. Gk. μονο- (*mono-*) 'one, single, alone' + τέσσαρα (*tessara*) 'of or pertaining to the number four' (OED)], i.e. a Gospel harmony), '*antiquus liber Germanicus*' (*an old German book*), '*manuscriptum verum Germanicum*' (*the doubtless Germanic manuscript*), '*versiculos*' (*passages*), etc. Thus, it would have been difficult for Eccard to know what to look for when and if he sought out other people's writings on the subject.

6.1.2 Linking the Latin *Prefaces* to the Old Saxon *Heliand*

Had Eccard been able to see MS M, or if he had had access to Smith's and/or Hickes' descriptions of MS C, he probably would have recognized the *Heliand* manuscripts as his predicted Old Saxon Bible. The *Prefaces* seem to describe with a degree of detail that which is now called the *Heliand* (Hellgardt 2004, p. 177-178; German translation, p. 181):

> [...] Ludouicus pijssimus Augustus [...] [p]ræcepit namq; cuidam uiro de gente Saxonum, qui apud suos non ignobilis Vates habebatur, ut uetus ac nouum Testamentum in Germanicam linguam poetice transferre studeret, quatenus non solum literatis, uerum etiam illiterates sacra diuinorum præceptorum lectio panderetur.

> [...] Ludwig, der sehr fromme Augustus [...] befahl nämlich einem gewissen Mann aus dem Stamm der Sachsen, der bei den Seinen als ein sehr angesehener seherischer Dichter galt, dass er sich anstrengen sollte, das Alte und das Neue Testament poetisch in die germanische Sprache zu übertragen, damit nicht nur den Schriftkundigen, sondern auch den Schriftunkundigen die heilige Lesung der göttlichen Gebote sich erschließe.

According to our current knowledge, the *Heliand* represents a retelling of the Gospels as an Old Saxon epic, a traditional poetic style that was readily recognizable to and popular among the Germanic peoples during the Medieval Period. Accordingly, the *Prefaces* mention a *Saxonum* ('Saxon') *Vates* ('poet, prophet, authority') who was called to *poetice transfere* ('to translate into poetic verse') the Old and New Testaments so that *non solum literatis, uerum etiam illiterates* ('non only the learned, but the unlearned as well') could understand.

Of course, it is only from our modern-day perspective that the language of the *Heliand* is known to be Old Saxon. By comparison, Hickes called the language of MS C "Franco-danish".[8] Yet, there it stands in the *Prefaces*: "uiro de gente Saxonum [...] in Germanicam linguam [...] transferre" ('a man of the Saxon folk [...] to translate [...] into the German language'). This should be taken in the context of the time the *Heliand* was written: assuming the Emperor Louis mentioned in the *Prefaces* to be Louis the Pious[9] (778-840), the combined work was written shortly after Charlemagne conquered

---

[8] *Franco-* meaning 'Frankish', not 'French'.
[9] A.k.a. Louis I. The alternative interpretation is his son, Louis the German (806-876), who, if assumed, implies an equivalent conclusion.

the Saxons after a long period of war. It is generally understood that the West Germanic languages (incl. Old English) were still mutually intelligible to a high degree during this period. It is apparent that the description of the language in the *Prefaces* comes from a Latin-centric viewpoint. Thus, that the *Prefaces* call the language of the translation "German" is to be expected: if at the time that the *Prefaces* were authored the Old Saxon language was not yet completely distinguishable from Old English, Old Frankish or even Old High German, what else would one call it but the Latin term by which these people and there language(s) were referred to collectively? Furthermore, if a distinction of the dialect need be read from the *Prefaces*, the author already specified the poet as being Saxon. Note that even by late seventeenth century a more specific name could not be offered for the language encountered on the *Heliand* manuscripts; from the English Hickes' perspective the language of MS C was, apparently, somewhere between Frankish and Danish. Geographically, the Saxons were just that. Considering the Continental West Germanic dialect continuum that had developed by Hickes' time, his was not a bad linguistic description of Old Saxon.

6.1.3 *Prefaces*' Proof of Authenticity

Despite the similarities between the *Heliand* and the *Prefaces* as presented, doubt has often been given to von Eccard's proposal: "Trotzdem haben die Stimmen nicht verstummen wollen, die glaubten, in den Vorreden die Fälschung eines gelehrten Humanisten erkennen zu können" (Eichhoff & Rauch, XII). Yet, as Georg Baesecke points out: "[e]in Satz der Vorrede [...] ist unverdächtig, weil ihn das germanische *fittea* trägt" (1948, p. 70). Here he refers to the mention in the *Prefaces* of the way the Old Saxon text had been divided into parts: "Iuxta morem uero illius poëmatis omne opus per *uitteas* distinxit, quas nos lectiones uel sententias possumus appellare" ('In keeping with the consistency of that poem, he divided the whole work into *fitts*, which we call passages or verses') (Hellgardt, emphasis mine). This was the practice of setting off the divisions through the use of initials, drop caps, and/or Roman numerals. The use of *fitts* is known from Old English epics, e.g. *Beowulf* and occasional Skaldic poetry. In the case of the *Heliand*, every manuscript displays evidence of *fitt* divisions except MS P.[10]

Indeed, the Old English form of the word is *fit*, and likewise means 'a stanza, verse paragraph' as well as 'a poem' (cf. Hofmann, Nachtrag 1972, p. 337). Thus, the Old Saxon poet was continuing a recognized Germanic tradition by dividing the *Heliand* into *fitts*. Furthermore, the author of the *Prefaces* gave a decisive clue toward verifying the authenticity of his work: though the word is attested in Old English, its Old High German equivalent is not attested. It was either likely lost very early in the latter dialect or never existed in it at all, having been retained only by the more northerly Germanic peoples. Thus, the Old English may have received the word from the Norse, and either of these could have lent it to the Old Saxons. Whatever the etymology of the word, the fact that it has no High German cognate is useful, because "[...] das Wort *Fitte* für die einzelnen Abschnitte der Dichtung den Humanisten [e.g. Illyricus] [...] nicht bekannt sein konnte [...]" (Eichhoff & Rauch). With Illyricus' chances of knowing this ancient word being slim to none, the appearance of the word in a work that might otherwise be deemed one of Illyricus' inventions effectively speaks against jumping to the conclusion that the *Prefaces* are a forgery. Moreover, the chances of Illyricus' creating the form *uitteas*—with its similarity in form and meaning to the otherwise attested form *fitt* from OE—are cosmically small. The presence of this word alone requires one to assume the easiest explanation, i.e., that the *Prefaces* are authentic.

In addition to this internal confirmation, there is external historical evidence speaking to the authenticity of what Illyricus printed as the *Prefaces*. This evidence comes in the form of letters from a contemporary of Illyricus, Georg Fabricius, who reveals a trail leading back to the document from which Illyricus obtained the Latin texts. Moreover, this evidence also speaks to the fact that the *Prefaces* belong to the *Heliand*.

6.2 Georg Fabricius: Scholar, Educator, Linchpin

In his 1939 paper "Die Lösung des Rätsels der Heliandpraefatio", Kurt Hannemann greatly advanced *Heliand* studies by sleuthing out previously un-

---

[10] MS P contains text that occurs in the middle of *fitt* XII and, therefore, can not serve as evidence of *fitt* division.

known information regarding the *Prefaces* in letters written by Georg Fabricius[11] to various acquaintances (Peter, 1892; Baumgarten-Crusius, 1845). Of particular importance is Fabricius' communication with Illyricus, who in the second edition (1562) of his Protestant tract *Catalogus testium veritatis* printed the two Latin Preface texts—the *Praefatio* and the *Versus*—under the combined heading "Praefatio in librum antiquum lingua Saxonica conscriptum". Illyricus does not reveal his source for what he prints, which is presumed long lost. Nevertheless, discussion of Illyricus' source is valuable toward determining concrete facts about the *Heliand*, such that a hypothetical document—indicated by me as *I (after 'Illyricus'; cf. Hannemann's "Codex Flacianus")—can be proposed.

Once printed by Illyricus, the *Prefaces* remained an isolated text until Johann Georg von Eccard first linked them to the *Heliand* in 1720. While the *Prefaces*' relationship to the *Heliand* is still disputed occasionally, current scholarly opinion overwhelmingly recognizes it as belonging to the Old Saxon epic.

In his writings, Fabricius alludes to topics mentioned in the *Prefaces*, in several instances even giving almost perfectly matching language. These allusions and transcriptions of *Prefaces* material suggest that Fabricius had access to the original manuscript. Similar to the documents Illyricus must have had, Fabricius' resource seems to be no longer extant. Thus, for the same reason as that cited for establishing a hypothetical Illyricus resource, a Fabricius resource is hypothesized and referred to by me as $*F_f$ (cf. Hannemann's "Codex Fabricianus").

Hannemann's brilliant contribution to Old Saxon studies was the discovery of evidence in Fabricius' writings that Illyricus had received his resource from Fabricius himself. Therefore, $*I$ and $*F_f$ were actually one and the same document. I will continue the tradition of Baesecke (1948) in calling this single source *F.

6.2.1 Matthias Flacius Illyricus, Protestant Firebrand and Printer

In a letter dated 24 March 1561 and addressed to his brother Andreas, Fabricius reveals that he himself possessed (or had access to) a codex with a

---

[11] (1516–1571): born Goldschmidt/Goldschmied in Chemnitz; matriculated at Wittenberg 1536 under "Georgius Fabricius Kemnitzensis" (AAV, vol. I p. 162).

preface that sounds remarkably like the one printed the following year by Illyricus (Peter, 16, emphasis mine):

> Mitto tibi ex antiquo libro Germanico praefationem, ex qua cognoscis opt(im)os Imperatores Germanorum vere Germanos non interdixisse lectioni sacrae vulgo hominum, vt nostri nunc faciunt Belgicis mandatis et vt totus Papatus facit: eam potes Ienensibus, qui historiam colligunt, communicare. Habet D. Illyricus Lotharii Saxonis Imp. genealogiam, quam si mihi impetrabis, facies rem omnium gratissimam.

> I am sending you a preface from an ancient Germanic codex, from which you will learn that the best and truly German Emperors of the German people did not prohibit the common folk from reading the Holy Word, as our leaders are now doing with the Belgian Mandates, and as the entire papacy does: you can pass this on to those who are compiling the history in Jena.[12] Dr. Illyricus has a genealogy of Lothar,[13] Emperor of the Saxons. If you can procure this for me, you will be doing me the greatest favor of all.

In this letter, Fabricius' asked Andreas to be the intermediary in an exchange with Illyricus. In keeping with his role in producing the *Magdeburg Centuries* in Jena, Illyricus had produced some genealogical materials for Fabricius, and the latter wished to repay the former with *F_f (or a copy of it). It is interesting to note that the genealogy Fabricius had requested was for Lothair, eldest son of Louis the Pious and leader of a number of revolts undertaken by the three of Louis' sons against their father. Fabricius had, no doubt, learned from the "preface from an ancient German codex" that of the men he called "the German Emperors of the German peoples" was one whom the *Prefaces* call *Ludouicus pijssimus Augustus* ('The most pious Emperor Louis'). Thus, Fabricius' desire to have Lothair's genealogy seems to indicate a desire to understand the background of the *Prefaces*, which arguably names Lothair's father, Louis the Pious, as commissioner of the Old Saxon biblical work. It is also remarkable that Fabricius called Lothair "Emperor of the Saxons"—certainly not a title by which Lothair was known, or at least not so in Fabricius' time. Rather, Lothair was known to history as "Emperor of the Franks".[14] That Fabricius linked him to the Sax-

---

[12] I.e. the Magdeburg Centuries.

[13] I.e., Lothair I (795–855).

[14] If there ever was use of 'Emperor of the Saxons', Lothair would have had access to the title by virtue of his being named co-emperor with his father in 823. Moreover, the situation of titles throughout history is slightly confused: the Holy Roman Empire was called *Gallia*

ons can only be seen as evidence that what he was sending to Illyricus via Andreas was the *Prefaces* material.

This quite doubtlessly establishes how Illyricus acquired *I, from which he would print the *Prefaces* in *Catalogus testium veritatis* (1562) the following year.[15] Note that one might also infer from Fabricius' description of his source for *F_f (i.e. "from an old German codex") that this codex was just that—a full codex not yet cut up into fragments, e.g. the Latin source of the *Prefaces*. In other words, it can be assumed that the *Prefaces* source material and the Old Saxon *Heliand* existed still as a unified book around the time of Fabricius' letter to Andreas. In fact, by paying attention to this seemingly minor inference, many details about the nature of the *Heliand* itself become clearer. This idea of a combined codex in the hands of Fabricius plays a central role in later discussions (cf. 13.1).

That Fabricius knew of the material that Illyricus would print as the *Prefaces* some months later in the following year is further corroborated in the dedication (penned 1562) to Fabricius' *Poetarvm veterum ecclesiasticorū opera Christiana* ('The christian work of the old ecclesiastical poets', 1564), in which he appeals to the layman's right to direct access to Scripture (Hannemann, 3, emphasis Fabricius'):

> Ludouici etiam Imp. cognomento Pij, sententiae piae aduersantur, qui librum quondam ab homine plebeio, uate tamen non ignobili, lingua Saxonica scriptum conseruari uoluit, ut NON SOLVM LITERATIS, VERVM ETIAM INLITERATIS, SACRA DIVINORVM PRAECEPTORVM LECTIO PANDERETVR. haec enim uerba epistolae sunt, quae libro Germanico, lingua Latina praefigitur.

> So it was that the dutiful judgment of Emperor Louis the Pious came about, that he once sought to promote a book written by a previously common man—albeit hardly an unknown poet—in the Saxon language, so that THE SACRED TEXTS RECEIVED FROM GOD MIGHT BE EXTENDED NOT ONLY TO THE LEARNED, BUT ALSO TO THE UNLEARNED. Indeed these are the words of the record in the Latin language, which is attached to the Germanic book.

Fabricius' language is almost an exact match of that in the printed *Prefaces* (exact all but for the intrusion of <n> into *illiteratis*).[16] To those who would

---

(i.e. 'France') in Latin (cf. von Eccard's quote in 6.1.1), despite the Franks having had nothing to do with the historical Gauls. Rather, such usage was purely geographical.

[15] Coincidentally, an oft reoccurring date in the history of the *Heliand* materials.

[16] The source of this intrusive <n> is unknown, but may have come from any number of places (Illyricus, the printer, etc.) and need not be seen as an error on Fabricius' part.

point to the publication dates of *Opera Christiana* (1564) and *Catalogus* (1562) to suggest that I am following a logical fallacy (i.e., that the evidence suggests the Illyricus had the material prior to Fabricius), Hannemann offers this explanation: "Ohne Kenntnis des Briefes von 1561 könnte man denken, das Zitat der Heliandpraefatio in den Opera Christiana stamme einfach aus Illyricus." That is, although Fabricius' is the later publication—and thus is suggestive of his having merely copied his material from Illyricus—Fabricius' allusion to *F_f* in the 1561 letter to his brother proves that the 1564 reference is neither a fake nor a borrowing from Illyricus. Moreover, Fabricius had penned the second reference two years prior to printing it—in 1562—astonishingly close to Illyricus' publication date (although it is unknown which came first). When the timing of all references is compared, it is Fabricius' 1561 reference that precedes all others between Fabricius' and Illyricus' collective writings. Thus, Fabricius had at least one and possibly two references penned prior to Illyricus' publication of the *Prefaces* material. This proves that Illyricus' knowledge of the material he printed originated from Fabricius, and not vice versa.

While Fabricius' 1561 reference provides evidence of the source of the *Prefaces*, his 1562 reference provides a more specific description of the nature of the manuscript *F, providing the parallel language to Illyricus' publication that links the two men's immediate sources (*F_f and *I) as (perhaps) two versions of the same original source. It is uncertain whether Fabricius handed over the manuscript he had to Illyricus, sent him a copy he had made of the manuscript of which he knew, or sent him a copy of a transcription he had made from the original. The greatest possibility for promulgation of any error occurs with the last of the three suggested means of transfer, considering the single spelling anomaly that separates Fabricius' and Illyricus' versions of the text.

Still more, Hannemann presents a third reference published in Fabricius' inscription to *Poemata sacra: [...] Poematvm sacrorvm libri XXV G. Fabricii* ('Sacred poems [...] G. Fabricius' letters of sacred poetry XXV'), part 2 (1567, p. 216). In it Fabricius provides possibly the rationale behind his interest in the document. In this reference, Fabricius defends the use of vernacular in preaching and for translating the Bible, reminding the Roman Church of its former acceptance of such activity (4, emphasis mine):

Legerunt sacram Scripturam (Graecos et Romanos excipio) sua olim lingua Syri: legerunt Dalmatae, interprete (ut ferunt) diuo Hieronymo: legerunt Gothi, expositore Vulfila episcopo: *legerunt Saxones, curante Ludouico Pio, Caroli Magni filio*: legerunt Indi et Armenii, et adhuc aliqua inter ipsos eius rei testimonia extare dicuntur. Franci historiam Euangelicam, aliquot item ueteris Testamenti libros, Otfrido Fuldano et Vuilramo Pabepergico auctoribus, legerunt. Eiusmodi libri, inualescente Romana tyrannide, aut suppressi, aut e minibus uulgi erepti sunt.

Besides the Greeks and the Romans, the Syrians of old read sacred Scripture in their own language; the Dalmatians read (and [still] boast of) the translation by St. Jerome; the Goths read the translation by Bishop Wulfila; the *Saxons read [it], having been provided for by Louis the Pious, the son of Charlemagne*; the Indians and the Armenians read [it], and to this day others living among them bear testimony of this very fact. The Franks read a Gospel narrative, as well as several books of the Old Testament, by the authors Otfrid of Fulda and Williram of Bamberg. Though such books had come into use in the Roman tyranny, they have [since] either been suppressed or are snatched away from the unfortunate folk.

Concealed among well-known examples of various peoples who had accessed holy writ in their own language is a detail that would have been otherwise completely unfamiliar at Fabricius' time, namely that the Saxons read sacred Scripture in their own language, and that such was provided to them by the "Emperor of Rome" himself. Fabricius' inclusion of this obscure knowledge serves today as proof of the influence that *F had on him.

In both the *Poemata sacra* (1564) and *Opera Christiana* (1567) references, Fabricius offers evidence supporting what I have hypothesized given his letter to Andreas: that Fabricius' request for a genealogy of Lothair came about because of the latter's relationship to Louis the Pious. Fabricius states: "[T]he best and truly German Emperors of the German people did not prohibit the common folk from reading the Holy Word" (24 March 1561) is equivalent in import to "the Saxons read [it], having been provided for by Louis the Pious, the son of Charlemagne" (1564, written 1562). It is apparent from Fabricius' letter to Andreas that he considered multiple "German Emperors" to have been responsible for providing scripture to the Saxons: certainly Louis the Pious, and perhaps either or both Lothair and Charlemagne.

It would be folly to look only at the publication date of *Poemata sacra* (1564) for evidence of when Fabricius' knew of the *Prefaces* material. Hannemann has shown that doing so for *Opera Christiana* (1567) would similarly lead to a false conclusion. While it has been shown through Fabricius' letter to Andreas that this knowledge preceded 24 March 1561, Hannemann shows that Fabricius was already well-acquainted with the document a full four years prior to writing to his brother: "die Widmung mit dem Heliandhinweis war schon am 1. 2. 1557—kein Druckfehler!—abgeschlossen" (5). Hannemann concludes that Fabricius must have been keeping his eye on the *Praefatio*-and-*Versus* manuscript during the intervening four years— either through regular trips to its home in Leipzig or by having brought it with him to Meissen. As stated above, also inferable from the 24 March 1561 letter to Andreas is the fact that the *Praefatio*-and-*Versus* manuscript was likely still combined in a single codex with the *Heliand* itself, meaning that both were being minded to on some level by Fabricius from February 1557 to at least March 1561. Yet the earlier of these dates can be pushed back even further still. To this very effect, Hannemann writes (35; italics his, bold mine):

> Man wird voraussetzen dürfen, daß Fabricius mehr von dem Praefatiokodex gewußt und wohl auch abschriftlich besessen hat, als er 1561 an Flacius gelangen ließ. So mußte er sich auch i. J. 1556 in einem leider noch nicht auffindbaren Brief an seinen „beständigen Gönner" Christoph v. Carlowitz in Dresden zum Heliand geäußert haben, wobei das „Treffwort" Schmellers natürlich immer fehlt. Das Brief echo Christophs vom **19. 10. 1556** lautet: **Quod autem non Saxones solum et Dalmatae, quos nominas, sed etiam multae aliae gentes sacras litteras iam inde a multis seculis in sua lingua legerent: id non modum verum esse credo, sed valde utile atque adeo necessarium etiam esse statuo.**

Thus, Fabricius' aforementioned 1567 *Poemata Sacra* reference to Saxon vernacular scripture was preceded by a decade by a very similar sounding claim in a letter to Christoph von Carlowitz, the head educational advisor to Duke Maurice of Saxony (cf. 13.2). Still more, as Hannemann reveals in a second article published several decades after his 1939 article, Fabricius left further writings in which he includes references to the *Prefaces* material. These citations stem from letters written in 1545—notably prior to Martin Luther's death in 1546.

6.2.2 Fabricius' Earliest Reference

In 1972 Hannemann offered a redaction of his 1939 piece, re-titling it more appropriately "die Lösung des Rätsels *der Herkunft* der Heliandpraefatio" (emphasis mine) and offering an addendum with the results of research from the intervening 33 years. Herein, he describes what he discovered in yet another published collection of Fabricius' letters (Baumgarten-Crusius, *Epistolae G. Fabricii Chemnicensis ad Wolfg. Meurerum et alios aequales* ['G. Fabricius' Letters to Wolfg. Meurer and other peers'], 1845). Hannemann found a gem of information in Fabricius' 7 January 1545 letter to Meurer (Baumgarten-Crusius, p. 17–18; cf. Appendix A.1):

> Velim igitur cum Bornero agas, ut praefationem illam Latinam sui manuscripti, quam ex Numburgensi bibliotheca habet, mihi describendam curet cum una atque altera pagina veri operas Germanici; cupio enim de eo doctorum et inprimis B. Rhenani cognoscere judicium atque sententiam.
>
> So, I would like you to try to convince Borner to take care when transcribing the Latin preface of his doubtless Germanic manuscript for me, which he has from the Naumburg library, every page of it, because I am interested to know the assessment and opinion of learned men concerning it, including the foremost B[eatus] Rhenanus.

Herein are two bombshells: (1) Fabricius reveals the source of his knowledge regarding *F as Borner, the very man who was charged with the founding of the UBL in 1543; and (2) he indicates a point of origin for *F: a library in Naumburg (cf. 13.1.3).

It is clear from the letter that Fabricius' goal was to put what would eventually be printed as the *Prefaces* into the hands of Rhenanus. The *Evangelienbuch*, itself a gospel harmony written in Old High German and dedicated to Louis the German in Old High German "Ludovvico orientalium regnorum regi sit salus aeterna" ("Ewiges Heil werde Ludwig zuteil, dem König des Ostreiches") (Widukind von Corvey, pp. 8–9), was penned by Otfrid ca. 865 and is thus remarkably similar in timing to the *Heliand*.[17]

---

[17] The *Evangelienbuch* is patterned after Latin verse, i.e. focused on end-rhyme. It is the first sizeable German-language work to operate so. This alone is indicative of the rather different set of circumstances under which the *Evangelienbuch* was authored as compared to the *Heliand*. Compare, however, Otfrid's self-declared purpose in penning the book (Reclam, 44–45, lines 113–122):

>   Nu will ih scríban unser héil,   evangéliono deil,
>   so wír nu hiar bigúnnun,   in frénkisga zungun;
>   115 Thaz síe ni wesen éino   thes selben ádeilo,
>   ni man in íro gizungi   Kristes lób sungi;
>   Joh er ouh íro worto   gilóbot werde hárto,
>   ther sie zímo holeta,   zi gilóubon sinen ládota.
>   Ist ther in íro lante   iz álleswio nintstaánte,
>   120 in ánder ginzúngi   firnéman iz ni kúnni:
>   Hiar hor er ío zi gúate,   waz gót imo gebíete,
>   thaz wír imo hiar gisúngun   in frénkisga zúngun.

Rhenanus' 1531 edition of Otfrid had gained international attention in great part because of the Calvinist movement started in 1536 in Switzerland and Alsace. There, Rhenanus' publication became a flash point in the Calvinist's battle against Rome. Thus, as its discoverer and publisher in the sixteenth century, Rhenanus was considered as the foremost expert on Carolingian-era biblical works and their tie to Charlemagne's descendants. Fabricius would have most certainly been aware of Rhenanus' reputation, and it is thus logical to assume that he should have wanted to get this expert's opinion of the Leipzig codex *F.

Following this initial letter to Meurer, Fabricius tried several more times to contact Borner to procure a transcription of the *Praefatio* in *F, namely through additional letters to Meurer, who was both physically and socially close to the UBL librarian.[18] A second letter, dated 16 September 1545, ends with a reminder to Meurer: "D. Bornerum mone de eo quod rogavi" ('Remind Dr. Borner about what I requested') (21-22; cf. Appendix A.2). Additionally, a final letter, dated 18 December 1545,[19] shows much more insistent language. Moreover, if there remains any doubt as to the location of Fabricius' desired document, he explicitly gives its whereabouts once again here (24; cf. Appendix A.3):

> Obsecro te, impetra nobis illam praefationem a D. Bornero, et illi adjunge literas tuas ad Rhenanum: nam cum primo accepero, ego reddam. Versiculos etiam Dantis Lipsiae in collegio Paulino, de quibus, ni fallor, in aliis literis egi, mitte.

       So will ich jetzt darangehen, unser Heil zu besingen, eine evangelische
                                                                         Geschichte zu schreiben,
       und zwar so, wie ich hier begonnen habe: in der Sprache der Franken –
115 damit sie nicht als einzige darauf verzichten müssen,
       daß man in ihrer Sprache Christi Lob singe;
       damit vielmehr auch auf fränkisch Er gepriesen werde,
       der sie zu sich geholt, in seinem Glauben versammelt hat.
       Wenn es jemand in ihrem Land gibt, der es anders nicht verstehen,
120 in einer anderen Sprache nicht aufnehmen kann,
       der höre hier nun zu seinem Heil, was Gott ihm bietet,
       hier in unserer fränkisch abgefaßten Dichtung.

---

[18] Meurer had served as Borner's deputy rector at the Thomasschule until 1535. He then served as rector of the Nikolaischule in Leipzig and, after 1549, became a professor of medicine at the University of Leipzig.

[19] Erroneously offered by Hannemann as Fabricius' 24 November 1545 letter (cf. Appendix A.4).

> I beg you, get me that preface from Dr. Borner, and attach your letter to Rhenanus to it. I will give it to him as soon as I receive it. As for you, send the passages that were donated to the Paulinum collection in Leipzig—you know, the ones I keep bugging you about!

The least that can be taken from Fabricius' 1545 letters is a new date by which the codex containing *F was located at the UBL. This *terminus ante quem* is effectively the date of the earliest of the aforementioned letters, namely 7 January 1545.

6.2.3 Brotherhood of Knowledge

Beyond pushing back the date by which Fabricius was aware of the codex by a decade, these letters also reveal Borner's relationship to the matter. Moreover, included in the second letter are "Grüßen [sic] an J. Camerarius und C. Borner", which might very well indicate that Joachim Camerarius also knew of the codex. After all, besides both these men's reputations as influential humanists of the time, Borner and Camerarius shared an additional common connection as, respectively, the first and second head librarians of the UBL (cf. 5.1.4). Given that the earliest of Fabricius' letters dates to the beginning of January 1545, it is therefore likely that not only Fabricius but also Borner—if not indeed Camerarius, as well—knew of the codex prior to 1545. Certainly, this triangulation of relationships points to a particular time—one of great transition in Saxony: Duke Maurice's educational reforms, including his awarding of the former Dominican monastery *St. Pauli* to the University of Leipzig in 1543, and therewith the establishment of the University's first central library in the same year.

Yet Borner and Camerarius shared their assignment to build up the UBL with a third man, who, if either of these two men knew of the *Heliand* codex, must have also been aware of it: Melanchthon. It is the last of these three men who garnishes a great amount of intrigue, considering his particular role as the pit-bull of Reformation Theology and close confidante of Luther: given their close ties, what is the likelihood that Luther, too, knew of the *Heliand* codex and the claims of its *Praefatio*-and-*Versus* dedication? It is simple enough to conclude that, once any of the three founders of the UBL knew of the *Praefatio*'s provocative claim in support of translating the Bible, Luther would have been informed.

Indeed, the relationships presented here is a rather tight-knit network of individuals deeply invested in promoting the goals of the Reformation, even if idiosyncratic agendas varied slightly between individuals. And although it may very well be impossible to ascertain which man informed Luther of the codex, such is really irrelevant: in effect, the tight relationship of the three UBL founders alone essentially makes them a single point of contact. The more important question, then, asks: "How did the codex in question end up in Leipzig?" In short, Fabricius' 1543 letter reveals a possible origin from which the UBL acquired *F: "the Latin preface of his doubtless Germanic manuscript [...], which [Borner] has from the Naumburg library." At a minimum, this detail provides a point from which to start looking (cf. 13.1.2).

Altogether, Fabricius' three letters, as discovered by Hannemann, reveal a patchy-yet-legible story about the document in question. What falls out of this storyline is (1) a short list of characters complicit in the knowledge of the document's existence; (2) the then-current location of the codex, i.e. at the new *Paulinum* among Borner's library collection; and (3) a measure of the importance of the message contained in the preface of the codex. This last detail comes from Fabricius' somewhat cryptic reference to his purpose in going to Beatus Rhenanus which, as stated in his 24 January 1545 letter, was to put *F—or at least a transcription thereof—into the hands of the "not-unfamous" scholar of ancient Germanic manuscripts. But whose idea was it?

Fabricius' first letter seems to indicate that it was Borner who was responsible for bringing the codex to Leipzig. It would have seemed equally obvious to Borner—as well as to Camerarius and Melanchthon—as it would have been to Fabricius to seek Rhenanus' interpretation of what seemed to be yet another work from the same time period. Yet Rhenanus lived and worked on the other side of the Empire—in Strasbourg—and considering the political climate of the time, sending this ancient and invaluable manuscript with just anybody would be dangerous and foolhardy. The legal repercussions of a document with the claims included in *F would have been questionable in the climate of religious fervor and militancy stirred up by Charles V's response to the Reformation movement, all the more so because of the Emperor's history of 'wishy-washy' threats (cf. 12.2.1).

If the supporters of Charles V's policy against Luther saw the *Praefatio-and-Versus* as a threat, would they hesitate to enforce capital punishment as per the Edict of Worms? Then again, would the deliverer of the document live long enough for the information to come out? Furthermore, even if the messenger to Rhenanus were to be carrying only a transcription of the original and this were to be compromised, the Empire could lie in wait for the original to surface elsewhere. For example, the Empire might then seek to counterfeit a contrary 'original' document. What kind of effect would it have on public opinion if the Reformers later published the information contained in *F? It seems that the importance of the document held at Leipzig would have been difficult to determine. All the more reason to seek an expert's opinion from Rhenanus, who himself was not an enemy of reform. At that, it would be far better and safer to have someone on the 'inside' to approach the expert with the subject. Enter Fabricius.

Borner had two connections to Fabricius: (1) a personal relationship that stemmed from a decade earlier, namely 1535, when Fabricius first arrived at the Thomasschule in Leipzig for instruction; and (2) through Meurer, who besides being involved with Camerarius in carrying out *Visitation* to one of the three *Fürstenschulen* established in Saxony under Duke Maurice's educational reforms,[20] worked with Borner in building another *Fürstenschule* at Pforta, and more importantly, was also a college buddy of Fabricius.

At 19, Fabricius enrolled at the Thomasschule in Leipzig, having finished his primary education at a Latin School in Chemnitz followed by a year under the tutelage of Johannes Rivius in Annaberg. When he arrived at the Thomasschule, then Rector Borner had just been called to his second tenure as vice-chancellor at the University of Leipzig. Feeling the strain of two time-consuming posts and a teaching position at the boys' school in Humanistic Studies (ADB, vol. 6, p. 510),[21] Borner turned his teaching duties over to the young-yet-blooming Latin poet in Fabricius. This was the first teaching position undertaken by Fabricius, who would later have a long career as an educator and rector, not to mention well-recognized Latin po-

---

[20] These were established simultaneously with the expansion of the University of Leipzig under the guidance of Borner, Camerarius, and Melanchthon, among others. Housed in former monasteries, these institutions served as feeder schools to the Reformation-controlled universities in Leipzig and Wittenberg (cf. 13.2).

[21] In fact, Borner had been committed to both posts since becoming rector of the Thomasschule in 1522 and subsequently given the professorship in Mathematics and Astronomy at the University of Leipzig the following year (NDB, vol. 2, p. 469).

et (ADB). After further teaching stints in Chemnitz and Freiberg, Fabricius returned to Leipzig in 1538, matriculating at the University in 1539[22] and then accompanying his friends Wolfgang von Werthern[23] and Wolfgang Meurer to Italy for the duration of his University studies.[24] The group of young men remained in Italy, making trips to various cities until 1543, when Fabricius returned to Beichlingen near Erfurt to fetch the younger brothers of his travel mate and recent benefactor, Wolfgang von Werthern, who had suddenly inherited his family fortune and protectorship of the young boys. Still in 1543, Fabricius escorted his charges to Strasbourg (where von Werthern had business to conduct), acting all the while as a science tutor to the two boys.[25]

So, suddenly finding himself in need of a trustworthy individual to undertake the task of approaching Rhenanus in Strasbourg with the contents of the Leipzig codex prefaces, Borner must have immediately seized upon the idea of employing Fabricius. To contact his former protégé, Borner would rely on Meurer, Fabricius' buddy since 1535, when they met at the Thomasschule (Lohr). When Fabricius went off to Italy in 1539, he originally left Meurer behind in Leipzig. In 1540 Meurer became dean of the Faculty of Arts at the Thomasschule. In February 1543, Meurer left Leipzig to join Fabricius in northern Italy (Lohr). By mid-October 1543, Fabricius had left Italy to transfer von Werthern's brothers from Beichlingen to Strasbourg, while Meurer stayed in Padua until February 1544 (Hannemann 1974), at which time he was called to return to Leipzig upon being given a new job as

---

[22] Appears under "Misnenses [nations]" (*Citizens of Meissen*) as Georgius Fabritius, enrolled Summer 1535 (*Jüngere Matrikel*).

[23] (1519-1583). He matriculated September 1542 under the name "Vuolphgangus von Werderen" [AAV vol. I, pg. 198] after transferring from Leipzig, where he began studying either in 1532 [as "Wulfgangus a Wertram"; CDS 16, 608] or 1539 [ADB, vol. 42 p. 119; not evident in CDS]). His younger brothers, Philipp (1525-1588) and Anton (1528-1579), are both also important to Fabricius' story. Both matriculated simultaneously at Wittenberg on 10 February 1541, appearing in AAV (vol. I, pg. 193) as "Philippus a Wertern" and "Antonius a Wertern".

[24] Fabricius' four years in Italy comprised his study of Roman antiquities, the published descriptions of which gained him great fame. He also gathered countless ancient manuscripts, including a rare Boethius text to be sent back to Saxony. Our modern knowledge of Boethius—if not also other ancients—is a product of Fabricius' actions (ADB, vol. 6, pp. 510-514).

[25] Fabricius would remain employed as the boys' teacher in Strasbourg for three additional years.

professor of Aristotelian Philosophy at the University of Leipzig—a position to which he had been recommended by Melanchthon (Roth, 477). Thus serving as a member of the faculty senate at the university of which Borner was now rector (since 1539, ABD), Meurer had immediate ties to Borner and Camerarius, who himself had arrived in Leipzig in 1541 as professor. Borner and company likely chose Meurer as their means of communication with Fabricius due to the regular postal communication maintained by the two men since their days in Italy. Meurer's history with Camerarius and especially Melanchthon also meant that his inclusion still kept the private knowledge of the contents of *F 'in the family'. Thus, included in this brotherhood of knowledge about the Leipzig *Heliand* codex were Borner, Fabricius, Meurer, Camerarius, Melanchthon, and likely by extension, Luther.

6.2.4 Overlooked Fabricius Reference

Proof of my ordering of events comes in the form of a fourth Fabricius letter—one apparently unbeknownst to Hannemann[26]—that makes reference to the task of getting the contents of the Leipzig codex into Rhenanus' hands. This letter—in actuality, the third in the sequence of four from 1545—had gone missing by the time Baumgarten-Crusius (i.e. Hannemann's source) investigated and published Fabricius' letters. Instead, Baumgarten-Crusius offers a part of the missing letter (dated 24 November 1545) from a copy taken down by Fabricius' biography Schreber (22–23):

> Ad hunc locum pertinet epistola ad Meurerum Argentorato XI. Cal. Decembr. a. MDXLV. scripta, quam Schreberus habuit, nunc amissa vel aliquo loco abscondita, cujus hanc partem ille exscripsit vitae Fabric. p. 71

> At one point there was a letter belonging to Meurer written from Strasbourg 24 November 1545. Schreber had it, but it has since been lost or misplaced. He copied the following part in *Vitae Fabricii, p. 71.*

This lost letter differs distinctively from the three other letters in which Fabricius mentions the *F codex: his discussion of the topic is much more

---

[26] Hannemann seems to have overlooked this third letter: he accidentally applied the date of the third (i.e. 'lost') letter to the fourth letter of the sequence (i.e. to the 18 December 1545 letter).

cryptic. Yet this letter occurs within the sequence that deals with the Leipzig manuscript and Borner, and it can be assumed that Fabricius' mention of "the matter that Borner wrote to me during the past year" is synonymous with his assignment to give *F to Rhenanus. The lost letter suggests a facet of the story heretofore unknown to Germanists, namely Fabricius' motivation in the matter. Despite this additional information, Rhenanus' role, as proposed by Hannemann, does not change with this new evidence. Rather, what changes is the interpretation that Fabricius was self-motivated in putting the codex in Rhenanus' hands.

Unlike the other letters of the sequence, in which Fabricius seems eager to perform the task, the 24 November 1545 letter reveals a tone of frustration and even disdain for it. Moreover, it redirects the chore as a favor that Borner asked of him, i.e. not a personal goal of Fabricius. If indeed Borner initiated the assignment for Fabricius to act as intermediary to Rhenanus, one must wonder why Fabricius had such a difficult time procuring a copy of the codex's preface. While I am unable to provide any answer to this question (other than proposing that changes in political currents of the time made those in Leipzig even more reticent to distribute the material), Fabricius does hint at why Borner and company would have been interested in Rhenanus' opinion of the piece. Namely, by expressing his fear apparently about the impending Schmalkaldic War, Fabricius implies how his task might play out in the larger scope of the Reformation (23, emphasis mine):

> Vocas me ad munus scholasticum: sed labor scholarum qualis sit ipse nosti, et ego, cum *lego Borneri epistolam ea de re scriptam ad me anno superiore,* quoquo modo illud onus fugere cupio; et ex iis, de quibus tu nunc scribis, dissensionibus ac periculis multis, quae quotidie intueor, plane exhorresco.

> You're calling me to do scholarly favor, yet you know as well as I do how much work this task is. Especially now, as I read *the letter about the matter that Borner wrote to me during the past year,* I just want to run away from the burden; and because of what you describe now, I'm completely terrified by the dissensions and the many perils that I observe daily.

It is evident that Fabricius has re-read a letter sent to him by Meurer concerning yet another letter sent by Borner earlier in the year. From context, I take that previous letter from Borner to be the one in which his request of Fabricius to approach Rhenanus was made. Note that Fabricius' wording suggests that Borner was aware that Fabricius knew of the *F codex, something that heretofore still remained to be established.[27] Since it is quite clear from all four letters that Fabricius did not have a copy of preface text with him in any shape, it seems that Borner's assignment was merely to approach Rhenanus and ask for his input about the matter, i.e., "would he be willing to take a look at a transcribed text?" Fabricius, however, seems to have felt uncomfortable about approaching the expert, and thus wanted a copy in hand to take to him straightaway. Consequently, Fabricius intends to lean on Meurer via the third (24 November) letter to go and persuade Borner to send a transcription. This explains Fabricius' language in the first (24 January) letter asking Meurer "to convince Borner" not only to transcribe the manuscript text, but to do so carefully. Fabricius' fourth (18 December) letter further suggests that he had not yet received the copy, despite nearly a year's time having passed. His imploring attitude in this final letter of the series belies Fabricius' discomfort with approaching the renowned scholar Rhenanus, which anxiety he also reveals in the third (24 November) letter when he states that he just "want[s] to run away from the burden."

Besides his unease with the situation, Fabricius speaks somewhat to the timing of Borner's request. Given that he describes the assignment in the fourth (18 December) letter stating, "the matter that Borner wrote to me during the past year," a rough timeline of approximately a year can be established, meaning Borner's letter must have been sent around twelve months prior to 18 December 1545. Furthermore, since Fabricius' first letter on the subject was sent on 7 January 1545, it can be concluded that Borner's letter arrived to Fabricius no later than the beginning of 1545. Thus, Borner's letter with the original request must have been written and sent in 1544. This is an important conclusion: it speaks to the timing of all the men's knowledge of the codex containing *F, pushing the *terminus ante quem* of the document's presence in Leipzig back to at least some time in early winter or late fall 1544. Estimating from the timing intervals between Fabricius' four letters in addition to the hint provided in his fourth letter, it seems safe to assume that Borner's letter of request was penned and sent some time in October or November 1544.

Furthermore, something must be said about the letter from Meurer to which Fabricius appears to be responding, which by necessity must have

---

[27] I.e., that both men recognized one another's acquaintance with the document.

dated to the period between mid-September and late-November 1545. Meurer's letter must have included some type of admonition for Fabricius' lack of action in contacting Rhenanus. This serves as another piece of evidence to suggest that Fabricius was uncomfortable about approaching Rhenanus empty-handed—and, thus, that he was holding out for a transcription to arrive.

Fabricius' 24 November response also entails that some earlier exchange began with his complaining in some way about his then-current status, to which Meurer responded with some advice. Meurer likely asked something about whether Fabricius missed traveling around as he did while in college: "Neque mihi desunt, quae me alio trahant [...]" (*"I do not miss the things that would take me elsewhere, [...]"*). The reason:

> [...] nam ut praesentem statum omittam, in quo studiorum meorum gratia acquiesco, hoc ipso mense Fuggerorum nomine in singulos annos LL. (fort. CL. v. CC) coronati cum victu, libris, vestibus oblati sunt, adjuncto etiam copioso honorario, si triennium cum Hulderico, quem tu Patavii vidisti, vivere velim. Judicium igitur Borneri, res ipsa, spes amplissimi praemii me facile deterrent ab eo munere, ad quod nemo nisi vi coactus aut impulsus inopia accedit

> [...] since I would have to give up my present situation, where I gladly give in to my endeavors, and for this reason: every year during this month 100 (sometimes 150 or 200) awards are offered in the name of the Fuggers[28] for living expenses, books, and clothes. This generous award would be of great help to me, considering I want to spend the next three years staying with Ulrich[29] (whom you visited in Padua). So, this is what is keeping me from performing that favor—which nobody else will even come close to unless forcibly bound and compelled out of necessity: Borner's decision, the matter of business itself, and the hope of receiving the ample prize

Fabricius' ultimate goal was to return to Italy, but to be able to afford this dream he was in need of one of the generous Fugger Awards. Perhaps Fabricius also hoped that by escaping to Italy, he would have an excuse to refuse to perform the favor for Borner. Given the sacrifice Fabricius made at age 19 to take up Borner's teaching duties at the Thomasschule, it is

---

[28] A wealthy Swabian family with headquarters in Augsburg known in the fifteenth century and sixteenth century for their international banking and venture capitalism. They gave their name to the *Fuggerei* in Augsburg, the oldest continuously-operating social housing project.

[29] Ulrich Hugobald? (1496–1571); a.k.a. Huldreich Mutius, Ulrich(us) Hugwald(us), Udalricus Hugualdus, etc. (PPN: 381564215).

evident that Fabricius had great respect for Borner. This might also serve as a sign of the depth of Fabricius' commitment toward any favor Borner might have asked from him. If Fabricius felt that turning Borner down was not an option, perhaps returning to his ground-breaking studies in Italy would serve as a decent enough excuse from performing Borner's task.

That Fabricius was responding to a now-missing advice letter from Meurer is further substantiated:

> Verum causas tui consilii affers magnas, caritatem patriae et studia juventutis, quae quidem apud bonorum animos non solum istis quae dixi praemiis, verum ipsi etiam vitae sunt anteponenda. Atqui non una ratio est demerendae patriae et consulendi studiis aliorum, quarum etiam aliquot continet Borneri epistola.
>
> You bring up valid reasons in your advice, I'll grant you that: yes, in the minds of good men, the prizes of which I speak are not what should be put first in life only, but also the love of one's country and of the passions of youth. Regardless, there is no one reason for lying under obligation of one's country and for considering pursuing other things, only some of which are contained in Borner's letter.

The nature of Meurer's advice can be deduced from this, as well as from the first sentence of the letter: that Fabricius' motivation ought to be (1) to his friends and colleagues ("You're calling me to do a scholarly favor") and, furthermore, (2) to his homeland ("the love of one's country", i.e., Saxony as opposed to Lothringen, Württemberg, or even Italy), and (3) to the quest for knowledge ("the endeavors of youth").[30]

Fabricius' rant about the heaviness of Borner's favor thus turns into a justification. Thereafter, Fabricius recommits himself, but not out of duty to country or to friends, but because of a promise he made to himself as a young boy:

> Quid igitur facies? inquis. Ego, mi Volfgange, laborem scholasticum neque fugio neque detrecto, imo hunc mihi a puero proposui et in eadem nunc quoque maneo sententia, quem etiamsi non uno aut altero etiam anno subeam et intra breve annorum spatium, non puto me idcirco patriae defuturum aut officio meo, et dum

---

[30] These motivations would have been understood with the Reformation cause in mind—what one could call the 'Lutheran-Humanist Complex'. This complex placed a huge emphasis on liberal education (cf. Tagungsbericht *Die Sächsischen Fürsten- und Landesschulen. Interaktion von lutherisch-humanistischem Erziehungsideal und Eliten-Bildung*). That is, the Protestant ideal was an intellectual who sought evidence to prove the error of Rome. This meant diligence to study on one hand, and giving oneself to new learning experiences on the other.

> illa mihi comparo argumenta (scr. adjumenta), quae ad tale negotium munusque necessario pertinent, et patria mihi ignoscet et amici viri boni atque aequi concedent. Tamen ad epistolae tuae partem praecipuam.
>
> 'What are you going to do?' you ask? Well, Wolfgang, I'm not going to run away from my scholarly work, nor will I shrink from it. Since I was a young lad, I have resolved myself to this, and I'm sticking to that same determination still—even if I do not succeed in one or even two years, and I am unable on account of my country or my office within the short space of the years to come, as long as I provide that evidence that applies inevitably to such business and service, and my country excuses me and my peers allow me—at least toward that particular part of your letter.

Recommitted thus, Fabricius' status is confirmed only weeks later by the fourth letter of the sequence provided by Baumgarten-Crusius, namely begging Meurer to put pressure on Borner to send him the text (18 December 1545): "I beg you, get me that preface from Dr. Borner [...] the one I keep bugging you about!"

Ultimately, it appears that Fabricius' hopes of receiving the Fugger scholarship went unfulfilled: the following spring (1546) he returned to Saxony to assume the position of rector of the newly established *Fürstenschule* in Meissen (1546). This was hardly a concession in the eyes of historians, since Fabricius' role as educator in Meissen is likely the role for which he is most recognized due to his having restarted the then-failing school and establishing the premier school's long-held reputation of producing influential scholars.[31]

6.3 Conclusions from Fabricius' Letters

It is clear from Fabricius' letters to Meurer that the codex containing *F was present at Leipzig prior to 7 January 1545. Furthermore, it is clear that

---

[31] Now the *Sächsische Landesgymnasium Sankt Afra zu Meißen*, another of Duke Maurice's educational institutions. He established two similar high schools: the first was in Schulpforte (*St. Marien*: 1543; now *Landesschule Pforta*) a district of Bad Kösen, ca. 5 km southwest of Naumburg (Saale) (cf. Ch. 13.2); the second was in Meissen; the third was in Grimma (*St. Augustin*: 1550). These "Landesschulen für Knaben" were known collectively as the *Fürstenschulen* and served as models for the establishment of similar institutions throughout the German lands (e.g. Schwerin, Heilsbronn, Joachimsthal [Brandenburg], Neutstadt). Notably, all three are still in operation today and can boast of some very notable alumni throughout their history.

Borner knew of the same codex and was likely the man behind bringing it to Leipzig from Naumburg. He was also aware that both Fabricius and Meurer were privy to this knowledge. Given that all three were involved at some point with the running of the four institutions established by Duke Maurice's educational reforms in Saxony—the timing of which places Meurer, Borner, Camerarius, and Melanchthon all in Leipzig at the same time, namely 1543—it is apparent that the latter two men in this list also knew of the document. As will be shown in the subsequent chapters, there is plenty of evidence to corroborate the idea that indeed Melanchthon was involved in the secret (cf. Ch 10). A bit more sleuthing will reveal additional evidence in support of Camerarius' involvement (cf. Ch. 11).

Additionally, it is apparent from the 1 February 1557 dedication to Part 2 of *Poemata sacra* that Fabricius had accessed the Latin text from the Leipzig manuscript some time in the period after his fourth letter to Meurer (18 December 1545). What remains, then, is a ca. 13-year window during which the status of the manuscript codex is unaccounted for by Fabricius. However, as will also be shown in subsequent chapters, there is evidence of a similar-sounding manuscript being present at the Leipzig *Paulinum* during this window.

Part III:

Reformation Rumors of an Old Saxon Bible

7. Prologue: the Rumors Recorded

7.1 Introduction to the Rumors

Continuing the discussion of Fabricius' letters, the next letter to Meurer was sent before Fabricius returned to Saxony, i.e., while he was still residing in Strasbourg. In this letter, dated 16 March 1546, Fabricius mourns Luther's passing and expresses dissatisfaction toward Emperor Charles V's impending military advance against the Schmalkaldic League. Neither in this letter nor any future ones to Meurer does Fabricius ever again mention the codex at Leipzig. Nevertheless, the timing of the March 1546 letter is conspicuous in one way: it was written *after* Luther's death. This tacitly reveals an obvious, yet valuable piece of information: the codex containing *F was without a doubt present at the *Paulinum* prior to Luther's death: all of Fabricius' previous letters to Meurer act as evidence toward this conclusion.

That *F was present in Leipzig during Luther's lifetime provides a link between that document and connection to another rumored (and thus hypothetical) document, the existence of which has been debated among scholars for at least the past three centuries. This second manuscript document has been referred to by Germanists over the past century as *L. The rumor associated with *L claims that it too was once present at the *Paulinum* in Leipzig. Moreover, the rumor describes *L as a codex that (1) credits its creation to a decree from Louis the Pious, (2) contained a preface in two parts—one in Latin prose, one in Latin verse—and (3) was once possessed by Martin Luther. The debate has raged on about the legitimacy of such claims because of a lack of material evidence in Leipzig. The discovery of MS L in 2006 has potentially delivered this material evidence.

7.1.1 The Reformers' Interest

It can be inferred from Fabricius' interest that the codex containing *F also included a Germanic text (cf. 6.1.2 "das Alte und das Neue Testament poetisch in die germanische Sprache" and 6.2.2 "doubtless Germanic manuscript"). Furthermore, as humanists, both Fabricius and Borner would have read and understood the Latin of the *Prefaces* without difficulty; on the other hand, the Old Saxon of the *Heliand* text to which the Latin *Prefaces* were attached would have most likely been somewhat recognizable, nevertheless quite enigmatic to them. Moreover, despite being a gifted poet,[1] Fabricius likely failed to see the poetic nature of the *Heliand* even in his writings after 1557. The poetic pattern of the *Heliand* is virtually unnoticeable when reading the text directly from the extant manuscripts. This was no doubt also true of the Leipzig manuscript that Borner had. Indeed, the first to recognize the metric layout of the *Heliand* was J. A. Schmeller in 1830.

There is an explanation for why even a gifted poet like Fabricius or the well-read Latin and Greek grammarians Camerarius and Melanchthon could miss the poetic patterns: the modern (and early-modern) mind is accustomed to seeing verse set off into lines in order to aid a reader's recognition of the meter and end-rhyme. When it was applied as ink on velum, the *Heliand* epic was apparently written to conserve precious materials. Thus, the text on the manuscripts appears to be prose. It is only upon closer investigation that one recognizes the poetic nature of the material: a pattern based not on a repeating meter and end-rhyme (the styles now most commonly associated with poetry), rather on alliteration—a native Germanic mnemonic tool.[2]

A classicist like Fabricius would have been quite unfamiliar with the ancient Germanic poetic form, because it had died out much before his time. This means of creating poetry was replaced on the Continent by the Latin style during the Middle High German period. Whether it is Borner, Fabricius, Camerarius or Melanchthon, all notable Latinists, the focus of education in the Early Modern Period was a return to Classical texts. All of these men were equally lost on the Old Saxon content, but were likely very interested in the value to them of it because of what they could glean from the Latin *Praefatio*-and-*Versus* material. Thus, Borner and company's interest in *F would not have come from the Old Saxon *Heliand* text, rather from the Latin *Prefaces*. Thus, their interest in receiving Rhenanus' interpretation of the codex serves as a tacit revelation that the codex containing *F must have included the *Heliand* text as well (cf. 13.1).

---

[1] He was declared poet laureate posthumously by Emperor Maximilian II.
[2] This difference between ancient native Germanic poetic verse and meter- and end rhyme-based Latin verse is one of the major differences between the *Heliand* and the aforementioned work published in 1531 by Rhenanus— Otfrid's *Evangelienbuch*.

7.1.2 From Fabricius to Eccard

Fabricius' personal letters remained inaccessible until published in 1845 by Baumgarten-Crusius. Yet, though these letters were thus available in the latter half of the nineteenth century, Germanists remained unaware of Fabricius' *Heliand*-related references because they saw him as a scholar of an unrelated field—Roman Antiquity. These Germanists were, however, aware of von Eccard's hypothesis from 1720 about the link between the *Prefaces* and an Old Saxon version of the Bible.

When Hannemann discovered Fabricius' epistolary references in 1939, he uncovered definitive evidence in confirming von Eccard's proposal that the Latin *Prefaces* had belonged to the *Heliand*. Therewith came the first real opportunity to date the composition of the *Heliand*: while the *Heliand* text provides no hint of authorial information, the *Prefaces* claim the Saxon poet was commissioned by "Ludouicus piisimus Augustus"—the pious Emperor Louis. This reference alone dates the poetic epic described in the *Prefaces* to the ninth century. Consequently, thanks to the efforts of Fabricius, the 1200 years that intervene between our current day and that of the *Heliand* poet have been bridged. Still, there is more to the story of the *Heliand*'s resurfacing during the Reformation—in particular, its link to Luther.

The modern knowledge of this additional evidence comes from the eighteenth-century librarian at the *Paulinum*, Joachim Feller, who passes along a rumor that Martin Luther once borrowed the codex (cf. 9.1).

7.2 Joachim Feller: Bridge between Periods

Despite Duke Maurice's success in filling the *Paulinum* with materials, neither Borner nor Cameriarius (nor their immediate successors for that matter) ever organized these holdings in any lasting systematic way. As a consequence of this, the Library fell into disrepair during the following century (ADB, vol. 6 pg. 615). In stark contrast to its being considered the foremost of libraries at its founding, the UBL had since suffered from old methodologies and years of grime. Nevertheless, the UBL still had countless rare works that remained un-catalogued until 1686, when Joachim Feller (1638-1691), then-sitting Head Librarian, published *Catalogus codicum manuscriptorum Bibliothecae Paulinae in Academia Lipsensis*, the University's first complete bibliographic reference. The task of compiling the catalogue was Herculean, as Feller described in the *Dedicatio* (1686, vii-viii):

> [...] Paulinum Lipsiensem reperi, confusam nempe ac pulverulentam, non æqve tamen male habitantem, cum Paulina nostra in loco illustri, amplo, pulcherrimisqve fornicibus exornato, non obscuro, angusto & lignis tabulato, qualem ibi Lambecius invenit, sit reposita. Novum itaqve Augiæ stabulum ut repurgarem, pulpita initio, qvæ pro libris supportandis una cum scamnis interpositis D. Caspar Bornerus SS. Theol. PP. & Primus Bibliothecarius An. CIƆ IƆ XLVII. exstrui fecerat, ex Academiæ decreto removi omnia; libros etiam catensis ferreis, qvibus alligati ab illo tempore in pulpitis jacuerunt liberavi, eosqve vice plus simplici propria excussi manu, & à pulvere aliisqve sordibus defecavi.

> [...] I found the Leipzig Paulinum in total disarray and covered in dust: a poor, uninviting use of the space, whereas the halls of our Paulinum could be restored to a distinguished position, spacious and furnished with the most beautiful vaulted ceilings; not how Lambeck[3] found it: dark, cramped, and with its floors covered in wood. And so, I cleared out Augeas' Stable[4] anew: at first the pulpits—ones with stools pushed in under them—that Dr. Caspar Bornerus (D.Th. and first librarian in 1547) had erected to pile up and store books on—I removed everything according to the University's decision. I also unleashed the books from the iron chains, which lay bound to the pulpits since Borner's time; I removed them from the dust and other filth, and spread them out by hand in turn on their own.

Before Feller's efforts to reorganize and re-enliven the UBL, both books and manuscripts had been treated without differentiation—left out in the open on lecterns, the more valuable materials simply chained down (*libri catenati*) through the spine to keep them from wandering off (cf. Appendix B.1). This precaution could only stop would-be thieves and vandals from taking an entire volume, but not from cutting out pages and even whole sections. Today, not only is it uncertain what was lost between Borner's time and that of Feller, it is equally impossible to tell what the University of Leipzig had acquired in the 274 years since its founding.

While cataloguing what remained of the Library's materials, Feller instituted the now-common practice of separating manuscripts from general usage books. This division is reflected in the format of *Catalogus codicum manuscriptorum*. A special mention of certain manuscripts occurs also in the catalogue's foreword, where one comment suggests that Feller had discovered the Leipzig *Heliand* manuscript. Besides an identifying description of

---

[3] Peter Lambeck (1628-1680).
[4] Referring to the legend of the Greek demigod, who in 30 years had never cleaned his stable full of 3000 cattle, until one day Hercules came and, in his might, cleaned it in one day (Lewis/Short).

the manuscript, Feller relates a rumor about one of its former owners (Præfatio, v, bold ed emphasis mine):

> Nec inter latinos non reperiebam raros oppido, ac memoratu omnino dignos. Nam præter illos [...], inveniebam *Monatessaron, seu Unum de qvatuor* jussi Ludovici Pii compositum h. e. Harmon. IV. Evangelistrum, qvo libro aliqvando Megalander Lutherus ex concessione amicissimi Borneri fuit usus, & cujus a Polycarpo Lysero in Harmoniæ part. I. p. 13. non fallax fit mentio: expressissima autem in *Traite des plus belles Biblioteqves de L'Europe par le Sieur Le Gallois* pag. 77. 78. qvi Tractatus Gallicus Parisiis A. 1685. denuo prodiit.

> Among the Latin [manuscripts] I did not find the exceptionally rare (not to mention entirely priceless) ones. In contrast to these [...], **I found a monotessaron—in other words, a one-from-four[5] composed by order of Louis the Pious, i.e. a harmony of the four Evangelists—a book which at some point the Great[6] Luther borrowed by permission of his very good friend Borner**, and of which a mention by Polycarp Leyser in *Harmoniæ* (part I, p. 13) is rendered true: printed also by Mr. Le Gallois in *Traitté des plus belles bibliotheques de l'Europe* (pp. 77-78), a French treatise that came out again in Paris in 1685.

Thus, Feller recounts information that links the Leipzig *monotessaron* to the Reformer Martin Luther (1483-1546). Indeed, without Feller's reference, modern knowledge of the connection between the *Heliand* and Luther might very well have been lost. Feller's position in Leipzig at the transition of the Early Modern Period (ca. 1500-ca. 1750.) into the Modern Period (ca. 1750-present) means that he acts as the bridge—in both timing and geography—connecting the manuscript fragments discovered in modern times with references to the *Heliand* in the Reformation period.

7.2.1 Pierre le Gallois, Rumor Intermediary

In his reference, Feller gives an indication of the course of the rumor prior to his time. He attributes his knowledge of the Luther-*monotessaron* rumor to two works: (1) Pierre Le Gallois' relatively recent *Traitté* (1680), in which (2) the "mention" made by Polycarp Leyser (cf. 7.2.2) in "*Harmoniæ* (part I, p. 13)" was reprinted (cf. Appendix C.1). Indeed, Le Gallois records the rumor, even claiming that Luther himself boasted about having the *mono-*

---

[5] Cf. Gk. *diatessaron*: literally 'through four', i.e. '[one thing] from four'.
[6] *Megalander* < Gk. μεγᾰλ-ᾰνδροι = μεγάλοι ἄνδρες: literally 'great men' (Liddel/Scott), whence the singular.

tessaron (77-78; translation attributed to Wm. Oldys [1739], p. 91-92; bolded emphasis mine):

> [...] Loüis le Pieux son [i.e. de Charles-Magne] fils succedant à ses genereuses inclinations, aussi bien qu'à son Empire, favorisa en tout ce qu'il put les Sciences, qu'il fit régner avec luy. **Ce fut ce Prince qui fit composer le Monotessaron, c'est à dire la Concodance des quatre Evangelistes , que Luther se vanta d'avoir en en sa puissance, & qui depuis a esté mis dans la Bibliotheque de Lypsic.** Que si ce devot Prince n'a pas érigé de Bibliotheques comme un glorieux monument à sa glorie, il a du moins beaucoup augmenté celle de son Pere.
>
> Lewis the Pious, his [i.e. Charlemagne's] Son, succeeded him well in his Great and Generous Inclinations, as in his Empire. He cherished the Arts and Sciences with all his Efforts; and we may say, they reigned with him: **The *Monotessaron* (*i.e.* The Concordance of the Four Evangelists.), which *Luther* boasted to have had in his Power, and has since been deposited in the Library of *Leipsic*, was of that Prince's composing**; and though he did not found Libraries, to render his Memory more glorious in the World yet it must be acknowledged, he made a great Addition to his Father's.

Le Gallois' work is encyclopedic in nature. Consequently, it is vague in reporting its resources. Ultimately, Le Gallois fails to mention where he gained his knowledge about the Leipzig *monotessaron*—of particular interest would be the source of Le Gallois' claim with regard to Luther's boasting about the manuscript. Nevertheless, Feller connected Le Gallois' statement and that printed by Leyser based on their similarity. In fact, he implies that Le Gallois' version is simply a reprinting of Leyser. As will be shown in Ch. 8 and Ch. 10, this is not true, since Leyser's version mentions nothing about Luther at all. This means Le Gallois had some other source about the Luther rumor. Thus, as early as 1680 it is evident that the Luther-*Heliand* story had begun taking on a life of its own, with multiple authors making mention of it to one degree or another.

In a similar fashion, Feller seems to add his own touch to the rumor by implicating Borner in providing the *Heliand* to Luther. This bit of information occurs neither in Le Gallois' original nor in his 1685 redaction. Also worthy of note is a slightly-abridged version of *Traitté* that appeared in English in 1739, translated and published cryptically "By a gentleman of the Temple" (as is given in lieu of the author's name on the title page). The Borner-Luther pathway is similarly missing in this English translation of Le Gallois, yet it further shows the Luther-*Heliand* rumor both spreading through Europe and picking up steam toward becoming legend by the end of the seventeenth century.

Meanwhile, Illyricus' *Prefaces* had been reproduced six times by Feller's time—albeit each with minor to sometimes major differences in spelling and/or lexical choice and by ever different publishers (Hellgardt 2004, 174-176). Yet, despite the number and timing of these reprints,[7] the knowledge of the *Prefaces*' relationship to the *Heliand* had apparently been long lost before Feller's time: neither he nor Le Gallois (in either French or English) seems to have been aware of it. If they had been, one has to wonder why both men failed to mention this curious connection.

7.2.2 Polycarp Leyser, Rumor Publisher but not Author

In 1593, Leyser published *Harmoniae evangelicae* ('Gospel harmony')— without a doubt the book to which Feller was referring. His mention of this source is a helpful clue about the rumor's origins, but it still only reaches back as far as 1593, 31 years after Illyricus' first printing of the *Prefaces* and 47 years after Luther had died. If the rumor has any truth to it, indications of its spreading need to be attested to at least the date of Luther's death, i.e. 18 February 1546. That is, if the claims of the rumor—i.e., that Luther possessed the *Heliand*—can be documented as having been known during the Reformer's lifetime, the chances of these claims being true are significantly greater.

Feller was only partially correct in his assumption about the source of the rumor: (1) Leyser was not the original author of *Harmoniae evangelicae*, merely the publisher; and (2) although the original author does indeed make reference to the Leipzig *monotessaron*, he never mentions it in connection with Luther. Again, this suggests that by Feller's time the Luther rumor had become muddled by myth.

On the other hand, an alternative hypothesis could be made: there once existed another source that implicated Luther in possessing the Leipzig *monotessaron*, and from which the information about the connection between the man and the manuscript merged with Chemnitz' account of

---

[7] In reprints of Illyricus' *Catalogus testium veritatius*: 1597, 1608, 1667/1668 and 1672 (i.e. 14 years before Feller's *Catalogus codicum manuscriptorum*. As an excerpt in Johannes Cordesius (1615) and Andreas du Chesne (Quercetanus; 1636) (cf. Hellgardt 2004).

events. Feller and Le Gallois could then be seen as recounting a form of this merged rumor. Indeed, the fact that Feller cites Leyser (who can then be traced back to Chemnitz) as the ultimate source of his and Le Gallois' knowledge suggests that not all of the information conveyed by the two men was mere folklore. That is, Feller, Leyser, and Le Gallois were all reciting a unified version of what was originally more than one account. The question remains: who besides Chemnitz fits the criteria of being both a contemporary of Luther (as well as of Borner, Cameriarius, Manlius, etc.), and was close enough to this intellectual circle to be able to record what I have to assume was at least somewhat privileged information?

7.2.3 Rumor Resources Revealed

A word of correction about Feller's assumptions: what this seventeenth-century Leipzig librarian attributes to the sixteenth-century Leyser—i.e. "*Harmoniae* part I., p. 13"—is *Harmoniae evangelicae* (1593), an 1800-page work consisting of two tomes, each divided into multiple (3 and 4, respectively) parts. The first tome stems from an even earlier undated, unpublished and presumably lost text written by Martin Chemnitz (originally titled *Harmonia quatuor Evangelistarum* ['Harmony of the four evangelists'], compare with Feller's "Harmon. IV Evangelistarum"). Chemnitz died before finishing the project that served as the impetus to his *Harmonia*—a harmonization of parallel passages in the Gospels, accompanied by commentary from contemporary leading Reformation theologians. Seeing value in continuing the project started by Chemnitz, Leyser edited and printed two of Chemnitz' unpublished works after the latter's death in 1596. That is, besides *Loci Theologici* (1591), Leyser put out *Harmoniae evangelicae* (1593), a continuation of Chemnitz' *Harmonia quatuor Evangelistarum* project. Yet, the scope of this project was indeed so vast that not even Leyser lived to see it finished. Rather, a third man, Johann Gerhard, finally finished the entire project a full quarter-century into the 1600s. By this time, the earliest words penned originally by Chemnitz were well over 50 years old— probably even older than 75.[8]

---

[8]   *Harmoniae evangelicae* was finally completed by Gerhard (1582-1637) and printed in 1626/1627; however, Leyser made several publications of the unfinished work.

Chemnitz had been a student at Wittenberg while Luther was teaching there, yet nowhere in Chemnitz' account of the Leipzig *monotessaron* does he ever implicate Luther, rather only Philipp—i.e. Melanchthon—in knowing of the *monotessaron* codex, i.e., what I have been calling *F. It is due to this lack of any mention of Luther in Chemnitz' account that I have furthered the hypothesis that multiple rumors have been merged into one. This merger had obviously occurred by Le Gallois' time in the late seventeenth century, i.e., some 150 years after Luther had died and nearly 100 years since Chemnitz did. Indeed, a second source does exist, and it provides the connection between Luther, Leipzig, and the *monotessaron* commissioned by Louis the Pious—whereas Chemnitz' account only links the latter two. I will describe the author of this second rumor source shortly.

Strangely, similar to his silence about the *Prefaces*, Feller mentions nothing about this second rumor source or its author, Ioannes Manlius—a man whose identity was likely as enigmatic in Feller's seventeenth century as it is now (cf. 9.2). In other words, Manlius' writings were likely unknown to Feller. This seems once again to verify the idea furthered thus far that separate Luther rumors had merged well before Feller's time. Nevertheless, despite the fact that Feller does not mention this Ioannes Manlius by name (nor Chemnitz for that matter), he does offer something rather astonishing: a description of the Leipzig *monotessaron* that uncannily echoes the language of three reports traceable to the 1540s: Fabricius' letters to Meurer (cf. Appendix A.1 and A.2), Chemnitz' *Harmonia quatuor Evangelistarum* (cf. Appendix C.1), and Manlius' *Locorum communium collectanea* ('Collection of shared references', cf. Appendix D.2)—information from three of Luther's contemporaries merged into one rumor and recorded by Feller.

7.3 Organizational Note

The following chapters (i.e. Chs. 8 and 9) deal with the latter two authors, i.e. Chemnitz and Manlius. Chapter 8 continues the discussion of Martin Chemnitz, his identity and history, as well as what his report entails. This insight into his past yields crucial information about his character, leading to a better judgment of the veracity of the rumor he recorded. Similarly, Chapter 9 introduces the second rumor and its author, i.e. reporter, Ioannes Manlius, and speaks likewise to clues about his identity. In both chapters, the examination of the men's personal histories will also establish windows of opportunity during which they likely recorded their knowledge. As will be shown, these measurements of the timing of the rumors can not simply be induced from the dates of publication for each man's book, since, for example in the case of Chemnitz, the book was published posthumously. Both he and Manlius likely wrote their rumor accounts well before the publication of the same.

Later, in Part IV, the language of the reports will itself be analyzed for further evidence for when they were penned. In both cases, the recording dates of both men will help further to establish when these reporters first learned about the Leipzig *monotessaron*, i.e. the transmission dates of this information. Thus, Parts III and IV investigate two facets to each rumor: (1) the external (historical) evidence, and (2) the internal (linguistic) evidence. As stated previously (cf. 7.2.3), the ultimate purpose of the examination is to discover whether the rumors can be traced back to Luther's lifetime. In that time, people and items moved quickly and freely between the Leipzig, Wittenberg, and the surrounding regions. The two cities lie very close to one another (ca. 60 km), allowing for intellectual interchange between the two universities. Consequently, both Wittenberg and Leipzig played central roles in Reformation events. Considering this, MS L was discovered in what is considered Luther's former backyard. Of course, that MS L was found in the University Library in Leipzig is intriguing because of the manuscript fragment's similarity to that which Fabricius described as a "*monotessaron* […] in Old Saxon". According to various reports, Fabricius' document was present in Leipzig—indeed, in roughly the same location that MS L was found in 2006—more than a year before Luther's death.

These coincidences of timing, location, and historical characters beg an important question: is the MS L the same document described by Fabricius and his contemporaries over 500 years ago? Two possible routes to answering this question lie in the language surrounding these documents: (1) "can the rumors/reports about Luther's Old Saxon *monotessaron* be verified in any way as authentic?", and (2) "what, if anything, can be discovered by comparing the language of Luther's biblical translations with, in particular, that of recorded on MS L (cf. 4.2.1 ff.) and, more generally, the *Heliand* as a whole?"

Before moving on to subsequent sections that deal with these questions, however, I wish to make note about the terminology and abbreviations I have been using and will continue to use.

7.4 Terminology

Since the two rumor sources offer similar information, a system of nomenclature to keep them apart will be useful. The indicators used hereafter refer to hypothetical manuscripts that are considered to have existed and acted in some manner as the basis for what Chemnitz and Manlius describe in their *monotessaron* statements. In the past, scholars have referred to the hypothetical Luther-*monotessaron* as **L*. I will continue to use this notation in a similar fashion. Again, the asterisk and italicized typeface denote that the manuscript indicated is not attested in reality; rather, its one-time existence has been deduced from modern-day clues. It is thus hypothetical in nature. The asterisk-and-italics notation stands in contrast to the use of Roman typeface alone. This marking denotes extent *Heliand* manuscripts and/or fragments, e.g. MS L.

As for the unattested resources that served as the basis of Chemnitz' and Manlius' reports, I introduce two new designations: when dealing with Chemnitz' account the hypothesized source document will be indicated as **Ch*; for the hypothetical manuscript behind Manlius' account, the label **L$_m$* will be used, wherein the subscript (the <m> refers to 'Manlius') distinguishes it from the unqualified **L*. That is, **L* is taken to subsume **L$_m$* because the latter implicates Luther (i.e., the <L> in **L* refers to Luther; cf. MS L, in which <L> stands for 'Leipzig'). Since **Ch* does not mention Luther, it has not been given a marker that might be confused as a reference to him. Therefore, **Ch* refers only to the means by which it is hypothesized, namely through Chemnitz. Indeed, a sub-goal of the following chapters is to determine whether **Ch* is also subsumed by **L*, despite its silence about the Reformer.

8. The Education of Martin Chemnitz

> Memini D. Philippum dicere, se vidisse monotessaron, sumptibus Ludouici Pii compositum, quod existimet in bibliotheca Lipsica haberi.
>
> I remember Dr. Philipp say that he has seen a monotessaron, composed at the expense of Louis the Pious, which he reckons is being held at the Leipzig library.
>
> — Martin Chemnitz (1593)

8.1 Biography of Martin Chemnitz

Martin Chemnitz (1522–1586) was born and raised in Treuenbrietzen, 30 km northeast of Wittenberg. In his youth he attended school in his birth town, as well as in Wittenberg (1536–1538), and Magdeburg (1539–1542). At the end of his schooling, he held aspirations of moving on to the academy, where he was intent on putting off the Latin and Greek studies of his youth and taking up the higher sciences, in particular Mathematics. The unexpected death of his father left him with no means to follow this dream, and so in 1542 he took a position as a school collaborator in Calbe, a town 25 km south of Magdeburg. Around Easter of 1543 Chemnitz made his first step into the Academy by enrolling at *Universität Viadrina* in Frankfurt (Oder),[1] to which he had been attracted by the presence of his cousin,[2] Prof. Georg Sabinus (1508–1560; a.k.a. Schuler).

8.1.1 First Studies under Melanchthon

Chemnitz grew tired after barely a year at Frankfurt (Oder) and so, having also spent his savings, he quit his studies and took up employment 50 km downriver at a school in Wriezen. Barely half a year later, in autumn 1544, he recommitted himself to university studies. Soon after this, Chemnitz gained access to Melanchthon by recommendation of Sabinus, who was both a beloved former student and son-in-law of Melanchthon (married Anna in 1536). The Wittenberg professor advised Chemnitz to take up a

---

[1] He appears in *Ältere Universitäts-Matrikeln, I.: Universität Frankfurt a. O.* as 'Martinus Kemnitz' inscribed on 23 April 1543, with the margin note "doctor theologiae" ("*doctor of Theology*") (p. 88).

[2] Described alternatively as his "entfernter Verwandter" in NDB (vol. 3 p. 201).

study of Mathematics, which he did in early 1545 after transferring to Wittenberg.[3] There Chemnitz also returned to studying Greek (under Melanchthon) and discovered Astrology, a subject at which he quickly excelled. The latter extracurricular subject eventually even offered Chemnitz a source of income as a consultant to George III, Prince of Anhalt-Dessau, to whom Chemnitz was recommended by Melanchthon. While at Wittenberg, Chemnitz also became mildly interested in Theology, but was altogether too busy with his other interests and consequently generally ignored Luther. Later, however, his interest in Theology grew and he began studying the subject autodidactically.

8.1.2 Königsberg Work and Studies

As a result of an argument brewing between Emperor Charles V and the Electoral Princes in 1546, the University of Wittenberg was soon astir in the confusion of the Schmalkaldic War.[4] Seeking to avoid any physical involvement in the skirmish, Chemnitz left his studies once again and escaped in the summer of 1547 to the safety of Prussia, where Sabinus was serving as the first rector of the 1544-established *Albertus-Universität* in Königsberg. There Chemnitz eventually took up employment as the principal of a school in the Kneiphof district. By autumn he had matriculated at the new university.[5] On 31 May 1548 he was called as rector of the Königs-

---

[3] Despite this, Chemnitz does not appear in *Album Academiae Vitebergensis*. His presence at Wittenberg is taken from DBA (II 222,376–405), which includes entries from 19 different biographical sources. Of these, Buck (1746) gives the clearest estimation of time between Chemnitz' leaving Frankfurt (Oder) and his arriving at Wittenberg, namely "nachdem er nehmlich daselbsten [Frankfurt (Oder)] nur ein Jahr mit Nutzen zurückgeleget [...] hatte" implies that he leaves university the first time around Easter 1544. In Wriezen he "[hatte] kaum ein halbes Jahr wieder glücklich ausgehalten," meaning he quit that position ca. mid-autumn 1544. Next "[e]r reiste nehmlich von Writzen weg und zog im Jahr 1545. nach Wittenberg." By this account, one should expect to find Chemnitz' name in the matriculation records (AAV) only as late as mid-April 1544 (Wittenberger academic year was e.g. 18 October 1544 – 17 October 1545, divided into two semesters), but indeed it is not there.

[4] Though considered a victory for the Catholic imperialists and a defeat for Protestant rebels, the Schmalkaldic War ironically aided in spreading Luther's teachings throughout the Empire.

[5] He appears in *Die Matrikel derAlberts-Universität zu Königsberg i. Pr., I Bd.* as 'Martinus Kemnitz' inscribed by Rector Sabinus between 1 August 1546 and 8 September 1547 (p. 7). He must have matriculated sometime in the summer of 1547, since he arrived in Königsberg on 1 May of that year (DBA: *Realenzyklopädie*).

berger Domschule, and on 27 September 1548 he received the degree of *Magister Philosophiae* as one of the first graduates of the *Albertus-Universität*.

In 1549 Chemnitz returned to Wittenberg with Sabinus to fetch the latter's children and bring them back to Prussia. Upon returning to Königsberg, Chemnitz found the region overcome by the Plague, from which he fled immediately with Sabinus to Saalfeld (Thuringia). From there he stepped down formally from his position at the Kneiphofer school on 28 July 1549. To bide his time in Saalfeld, Chemnitz began his autodidactic study of Theology.

After the effects of the Plague had passed in early 1550, Chemnitz returned to Königsberg but soon wanted only to leave Prussia again for good. Before he was able to devise a plan to leave, Chemnitz was called upon on 5 April 1550 by Duke Albert of Hohenzollern (Albrecht I. von Brandenburg-Ansbach, founder of the Duchy of Prussia and the Hohenzollern dynasty) to manage the ducal library in Königsberg, a position extended due to the Duke's fondness of an astrological calendar produced by Chemnitz and printed while the latter sought refuge from the Plague. The position came with its perks: full use of the Duke's books, space, writing materials, clothing, firewood, etc. Chemnitz later described this as the best three years of his life. During this period he also began a more formal pursuit of his theological interests by attending lectures by Friedrich Staphylus at the University.

Chemnitz had all but decided to stay indefinitely in his auspicious position when an issue of local inter-Protestant tension took a turn for the serious. Pressure had been swelling behind the theological radical Andreas Osiander, a former member of the Schmalkaldic League to whom Duke Albert had granted a professorship at his eponymous university in 1549. This move by the Duke aroused controversy and, ultimately in 1551, conflict. In this conflict, Chemnitz openly sided against Osiander, while the Duke maintained his support for the radical. Thus, Chemnitz and the Duke were at odds, and having thus lost a level of the Duke's favor, Chemnitz began reconsidering his long-term plans. Despite some reluctance on the part of Duke Albert to let him go, Chemnitz resigned from his position and left Prussia on 3 April 1553 with the intent of returning to Wittenberg.

8.1.3 Second Studies under Melanchthon

After arriving on 29 April 1553, Chemnitz gave himself wholly to theological studies under the guidance of his old mentor, Melanchthon. His zeal so impressed the Faculty of Philosophy that it offered him a teaching position on 15 January 1554, despite Chemnitz' being only at the rank of *Magister*. He began teaching on 9 June, lecturing on Melanchthon's *Loci communes* (1521), for which he gained great praise. On 6 August 1554 Chemnitz traveled to Braunschweig to fulfill an invitation to preach there on 12 August. The event so pleased Chemnitz' host, Superintendent Joachim Mörlin, that he offered Chemnitz a position as his coadjutor bishop. After this, Chemnitz returned to Wittenberg for only a few months before leaving permanently on 30 November 1554, thereafter assuming his new position in Braunschweig.

8.2 Circumstances of Chemnitz' Report

Although from this point Chemnitz continued on to an active career for which he traveled frequently, his November 1554 move from Wittenberg represents the end of the familiar contact he had kept with Melanchthon. It is from this relationship with his one-time mentor that Chemnitz knew about the Leipzig-*monotessaron*. Furthermore, since Chemnitz' report of Melanchthon's claim about the *monotessaron* ultimately served as the basis for the rumor recorded by Feller in 1686, a closer observation of Chemnitz' association with Melanchthon is required. The goal of such an observation is to determine the date at which Chemnitz heard Melanchthon make his claim. From this date more can be determined about when the *monotessaron* was present where Melanchthon claims to have seen it.

8.2.1 Dates to Consider

At an unspecified date, Chemnitz penned his manuscript *Harmonia quatuor Evangelistarum* (Hannemann, 328; also Eichhoff & Rauch, 5), the unfinished work that Polycarp Leyser later edited and published in 1593 as Part I of *Harmoniae evangelicae*. Here in the Prolegomenon, Chemnitz relates his memory of Melanchthon claiming to have seen the Leipzig *monotessaron*. The 1593 publication date of *Harmoniae evangelicae* belies the actual date of the occurrence of Melanchthon's claim. Nevertheless, it is clear that this event, i.e., the Transfer Event (TE) at which Chemnitz first learned of the Leipzig *monotessaron*, must have occurred considerably earlier than the publication of *Harmoniae evangelicae*. First of all, both Melanchthon and Chemnitz had long since passed away by the time the book was printed. Moreover, Chemnitz must have recorded his knowledge—i.e. the Recording Event (RE)—at some point between hearing Melanchthon make his claim and his own death in 1586. Since it is not clear when before his death Chemnitz penned his original manuscript, the timing of Melanchthon's claim can not be ascertained from that event. With no clues being offered from the text of Chemnitz' report, the only recourse is to consider the events in Chemnitz' lifetime during which Chemnitz was in contact with Melanchthon and was therefore likely to hear the *Praeceptor Germaniae* ('The Teacher of Germany') speak about his seeing a *monotessaron* with ties to Louis the Pious and Leipzig, since it is as a personal memory of Melanchthon speaking that Chemnitz describes his TE.

8.3 Chemnitz' Contact with Melanchthon

Chemnitz and Melanchthon had the greatest contact with one another when both lived in Wittenberg simultaneously. As for Melanchthon, a residence at Wittenberg is documented starting 25 August 1518, the date he arrived at the University of Wittenberg as a young professor of the Greek language, and from which date he maintained a continuous academic career until his death on 19 April 1560. For the most part, his only departures from Wittenberg amounted to short stays—mostly to establish schools in surrounding cities in today's eastern Germany (e.g. Magdeburg 1524, Eisleben 1525, and Nuremburg 1526).

Chemnitz was present in Wittenberg for fewer than a total of 6 years throughout his life, split into three roughly equal periods: (1) as an adolescent: 1536–1538; (2) while attending university: Early 1545 – May 1547; and (3) as an adult: 29 April 1553 – 30 November 1554. Since it is during only these three windows of time that Chemnitz lived within proximity to Melanchthon, it can be assumed that these periods offered the greatest opportunity for Chemnitz to hear Melanchthon talk about "a monotessaron commissioned by Louis the Pious [...] at the Leipzig library" (cf. Appendix C.1). Following the third of these periods, the two men had only limited (and tense) interaction, either through intermediaries or while at a small number of (often contentious) Reformation conventions.

8.3.1 First Period in Wittenberg

Both Chemnitz and Melanchthon were indeed present in Wittenberg during the first period (1536–1538). Nevertheless, a considerable problem with this period can be found in Chemnitz' age: although it is imaginable that the ca. 15-year old Chemnitz could have had occasion to hear the already-famous Melanchthon speak, such an event would have been both formal and infrequent. Moreover, the adolescent Chemnitz' interest during this period moved from the *trivium* subjects to the *quadrivium* subjects: by 1538 he had decided to advance to the university and to study the hard sciences there. It is also apparent from later comments by Chemnitz that he had paid little attention to Luther while at Wittenberg. It can be surmised then that Chemnitz would have been generally uninterested in the religious debates surrounding him while attending secondary school in Wittenberg during the first period. His mind had become focused on the practical nature of Mathematics—an impulse likely strengthened by the death of his father, a once-successful clothmaker. In any case, the chances of Chemnitz encountering Melanchthon during this first period would have been notably low, especially when compared to the later two periods—when both a) Chemnitz' presence at the University is documented, and b) Melanchthon held obvious influence over Chemnitz. For these reasons, I find it acceptable to disregard the first period as a time when Melanchthon could have made his claim of seeing the *monotessaron*.

8.3.2 Second Period in Wittenberg

Melanchthon's first influence over Chemnitz seems to be slightly prior to the student's transfer to Wittenberg in early 1545. It is unclear where the two men were when Melanchthon offered his advice (i.e., was Melanchthon visiting Frankfurt (Oder) or was Chemnitz visiting Wittenberg, or was the advice transmitted through an intermediary?). Whenever their meeting did occur, this was the beginning of Melanchthon's influence over Chemnitz. It is also evident from this and later experiences that Chemnitz regarded Melanchthon as a mentor. As such, Melanchthon must have had Chemnitz' ready attention. It is also clear that Chemnitz intended to take full advantage of his proximity to the notable professors (who coincidentally also served as the fathers of Reformation), especially when they lectured on subjects related to Mathematics, namely on Astrology. Chemnitz certainly attended courses in the Greek language instructed by Melanchthon. Thus, the ca. two-year long second period in Wittenberg was likely full of opportunities for Chemnitz to listen to Melanchthon. In fact, due to the men's respective roles during this period as teacher and student—namely Melanchthon's position to lecture freely about Reformation ideas to a notetaking Chemnitz—it is likely during this second period (early 1545 – 18 May 1547) of Chemnitz' three stays in Wittenberg that he heard Melanchthon made his claim.

8.3.3 Third Period at Wittenberg

During Chemnitz' third stay in Wittenberg (29 April 1553 – 30 November 1554), he spent the final ten months as official faculty at the University. Chemnitz had left Prussia as a result of the Osiandrian Controversy and returned to Wittenberg specifically in order to be near Melanchthon. Considering that Chemnitz jumped immediately into his theological studies under Melanchthon, the two men had considerable contact in the ca. seven-month period before Chemnitz became a university lecturer (January 1554). Similarly, later as a lecturer on Melanchthon's *Loci communes*, Chemnitz would have had both access and reason to consult with Melanchthon about the topic of the course, as well as to continue to attend Melanchthon's lectures. For these reasons, it is also quite probable that Chemnitz heard Melanchthon's claim at some point in the third period.

Interaction between Chemnitz and Melanchthon most likely stopped some time between autumn and early winter in 1554. Shortly before this, Chemnitz left Wittenberg in order to visit to Braunschweig (arrived 6 August 1554). He occupied the post as coadjutor for "Superattendent" (ADB) Joachim Mörlin less than four months later on 30 November 1554. From this point on, Chemnitz distanced himself increasingly from Melanchthon. This posturing proved to be a growing rift in his allegiance to his former mentor. If Chemnitz had any contact with Melanchthon after this date, it would have been limited, due only in part to their geographic separation. Their relationship ended formally in 1557 when, at the Colloquy of Worms

(11 September – 8 October 1557), Chemnitz disappointed Melanchthon by siding with the Gnesio-Lutherans, Melanchthon's opponents in the Adiaphoristic Controversy.[6]

8.4 Dating via Parallel Historical Evidence

30 November 1554 serves as the latest realistic opportunity for Chemnitz to hear Melanchthon's claim about the *monotessaron* (i.e. TE). Thus, the window of opportunity for this exchange of information falls between Chemnitz' transfer to the University of Wittenberg in early 1545 and his leaving Wittenberg permanently on 30 November 1554—a period of approximately nine years. This window of opportunity can be winnowed down further still: while it is certain that Chemnitz maintained an allegiance to Melanchthon after leaving Wittenberg for Königsberg prior to 18 May 1547, their geographic separation during Chemnitz' Königsberg period would suggest that there was little opportunity for the two men to interact other than by letter.[7] This is unlikely to be the means by which Chemnitz learned of Melanchthon's claim, since in recording his memory of the event Chemnitz uses "dicere"— i.e., "I remember Dr. Philipp *say*"—denoting an oral exchange. Such would preclude Chemnitz' Königsberg period from being considered for the timing of Melanchthon's claim. It might simply be disregarded for the same reason that Chemnitz' first (i.e. childhood) period in Wittenberg has been, or for the reason any other unmentioned period has been ignored. Namely, geographic distance limits the interaction between the two parties involved, making the probability of the event of Melanchthon's claim during the first period very low.

What remains are two relatively restricted windows during which Melanchthon's claim regarding *Ch would have occurred: some time from early (April?) 1545 to 18 May 1547 and/or from 29 April 1553 to 30 November 1554. What can be taken from these dates is an effective *terminus ante quem* for Chemnitz' TE. This rough terminus is valid for working purposes, serving a double role: Melanchthon must have seen the *monotessaron* before he

---

[6] Another side-effect of the conflict at the Colloquy was Flacius' 1559 banishment from Jena.

[7] Their personal contact in this interim period was limited to a short encounter during Chemnitz' 1549 return to fetch Sabinus' children, a trip that took approx. two weeks including travel (DBA: Buck).

ever told anyone that he had done so. This is an obvious statement that is also noted in the language of Chemnitz' report ("vidisse": perf. inf. act. = "[he] has seen"; cf. 10.2.2).[8] Thus, the steps in logic are the following: (1) the latest Melanchthon could have conceivably seen the *monotessaron* would have been immediately prior to talking about it within earshot of Chemnitz; (2) Chemnitz most probably heard Melanchthon while present at the University of Wittenberg; (3) Chemnitz quit Wittenberg no later than 30 November 1554. Based on external evidence, this date is the *terminus ante quem* for the event (TE) at which Chemnitz heard Melanchthon claim to have seen the *monotessaron*. In Chapter 10, evidence will be presented to push this terminus back in time to 1547.

8.4.1 Chemnitz' Reliability

There may be some who question the reliability of Chemnitz as a reporter of the existence of the Leipzig *monotessaron*. [Indeed Hannemann cites somebody for seeing it as hearsay]. Three potential arguments come to mind: (1) Chemnitz' claim is useless because it is hearsay; (2) Chemnitz was motivated by other factors—either for his own gain or that of Melanchthon—and thus his report is of dubious value; and (3) even if Chemnitz' report is accurate and objective, his Latin was poor; this leads to difficulty in interpreting the details of Melanchthon's claim. The following subsections will speak briefly to these assertions.

8.4.2 Devil's Advocate: Arguing Hearsay Evidence

Chemnitz' knowledge of the existence of the *monotessaron* is indeed hearsay. This does not discount his report of what he heard Melanchthon say. The veracity of the existence of the document depends not on Chemnitz', rather on Melanchthon's character. While one may wish to question Melanchthon's truthfulness, doing so does not negate the historical occurrence of his claim. At the worst, Chemnitz has only acted as the medium for Melanchthon's lie. At the best, he offers us a very rare piece of information about knowledge that has otherwise been lost. Whether true or not, the

---

[8] "The Perfect Infinitive represents an act as *prior to* the time of the verb on which it depends" (Bennett, §270.1.a).

exceptionality of Chemnitz' report makes it worthy of investigation. The veracity of Melanchthon's claim will be borne out by the existence—or lack—of external evidence that can be linked to the existence of a similar document in the same place at the same time.

8.4.3 Motivation for Reward

The heart of the concern in argument (2) is whether Chemnitz fabricated the story of his memory. Perhaps he thought that some sensational story about the existence of a vernacular treatment of the Bible—especially one with ties to the current Emperor's predecessor—would be worth something during a time when an Imperial inquisition was in place. All that can be offered as defense against this kind of conclusion is that, on the contrary, it appears that Chemnitz had little to gain for passing along this story. Indeed, whether true or false, the assessment that Chemnitz fabricated the story due to ulterior motives is faulty because:

a. he acts merely as the messenger of the claim that the document exists, and not as the claimant;
b. Chemnitz' relationship with Melanchthon had soured in the time between when Melanchthon made his claim and when Chemnitz penned his manuscript; and
c. Chemnitz' book was published seven years after his death.

8.4.3.1 Greater Risk than Reward

The implication of a) is that, had the *monotessaron* information been worthy of reward or fame, Chemnitz would not have been the one to receive it. Moreover, the risk of punishment was greater than the chance of reward (8.4.3.3), since according to the inquisition imposed by Charles V in an attempt to stem the Protestant tide, any information that aided the Protestant cause was punishable by death, as was declared in Charles V's Edict of Worms (1521; translation Batcher 2006; bolded emphasis mine):

> Against each and every one of the books and writings under the name of the said Luther already published or to be published, and also against those who henceforth will print, buy, or sell those books and writings.

> Item. Against accomplices receiving or favoring Luther and his works in any way.
> Item. Against **all insulting and libelous** books, and other such **writings** and illustrations, and also against **writers, printers,** buyers, or **sellers**, whoever they are or whatever social status or condition they have.
>
> Law for printers to defend against the evils which come from the abuse of the praiseworthy craft of printing.
>
> Punishments
>
> For the crime of *lèse majesté* [high treason] and for very serious offense and indignation against the prince.
> Item. **Confiscation and loss of body and belongings and all goods**, fixed and movable, half of which will go to the Lord, and the other half to the accusers and denouncers. With other punishments as given more fully in the present edict and mandate.
> [...] we forbid anyone from this time forward to dare, either by words or by deeds, to receive, defend, sustain, or favor the said Martin Luther. [...] Those who will help in his capture will be rewarded generously for their good work.
> [...] we forbid anyone, regardless of his authority or privilege, to dare to buy, sell, keep, read, write, or have somebody write, print or have printed, or affirm or defend the books, writings, or opinions of the said Martin Luther, or anything contained in these books and writings, whether in German, Latin, Flemish, or any other language. This applies also to all those writings condemned by our Holy Father the pope and to **any other book written by Luther or any of his disciples**, in whatever manner, even if there is Catholic doctrine mixed in to deceive the common people.
> For this reason, and to kill this mortal pestilence, we ask and require that no one dare to compose, write, print, paint, sell, buy, or have printed, written, sold, or painted, from now on in whatever manner such pernicious articles so much against the holy orthodox faith and against that which the Catholic Apostolic Church has kept and observed to this day. We likewise condemn **anything that speaks against** the Holy Father, against the prelates of the church, and against **the secular princes**, the general schools and their faculties, and all other honest people, whether in positions of authority or not.

Chemnitz certainly fell into the group of "writers, printers [...] or sellers" of "all insulting and libelous [...] writings" "favoring Luther and his works in [some] way." Therefore, if he printed his Leipzig *monotessaron* report with the hopes of publicizing that document, Chemnitz was susceptible to corporal punishment. After all, he printed this information instead of turning it over to Imperial authorities. Moreover, the entire scope of *Harmoniae evangelicae* was to offer side-by-side comparison of parallel biblical passages accompanied by copious amounts of justifying commentary by the likes of Luther, Melanchthon, and other Reformation leaders.

That Charles V equated religious heresy with political treason is clear: "Action will be taken [...] against those who commit heresy or the crime of *lèse majesté*." Thus, "it is our duty to help subdue the enemies of our faith [...] and to keep the Christian religion pure from all heresy or suspicion of heresy [...]."

Though Charles V's threats were harsh, it is questionable whether they were ever truly enforced, since the Emperor soon became swept up in other political and military campaigns after issuing the Edict of Worms. Yet, still two decades later at the Revolt of Ghent (1540), Charles V proved again his favor of using draconian methods in order to control political dissent: he forced the tax-protesting Flemish nobles to march before him through town, barefoot and with nooses about their necks.[9] Furthermore, he reinstated the death penalty for heresy after having personally led his forces in defeating the Schmalkaldic War (1548) and forcing the particularistic Pragmatic Sanction of 1549 on the Seventeen Provinces,[10] therewith humiliating the Low Countries once again. Surely, the Emperor's threats were seen by no means as idle. Therefore, Chemnitz would have been just as likely—if not more so—to receive punishment as he was to gain reward, considering the implications against the Emperor that extended from the Leipzig *monotessaron* report.

8.4.3.2 Possibility of Charitable Selfishness

The implication of (b) in 8.4.3 is that Chemnitz was unlikely to be seeking reward for Melanchthon. If Chemnitz recorded his memory (RE) after November 1554, Chemnitz would have been unlikely to seek the fame for Melanchthon, because their relationship faltered then and ultimately failed in 1557. For those who might see Chemnitz' printing of the *monotessaron* rumor as a way for him to mend this relationship by bringing attention to Melanchthon, there are two counter arguments:

---

[9] Whence the nickname for Ghenters: *stroppendragers* 'noose wearers'.
[10] Charles V's enforcement of religious laws ultimately led to the Eighty Years' War of the Dutch Revolt (1568-1648).

i. Melanchthon had plenty of his own fame prior to this, and this small attribute in Chemnitz' unprinted text would have not brought much positive attention even if it had been printed within the Melanchthon's lifetime.
ii. The attention it would have likely brought Melanchthon—had the publication date of the information allowed it—would have been at least as equally negative as positive (cf. 8.4.3.1), i.e., all the more reason for the Imperial powers to punish the man whose name was included in the 1559 *Index Librorum Prohibitorum*[11] (*List of Prohibited Books*) under the heading "Auctores quorum libri, & scripta omnia prohibentur" (*Authors whose books and entire writings are forbidden*).

Perhaps, then, one might see Chemnitz' report as an attempt to injure Melanchthon, i.e., to seek revenge against him. However, had this been Chemnitz' goal (cf. 8.4.3.3), he would have been making himself equally susceptible to Imperial punishment (cf. 8.4.3.1). Moreover, Chemnitz' report was printed during neither Melanchthon's nor Chemnitz' lifetime.

8.4.3.3 Easier Means to Reward

Such is also the implication of (c), i.e., that Chemnitz had been long dead by the time *Harmoniae evangelicae* was published in 1593, and therefore unable to benefit/suffer personally from it in any way. Indeed, the scope of Chemnitz' project undertaken originally as *Harmonia quatuor Evangelistarum* was very large and long-term. Chemnitz ultimately only worked through a fraction of what Leyser later completed and published. If Chemnitz was seeking to benefit from the information provided by the single-sentence mention of the *monotessaron*, he would likely have cited it in a shorter, more immediately printable work—or perhaps taken the Emperor at his word from the Edict of Worms: "[t]hose who will help [...] in apprehending [...] those who seem rebellious [...] and to punish them according to the penalties set out by law-Divine, canon, and civil" "[...] will be rewarded generously for their good work."

---

[11] Published by Pope Paul IV in 1559, the first edition was titled *Index Auctorum Et Librorum Prohibitorum* (a.k.a. the *Pauline Index*) and was the Vatican's first official list of banned materials.

8.4.4 Chemnitz' Knowledge of Latin

Concerning Chemnitz' skill in the Latin language, it can not be claimed that his usage of that language was somehow substandard, and thus imply that an accurate reading of his language is impossible. On the contrary, Chemnitz was notably capable in Latin, as Buck describes (1746):

> [...] Da er aber hiezu [i.e. zur Tuchmacherhandwerk][12] keinen natürlichen Antrieb bezeugte, und folglich den mütterlichen Wünschen kein Genüge leisten konnte, so behielte ihn die Mutter wieder zu Hause, und erlaubte ihm, ohne weiter die Schule zu besuchen, in der lateinischen Sprache eigenmächtig sich zu üben. Bey dieser Verfassung blieb er in seiner Vaterstadt so lange, bis im Jahr 1539. zwei weitläufige Verwandte, Peter Niemann, Secretatius des Raths zu Magdeburg, und Benedickt Köppen, Schöppenschreiber der besagten Stadt, Geschäfte halber dahin kamen, denen er ein selbst verfertigtes lateinisches Sendschreiben überreichte, und hiedurch sich bey ihnen in solche Gunst setzte, daß er von ihnen nach Magdeburg mitgenommen, in die dasige Schule gegen das Ende des Jahres 1539. hineingegeben, und durch ihre Vorsorge mit freyen Tischen und anderen Nothwendigkeiten unterhalten wurde. Da er in diesen Anstalten fast drey Jahre verblieben war, eerward er sich nicht allein in der lateinischen Sprachkunst, sondern Dichtkunst, Dialecktick und Rhetorick die nöthige Geschicklichkeit, sondern legte auch hieselbsten den ersten Grund zu Mathematik. [...]

This indicates that Chemnitz had an advanced facility for Latin, even at a young age. Consequently, it is safe to assume that he was aware of the syntactic, morphological, and semantic peculiarities of the language and their logical implications. Therefore, he can be considered quite deliberate in his manner of expression.

---

[12] His father was a clothmaker, and Chemnitz' mother initially intended for her son to learn the same trade.

9. The Enigmatic Ioannes Manlius

> Ludouicus Pius curauit fieri Monotessaron, id est, concordantias quatuor Euangelistarum, magno sumptu. Quem librum diu habuit apud se Lutherus, & hodie est in Lipsica bibliotheca. Præfatio est partim Latinis uersibus, q̨ ualde boni sunt, partim prosa oratione, etiã bene et Latinè scripta.
>
> Louis the Pious saw to it, at great cost, that a monotessaron was made, i.e. a harmony of the four Evangelists. Luther had this book with him for a long time, and which today is in the Leipzig library. The preface is partly in Latin verses, which are very good, and partly in prose language, also good and written in Latin.
>
> — Ioannes Manlius (1562)

9.1 Rumor of a Luther Codex

The excitement over the discovery of MS L stems in great part from information passed down by a man named Ioannes Manlius, for it is only through him that the rumored link between the *Heliand* and Martin Luther is known. That this plausible historical connection was on the minds of L's discoverers is clear from Hans Ulrich Schmid's first periodical report of the fragment after its discovery in 2006 (322–323):

> Eine weitere Frage, die hier nur gestellt, aber nicht beantwortet werden kann, ist die, ob L – möglicherweise zusammen mit P – jenem rätselhaften Codex entnommen worden ist, der in humanistischen und reformatorischen Kreisen im Raume Naumburg – Leipzig – Wittenberg benutzt worden ist [...]. Mit großer Vorsicht hat Kurt Hannemann die Möglichkeit in Erwägung gezogen, daß P letzter Überrest dieser Handschrift sein könnte. Daß nun ausgerechnet unter den in der Universitätsbibliothek Leipzig deponierten Beständen der Thomas-Kirche ein Fragment entdeckt wir, das beträchtliche formale und sprachliche Übereinstimmung mit P aufweist, verleiht dem ganzen Fragenkomplex einen neuen Aspekt. [...] Sollte etwa ein indirekter Weg von Leipzig zurück in die weitere Heimat des 'Heliand' führen? Und sollte diese Hs. wiederum identisch sein mit dem 'Luther-Heliand', von dem wir nur aus einer Bemerkung Melanchthons wissen? Und kann Flacius genau dieser Hs. seine 'Praefatio' entnommen haben?

Schmid remarks that, due to L's similarities to P (cf. 2.1.2), a new facet has been introduced to the hypothesis presented by Hannemann in the 1972 redaction of his 1939 paper "Die Lösung des Rätsels der Heliandpraefatio".[1]

---

[1] Renamed in 1972 as "Die Lösung des Rätsels der Herkunft der Heliandpraefatio".

There, Hannemann discusses the centrality of Leipzig in the resurfacing of the *Heliand* during the Early Modern Period. His approach is cautious, noting a previous, failed attempt to link Luther to MS M. Instead, he proposes an alternate theory, first linking *F and *L (p. 11: "[...] der Briefhinweis auf die Naumburger ‚Praeexistenz' der Hs., deren Identität mit dem Lutherheliand wahrscheinlich ist"), then connecting *L to MS P (13):

> Krokers Frage [...]: „Soll der Codex Flacianus für immer verschollen bleiben?", ist noch nicht endgültig negativ entschieden. Die Möglichkeit, daß der Monacensis der Luther- und Praefatiokodex wäre, schloß W. Krogmann in seiner Praefatiountersuchung [...] aus. Der Gedanke, daß etwa das Bruchstück P ein Rest des ›Monotessaron‹ sein könnte, ist noch nicht erwogen worden. So gewagt die hier zuerst entwickelte Naumburger Hypothese in ihrer Koppelung mit dem Prager Bruchstück erscheinen mag, sie sollte doch durchdiskutiert werden.

Hannemann concludes that the lack of an answer to the questions did not entail a negative answer. He suggests that further research be directed toward investigating the link between MS P and his Naumburg hypothesis. Put simply, Hannemann's hypothesis is this: the Naumburg-resident *F was moved to Leipzig, where it was housed at some point in the UBL, where Luther accessed it in some fashion (as *L), from which Fabricius took the *Prefaces* that he sent to Illyricus to be printed, and also from which MS P was later separated and subsequently sent to Prague, where it was discovered in the late nineteenth century. In other words, MS P, *F, *L and Luther are all linked via Leipzig. In light of this, the discovery of MS L in Leipzig comes as potential proof of Hannemann's hypothesis. Moreover, it may be the missing link to finally substantiate the rumor that Luther made use of the *Heliand*. The question remains: Does MS L really corroborate Hannemann's hypothesis? Also, what else does MS L have to reveal regarding the history of the *Heliand*?

The alleged connection between Luther and the *Heliand* is not in any way new. Hannemann briefly touches upon the previous hypothesis that sought to unite Luther and MS M—a theory ultimately disproved by Willy Krogmann in 1948 (Niederdeutsches Jahrbuch 69/70). Furthermore, Hannemann himself hinted at the sources of the centuries-old Luther rumor in the 1939 version of his paper on the provenance of the *Prefaces*. Yet, strangely, in a move that serves only to frustrate current research into these questions, Hannemann ultimately fails to cite these sources explicitly. He states (328; also Eichhoff & Rauch, 5):

Schülernachschriften in einer Pariser und in einer Leipziger Handschrift und eine seit 1562 oft gedruckte Sammlung von Melanchthonanekdoten, die ein Jh. Manlius zusammengestellt hatte, melden von einem Monotessaron, das Ludwig d. Fr. angeregt, Luther lange besessen und eifrig gelesen habe und das heute, d. h. zunächst etwa 1555, in der Leipziger (Pauliner) Bibliothek sei.

Hannemann provides herein very valuable information; yet, that none of the sources mentioned are ever given outright should immediately raise suspicion. Luckily, he does provide a pair of hints: the name "Manlius" and the date "1562".

9.1.1 Source of the Rumor

The Manlius referred to by Hannemann is doubtless Ioannes Manlius, author of three Melanchthon-related books between 1562 and 1565. Already noted in Chapter 6 is the connection Martin Chemnitz provides between Melanchthon and *Ch. Thus, the topics of Manlius' books seem to verify him as the correct individual. Yet, despite being described by Hannemann as "oft gedruckt", the works of Manlius are rare: there has not been a renewed edition of any of Manlius' works since the late sixteenth century. More specifically, what Hannemann assumes to have been readily copied are merely extracts of certain more interesting elements from Manlius.[2]

The quotation at the top of this chapter occurs on pages 99–100 of Manlius' *Locorum communium collectanea*. This extract has likely had a great deal of influence on the Luther-*monotessaron* rumor. In fact, it is the only extant source to explicitly state Luther's name. Chapter 11 will examine the influence of this citation in more detail. Until then, the remainder of the current chapter will establish the identity of Ioannes Manlius—not an easy task, since history provides little to work with.

9.2 Identifying *Ioannes Manlius*

Other than three works published by Manlius (*Locorum communium collectanea* 1562; *Libellus medicus variorum Experimentorum* ['Medical booklet of various experiments'] 1563; *Epistolarum Philippi Melanchthonis farrago* ['Assort-

---

[2] E.g., it is through Manlius' 1562 book that the first references to a man named Johann Faustus—Goethe's eponymous anti-hero and evidently a childhood acquaintance of Melanchthon—is known.

ment of Philipp Melanchthon's letters'] 1565), there is very little direct record of his existence. For example, he does not appear in the perennial biographical standards *Allgemeine Deutsche Biographie* (ADB) or *Neue Deutsche Biographie* (NDB). To be sure, the only form of Manlius' name that ever occurs in his three publications is *Ioannes Manlius*—generally printed in letter-spaced small caps, i.e. I O A N N E S   M A N L I V S (or its equivalent when declined, i.e. acc. Ioannem Manlius, etc.). I have sought the identity of Manlius using as many of the most obvious various ways to spell this name (e.g., Jo[h]an[n][es], Io[h]an[n][es], etc.) as possible; however, for the ease of the reader, I will refer to him henceforth only by the spelling *Ioannes Manlius*, since this is the only form that is actually recorded in historical documents attributable directly to his hand. Therefore, when I offer in subsequent discussion what appear to be other spellings of this name, it is either to quote some other author's usage (which will be made obvious because of the name's occurrence within a quotation) or in reference to a (possibly) different individual attested in other historical records (e.g., Johannes Menlin). The point in introducing the names of such other individuals is to investigate whether they can be identified as the author of the aforementioned passage.

9.2.1 Similar Names in Biographical Resources

The name "Manlius" appears to be a Latinized form of a German name, and indeed a search of this name at the *Personennamendatei* (PND) at the Deutsche Nationalbibliothek (DNB) website reveals multiple possibilities: Hans Mandl (PND working date: 1581) and Jakob Mennel (PND vital dates: 1460–1526), Johannes Jakobus Manlius de Bosco (PND working date: fifteenth century), Johannes Manlius (no dates), Johannes Manlius (1588), and Johannes Manlius (1562–1600). The *Digitales Register* for ADB/NDB yields the entries for the first two men as results for a query of the name *Manlius*.

9.2.1.1 Hans Mandl

Hans Mandl (a.k.a Mennel, Mannel, *Slovenian*: Mandele) (PND: 137083378) was a wandering publisher (*Wanderbuchdrucker*) in the latter half of the sixteenth century (ADB offers the range 1575–1582), who also went by the pen name Johannes Manlius. Mandl's activity appears to have been confined to

Hapsburgian Carniola and Styria, as well as western Hungary and Saxon Transylvania. The possibilities of equating Mandl with Ioannes Manlius are discussed further in 9.2.2.4.

9.2.1.2 Jakob Mennel

Jakob Mennel (PND: 118580876) was a historiographer at the court of Maximilian I. His profession might therefore seem to fit the character of the editor Ioannes Manlius. Indeed, Mennel was also known to use this Latinized surname in publication; however, his first name and his death—roughly 30 years before the 1562 publication of *Locorum communium collectanea*—ultimately speak against the possibility of equating Mennel with Manlius. Nevertheless, Jakob Mennel's existence seems to have had an influence on modern scholarship attempting to identify Ioannes Manlius, since a combination of all three names "Johannes Jacobus Manlius" is often associated in bibliographic databases with the three aforementioned publications of Ioannes Manlius.

9.2.1.3 Johannes Jacobus Manlius de Bosco

A simple search of a number of combinations of the three names at WorldCat yields results that include at least one of the three books cited in 9.2. Thus, it appears that the bibliographic databases confuse the identities of at least two if not several men. It is likely this corruption of Ioannes Manlius as "Johannes Jacobus Manlius" in bibliographies that has caused some scholars to confuse the Melanchthon-anecdote writer with a slightly earlier historical persona: Johannes Jacobus Manlius de Bosco (a.k.a. Giovanni Giacomo Manlio de Bosco; PND: 100202837), the fifteenth-century Italian author of *Luminare maius* (variably 1517 or 1536). Adding to the confusion, it is possible that de Bosco authored a second book, *Loci communi* (publish 1556), which carries a title very similar to that of Ioannes Manlius' *Locorum communium collectanea*. Indeed, the former name is often used as a shortened form for the latter in German research. Thus, two similarly named authors who penned two similarly named books within a century of one another has led to an inevitable misunderstanding by those not careful enough to keep the two men apart.³ Consequently, many bibliographic and biographic resources have merged these two distinct persons into a single historicized character. So it is that our modern-day resources seem to disagree on to whom to credit which publications. No birth date or death date is available for de Bosco; only the PND's working date "15. Jh." places him in time. His publication(s) would have therefore been posthumous. As such, de Bosco can be stricken from the list of identities with which to associate the reporter of the Luther rumor.

9.2.1.4 Einer aus Ansbach, einer aus Auerbach

As if this has not caused enough confusion, there are still the three other PND entries under the name *Johannes Manlius*. Two or even all three of these entries may in fact refer to one individual, since each record reveals slightly different yet similar information.

Record 103121145 offers the least information, giving as "weitere Angaben" the profession "Gelehreter", but offering no dates or origin whatsoever. This is likely a duplicate record of some sort. Record 119752220 gives the working dates 1562–1600⁴ and, as additional information, the location "Ansbach", i.e. "Manlius, Johannes aus Ansbach". Record 119752212 gives the working date 1588 and, as additional information, the location Auerbach, i.e. "Manlius, Johannes aus Auerbach".⁵ The source of the final two is listed as VD 16 (*Verzeichnis der im deutschen Sprachbereich erschienenen Drucke des XVI. Jahrhundert*). Since both of these records stem from the same source with corresponding working dates, it is possible that one represents a misspelling of the other city, which—should Auerbach be assumed to be Auerbach in der Oberpfalz—happen also to lie in proximity to one another: Ansbach in the west, Auerbach in the east, roughly equidistant on either side of Nuremberg (ca. 45 km each).

---

³ Even the Munich Digitisation Centre at the Digital Library Department of the Bavarian State Library (BSB, <http://www.digital-collections.de/>) has posted (16 March 2009) the images of Manlius' 1563 *Libellus medicus variorum experimentorum* with the author erroneously given as "Manlius, Johannes Jacobus".
⁴ This date range supports Kohnle's hypothesis linking Ioannes Manlius with Hans Mandl (cf. 9.2.2.4).
⁵ This name and date are corroborated in the *Leipziger Matrikel*. If the scenario presented in 9.2.2.4 is valid, the man from Auerbach was in all likelihood a different individual.

9.2.2 Establishing working dates

The Deutsches Biographisches Archiv (DBA) also contains information for a "Manlius, Johann": two frames (I 800, 395-396) reproduce the *Allgemeines Gelehrten-Lexicon* (Jöcher, 1813), with the following information (emphasis mine, cf. Appendix D.1):

> Manlius (Johann), ein seinen Lebensumständen nach wenig bekannter Gelehrter, von dem G. Th. Strokel in Hummels Bibliothek von seltenen Büchern Band II. p. 310 f. einiges anführt. Er war *ohne Zweifel aus dem Marggrafthum Anspach gebürtig, studierte zu Wittenberg und war ein großer Verehrer Melachthons, dessen Reden und Gespräche er fleißig aufzeichnete*, 1562 hielt er sich zu Basel auf, und nahm zu Wittenberg 1563 die Magisterwürde an. Darauf reisete er durch Teutschland und in einige angränzende Oerter, Briefe von Melanchthon aufzusuchen, die er hernach auch wirklich herausgab. Wann und wo Manlius zu einer Bedienung beföderet worden sey, weiß ich nicht. 1570 bekleidete ein Bruder von ihm ein geistliches Amt zu Kitzingen. Er gab heraus:
>
> Epistolarum D. Philippi Melanchthonis [...]. Basil, per Paulum Queckum. 1565 [...] Nürnb. und Altdorf 1784.
>
> Locorum communium collectanea [...] ex lectionibus D. Philippi Melanchthonis. Basil. per Jo. Oporinum (1563) [...] Teutsch übers. Jo. Manlii, [...] gemehrt durch Joh. Huldreich Ragor. Frankf. 1574. Fol.
>
> Libellus medicus variorum experimentorum [...] ex plurimis D. Philippi Melanchthonis [...]. Basil. 1563. [...] S Baumgarten [...]. Francf. 1566.

This resource reflects the publications of Ioannes Manlius, corroborating at least that all three were not authored by three similarly named men. The publication date of *Locorum communium collectanea* is erroneously give as 1563,[6] close to the PND's working date of 1562 for "Manlius, Johannes aus Ansbach". Similarly, Jöcher traces his Manlius back to Ansbach. Thus, here is an intersection between three sources: the PND, the DBA and Ioannes Manlius' own publication, yielding an expanded working date range (1562–1600) for the reporter of the Luther rumor. From this point on, I will therefore assume that all three sources refer to the same individual, i.e., the man I am calling *Ioannes Manlius* after the inscription in *Locorum communium collectanea*, etc.

Furthermore, Jöcher indicates that Manlius stopped over in Basel in 1562. This date corresponds with the publication date of the Luther rumor book. He also places Manlius at Wittenberg in 1563. His presence in Witten-

---

[6] Bibliographies vary between 1562 and 1563, likely due to the fact that the publication date does not appear on the title page of the book.

berg as well as his apparent status as a student of Melanchthon's—not only does Manlius diligently take down that professor's "Rede und Gespräche", but later publishes so-called "Melanchthon dicta und exempla" (Kohnle 2009) in three volumes—seems to suggest that he was present at Wittenberg even earlier than 1563. This would have been necessary, since Melanchthon died on 19 April 1560. Thus, it would seem that Manlius' studies at Wittenberg and under Melanchthon must have begun several years prior to this date, e.g. some time in the mid-1550s. All this suggests the need to search the matriculation records of Wittenberg to discover the actual dates that Manlius was present there.

9.2.2.1 Wittenberg Matriculation

The information provided by the DBA entry for Manlius led me to investigate the matriculation records for the University of Wittenberg, since it is stated that he was a student there. The DBA entry also allows for a rough timing of Manlius' presence at Wittenberg, since it is stated that Manlius eagerly took notes of Melanchthon's lectures. Melanchthon can be placed at Wittenberg from 25 August 1518 until his death in 19 April 1560. Interestingly enough, there are in the Wittenberg matriculation records (*Album Academiae Vitebergensis* ['Album of the University of Wittenberg'; henceforth: AAV], vol. III, p. 297) four entries under the surname *Manlius*, one of which lists the student's origin as Ansbach. However, this entry contains the first name "Nic[olaus]". To be sure, vol. III of the three-volume AAV is a registry created by its 1905 editor to list all the inscribed individuals by common last name. The various oddities of spelling for both names and places of origin are modernized and abbreviated. Thus, the registry points to the first two volumes to discover more accurately the information taken from the hand-written matriculation rolls. In the case of the entry for Manlius, Nic[olaus], it is in vol. II, p. 329 col. b line 23, where the actual inscription is "Nicolaus Manlius Onolsbacen", listed under the date 12 May 1585. Ansbach was indeed known as Olonzbach (*Meyers*, p. 614) until the eighteenth century, however no indication is given to suggest Nicolaus Manlius had an additional name Johann, or anything like it. Moreover, the date of matriculation, 1585, comes a decade-and-a-half too late for him to have studied under Melanchthon, who died in 1560. Therefore, it is unlikely that

Nicolaus Manlius from Ansbach can be identified as Ioannes Manlius from Ansbach.

An additional three names are listed in AAV under "Manlius", none of which has Johann as a first name, nor Ansbach as an associated place, and all of which appear under dates at least a decade after Melanchthon had died. There are two notes associated with the registry entry for the name *Manlius*: "—s[iehe] a[uch] Maul (Auerbach), Menlin."

Under the heading *Maul, Maulius* (III, 302), of which the second might represent a misreading of a handwritten <n> as <u>, there are four entries, one of which contains the name Johann: "Auerbach i. Oberpfalz: J[ohann] (= Manlius?)" and appearing in vol. II p. 348 as "Iohannes Maulius Aurbacensis." This would seem to be the individual cited in PND record 119752212. It seems that the editors of AAV were perhaps already trying to associate Ioannes Manlius with an entry in the matriculation records, or perhaps they were simply admitting that they could not make out the handwriting of this particular entry. In any case, the individual referred to in this entry also fails as a match for the editor of the Melancthon anecdotes, again for reasons of age: this Johann(es) Maulius (Manlius?) matriculated 1586–88—too late to have any personal interaction with Melanchthon.

The second "*s. a.*" given under the registry heading for Manlius, i.e. "Menlin" (III, 309), proves its worth: "Ansbach. J[ohann]" referencing vol. I p.237: "Johannes Menlin Onoltzbachensis" under the matriculation date 8 January 1546. This entry matches the DBA and PND information in both name and location. It also conforms to a time when Melanchthon was active at both Wittenberg and Leipzig. Strangely, however, it would mean that Manlius would have begun attending university a decade earlier than predicted.

To be sure, I have verified all headings in the registry (i.e. vol. III) of AAV that include surnames that resemble *Manlius* including the following:

> Mandlinus; Manica, Manicke, Manecke, Manick, Manike; Manlius; Mann, Man, Mannus; Manne; Mantel, Mantelius, Mantell; Maul, Maulius; Mende; Mendius; Mendel; Mendius; Mendle; Mendlen; Mener; Menlin; Mentz, Mencius, Mens, Mencz, Menzius; Mentzel, Mencelius, Menczel, Mentzelius, Menczell, Menzelius; Mintzelius; Ment; Mente; Menten, Menden, Mentenius.

A full list of the entries under these surnames is given in Appendix D.4.

The basis for determining what "resembles" *Manlius* was made first and foremost by the inclusion of the base form *Man-* or *Men-* (or forms that might be mistakenly read as such), and secondarily by inclusion of an <l> in a second or third syllable, or a character that might have been misread as an <l> by a printer (and which Latinized form the author subsequently took up as a *nom de plume*).

Out of 45 entries that result from the search described above, 17 contain the name Johann. An eighteenth entry contains the name *Jonas* which appears similar enough to be considered. Of these 18, only 6 matriculated prior to Melanchthon's year of death, 1560. Of these 6, not one had matriculated in the 1550s such that one could reasonably conclude that any one of them was still present as a student at Wittenberg to attend lectures by Melanchthon and record his *monotessaron* claim. However, if it can be assumed that Melanchthon's first encounter with the Heliand document occurred not just prior to his study of world history in 1555, rather more than a decade earlier when he played part in the reorganization of the University of Leipzig and the establishment of UBL in 1543, then Melanchthon could have presumably spoken about seeing the *monotessaron* in the 1540s. With this new guideline, three entries with the name *Johann* appear in the matriculation list: Jonas Mantel from Wittenberg (enrolled 25 September 1540), Iohannes Menlin from Ansbach (enrolled 8 January 1546), and Johannes Mentzel from Döllstädt (enrolled 30 May 1545). If *Ioannes* is neither pseudonym nor middle name, the men listed in these three entries represent the best possibilities at determining more about the identity of the author/editor Ioannes Manlius.

My preferences lie with Iohannes Menlin (written as it occurs in the matriculation record): the surnames of the other two men are problematic. These names would require syncope of the word-internal dental stop or affricate in order to come to the form Manlius. In both cases, AAV gives equivalent Latinized forms for these names: "Mantelius" for Mantel and "Mencelius, Mentzelius, Menzelius, Mintzelius" for Mentzel. Compare this to the relatively simple derivation of Manlius from Menlin: one might simply attach a Latin nominal suffix to create Menlinus or Menlius[7], which then by analogy brings to mind the famous Roman *gens Manlius*. It is also possible that the name Menlin invoked the meaning apparent in NHG *Männlein*, which stems from MHG *menlîn*, i.e. the diminutive of *Mann*. While

---

[7] Apocope of syllable final *-n* from German names when creating Latinate forms is attested, e.g. Wittenberg > Viteberg.

not a true diminutive, Manlius does contain in its second syllable something akin to the Latin diminutive suffix *-uleus*. Perhaps a combination of analogy and appeal to popularity could have driven Johannes Menlin to assume *Manlius* as his Latin name.

9.2.2.2 Basel Matriculation

As for Manlius' presence in Basel, a matriculation record from the University speaks to his arrival there some time between 1 May 1561 and 30 April 1562 (*die Matrikel der Universität Basel*, vol. II, 1956, p. 135). Manlius must have arrived toward the end of this period, i.e. in early 1562, or so his name appearing in the list as 62 of 69 matriculates would suggest.

An interesting detail also arises: the entry lists "magister Johannes Manlius Onoltspachiensis", so that not only do the name and derivation match, but it is evident that Manlius had already received his advanced degree. This contrasts with Jöcher's account in which Manlius returned to Wittenberg in 1563 to take up his master's studies. Moreover, the editors of the *Basler Matrikel* have apparently already been on the same hunt after the identity of Manlius: given below the entry is "1548[8] I. Wittenberg (Jo. Menlin Onoltzbachensis) [...]" (cf. Appendix D.5). They, too, have linked Manlius to Johannes Menlin as was hypothesized in 9.2.2. Additionally, in an addendum (p. 624) to vol. II of the *Basler Matrikel*, the editors include two

---

[8] This year is clearly an error on the part of the Basler Matrikel editors, who were searching a great number of other matriculation lists and other genealogical records for as many alumni as possible as part of their stated purpose: "möglichst alle Studierenden, die einst an der Basler Universität immatrikuliert gewesen waren, genau zu identifizieren" (vol. I, 1951, p. VII). Consequently, they likely came upon Jo. Menlin in the *Register*, i.e. vol. III of AAV, which was organized by the editors for ease of finding the true entries in vols. I and II. There, the names are listed alphabetically, with three indicators given: volume number (blank for vol. I or "II" for vol. II), page number, column ("a" or "b") and a position ordinal. The registry entry for "Manlius, Jo." is "257b,11", i.e. vol. I, p. 257 column b, no. 11.

On the last page of the register is the "Gegenüberstellung der Jahres- und Seitenzahlen", a table listing page ranges next to their associated academic years. In several cases, an academic year had gone by with no new students having matriculated. Such was the case in Wittenberg for the year 1547-1548. Consequently, the year range given for pages 236-242 is 1546-1548, the year range associated with the page range. However, once "Johannes Menlin" is located in vol. I, it is clear that his entry occurs under the year 1546 with the date "8 Ian." beside it. Not far after Menlin's name, a new section begins for the school year starting August 1548.

further spellings—"Männlein, Mendlein"—that corroborate my earlier appeal to the diminutive nature of the name. They also provide further information tracking Manlius' movements: "1558 4. VIII. m. a. Wittenberg – 1564 S Leipzig.[9] – Pfarrer: 1565 Langenzenn; 1569 Wiesentheid." Thus, as suspected, Manlius was present at Wittenberg as late as 4 August 1558, the date of his graduation as *magister artium*. In other words, Manlius was present as a student at Wittenberg prior to Melanchthon's death in 1560. More revealing, however, is the fact that he was a student there also in 1546, i.e. well before anticipated. That Manlius was at Wittenberg for 12 years is unexpected, but not unheard of. He may well have left and returned to his studies during this period.

9.2.2.3 Return to Mittelfranken

According to Jöcher, Manlius set off on a tour of Europe after 1563 to collect the letters Melanchthon had sent out to acquaintances over his lifetime. Supposedly, from these he published *Epistolarum* (1565), also printed in Basel. Yet, according to the addendum in the *Basler Matrikel*, Manlius enrolled at Leipzig in the summer of 1564. Indeed, Kohnle has discovered evidence that Manlius was presumed to be in Wittenberg in 1563, but went missing after traveling about the region to sell his *Locorum communium collectanea* (p. 7). Kohnle cites from Theodor Wotschke (1927) a statement from a letter written by Paul Eber about Manlius' activities around this time. Eber had been charged with reporting to Count Georg Friedrich of Brandenburg-Ansbach about the recipients of ducal scholarships for attendance at Wittenberg. Manlius was apparently one of Eber's charges[10] (Kohnle 2009, p. 7):

> Der für die Ansbacher Stipendiaten zuständige Paul Eber in Wittenberg erstattete nämlich am 19. September 1563 an Markgraf Georg Friedrich von Brandenburg-Ansbach einen Bericht, in dem es heißt, Magister Johnanes Menlin sei derzeit nicht in Wittenberg anwesend, und dann wörtlich: *welcher mit seinem Buch im Land unzieht und ihm dasselb nütz machet mit Versäumnis der Studien. Weiß jetzt niemand, wo er ist ...*

---

[9] Indeed: "Manlius Ioh. Onoltzpacen. m. Vitebergen. 6 gr. i S 1564" (*Die Jüngere Matrikel der Universität Leipzig*, p. 279).
[10] Cf. Gößner (2003).

Consequent to his giving up his studies, Manlius' scholarship was revoked.

Kohnle presumes that ca. 1565 the Count must have had reason to forbid Manlius from printing any more of his Melanchthon-themed books after these were openly criticized. Around this same time, Caspar Peucer (1525–1602), then Wittenberg rector and himself also a publisher of Melanchthon anecdotes, complained to the Count about a dire lack of material left among the Melanchthon letters. Of course, this might have been due to Manlius' 1565 publication of *Epistolorum*. Perhaps Manlius made an enemy of Peucer by beating him to the punch or even stealing material from the collection. Whatever the situation, it seems that Manlius gave up publishing shortly after this. His final published words were penned by him on 6 April 1565—the dedication to a German version of *Locorum communium collectanea* translated by Johann Huldreich Ragor printed in Frankfurt, but not until 1574.

In 1565 Manlius appears back home in Mittelfranken, where his presence in the general area is more or less accounted for over the next six years. Kohnle suspects the censoring of Manlius because of the proximity of *Epistolorum* and Peucer's complaint. Such censoring would have had a financial implication for Manlius, who had already lost his scholarship support. Kohnle cites debt as the motivation behind Manlius' move. Indeed Simon (1955) indicates that Manlius was in a significant amount of debt (approx. 243 Gulden[11]). Hence, Manlius must have made use of his connections at home to come by a paying position, which he fills in 1565 in Langenzenn. This corresponds to the "Pfarrer" post noted by the *Basler*

---

[11] Equal to 121½ Speciesthaler, the international standard currency of the time. In 1566, 1 Speciesthaler = 29.23 g silver (889/1000 fineness [Simons 2008: "Reichsthaler"]). Thus, 243 Gulden (fl.) = 7102.89 g silver. For comparison, the average daily wage of a building laborer in 1566 Augsburg was 3 g silver (IISH: Allen); that of an agricultural worker in 1566 Frankfurt (Main) was 4.23 g silver (IISH: Elsas). Assuming the unlikely measure of 365 days of work per year, the two workers could expect a max. yearly salary of ca. 37.5 Speciesthl. (74.9 fl.) and ca. 52.8 Speciesthl. (105.6 fl.), respectively. Thus, Manlius' debt was more than double the max. yearly salary for the average farmer from Middle Germany.

For comparison of purchasing power, 1 fl. in 1566 was roughly equivalent to €31 or $44 in 2010 (IISH: Calculator; USD:EUR exchange rate listed on 2 November 2010 [Google Finance]). Thus, Manlius' debt was roughly equivalent in purchasing power to €7489 or $10518 when adjusted to for inflation to 2010 values (IISH: Calculator).

Thus, whether compared to the double of an average worker's salary in modern times or to its relative purchasing power in 2010, Manlius' debt of 243 Gulden was indeed a significant value in his own time.

Matrikel editors, which Kohnle clarifies to be a "Kanzlei", a chaplaincy—i.e. an extraterritorial pastoralist over a certain segment of society, e.g. hospital patients, the elderly, etc.

After only a year at Langenzenn, Manlius moves yet again. Kohnle cites unprinted materials toward his conclusion that the Langenzenn post did not bring in enough income for Manlius. The move was thus a second money-motivated decision for Manlius, who took over the parish in Wiesenbronn near Castell. Two more years of unfulfilled expectations were likely the impetus for a third move in 1569, this time only 6 km away to the parish in Wiesentheid, noted also in the *Basler Matrikel*. Finally, on 15 February 1571, in keeping with his capricious nature, Manlius requested that the Counts of Castell transfer him to a better parish or allow him to leave freely. Coincidentally, Jöcher also mentions that a brother of Manlius' took a clerical post in Kitzingen (ca. 15 km west of Castell) in 1570. It would be no surprise if it were discovered that Manlius was personally responsible for his brother's good fortune. From this point on, however, Manlius is lost to history.

9.2.2.4 A New Life in Slovenia

The 1571 request made by Manlius is the last known indication of the man traceable to Wittenberg as Melanchthon's student, to Basel as both student and publisher of *Locorum communium collectanea*, and to Leipzig/Wittenberg as the graduate school drop-out/wandering book salesman. Kohnle makes a convincing argument—first suggested by Boris Bálent (Borsa 1979)—that our Ioannes Manlius was the same character as Hans Mandl presented above (9.2.1.1). Indeed, Hans Mandl first appears on the historical radar in 1575 (ADB, vol. 20, p. 176–178):

> Zwar lautet ein „Beschluß" der Herren der krainischen Landschaft vom 21. April 1575, an welche M[andl] seine „Supplication" gerichtet, „Ime zu vergünstigen, ainen Druckh auff seine vnkosten vnd Verlag alhie anzurichten", ablehnend: „nachdem auß allerhand bewegungen mit fürthuenlich noch Ime Supplikanten für nutzlich befunden wirdt alhie ainiche Buchdruckerey auffzurichten demnach so wissen die bey gegenwärtigen hoffthäding versambleten Herrn vnd Landleut in def; Supplikanten begehren nit zu bewilligen", aber dieser Schluß muß doch noch in demselben Jahre eine Reformation erfahren haben, denn es erschien (die Vorrede ist datirt vom 11. Oktober 1575) in seiner Druckerei zu Laibach 1575 als erstes in Krain gedrucktes Buch eine slovenische Uebersetzung des Jesus Sirach.

The connection between Manlius and Mandl is tenuous, and suffers from a lacuna of four years. Nevertheless, the two men share a number of personal characteristics and associates that make the interpretation seem probable that both identities are the same individual.

Manlius, having graduated with his M.A. from Wittenberg in autumn 1558, must have been present at that university for several years prior. This would mean that his time there overlapped with another man of influence in the Slovenian sphere: Hans Ungnad Freiherr von Sonneck (1493–1564). Ungnad was a fiery statesman in the Hapsburg circle, noted for his furiousness against the Turks. He was raised in the court of Emperor Maximilian I. In 1519, he accompanied a retinue of Hapsburgs on a visit to their Spanish relatives at the occurrence of Charles V Imperial enthronement. By 1530, he was made governor of Styria and regent at Celje (near Ljubljana). That same year he attended the Imperial Diet at Augsburg, and hearing the cause of the Protestants, was converted to it in heart and soul. In 1541, as "Oberster Feldhauptmann" (a title earned through his accomplishments during the first Turkish Siege of Vienna), he pleaded for the allowance from King Ferdinand to convert officially, which the staunch Catholic liege promptly refused. Ungnad made his request twice more, in 1548 and 1556, appealing the last time to the 1555-established Peace of Augsburg treaty. The Hapsburg King's retort mimicked the "cujus regio, eius religio" with the addendum "wem diese nicht gefalle, dem stehe es frei Hab und Gut zu verkaufen und anderswohin zu ziehen" (ADB). Ungnad followed the last remark literally and left with hearth and home for Wittenberg. He remained there for two years, during which he enjoyed the friendship of Melanchthon. During this time he must have also become acquainted with Ioannes Manlius. Serving as evidence toward this is the preface to Ragor's German translation of *Locorum communium collectanea* (1574), which preface Manlius had penned in 1565. In it, he dedicates the book to two men, one being Ludwig Ungnad (1530–1607), son of Hans Ungnad, likely in an attempt to attract him as a patron, since by this time the Ungnad family's new venture in Württemberg had become successful and Manlius was still in debt.

Ca. 1558, Hans Ungnad and family left Upper Saxony for Württemberg due to the tensions of the Adiaphorist Controversy[12]. The family took up

---

[12] The same tensions that ruined Chemnitz' friendship with Melanchthon.

residence at an unused monastery in Urach, where Hans established a printer's shop where he began printing Reformation materials in Slovenian and Croatian. Ungnad acquired funding for his press through a cunning maneuver: he appealed not only to his Württemburgian patron Duke Christoph and other Protestant princes, but also to the future Emperor Maximilian II to support the creation of typeset in Cyrillic (actually Glagolitic). Thus, he keenly manipulated a Catholic Hapsburg to defray the cost of printing Protestant material for a mission to the Slavs. The Carniolan Reformer Primus Truber (Primož Trubar; 1508–1586), a native of Celje and translator of the first Slovenian translation of the New Testament, came to Ungnad in 1560 to ask him to print his Bible. Furthermore, a young Slovenian named Leonhard Maraula (Maravlja) trained at Ungnad's press while attending the University of Tübingen. Maraula surfaced in the late 1570s at Hans Mandl's press and bookshop in Ljubljana—the first Slovenian printing press.

Mandl had been printing in Ljubljana since 1575, putting out Slovenian, Croatian, German, Italian and Latin books. Among these was a translation of Spangenberg's 1544 *Postille*. Cyriacus Spangenberg (1528–1604) attended Wittenberg, studying under the direction of Melanchthon from 1544 to 1547, after which he graduated at age 19 as a *magister*. It is possible, then, that Manlius (i.e. Menlin) became acquainted with Spangenberg in the former's first year at university. Mandl's printing of Spangenberg in translation might therefore be seen as a throwback to his old college days, and thereby provide the link between Mandl and Manlius. Moreover, after Mandl's forced closure in 1582, his associate Maraula appears enrolled at Wittenberg the following year. Perhaps Mandl's connections to that University as Manlius can account for this.

A second famous work printed by Mandl in Ljubljana is the publication of the first part of Dalmatin's Bible in Slovenian. Jurij (Georg) Dalmatin (1547–1589) was a native of Ljubljana who attended secondary school in Tübingen 1565–1566 and attended university in the same city 1566–1572, where he was the student of Primus Truber, the aforementioned translator of the New Testament in Slovenian. Dalmatin began translating the Book of Genesis from the Old Testament in 1572. That same year he was anointed as priest in Ljubljana. In 1578, Dalmatin's full Bible translation was printed on Mandl's press. It was printed in full 1584 in Wittenberg. This timing corresponds with Maraula's appearance at Wittenberg, where it is known that he worked on an edition of Dalmatin's Bible translation (cf. Dimitz 1883).

Kohnle cites Borsa in calculating 30 known works printed by Mandl in Ljubljana between 1575 and 1580. Of these 14 are in German, four in Latin, one in Croatian and 11 in Slovenian. Mandl not only printed books, he also sold them from a bookshop opened in 1575, which likely carried books from abroad. Moreover, Mandl produced "Gelegenheitsschrifttum genealogischer Art, lateinische Hochzeitsgedichte und Nachrichten über den Türkenkrieg," much of which was apparently created by Mandl himself. In other words, the entrepreneur book salesman was more than the average businessman, rather highly educated. Moreover, he was industrious—which quality can be interpreted as a kind of directed capriciousness for which Manlius was apparently known. Manlius turned quickly to selling his books while wandering the land. This entrepreneurial spirit might have translated equally as well into a do-it-yourself attitude that would have driven him to print books on his own. Money seems also to have been a motivation, and the printing press in the mid-sixteenth century was a money-maker. A network of individuals links Mandl from Ljubljana to Tübingen and Urach and northward to Wittenberg; similarly, Manlius is linked to Wittenberg, Basel, and Franconia. The motive and circumstantial evidence leans toward identifying Mandl as Manlius; only the smoking-gun evidence is lacking. In short, moving out of the Holy Roman Empire to an Austrian territory might have seemed to Manlius like a chance to start over.

9.2.2.5 Banishment from Hapsburg Lands

The final chapter in the Mandl saga—and therefore possibly that of Manlius as well—begins ca. 1580, by which time Mandl was in trouble with the powers-that-be in the Austrian lands (ADB):

> Leider war dem Geschäfte dieses tüchtigen Mannes, der in dem kurzen Zeitraume von fünf Jahren gegen zwanzig größere und kleinere Schriften publicirt hatte, nur eine kurze Dauer beschieden: antikatholische Flugschriften, durch unbefugte Colporteure durch das Land verbreitet, mußten den Grund hergeben, daß auch seine Druckerei und Buchhandel verdächtigt und verfolgt wurden. Den nächsten greifbaren Anlaß hiezu gab M[andl] durch die Herstellung und Ausgabe der evangelischen Schriften in windischer Sprache und ganz besonders wegen des Druckes der windischen Bibel Dalmatin's.

Thus, a somewhat flippant attitude landed Mandl in trouble, another characteristic that ties him to Manlius. Archduke of Austria Charles II banished Mandl on 13 October 1581 and again on 30 December 1581 (ADB). In 1582 Mandl relinquished his press into other hands. On 8 April 1582, the Carniolan Parliament decided to award Mandl 50 Gulden in compensation, "weil er ein Bürger ist." At this point the ADB record loses track of the wandering book-printer. Kohnle suggests that Mandl had gained citizenship in Ljubljana as early as 1580. Kohnle also mentions an invitation Mandl received to go to Württemberg (Semmelweis 1972). Instead, after appealing his banishment at Graz, Mandl moves to Güssing in western Hungary (now Austria), where the Protestant Stephan Beythe, court chaplain to the Batthyány, took him in. Baron Balthasar Batthyány then made use of him as his book and manuscript collector, turning Güssing into a center of Humanism in Hungary. Kohnle produces a list of known localities in which Mandl surfaces until his presumed death in 1604/1605: Güssing (1582–1585), Varaždin (1586/1587), Eberau (1587–1589), Güssing (1589), Eberau (1590–1592), Deutsch-Schützen (1592–1593), Güssing (1595–1597), Deutschkreuz (i.e. Criț, Romania; 1598–1599), Sárvár (1600), Deutschkreuz (1601), Sárvár (1602), Deutschkreuz (1603–1605).

9.3 Implications of Manlius-Menlin-Mandl

However one looks at the evidence provided toward identifying Manlius, one thing is certain and unarguable: it is known from Manlius' books that he was a student and that he published classroom material attributed to Melanchthon. Moreover, the *Basler Matrikel* links the author of these books to the student Johannes Menlin, who matriculated at Wittenberg in 1546 and graduated with an M.A. in 1558. Assuming the typical age range for a university student, Manlius was likely 17–20 years old at the time of his matriculation at Wittenberg. This translates to a birth year some time after 1525. If Manlius and Mandl are indeed the same individual, he would have been between 77 and 80 years old at his death in ca. 1605. A lifespan of this length was not unexpected for this period, as can be seen from the age of some of Manlius' peers at their deaths: Spangenberg (76), Ludwig Ungnad (77), and Peucer (77).

The resources discussed describe Manlius as a student of Melanchthon's. Considering the connection between Melanchthon and a Leipzig *monotessaron* as offered by Chemnitz (cf. Ch 8), it is not wholly unreasonable to expect that Manlius heard Melanchthon speak about seeing the Leipzig *monotessaron* in a manner much like Chemnitz claims to have. Coincidentally, Johannes Menlin's matriculation at Wittenberg in 1546 puts him at that university concurrent with Chemnitz. Perhaps, then, the two men were reporting the same event.

Hannemann proposes 1555 as the date for Manlius' TE—specifically "zunächst 1555", implying that no earlier date is possible for Manlius' reported RE (and, therefore, neither for Manlius' TE). From this, it can be assumed that Hannemann interprets the RE as having occurred some time between 1555 and the 1562 printing of *Locorum communium collectanea*. Hannemann bases his estimate on what is known about Melanchthon's lecture series on Louis the Pious and this emperor's role in world history. Melanchthon began these lectures in July 1555 (Hannemann 1939, pg. 328; Eichoff/Rauch, pg. 5; cf. Hannemann 1974, pg. 53), and they continued until his death in April 1560. Though based thus on established historical fact, there is a weakness to Hannemann's estimate, namely that he focuses on Melanchthon as the reference point. This approach is problematic: it relies on only one reference point—and the wrong reference point at that. The source of the rumor as we have it is not Melanchthon, but Manlius. Moreover, the report at the heart of that rumor mentions nothing about Melanchthon. That connection has been ascribed to it from elsewhere.

A different interpretation develops when one attempts to date the RE by focusing on Manlius: (1) the publication date (1562) of *Locorum communium collectanea*—and not Melanchthon's death in 1560—provides a *terminus non post quem* for the TE; (2) the discovery of Manlius as Johannes Menlin provides a range of time stretching back to 1546, placing him there in relative proximity—both in space and time—to the date established for *F; (3) Manlius' presence at Wittenberg in 1546 means that his time there overlapped with that of Martin Chemnitz, the other source of the Leipzig *monotessaron* rumor. Thus, the year range 1546–1562 becomes the working time window for Manlius' TE and RE.

Strangely, Hannemann ignores the possibility that the two men were both witnesses to the same event. Instead, he sees Manlius as the only witness to Melanchthon's claim. Moreover, he refuses to see that event happening before 1555. Since Chemnitz' *Harmoniae evangelicae* (1593) was published after Manlius' *Locorum communium collectanea* (1562), Hannemann concludes that Chemnitz was either just referencing or even outright copying Manlius' story. This is a strange conclusion, since (1) it ignores all evidence prior to 1555, (2) Manlius is rather clear about stating that his source was not Melanchthon, and (3) Chemnitz is very explicit in attributing his information to Melanchthon. Thus, Hannemann's deduction is paradoxical: it values the *monotessaron* information provided, but completely discounts the reporters' statements regarding their sources.

A close analysis of Chemnitz' (Ch. 10) and Manlius' (Ch. 11) language will be the focus of Part III. In this analysis, evidence will be extracted from the men's own language toward establishing when the men first penned their *monotessaron* reports. Since the RE necessarily followed the TE for both reporters, pinning down a date for the former will yield a *terminus non post quem* for the latter. These dates will reflect a relationship between Luther's lifetime and the presence of the Fabricius codex at Leipzig, thereby suggesting that Luther's knowledge of the same document was quite probable.

Part IV:

Dating and Verifying the Rumor Reports

10. Chemnitz' Report Dissected

10.1 Significance for Dating the Rumors

The language of Chemnitz' report provides critical evidence about the timing of two events:

1. A transfer event (TE)
2. A recording event (RE)

The TE indicates the time at which Chemnitz heard Melanchthon claim to have seen a *monotessaron* in Leipzig that invoked Louis the Pious. The RE indicates the time at which Chemnitz wrote his memory of the TE in his otherwise un-datable (and missing) manuscript *Harmonia quatuor Evangelistarum*.[1] Chemnitz' report is important because it is one of the two earliest sources currently known from which we can now expect that the Luther *Heliand* rumors were promulgated. The problem with Chemnitz' report is that it was first printed in 1693, both several years after the author's death and several decades after Melanchthon died (1560). It seems that much scholarship has overlooked the historical timing of events necessary for Chemnitz' report to be true. The following linguistic analysis elucidates the timing of events surrounding Chemnitz' RE and TE.

10.2 Published Report

In his *Harmoniae evangelicae* report, Chemnitz records what appears to be a first-person encounter, i.e., that he heard Melanchthon's claim firsthand (p. 13):

> Memini D. Philippum dicere, se vidisse monotessaron, sumptibus Ludouici Pii compositum, quod existimet in bibliotheca Lipsica haberi.
>
> I remember Dr. Philipp [Melanchthon] say that he has seen a monotessaron, composed at the expense of Louis the Pious, which [he, i.e. Melanchthon] reckons is being held at the Leipzig library.

---

[1] The basis for Part I of *Harmoniae evangelicae* (1693).

Chemnitz' description of the TE is in the form of a personal memory. If the tense of the verbs in Chemnitz' statement provide any indication of timing his TE must have occurred while Melanchthon was still alive. Some confusion arises because of Chemnitz' combined use of a defective verb[2] of reporting (*memini*)[3] with successive dependent clauses containing infinitival verb forms (*dicere, vidisse,* and *haberi*) with subjects (*Dr. Philippum, se,* and *quod*) in the accusative case. This grammatical phenomenon is an example of the well-known Latin indirect statement, also called *Accusativus cum Infinitivo* (AcI).[4]

Three recurring instantiations of AcI have the effect of obfuscating the timing of events in Chemnitz' statement.[5] Consequently, any translation from the Latin into a language that is less permissive of the AcI structure (e.g. German and English) must re-establish the temporal relationships implied by the author.[6] The English translation printed above reveals an ordering of events that disproves Hannemann's aforementioned claim that Chemnitz' knowledge of the Leipzig *monotessaron* was merely a reprinting of Manlius' report on the same document.

10.2.1 *Clusivity*: Chemnitz as an 'Eyewitness'

It is important to note that the semantics of *memini* involve certain specific implications. In particular, these regard the relationship of the reporter to the reported information, so-called *clusivity*. Charlton Lewis and Charles Short sum this relationship up nicely in their dictionary entry for the verb in question (1879, pp. 1129-1130):

---

[2] Baermann describes this as "a mismatch between form and function" (p. 1).
[3] A "verb of [...] thinking" (Jones & Sidwell, p. 534) that, though "Perfect in form, [is] Present in sense" (Bennet, §133.2).
[4] "When words are not quoted direct[ly] but given in reported form [...], Latin [...] [u]ses the accusative and the infinitive to express indirect statements [...]" (Jones & Sidwell, p. 533-34, also Notes 1 and 2).
[5] "The tenses of the Infinitive denote time not absolutely, but with reference to the verb on which they depend. Thus [...] [t]he Present Infinitive represents an act as contemporaneous with the time of the verb on which it depends [...]" (Bennet, §270.1a).
[6] For the usage of the defective verb *memini* with AcI constructions, cf. Lewis & Short, 1129-30.

mĕmĭni, isse, v. n. [...] **7** With acc. and *inf.* **(a)** With *pres. inf.* (so usually of the direct memory of an eyewitness): [...] — **(b)** With *inf. perf.* (so usu. when the subject is not an eye-witness; esp. with second and third persons of memini): [...]

Without calling it such, the dictionary editors describe the usage of this verb as the independent verb in an AcI construction (i.e. "with *pres. inf.*", "with *inf. perf.*"). Moreover, they provide the means by which to determine whether the speaker was directly involved in the action being remembered or not. That is, the distinction in speaker-subject's *clusivity* can be deduced from the infinitival form used for the dependent verb, namely: the *present infinitive* implies the speaker is an eyewitness to the event at which he heard what he now offers as indirect speech, while the *infinitive perfect* would be used for hearsay information only, i.e., that the speaker-subject was not present at the event in question and only knew of it through a third person.

Lewis & Short's explanation is a revelation with direct impact on the interpretation of Chemnitz' *monotessaron* report: Chemnitz reveals that he personally heard Melanchthon's claim of seeing the Leipzig *monotessaron*. He does so by his use of the present infinitive *dicere* and not the infinitive perfect *dixisse*: "Memini D. Philippum dicere, [...]". With this in mind, no reasonable argument can be made to support Hannemann's interpretation that Chemnitz was either passing along second-hand information or that he copied his information from another source, e.g. Manlius. On the contrary, Chemnitz must have been present physically when Melanchthon claimed to have seen the Leipzig *monotessaron* and revealed that document's presumed whereabouts.

10.2.2 Finite Equivalents to Latin Infinitives

Chemnitz' indirect quotation of what Melanchthon said begins after the first comma "Memini D. Philippum dicere, se vidisse monotessaron, [...]." The first item of interest in the indirect quote is "vidisse", the perf. inf. act. form of *video*. Similar to *dicere* above, *vidisse* is an infinitival form and thus is not inflected for tense. Consequently, the truncated statement is roughly equivalent to "I remember D. Philipp tell of himself having seen a monotessaron, [...]." Taken as such, it is only clear that Melanchthon saw the document prior to telling Chemnitz (and prior to Chemnitz remembering). This is hardly anything out of the ordinary. All the same, within this quote are small but significant clues that act as evidence of the timing of when Chemnitz wrote his report.

As stated by Bennett, the three Latin infinitival forms "denote time [...] *with reference to the verb on which they depend*" (Cf. previous footnote, emphasis mine). Since the Latin infinitive comes in only three temporal varieties, it can only connote relative timing: an action *prior to* (perfect infinitive), *contemporaneous with* (present infinitive), or *subsequent to* (future infinitive) the action expressed by the independent verb.

The perfective active infinitive *vidisse* "represents an act as *prior to* the time of the verb on which it depends." Yet determining the relative timing of *vidisse* is complicated by the fact that the independent verb upon which it depends i.e. *dicere*, is itself an infinitival form (cf. 10.1.1). It has already been established that "dicere" is dependent upon and references the timing of "Memini", and that although the *memini* is perfective in form, it conveys a sense of the present. It is hardly surprising that the order of events conveyed in Chemnitz' report entails the following order: (1) Melanchthon saw the *monotessaron*, then (2) he told Chemnitz about it, and finally, (3) Chemnitz remembered this discussion and wrote it down. This much is fairly obvious; the surprising element comes from what is *not* implied by the perfective infinitival form.

It is important to note what the perfective infinitival verb form can not do. When the independent verb (*dicere*) in the AcI construction conveys the present, the dependent verb (*vidisse*) is unable to express the concept of a "more distant past," i.e. anything resembling the pluperfect tense. Had Chemnitz intended the sense of the pluperfect for "vidisse", he would have expressed that function periphrastically, i.e. through the use of a separate clause with finite verb form, e.g. pluperf. act. subj.: "quod [...] vidissem monotessaron" ("that [...] he *had* seen a *monotessaron* [...]"). This is clearly not what Chemnitz wrote.

Since Chemnitz did not use a finite form like the one suggested above, one must conclude that he used the perfective infinitival form *vidisse* deliberately, i.e., because that form expresses precisely the sense that he intended: "[...] he *has* seen a *monotessaron* [...]." Clearly, Melanchthon was still alive when Chemnitz learned of the Leipzig document. This serves as further evidence disproving Hannemann's belief that Chemnitz was merely relaying what he had read in Manlius' writings.

10.2.3 The Extended Modifier

The next syntactic element in Chemnitz' report is the extended modifier "sumptibus Ludovico Pii compositum", which is essentially a drawn-out adjective. The head of this clausal adjective is the past participle *compositum*, which is built from the verbal stem and conveys the passive voice (but no tense). The Latin past participle is equivalent in function to that of both English and German. The usage of a past participle in an extended modifier is common in German; however, its usage is much more reduced in English—especially when the extended modifier involves more than just the verbal adjective and one other adverbial and/or nominal argument. Such is the case with Chemnitz' Latin, thus the English translation is unable to handle the extended modifier in the equivalent formulation, rather it requires the clause to be postposed in a relative clause: "[monotessaron], which was composed at the cost of Louis the Pious". Due to its case-marking morphology, German readily handles even lengthy extended modifiers with multiple arguments, etc., yielding the translation: "auf Kosten Ludwigs des Frommen verfasstes [Monotessaron]".

10.2.4 Triangulating the *monotessaron*, Melanchthon, and Leipzig

The final clause of Chemnitz' report, i.e., "quod existimet in bibliotheca Lipsica haberi" is in fact two clauses: "existimet" is the verb of the independent clause, and "haberi" is the verb of the dependent clause. As an infinitival form (present passive infinitive of *habeo*) *haberi* expresses temporality only in reference to the tense of the verb in the preceding independent clause, i.e. *existimet*.

The form *existimet* is the present active subjunctive form for third person singular. The subjunctive indicates that the clause is subordinate to a preceding clause—i.e., the clause headed by the verb *dicere*—much like the infinitival forms discussed previously, except that *existimet* '[that] he reckons'[7] does provide tense. Chemnitz' use of this particular verb form is indicative: Melanchthon was still alive as Chemnitz put his pen to page.

---

[7] The clearest way to express the function of the Latin subjunctive in English is through the use of a conjunction in association with a finite verb. German allows for something a bit closer to the original Latin structure ('er schätze'), i.e. a clause unpreceded by a conjunction but headed by a verb in the subjunctive mood (e.g. Konjunktiv I).

The presence of the present infinitive passive *haberi* is somewhat problematic, since neither English nor German has infinitival forms that can express relative tense (cf. 10.1.1) or voice, e.g. passive. In both English and German, the passive voice is indicated via periphrastic construction (i.e. English: *to be* + past part.; German: *werden* + past part.). Thus, a combination of the translation method used for *dicere* with the English and German periphrastic passive formulation is required: Latin *haberi* is equivalent to English 'to be had' and German 'gehabt zu werden'. An alternate translation of Latin *habeo*, particularly in the passive is 'to hold', i.e. 'to be held', 'aufbewahrt zu werden'. Moreover, because *haberi* occurs in an AcI construction, the tense originally associated with Melanchthon's utterance is obscured. All that remains is a hint of tense relative to the independent verb (cf. 10.1.1). Indeed, a very crucial detail—a second clue regarding when the *monotessaron* was present in Leipzig—is highlighted by converting these translated verbs into finite forms in English. In this case, *haberi* depends upon *existimet* (pres. subj. act. 3ps) '[that] [he] reckons [...]'. The same effect of *haberi* can be expressed in English as 'is held' or 'is being held'. The two options exist because English divides the present tense into simple present (i.e. perfective aspect) and progressive/continuous present (i.e. imperfective aspect). I would argue for the progressive reading ('is being held'), since it seems to fit better in juxtaposition with Chemnitz' usage of *memini* 'I remember' and *vidisse* "he has seen" (cf. 10.1.2). Overall, Chemnitz use of *haberi* provides another important clue: the *monotessaron* was present in Leipzig at the time of the RE.

Taken together, the two clues provided by this analysis reveal a wealth of information: as Chemnitz wrote, the still-living Melanchthon reckoned that the *monotessaron* was still being held at Leipzig:

> Memini D. Philippum dicere, se vidisse monotessaron, sumptibus Ludouici Pii compositum, quod existimet in bibliotheca Lipsica haberi.

> I remember Dr. Philipp say that he has seen a monotessaron, composed at the expense of Louis the Pious, which he reckons is being held at the Leipzig library.

> Ich erinnere mich daran, D. Philipp sagen zu hören, er habe ein auf Kosten Ludwigs des Frommen verfasstes Monotessaron gesehen, [und] er schätze, es wird in der Leipziger Bibliothek aufbewahrt.

That is, all three events are contemporaneous: (1) Chemnitz' RE, (2) Melanchthon being alive, and (3) the *monotessaron* being held at the Leipzig library (at least according to Melanchthon's reckoning).

10.3 Conclusions about Chemnitz' Report

That Chemnitz is speaking about a still-living Melanchthon means that Chemnitz' RE must have occurred prior to Melanchthon's death in 1560. His report also indicates that the *monotessaron* was present at Leipzig prior to his RE. Therefore, 19 April 1560 acts as a working *terminus ante quem* for both Chemnitz' RE and the presence of *Ch at the Leipzig library (i.e. the *Paulinum*). Furthermore, this date bears important significance for the discussion of Manlius in Chapter 11, because Manlius' report of the *monotessaron* was not published until 1562. Yet Hannemann (1939, p. 6) argues that Chemnitz merely copied his report from Manlius'. The *terminus ante quem* presented above proves that Chemnitz could not have learned of the Leipzig *monotessaron* from Manlius' book, nor copied the idea from it.

Moreover, when comparing the proposed *terminus ante quem* of 19 April 1560 to the historical evidence of Chemnitz' relationship with Melanchthon as discussed in Chapter 8, it is possible to deduce an even earlier date for Chemnitz' RE. Melanchthon's lecture series on Louis the Pious' role in world history occurred between July 1555 and April 1560. Although this would have been a perfect setting for Melanchthon to mention his experience with the Leipzig *monotessaron*, it can not have been the setting at which Chemnitz heard of it (TE). This is because Chemnitz was no longer a student or faculty member of the University of Wittenberg when Melanchthon's course was taking place. Rather, Chemnitz had left Wittenberg eight months before Melanchthon's university course began. Also, Melanchthon must have prepared for his course prior to July 1555, and very well could have—and truly must have—learned about the *monotessaron* prior to the start of the course. The question then is "how much earlier?"

Chemnitz makes it clear that he heard of the *monotessaron* from Melanchthon directly, i.e. not as a rumor via a third party. Chemnitz' closest and most durative contact with Melanchthon occurred in Wittenberg over two periods, namely as a student from early 1545 to mid-May 1547 and as a doctoral student/instructor from late-April 1553 to late-November 1554. This last date seems recent enough to suggest that Melanchthon could have been preparing material for his course before Chemnitz left Wittenberg for Braunschweig. Yet there is one more piece of evidence to suggest that Melanchthon was aware of the Leipzig *monotessaron* much earlier: in Chapter 4, it was shown that Fabricius wrote four letters in 1545 (7 January, 16 August, 24 November, and 18 December) indicating that a "doubtless Germanic manuscript" with a "Latin preface" had been "donated to the Paulinum collection in Leipzig". Implicated in the knowledge of the existence of this document was C. Borner, the first Head Librarian and one of the three founders of the *Paulinum*-housed UBL, established in 1543. There were two other founders: J. Camerarius and P. Melanchthon.

If Borner knew of *F prior to 7 January 1545, can there be any doubt about whether Melanchthon knew of it also? Furthermore, considering that Chemnitz must have heard Melancthon speak about the Leipzig-housed, Louis the Pious-commissioned *monotessaron* at some point in early (April?) 1545, can there be any serious doubt that *F was not the same document as *Ch?

We know from Chemnitz that the Leipzig *monotessaron* was originally commissioned by Louis the Pious. On the other hand, we know that Fabricius' document had a Germanic part and a Latin Preface. Moreover, we know that later he gave to Illyricus what was printed as the Latin *Prefaces* in 1562. Finally, we know that nowhere in the Old Saxon *Heliand* is there a mention of Louis the Pious. Rather, that information—and the story of the commissioning and composition of the attached Germanic verse, divided into "vitteas", i.e. *fitts*—comes only from the *Prefaces*. Chemnitz therefore tells us something he could not have known otherwise: *Ch = *F. Consequently, the Leipzig *monotessaron* was a full codex, containing both the *Prefaces* and the *Heliand* epic together as one.

11. Clues from Manlius

11.1 Differential between Two Rumor Reports

In discussing his assumption that the event recorded by Manlius took place no earlier than 1555, Hannemann states the following about the source of Martin Chemnitz' report (328; also Eichhoff & Rauch, 6):

> Chemnitz hatte 1545–47 und 1553–1554 in Wittenberg studiert und sich des nahen Umgangs mit Melanchthon erfreut. So könnte er aus dem Munde des Lehrers im Privatgespräch schon vor 1555 vom Leipziger Heliand gehört haben. Auf persönliche Erinnerung scheint das Memini zu deuten. Allerdings nähert sich „sumptibus" [aus Chemnitz' Vorbericht] bedenklich dem Ausdruck Manlius': magno sumptu, so daß man vermuten könnte, der Theologe Chemnitz verdanke die Nachricht erst Manlius, der später ausgeschrieben wurde.

Despite recognizing that Chemnitz would have likely heard Melanchthon make his claim prior to 1555 (cf. 8.2.1), and despite noting the personal nature of Chemnitz' account (cf. 8.2.3), Hannemann ultimately discounts Chemnitz' report. Instead, he bases his opinion on a single occurrence of similar language in the two reports, namely (a) Chemnitz' usage of "sumptibus" (*Harmoniae evangelicae*, p. 4) with (b) Manlius' "magno sumptu" (99-100, emphasis mine):

> Et memini D. Philippum dicere, se vidisse Monotessaron, *sumptibus Ludouici Pij compositum*, quod existimet in bibliotheca Lipsica haberi.

> I also remember Dr. Philipp say he had seen a monotessaron, *composed at the expense of Louis the Pious*, which he reckons is being held in the Leipzig library.

> Ludouicus Pius curauit fieri Monotessaron, id est, concordantias quatuor Euangelistarum, *magno sumptu*. Quem librum diu habuit apud se Lutherus, & hodie est in Lipsica bibliotheca. Præfatio est partim Latinis uersibus, ɋ̄ ualde boni sunt, partim prosa oratione, etiã bene et Latinè scripta.

> Louis the Pious saw to it, *at great cost*, that a monotessaron was made, i.e. a harmony of the four Evangelists. Luther had this book with him for a long time, and which today is in the Leipzig library. The preface is partly in Latin verses, which are very good, and partly in prose language, also good and written in Latin.

If the similarity in the two men's language is to be taken as more than mere coincidence, it need not be seen as evidence of copying. Rather, both may very well be citing the original language of a common source, i.e. Melanchthon's own wording. This conclusion would appear to be supported further by the two men's simultaneous presence at Wittenberg. Indeed, Hannemann seems to forget completely that of the two men, it is Chemnitz who states outright that he heard his information from Melanchthon. Furthermore, Hannemann assumes Manlius' source is Melanchthon, even though Manlius gives an indication to the opposite effect (cf. 9.3.4).

To clarify Hannemann's position, his interpretation of the timeline of events can be reconstructed thus:

1. Melanchthon sees the *Heliand* manuscript at Leipzig ca. 1555, perhaps earlier, but certainly in connection with his study of world history and Louis the Pious.
2. In lectures on material gleaned from his study, Melanchthon mentions the Luther-*monotessaron* relationship, citing Louis the Pious as having been the sponsor for the expense of the *Heliand* project.[1]
3. Manlius, still a student of Melanchthon in 1555, faithfully records his teacher's discussions. Manlius eventually puts these notes up for publication while in Basel in 1562, during a stop-over from his travels across Europe to gather the now-deceased Melanchthon's letters for a subsequent publication.
4. Chemnitz reads Manlius' 1563-published *Locorum communium collectanea* and, when penning the Prolegomenon to *Harmonia quatuor evangelistarum* at an unspecified date (nevertheless, assumed by Hannemann to be after 1563; cf. 8.2), takes what he has learned about the *monotessaron* (i.e. Chemnitz' RE) from reading Manlius and attributes this information to Melanchthon. Chemnitz' *Harmonia quatuor evangelistarum* remains an unfinished work after his death in 1586, which is later published in 1593 as Part I *Harmoniae evangelicae* by Polycarp Leyser.

Thus, because Hannemann takes Chemnitz' report to be a derivative of Manlius', he sees *Ch as the same hypothetical document as *L_m. In coming to this conclusion, however, Hannemann ignores a lot of additional evi-

---

[1] A piece of information, by the way, that Melanchthon could have only known from the Latin *Prefaces*.

dence about the timing of the two reporters REs. Ultimately, I agree with his proposition that both hypothetical documents are the same, i.e., that both refer to the same codex present at Leipzig at the time. However, the evidence in 8.3 and 9.4.4 suggests that neither Chemnitz nor Manlius is using one another as a resource, rather that both bore separate witness to the knowledge that they reported.

Regarding the similarity in the language of the two reports: the semantic similarity of one word—Chemnitz' *sumptibus* and Manlius' *sumptu*—is hardly exhaustive proof of copying. Neither is it evidence that the two reporters heard the information from the same source, i.e. Melanchthon. This is because there are only a relatively small number of ways to express the semantic notion of 'at the expense' in Latin.[2] Depending on the size of the group that knew about the Leipzig *monotessaron*, the one expression that roughly coincides between the two reports may be due to the development of an idiomatic expression that was used in description of the *monotessaron* in all circumstances when discussing it. This means that several, if not many, different people could have described the same document using similar terminology over a diffuse time period. That having been said, the minimal indication of similarity between Chemnitz' and Manlius' reports is not enough to assume that both men were present at the TE to hear Melanchthon's claim of having seen the *monotessaron*. Moreover, the two reports differ significantly, since (1) it is only Manlius who links the *monotessaron* to Luther (cf. 9.3.3), and (2) Manlius is relatively clear about stating that his source is *not* Melanchthon (cf. 9.3.4).

11.1.1 Assertions about Luther

Regarding Luther's relationship to the Leipzig *monotessaron* as reported by Manlius, Hannemann states the following (5, emphasis mine):

> [...] eine seit 1562 oft gedruckte Sammlung von Melanchthonanekdoten, die ein Jh. Manlius zusammengestellt hatte, melden von einem Monotessaron, das Ludwig d. Fr. angeregt, Luther *lange besessen* und *eifrig gelesen habe* und das heute, d. h. zunächst etwa 1555, in der Leipziger (Pauliner) Bibliothek sei.

---

[2] Lewis & Short list the following as possibilities: *jactura, onus, pensiatio, sumptus*. Not all of these would necessarily fit with the context of Chemnitz or Manlius (e.g. *onus* = 'a load, a burden, a tax or an expense [usually in the plur.]').

That is, according to Hannemann, Luther not only "possessed", but "diligently/eagerly read" the *Heliand* manuscript. That Hannemann reads more into Manlius' report is clear when one reads the latter's actual language (99-100, emphasis mine):

> Ludouicus Pius curauit fieri Monotessaron, id est, concordantias quatuor Euangelistarum, magno sumptu. Quem librum *diu habuit apud se* **Lutherus**, & hodie est in Lipsica bibliotheca. Præfatio est partim Latinis uersibus, ɋ̃ ualde boni sunt, partim prosa oratione, etiã bene et Latinè scripta.
>
> Louis the Pious saw to it, at great cost, that a monotessaron was made, i.e. a harmony of the four Evangelists. Luther *had this book with him for a long time*, and which today is in the Leipzig library. The preface is partly in Latin verses, which are very good, and partly in prose language, also good and written in Latin.

While Manlius does state that Luther had the *monotessaron* with him, i.e., presumably borrowed from the UBL, he makes no mention of *how* Luther read it, whether diligently, eagerly or not. This additional detail invented by Hannemann has had an effect on scholarship until today; it can be seen repeated in Schmid's announcement for the discovery of MS L reprinted at the beginning of the chapter. It appears that these "facts" have become part of the folklore surrounding the Luther *Heliand*. The fact of the matter is that nowhere yet has there been found any indication of *why* Luther had the *Heliand* or *what* he did with it (cf. 4.2.1.3). Furthermore, Hannemann assumes that the collection of materials printed by Manlius in *Locorum communium collectanea* is completely attributable to Melanchthon.

11.1.2 Anonymous source(s)

As stated previously (cf. 9.3), while Chemnitz explicitly names Melanchthon as the source of his knowledge of *Ch, Manlius is less clear about where his knowledge of *L_m came. In fact, although Hannemann made an outstanding contribution to Germanic studies by linking Fabricius' epistolary comments to the *Prefaces* (Hannemann, 8-13), he ultimately blundered in treating Manlius by assuming Melanchthon-devoted material as the sole focus of *Locorum communium collectanea*. Even the full title[3] of this work

---

[3] *Locorum communium collectanea a Jo. Manlio per multos annos, pleraque tum ex lectionibus D. Philippi Melanchthonis, tum ex aliorum doctissimorum virorum relationibus excerpta, et nuper in ordinem ab eodem redacta etc.* ('A collection of parallel passages gathered over many years by

seems to suggest more than what Hannemann assumes. Moreover, Manlius explicitly states in his *Epistola dedicatoria* that among the Melanchthon anecdotes are those of other great men as well (Tomus I, p. IX-X, emphasis mine):

> Nunc ueró serenissime rex M A X AE M I L I A N E , S.R.M.T. offero primitias huius mei laboris: quē ex prælectionibus Philippi Melanchthonis, *alijsq; clarissimorū uirorum relationibus*, non sine studio atq; labore per multos annos collegi, ac in hunc ordinem digessi.

> To His Royal Highness the ever serene Emperor M A X A M I L I A N I now offer the first-fruits of my labor, from the lectures of Philipp Melanchthon *and other reports of the most brilliant men*, which I have diligently and tirelessly collected over many years and arranged in the following order.

Manlius repudiates Hannemann's assumption again in the preface to Part Two (Tomus II, p. I, emphasis mine):

> Non temerè aut inconsideratè labor hic noster, amice Lector, *collectus ex ore D.* P H I L I P P I *Melanchthonis, alijsq; clarissimis uiris* (qui nunquā cogitarūt fore ut ipsorum dicta typis commendarentur) in lucē prodit:

> Neither by chance nor without thought, dear reader, does this work of ours come to light, *collected from the mouth of Dr. Phillip Melanchthon and other very brilliant men* (who never considered that their words would be committed to print);

Moreover, here in the preface to part two he also explains his usage of a marking that he uses in all three parts of *Locorum communium collectanea*, whereby he formalizes his treatment of material for which he does not provide the original author's name (2-3):

> Quod attinet ad signum C O L L. sciendum est, *non esse ea Philippi, quæ post hoc signū inueniuntur:* quamuis fortè semel atq; iterum illud non obseruatum est. Præterea *quædam nomina in quibusdam narrationibus sunt suppressa:* quod fecimus non sine consilio quorundam doctorū & bonorum uirorū.

> What pertains to the heading C O L L.[4]: it is to be understood that *the words that follow this mark are not Philipp's* [i.e. Melanchthon's], even if it [i.e. the rule] is not adhered to from time to time. Moreover, *in some commentaries certain names have*

Jo. Manlius, and mostly from both the lectures of Dr. Philipp Melancthon and the communications of other very learned men, and recently edited according to the sequence of these and others.')

[4] C O L L. = *collega* (i.e. 'colleague')?

been concealed—something we have not done without the recommendation of those doctors and good men.

Due in part to the large number of such inclusions, Manlius' system of demarcating anonymous quotes is necessary. As a consequence, there is no way to determine who offered the quoted text, nor when it was uttered.

What seems clear, however, is that Manlius reserves anonymity for only some of his sources. The description he offers of his placement of text under the heading "C O L L." is quite unmistakably exclusive of Melanchthon: "[...] the words that follow this mark are not Phillip's [...]". Manlius even provides a condition for those areas of text that he might have forgotten to demarcate appropriately: "[...], even if it is not adhered to from time to time." This implies that anonymously cited information should be expected to be demarcated with "C O L L." in the heading, but that from time to time Manlius forgets to apply this rule. What it does not imply logically is that Manlius includes under the heading "C O L L." information that stems from Melanchthon. In other words, Manlius' rule can be reworded as follows:

> Whatever follows a heading marked "C O L L." are not Melanchthon's words, but those of an anonymous source. In the event that I have forgotten to mark an anonymous source's words with "C O L L." in the heading, it should be understood that these are still not Melanchthon's words.

Of course, it is impossible for the reader to differentiate between the words of an anonymous source and those of Melanchthon when Manlius fails to give an indication of who shared the information with him.

In any case, Manlius' desire to distinguish between the sources of his information has direct impact on the analysis of his report of $*L_m$, since the entry that includes the reference to the Luther-*monotessaron* is immediately preceded by Manlius' demarcation "C O L L." (99–100; cf. Appendix D.2):

> COLL.
> [...]
> Ludouicus Pius curauit fieri Monotessaron, id est, concordantias quatuor Euangelistarum, magno sumptu. Quem librum diu habuit apud se Lutherus, & hodie est in Lipsica bibliotheca. Præfatio est partim Latinis uersibus, q̃ alde boni sunt, partim prosa oratione, etiã bene et Latinè scripta.

COLL.
[...]
Louis the Pious saw to it, at great cost, that a monotessaron was made, i.e. a harmony of the four Evangelists. Luther had this book with him for a long time, and which today is in the Leipzig library. The preface is partly in Latin verses, which are very good, and partly in prose language, also good and written in Latin.

Thus, according to his own rule, Manlius indicates that he learned of $*L_m$ from someone other than Melanchthon. By using his demarcation rule, Manlius is explicit only in stating that the source of the above quote wished to remain anonymous. That is, keeping the speaker's anonymity was "something [...] not done without the recommendation of th[at] doctor[...] and good m[a]n." Yet, notwithstanding Manlius' own explanation, the assumption that Melanchthon was Manlius' source has been taken for granted in academia.

Despite not wanting to reveal his anonymous sources, Manlius seems to slip from time to time. Occasionally, he offers a source's name despite placing that person's words under the anonymous heading. This occurs once within the section in which the $*L_m$ reference occurs, allowing another glimpse into the timing of that report.

11.2 Historical Hints at Manlius' Source

Though Manlius offers no clues toward determining where he learned of the *monotessaron* that he links to Luther, Louis the Pious and Leipzig, there are hints at least to the timing of when Manlius penned the entry (i.e. Manlius' RE). While this does not offer the exact timing of when Manlius heard his anonymous source's *monotessaron* claim, the date at which Manlius wrote his account does function as a *terminus ante quem* for that event.

In Manlius' report, Louis the Pious occurs among a list of other historical figures who are praised for their dedication to the cause of literacy, as is stated in the section heading under which the $*L_m$ reference occurs (99–100):

ENUMERATIO QVORVN dam præstantissimorum uirorum, cùm ex magnatum, tum ex alijs familijs ortorū, qui uel ipsi literarū cognitione studioq[ue]; indefesso, uel liberalitate & alijs beneficijs de Ecclesia benemeriti sunt, & adhuc in id incumbunt.

AN ACCOUNT OF some of the most outstanding men (while they stood out from great men, they do so all the more now from those of other groups) who either were aware of their own literacy and worked tirelessly at it, or have benefited greatly from other services of the Church and devote themselves to it until now.

The list of "outstanding men" notes seven powerful men who make education a priority: "Philippus rex Macedoniæ" (Philip II of Macedon), "Ludouicus Pius" (Louis the Pious), "Eberardo Vuirtenbergensi" (Eberhard, Duke of Württemberg—either I or II), [5] "Carolus Magnus" (Charlemagne), "Otto Secundus" (Otto II), "rex Portugalensis" (either John III "the Pious" [reigned 1521-1557] or his grandson and heir Sebastian I "the Desired" [born 1554, reigned 1557-1578]), and "Carolvs Quintus" (Charles V [HRR, reigned 1506-1556]).

Hannemann connected Manlius' reference to Louis the Pious with Melanchthon's well-known study of that emperor's contributions to world history, which he began in July 1555. From this, Hannemann determined the approximate date of 1555 for Manlius' report of the Luther-*monotessaron*. Yet, as presented above, there is at least cause to doubt Melanchthon as Manlius' source. Moreover, even if Melanchthon did serve as the source, his 1555-1561 world history review only provides the upper boundary of a window of time during which Manlius was able to have learned about $*L_m$. In reality, this event probably took place some time earlier than 1555, as is evident from clues provided by Manlius in the text section he titles "Enumeratio quorundam præstantissimorum virorum" (henceforth: "Enumeratio").

---

[5] There were a total of eight men named Eberhard of Württemberg that held the title referred to as *dux* or *comtes* in Latin, for which there are two possible German equivalents: 'Herzog' and 'Graf', both equivalent to English 'duke' and 'count'. These titles eventually became interchangeable, leading to some confusion. More confusion came in 1495, when Württemberg underwent a transition from a *Grafschaft* (county) to a *Herzogtum* (duchy). Fortunately, two men named Eberhard of Württemberg were born in or after the seventeenth century and therefore can not be the subject of this quote. The other six are: Eberhard I "der Erlauchte" (1265-1325); Eberhard II "der Greiner" (1315-1392); Eberhard III "der Milde" (1362-1417); Eberhard IV "der Jüngere" (1388-1419); Eberhard V "Eberhard im Bard" (1445-1496, also called Eberhard I as the first to hold the title of duke); and Eberhard VI (1447-1504, also called Eberhard II as duke). Ultimately, all six men had died before the window of time established for the intersection of Luther and the *Heliand*, and so are not useful in determining the date of Manlius' report.

11.2.1 Concurrent reigns of an emperor and a king

If the 1563 publication date of *Locorum communium collectanea* is taken as the firm *terminus ante quem*, the unnamed "rex Portugalensis" can only be one of the two men offered as an interpretation above. However, a second reference point toward establishing this as John III exists in the "Enumeratio" reference to Charles V, since the end of both men's reigns coincided closely: John III of Portugal on 11 June 1557, and Charles V (as Holy Roman Emperor)[6] on 16 January 1556. Indeed, Manlius' language indicates that Charles V had not yet died when he wrote the section containing the $*L_m$ reference, as can be seen in the use of the present tense in describing the Emperor's behavior (100–101, emphasis mine):

> Audiui ab Appiano & Hūmelio, amicis notris, se miratos esse, nostrum Imperatorem Carolum V. uiruū occupatum tanta gubernatione Imperij, tamen domi & militiæ contemplationibus & meditationibus in doctrina Astronomiæ adeò deditum esse, ut etiam *disputet* multa quæ ignorant docti in schola.
>
> Audiui dici à sapiente uiro, nec auditum nec lectum esse, ullum principem tam studiosum fuisse literarum, atq; Carolvm V. Imperatorem, præcipuè cum *sit* obnoxius multis calamitatibus seu morbis.

> I have heard from our friends, [Peter] Apian and [Johannes] Hommel, that they marvel at our Emperor Charles V, a man occupied entirely by the management of the Empire, yet at home and at war is still given to studying and contemplating Astronomy so much, that he *considers* many things that the educated ignore in school.
>
> I have heard it said by a knowledgeable man, that it is neither heard nor read that any ruler was ever so studious in the letters as Emperor Charles V, especially when one considers that he *is* subject to great misfortune, that is to say, bad health.[7]

---

[6] Charles was the heir to four of Europe's great dynasties and was thus the culmination of centuries of political matrimonial jockeying. Besides that of Holy Roman Emperor, he held regnal titles as Duke of Brabant, Limburg, Lothier and Luxembourg; Count of Artois, Burgundy, Flanders, Hainaut, Holland, Namur and Zeeland; King of Aragon, Majorca, Valencia, Navarre, Naples and Sicily; Count of Barcelona; King of Castile and León; Duke of Guelders; Count of Zutphen; Archduke of Austria; Duke of Styria, Carinthia and Carniola; Count of Tyrol; King of the Romans (i.e. German King), King of Italy, and Prince of Asturias, as well as being a pretender for Byzantine Emperor. From some of these he abdicated simultaneously when he stepped down as Holy Roman Emperor, from others at some other occasion.

[7] Charles V suffered from an enlarged lower jaw—a genetic result of Habsburg endogamy—making it difficult to chew, which in turn caused him severe indigestion. He also suffered from epileptic seizures. Moreover, he subsisted on a diet consisting mainly of red

Thus, since he describes a still-living Emperor Charles V, Manlius must have written his report of $*L_m$ prior to January 1556, which therefore becomes a new working *terminus ante quem*. While this date would allow for Hannemann's estimate of "approximately 1555", there is still further internal evidence that allows for Manlius to have learned of $*L_m$ earlier.

11.2.2 Private information about the Emperor

Strangely, despite indicating in the section heading that the information given was from an anonymous source, Manlius felt the need to add a remark about the quality of that source, calling him "a knowledgeable man," and continuing his description of him in the following sentence, given here (101):

> Ille plurimùm legit Thucydidem, qui admodū difficilis est intellectu: bene etiam nouit paternam historiam suam: & est consuetudo cubiculariorum suorum, [...]

> That same man [who told me] has read a lot of Thucydides, who is difficult to understand correctly; nevertheless, he has learned well the history of his fathers and the traditions of the women's chamber-servants, [...]

After this Manlius continues by reporting what the "knowledgeable man" had told him concerning the traditions and daily habits of the Imperial household of Charles V, noting particularly how fond the Emperor was of reading Thucydides in the morning with the servants. It seems an interesting topic, and one that is full of privy information—the kind of information only an insider would have access to, and for this very reason all the more likely to cause its sharer to wish to remain anonymous.

In Manlius' preceding paragraph, he offers the names of two men with whom he was personally acquainted, who are known to have served at two separate imperial residences, and who had close access to the Emperor himself—especially close in one case. The two residences were fewer than 75 km apart, meaning that Apianus (i.e. Apian), at Ingolstadt, and Humme-

---

meat, from which he developed by age 28 a crippling case of gout that plagued him throughout his life (Alonso, 2006). It has been suggested that Charles' ultimate abdication as Holy Roman Emperor resulted after a particularly serious gout attack forced him to postpone a military advance to recapture Metz from rebelling German princes who were supported by Charles V's enemy, Henry II of France, as part of the Habsburg-Valois War, also called the Italian War of 1551–1559.

lius (i.e. Hommel), at nearby Augsburg, were within a day's trip from one another. Their service at the imperial court is useful as a reference for timing because their tenures only overlapped for a period of approx. two years, from 1548–1550.

Johannes Hommel (1518–1562; a.k.a. Homel, Hummel, Homelius, Homilius, Hummelius [WBIS]) served the shorter amount of time, which corresponds precisely with the period of overlap between the two men. He was born in Memmingen in Schwaben, attended university in Strasbourg shortly some time in the 1530s before transferring to Wittenberg in 1540 (Zedlers, 734), where he earned the degree of *Liberalium Artium Magister* and where he was in close contact with Luther, Melanchthon and Erasmus Reinhold. In 1548, Hommel returned to Memmingen, specifically to Bläß, where he took a position as a pastor. In 1548, the advent of the Augsburg Interim required him to forfeit his ministry, and a fine knowledge of mathematics earned him his position that same year at the imperial residence at Augsburg. There, he produced a clock as a gift from the Emperor to Sultan Suleiman I. Ultimately, the Protestant Hommel felt uncomfortable in the catholic Emperor's service. Despite invitations to stay, he left in 1550 for Leipzig, where he was given a professorship at the University in 1551 and soon came into the favor of the Saxon Prince-Elector. At Leipzig, Hommel would later have an influence on renowned astronomer Tycho Brahe (ADB, vol. 3 pg. 58). Also important to note: he was the son-in-law of J. Camerarius (Zedlers).

Peter Bienewitz (1495–1552; a.k.a. Bennewitz, Petrus Apianus, Apian, Apisfilius [WBIS]) was born in Leisnig, Saxony and grew up in nearby Rochlitz. He began university in 1516 at Leipzig, where he translated his bee-themed surname into the Latin *Apianus*.[8] In 1519, Apian transferred to Vienna, then the leader in geography and mathematics, where he studied under Georg Tannstetter. In 1521, the plague hit Vienna, forcing Apian to flee the city after completing his baccalaureate. He moved first to Regensburg, then to Landshut in 1524, where he published his famous astronomical treatise *Cosmographicus liber* ('Cosmographic book', ADB). In 1527, he accepted a faculty position in mathematics at the University of Ingolstadt,

---

[8] Like Menlin, who likely leaned on the well-known Roman *gens Manlius* in choosing his Latin surname, Bienewitz assumed an already established Latin name as a rough translation of his native surname, relying on the success of the Roman historian Appianus of Alexandria (ca. 95-ca. 165).

where he also set up a printer's shop and began printing the works of Luther-contrarian Johann Eck, as well as many now-famous maps. By the 1530s, he was so beloved by the Emperor, that he was granted a printing monopoly in Ingolstadt. It was around this time, more precisely in 1531, that Apian observed Halley's Comet and was the first to recognize that its tail always points away from the sun (NDB). Apian's interest in mathematics was likely the catalyst for his relationship with fellow mathematician Hommel. His prowess at astronomy earned him the position as teacher to Charles V, who shared an interest in the stars, as is noted by Manlius in the citation provided above. Apian's duties as Imperial Instructor would have offered him rare insights into the private behaviors of Charles V's court.

The link between Hommel and Camerarius ultimately reveals the identity of Manlius' source. Camerarius was a great scholar of Greek. He held early employment as a teacher of the subject: "auf [Melanchthons] Empfehlung [wurde] er 1526 an dem neugegründeten Ägidiengymnasium in Nürnberg Lehrer des Griechischen und Lateinischen" (BBKL, vol. 1, pp. 891–892). Moreover, Camerarius' prowess with the language, such as to be able to read Thucydides "correctly" (as per Manlius) is also verified:

> C[amerarius] war nach dem Tod des Erasmus von Rotterdam der hervorragendste deutsche Philologe des 16. Jahrhunderts. Das beweisen seine zahlreichen Ausgaben und Kommentare griechischer und lateinischer Schriftsteller sowie seine Beiträge zur griechischen und lateinischen Grammatik und Altertumskunde.

Among his "numerous publications and commentaries on Greek [...] authors" is one entitled *Thucydides cum scholiis et antiquis et utilibus, sine quibus autor intellectu multum est difficilis* ('Thucydides: with both ancient and useful exercises without which the author is very difficult to understand'), published 1540. Manlius' language even reflects the title of this book, including the supine construction: "Thucydidem, qui admodū difficilis est intellectu" ('Thucydides, who is difficult to understand correctly').

It appears that Manlius accidentally names his sources about the Emperor's daily routine. There would have been no danger to either Apian, Hommel or Camerarius to be cited openly praising the sitting Emperor, but to be implicated in sharing sensitive information about his habits, which must have been taboo, certainly came with risk. Thus, it seems probable that Manlius' mention of a "knowledgeable man" who told him some imperial gossip is merely a shallow attempt at veiling the identity of Camerarius. How Camerarius acquired this dangerous information is not known; however, it might well have been through his son-in-law Hommel, whom Manlius also calls a personal friend.

What develops from the interaction of Hommel with Charles V and Apian is the formation of a means to date Manlius' report. To this end, it is unimportant whether Hommel himself is the ultimate origin of Camerarius' information or whether it traveled via Hommel from Apian: the fact is that Hommel's three year stint at the Augsburg residence is the only time during which Hommel could have come to know of Charles' routines—either from personal observation or as the result of friendly gossip with Apian. Once relocated to Leipzig, Hommel was in relatively close proximity to Manlius who—should he be identified as Johannes Menlin as proposed—had been studying at Wittenberg since 1546.

That Manlius and Hommel were in contact is not in doubt, since Manlius confirms this explicitly. It is uncertain when Manlius and Hommel became acquainted; however, it is known that Hommel moved to Leipzig prior to taking his position at the University of Leipzig in 1551. Therefore, approx. 1550 is a reasonable early estimate for Manlius to learn about Emperor Charles V's literacy and morning rituals from Hommel. This date then serves as the *terminus post quem* for Manlius' penning of the "Enumeratio" section. The 1550 date also appears to be confirmed by yet another clue provided by Manlius concerning Granvelle.

11.2.3 The Emperor's counselor Granvelle

Presented so far is a window of time that stretches from 1550 to 1556, yet the upper limit of this window can be narrowed down further still by analyzing one other statement offered by Manlius in "Enumeratio". This statement revolves around Manlius' mention of a man with the surname Granvelle (102):

> Granuelus adferens imperatori Thucydidē primò Gallicè uersum, dixit: Hunc librum dono Tuæ Maiestati, sed ea cōditione, ut ea promittat mihi, quòd uelit illum perlegere. Euolutis uerò in eo libro ab imperatore aliquot pagellis, ita placuit, ut tertià perlegeret.

> When he first suggested Thucydides' verse in French to the Emperor, Granvelle said: "I present this book to Your Majesty, but on the condition that he promises me that he will read it." Truly, the reading of several passages in that book by the emperor has so pleased him that he is reading it for the third time.

The timing of this event is rather complicated, as there were four men with the surname "Granvelle" who served in the courts of either Charles V or his successor to the Imperial throne, his brother Ferdinand I.

The first was Nicolaus Perrenot de Granvelle (1484–1550), who was also the father of the other three. He was born in Burgundy, studied law at Dole, and received his first imperial assignment as *maitre de requêtes*[9] in the Habsburg Netherlands (ADB, 580). He accompanied Grand Chancellor Mercurino Gattinara to the momentous negotiations[10] of 1521 between Emperor Charles V and French King Francis I, which were presided over by Cardinal Thomas Woolsey.[11] The elder Granvelle gained notoriety within the royal circle and was promoted to ever more influential positions. By 1525 he had been raised to a functionary within Charles V's own court, where he served in several different functions before the Emperor named him as his Chancellor, replacing Mercurino Gattinara after that man's death in 1530. Regarding Granvelle's influence over the Emperor (ADB, 580–581):

> Im Großen und Ganzen wird Kaiser Karl persönlich für die von seiner Regeirung befolgte Politik die Verantwortlichkeit zu tragen haben; im Einzelnen wird man sagen dürfen, daß sein Minister Granvelle in den meisten Fällen ihm die friedlicheren Wege anempfohlen und oft ihm von raschen Thaten abgerathen habe. Wie Granvelle über eine gewisse Meisterschaft diplomatischer Technik verfügte, so zog er meistens geschicktes Verhandeln und eifriges Negociiren den gewaltsamen Maßregeln vor, er liebte zu beschwichtigen und besänftigen, die Gegensätze zu mildern und die Gegner zu gewinnen. Friedlicher Ausgleichung mit Frankreich redete er wiederholt das Wort. Die Eintracht des Kaisers mit dem Papste meinte er wiederholt weniger durch Brüskiren und Einschüchtern als durch Schmeicheln und Zureden zu erringen; selbst die deutschen Protestanten wünschte er durch friedliche Mittel von dem definitiven Bruche mit der katholischen Kirche zurückzuhalten und ihre Rückkehr in den Schooß [sic] der Kirche schmeichelte er sich durch Vergleichshandlungen zu erzielen.

---

[9] Roughly equivalent to a District Attorney or State Prosecutor in the United States today.

[10] This ended in the Italian War of 1521–26, also called the Four Year's War, between the alliance of France and Venice and the alliance of the Holy Roman Empire, Spain, England and the Papal States.

[11] The most powerful man in England at the time, he was English King Henry VIII's closest advisor and often was branded *alter rex* (the second king). Prior to the 1521 Calais negotiations, he presided over the momentous "Field of the Cloth of Gold" meeting between Francis I and Henry VIII in Balinhem, just outside Calais.

This establishes the character of Granvelle as a thoughtful mediator who sought to assuage societal problems that arise from differences in personality, using his sway over the Emperor to attempt to accomplish his own moral goals. He is just the character to find value in Thucydides' theme of ethical imperialism (cf. Romilly 1947).[12] Furthermore, his relationship with the Emperor was of the very nature that would have allowed Granvelle to suggest that Charles V read Thucydides, with the hope that, by appealing to Charles V's love of reading, the Emperor's acknowledged belligerence might be softened through reason and rationality. Granvelle may have also been attempting to coax the Emperor toward thinking more empirically instead of superstitiously "giv[ing himself] so much to studying and mulling over astronomy" (*Locorum*, 101).

Nicolaus Perrenot de Granvelle fathered five sons (ADB, 582); however, only three sons ever played roles in court politics, and only the eldest son was old enough to rise in the Emperor's court to prominence equivalent to that of his father.[13] Antoine Perrenot de Granvelle (1517-1586) received his first position as bishop of Aras, Navarre in 1540. Antoine proved himself in 1543 by publicly explaining the Emperor's political view of the Church during a dispute between the Trident town council and papal legates. His action was rewarded (ADB, 582):

> Nachdem diese erste Probe öffentlichen Auftretens mit Beifall belohnt war, zog ihn der Vater mehr und mehr in die Staatsgeschäfte hinein: von 1545 begegnen wir auf Schritt und Tritt in den Staatshandlungen und in den Staatspapieren Karls V. den Arbeitsspuren des jüngeren G[ranvelle].

Thus, Antoine's accession into his father's role was a slow process starting in 1545. From this point on, Antoine was being groomed openly to succeed his father as Chancellor, which he did when the father Granvelle died on 28 August 1550. This date is the crucial piece of evidence toward the timing of Manlius' writing of "Enumeratio". There, the man who presented a copy of

---

[12] The issue of ethics in relation to Charles V is monumental: he reigned over the largest empire in the world at the time: as a Habsburg, his personal holdings stretched across Europe; as the King of Spain, they extended over the ocean to the New World at the beginning and height of the Spanish Conquest of that continent.

[13] Thomas Perrenot de Granvelle (1521-1571) was prominent in his own right, but even more so within the court of Charles V's son Philip II, King of Spain. Friedrich Perrenot de Granvelle (1536-1600) was a militant, serving in the Emperor's guard. Like his older brother Thomas, Friedrich came into his own after the death of Emperor Charles V.

Thucydides in French to the Emperor is only referred to by the Latinized surname "Granuelus" (102):

> Granuelus adferens imperatori Thucydidē primò Gallicè uersum, dixit: Hunc librum dono Tuæ Maiestati, sed ea cõditione, ut ea promittat mihi, quòd uelit illum perlegere. Euolutis uerò in eo libro ab imperatore aliquot pagellis, ita placuit, ut tertià perlegeret.

> When Granvelle first recommended Thucydides' poems in French to the Emperor, he said: "I present this book to Your Majesty, but on the condition that he promises me that he will read it." Truly, the Emperor's reading of several passages in that book has so pleased him that he is reading it for the third time.

With as many as four Granvelles present at the court of Charles V at this time, one would expect Manlius to be more specific about whom he means, unless (1) Manlius wrote "Enumeratio" when only the senior Granvelle was active, or (2) Manlius is referring to the first man known widely and broadly as Granvelle (viz. Nicolaus) and is writing before the junior Granvelle had gained international recognition.[14] Both are viable scenarios; both also lead to the same conclusion: Manlius wrote "Enumeratio" before Nicolaus Perrenot de Granvelle had died. Thus, the *terminus ante quem* for Manlius' penning of "Enumeratio" is revised to late August 1550. Between the working *terminus post quem* of 1550 that was deduced earlier from the relationship between Manlius and Hommel in Leipzig, and this new *terminus ante quem*, there is only a very small window of time during which Manlius likely wrote the contents of the "Enumeratio" section, later published in 1563 as Part III of *Locorum communium collectanea*.

11.2.4 Manlius' link to Camerarius

If Manlius' friend Hommel was indeed his source for the parts of "Enumeratio" that tell about Charles V (cf. 9.4.2),[15] then perhaps Manlius' information about $*L_m$ can be traced back through Hommel to his father-in-law,

---

[14] Much like a father who wishes to name his son after himself does not need to be distinguished by the suffix "Sr." until the actual existence of the junior makes it necessary.

[15] The part lauding Charles V's diligent study of Astronomy was, without question, from Hommel.

Joachim Camerarius.[16] It was shown in Ch. 4 that Camerarius was one of three men—along with C. Borner and Melanchthon—who were given the task of establishing the University Library at Leipzig as part of Duke Maurice's educational reforms for Saxony. It has already been established through Fabricius' letters that Borner knew of this *Heliand* codex, including its Naumburg origin (cf. 6.2.2). Likewise, Melanchthon's knowledge of a *Heliand* codex at Leipzig is confirmed by Chemnitz in *Harmoniae evangelicae* (cf. Ch. 8). That two of the three founders of the UBL are attested to have known of the existence of a (Germanic) document in the holdings of the Pauliner-housed library that attributes its own creation to Louis the Pious seems to suggest that the third man of that group, viz. Camerarius (who was also Borner's successor as that library's director) would have been as aware of a *Heliand* codex as the other two men were. Therefore, it should not be surprising that evidence from Manlius' account of the Leipzig-*monotessaron* indirectly implicates Camerarius as its source. Of course, there is most certainly an element of surprise in this revelation: it is not that Camerarius knew about the *Heliand* codex, but that he was Manlius' anonymous informant.

Compare Manlius' treatment of his supposedly anonymous source(s) for "Enumeratio" with that of another Luther rumor, which he attributes to Albrecht Dürer (1471–1528), and is also likely information that he received from Camerarius. The following quotation stems from a section in Part II of *Locorum communium collectanea* entitled "Iudicia et monumenta uarijs rebus" ("*Judgment of and testament to various facts*"; cf. Appendix D.3). Here Manlius gives a rather stream-of-consciousness account of several unique Bibles known to exist at the time, e.g. (285):

> Ratisbonæ in monasterio est Testamentũ nouum, scriptũ aureis literis in mẽbrana: quod uidi.
>
> Basiliæ fuit etiam nouum Testamentum græcum, aureis literis scriptum: quo ego usus sum adolescens. Erasmus eius etiam facit mentionem, quia eo est usus in emendatione noui Testamenti.

> In a Regensburg monastery there is a New Testament, written in gold letters on parchment, which I have seen.

---

[16] Or perhaps Camerarius served as Manlius' source for both the *L_m information and the gossip about Charles V, the second of which Camerarius could have received prior to Hommel's move to Leipzig. This line of thinking can only push the date of Manlius' knowledge of both pieces of information in one direction, namely to an earlier date than even 1550.

> There was also a Greek New Testament at Basel, written in gold letters, which I used as a young man. Erasmus makes mention of it because he makes use of it in [his] revision of the New Testament.

Manlius transitions from here into why Luther's translation of the Bible is, according to Dürer, superior to Erasmus and others:

> Albertus Durerus, pictor Norinbergensis, sapiens uir, dixit: hoc interesse inter Lutheri & aliorum Theologorum scripta, quòd ipse legens in prima pagina tres uel quatuor periodos scriptorum Lutheri, scire posset, quid esset expectandum in toto opere. Et hanc esse laudem scriptorum Lutheri, uidelicet illam perspicuitatē & postquam perlegisset totum librum, oporteret attentè cogitare quid uoluisset author dicere, uel de qua re disserat.

> Albrecht Dürer, the artist from Nuremburg, an intelligent man, said: the Scriptures differ between Luther and the other theologians to the extent that, within three or four sentences on the first page of Luther's Scriptures, the reader can know what to expect from the whole work. Indeed this is what is good about Luther's Scriptures, namely this clearness and inasmuch as one finishes reading the whole book, it is necessary to reflect carefully upon what the author was wanting to say, specifically, what he was arguing about.

This mention of Albrecht Dürer gives some insight into Manlius' source for *L_m: Dürer formed a close friendship with Camerarius when the latter lived in Nuremburg from 1526–1535. During that period, Camerarius served in the prominent role as the first rector at the then-new *Egidiengymnasium* (renamed *Melanchthon-Gymnasium* in 1993). Note that Cameriarius' presence at Nuremburg only allowed for his friendship with Dürer to last approximately two years: Dürer died on 6 April 1528. Thus, Manlius could not have heard Dürer's opinion from the artist himself, since he would have either not been born by the time of Dürer's passing, or if he had been, he would have been far too young to remember.[17] Yet another simple connection between Manlius and Dürer does exist that allows for Dürer's statement to reach Manlius: Manlius' connection to Camerarius, whether through Hommel or not. Thus, there is evidence to suggest that at least two of the "other very brilliant men" described in the *Epistola dedicatoria* were Man-

---

[17] There is no birth date available for Manlius, although it has been assumed (cf. 9.3) that he was born after 1525. Thus, Manlius would have certainly been younger than three years old when Dürer died—if he had been born yet at all. Even if the maximum age of three is to be taken, Manlius would have not likely understood the topic of Dürer's opinion, let alone remember it in detail as an approx. 22–25 year-old man in 1550.

lius' friend Johannes Hommel and Hommel's father-in-law Joachim Camerarius. Finally, there is clear evidence that points to all three UBL's founders' knowledge of a *Heliand* codex: *F is linked to Borner by Fabricius, *Ch is linked to Melanchthon by Chemnitz, and *L_m is linked to Camerarius by Manlius. What is more, that all three UBL founders knew of a document that is described by three outsiders using very similar language further suggests that the three individual hypothetical documents are one and the same document, i.e. viz. *F = *Ch = *L_m (cf. 13.1).

11.3 Conclusions about Manlius' report

The link between the *Heliand* and Martin Luther is only attestable to one source: Manlius' account. To date, neither Chemnitz nor Fabricius—for that matter, Flacius or any other contemporary—has been discovered making this connection between document and Reformer. While Chemnitz and Fabricius offered the sources of their knowledge of the Leipzig *monotessaron*, Manlius allowed his to remain anonymous. Furthermore, Manlius is explicit in stating in his preface that the anonymous information that he recounts is not attributable to Melanchthon, but to other "very learned men". Why he keeps some informants anonymous is uncertain. However, in the "Enumeratio" section, Manlius shares at least two pieces of information that were likely sensitive at the time: (1) a rumor regarding the private habits of Emperor Charles V, and (2) an account relating the existence of a Bible translation commissioned by a previous Emperor, viz. Louis the Pious, that could serve to defame the political policies of Emperor Charles V.

The source of the rumor about the Emperor's daily routine is veiled only loosely: in the previous sentence, Manlius relates how two of his friends, Apian and Hommel, praise the Emperor for his studious nature. That Apian and Hommel shared this seemly gossip about the Emperor comes as no surprise: both men were present at the Imperial court—Apian as the Emperor's Astronomy instructor, Hommel as his Mathematics tutor (ADB, vol. 13 pg. 58) and horologist. Either man could have been present when Granvelle the Elder gave a copy of Thucydides in French to Charles V (or at least knew of this event from another member of the Imperial inner circle). Eventually, just shortly before Granvelle Sr. passed away, Hommel grew weary of being a Protestant amongst the Catholic Habsburgs and moved to

Protestant-friendly Saxony to teach at the University of Leipzig. In light of this move (1550), Granvelle's death (1550) and Charles V's ultimate abdication (1556), a *terminus ante quem* for Manlius' penning of the Emperor rumors can be established for 28 August 1550 (cf. 11.2.3). This same date also acts therefore as the *terminus ante quem* for Manlius' RE of the Luther-*monotessaron* report.

After moving to Leipzig, Hommel married Camerarius' daughter Magdalena. Some time after this, Hommel took Camerarius' suggestion to formalize the usage of his Latin surname to *Homilius* (DBA, I 565, 127). Hommel's relationship to both Camerarius and Manlius would seem to imply that he was the intermediary of information between the latter two, but there is no reason to suggest that Camerarius and Manlius did not know of each other through other means as well. Nevertheless, their common link via Hommel strengthens the idea that Camerarius and Manlius had some sort of contact with one another. Therefore, it can be stated that either (1) Camerarius shared Hommel's rumors about the Emperor with Manlius or (2) Hommel shared Camerarius' knowledge of the Luther-*monotessaron* with Manlius. Either scenario must have occurred prior to 28 August 1550. Since Manlius is known to have been present at Wittenberg in 1546, it is not hard to imagine that he came into contact with Camerarius at some point in the intervening four years. That is, Camerarius had colleagues (Melanchthon in particular) in Wittenberg, meaning he likely had reason to travel to the nearby city. Moreover, given Manlius' later surfacing in Leipzig and his apparent wanderlust in the 1560s (and as Mandl in the 1580s and 1590s), it is not hard to assume that he had this trait even earlier in life. Such would at least offer reason to expect that he showed up in Leipzig from time to time while a student at Wittenberg the first time around. If his connection to Camerarius had truly been established before his friendship with Hommel, it is not hard to imagine that it would have come about by the sheer fact that both Manlius and Camerarius belonged to the same circle, with at minimum a tenuous connection provided via Melanchthon. Given that Manlius excludes Melanchthon as the source of his knowledge of $*L_m$, the next most likely candidate would be Camerarius—whether directly from him or via Hommel—who most certainly had a knowledge of the Leipzig *monotessaron* equal to that of Borner and Melanchthon (cf. 5.1.4).

As discussed in Ch. 6, the presence of the Leipzig *monotessaron* can be traced back nearly to the founding of the UBL. As one of the three founders of that Library, Camerarius must have known very early about the existence of the Leipzig *monotessaron*. Therefore, we can take the founding date of the UBL as a rough working date for Camerarius' knowledge of the document. Due to the intertwined nature of Camerarius' and Hommel's rumors, the window of time during which Manlius learned about $*L_m$ stretches from 1543 to 1550. Again, Manlius' matriculation as Menlin at Wittenberg places him in that city as late as 1 May 1556, i.e. right in the middle of the aforementioned time window.[18]

In conclusion, Manlius' knowledge of the rumors mentioned in the "Enumeratio" section of *Locorum communium collectanea* must have come about prior to Autumn 1550. Whether Manlius is identified with Johannes Menlin at Wittenberg in 1546 or Ioannes Mendel at Leipzig in 1544, his report of $*L_m$ coincides with the timing established in Ch. 8 for Chemnitz' knowledge of $*Ch$. Barring the existence of two or more of the same rare medieval document, it must be concluded that $*Ch$ and $*L_m$ are the same *Heliand* manuscript. Also, Chemnitz and Manlius stand as separate witnesses—or at least reporters of two separate witnesses, i.e. Melanchthon and Camerarius—to the existence of the *Heliand* at Leipzig prior to and shortly after the death of Martin Luther in 1546, and implying that Manlius' rumor that the Reformer once possessed a Louis the Pious-commissioned *monotessaron* is based on fact.

---

[18] Likewise, should one wish to claim as folklore the information used from the DBA (Wittenberg student, originated from Ansbach) to link Ioannes Manlius to Johannes Menlin, then a second attested person stands ready to be associated with Manlius—namely, Ioannes Mendel of Auerbach, who matriculated at Leipzig in Summer 1544. This places him under the nose of Camerarius (and Borner) a mere year after the founding of UBL. Furthermore, some effort might yield a link between Menlin and Mendel that suggests the same individual transferred from one school to the other (cf. Kohnle's findings in footnote 25).

Part V:

Religious Politics of a Secular Empire

12. An 'Ace Up the Sleeve' in a Religious War

12.1 Imperial Reaction to the Reformation

Between the Edict of Worms (1521) and the start of the Eighty Years' War (1568), i.e. for more than a half-a-century, a regally-sanctioned (for most of which time it was also sanctioned imperially) inquisition was state policy, held back from full force only by a tenuous peace proclaimed from the Diet of Augsburg in 1530. During this stretch of time, the theater of the conflict moved about the German lands—from Swabia to Saxony and then to the Netherlands—and though a period of peace existed after 1530, the purpose of the Edict of Worms policy remained intact. This purpose was to prevent Protestantism from expanding and, if possible, to regain territories lost to "heresy". Initially, the strategy was to threaten the Protestants with the loss of property and life. In pursuance of the Edict of Worms, such punishments could be applied for so much as owning an unauthorized translation of the Bible.

12.2 Threats from Worms

One effect of the Diet of Worms in 1521 was an Imperial decision that proved to be both long-lasting and widespread: the Edict of Worms. Upon seeing the German princes' reluctance to pursue Luther by committee, the Emperor Charles V issued this rash imperial edict to outlaw the Reformer officially—effectively placing a price on Luther's head. The purpose of this banishment is explained in parallel with Luther's excommunication (Edict of Worms, emphasis mine):

> We have declared and hereby forever declare by this edict that the said Martin Luther is to be considered *an estranged member, rotten and cut off from the body of our Holy Mother Church.* He is an obstinate, schismatic heretic, and we want him to be considered as such by all of you.

Hoping to guarantee Luther's arrest, Charles V attempted to foment mutiny within the ranks of the Protestants: "Those who will help in his capture will be rewarded generously for their good work," while those capable of doing so but choosing instead to maintain or join the alliance with Luther would be duly punished (emphasis mine):

> As for his accomplices, *those who help or favor the said Martin in whatever manner* or who show obstinacy in their perversity, not receiving absolution from the pope for the evils they have committed, we will also proceed against them and will *take all of their goods and belongings*, movable and fixed, with the help either of the judges in the area in which they reside or of our parliaments and councils at Malines or in other cities in which these events are made known.

Yet financial punishment was not the only means the Emperor was willing to use toward his ends. In fact, he threatened the most severe penalty possible: capital punishment. To support such severe action Charles V equated support for Luther to be comparable with *lèse majesté*, i.e. high treason—the most severe crime of all (bolded emphasis mine):

> Action will be taken according to the desire of the accusers or of our fiscal procurators, but always according to the constitution and the laws, whether canon, civil, or divine, written against **those who commit heresy or the crime of *lèse majesté***. These laws will be applied regardless of person, degree, or privilege if anyone does not obey our edict in every manner.

Here Charles V openly equates religious heresy with political treachery. The equivalence of these crimes in his mind justified the most severe punishment for those who spoke out against the Catholic Church (emphasis mine):

> Punishments.
> For the crime of *lèse majesté* and for very serious offense and indignation against the prince.
> Item. Confiscation and *loss of body* and belongings and all goods, fixed and movable, half of which will go to the Lord, and the other half to the accusers and denouncers. With other punishments as given more fully in the present edict and mandate.

Clearly, Charles V intended that his quiver of punishments would not end at "loss […] belongings and all goods", rather should also allow for "loss of body", i.e. execution. All the same, the Emperor's attempts to be vague about how he intends to punish Luther (emphasis mine):

> […] we want him to be apprehended and punished as a notorious heretic, as he deserves, to be brought personally before us, or to be securely guarded until those who have captured him inform us, whereupon we will order the *appropriate manner* of proceeding against the said Luther.

Yet, he does give clues as to what Luther's impending punishment would entail. This included an extraordinary trial in which Luther would have no chance to defend himself (emphasis mine):

> Namely, that a man like the said Luther, already condemned and still persisting in his obstinate perversity, separated from the way of life of Christians, and a notorious heretic, *should not be listened to nor questioned*, according to the law, in order to prevent every opportunity for those who favor the said Luther and his errors to do evil.

Furthermore, if there is any doubt about what punishment Charles V deemed "appropriate" for Luther, he alludes to it earlier in the edict when comparing Luther to Jan Hus (emphasis mine):

> He wants to bring dishonor upon all of Christendom by calling this council "Satan's Synagogue" and by insulting all those who attended it, namely, "Sigismund of curious memory, emperor; and the princes of the Holy Empire, antichrists and apostles of the antichrist, murderers and pharisees," because, following an order from that council, *they burned the heretic John Hus*. Luther also added that all John Hus's articles, condemned during the council as wrong and heretical, were evangelical and Christian, and he wanted to defend him and approve of what he did. But he rejects and refuses whatever articles were approved by the council, protesting like a madman that *if John Hus was once heretic, he* [Luther] *is proud to be ten times more heretic*.

Charles V uses Luther's self-description of being "ten times more heretic" as Hus to justify executing Luther in that same way that "several [other] heretics [...] have already been condemned, excommunicated, and buried in hell for a long time". That is, if Hus was executed for heresy, surely the man proclaiming to be ten times the heretic as he should also be dispatched with in defense of the Church.

Moreover, as indicated previously, Charles V included language allowing for the execution of Luther's sympathizers. The edict specifies by what actions "those who help or favor the said Martin in whatever manner" made themselves "his accomplices" (emphasis mine):

> [...] we forbid anyone from this time forward to dare, either by words or by deeds, to receive, defend, sustain, or favor the said Martin Luther. [...]
> We order, upon the penalties contained herein, that the contents of this edict be kept and observed in their entirety; and we forbid *anyone, regardless of his authority or privilege, to dare to buy, sell, keep, read, write, or have somebody write, print or have printed, or affirm or defend the books, writings, or opinions of the said Martin Luther, or*

> *anything contained in these books and writings,* whether in German, Latin, Flemish, or any other language. [...]
>
> [...] to kill this mortal pestilence, we ask and require that no one *dare to compose, write, print, paint, sell, buy, or have printed, written, sold, or painted,* from now on in whatever manner such pernicious articles so much against the holy orthodox faith and against that which the Catholic Apostolic Church has kept and observed to this day.

Thus, Charles V offers a widespread gamut of possible actions that could be considered treason and, therefore, be punishable by execution. Still more, *habeas corpus* was lifted: guilt could be determined by observation of a person's demeanor alone (emphasis mine):

> We ask you to be diligent in apprehending and confiscating all the belongings of *those who seem rebellious* to the ordinances herein mentioned and to punish them according to the penalties set out by law-Divine, canon, and civil.

With such rash language and unfettered logic, Charles V essentially initiated a witch hunt—or expressed more formally, an inquisition—that directly affected the Habsburg Netherlands, a territory which Charles V had inherited (as Duke of Burgundy) from his paternal grandmother, Mary of Burgundy. In 1543, Charles V added to this the Duchy of Guelders, and in 1549 he enforced the Pragmatic Sanction—a particularist policy that created a unit-state out of the Netherlands, outside of the Holy Roman Empire and wholly in control of the House of Habsburg. Throughout this state—the "Seventeen Provinces"—Charles V reorganized the Church dioceses in an attempt to control the religious situation.

12.2.1 Breaking the Revolt of Ghent

Already by 1521 the Reformation spirit had gained strong footing in the Netherlands. A majority of these lands were personal holdings of the Habsburg dynasty. Consequently, Charles V's inquisition had its strongest effect here. As both the supreme (albeit in reality more or less titular) political authority over the Holy Roman Empire and a devout catholic, Charles V felt it his God-given duty to defend the Church from the onslaught of Protestant heresy (emphasis mine):

> To the honor and praise of God, our creator, through whose mercy we have been given kingdoms, lands, and domains hereabove mentioned, *it is our duty to help subdue the enemies of our faith and bring them to the obedience* of the divine majesty,

magnifying the glory of the cross and the passion of our Lord (insofar as we are able), and to keep the Christian religion pure from all heresy or suspicion of heresy, according to and following the ordinance and custom observed by the Holy Roman Church.

This meant ridding at least the Habsburg-held lands—territories where Charles' authority was less a question—of what he considered a spiritual plague. Some of his means of doing so have already been introduced.

One might now consider Charles V's introduction of the death penalty for treason "unenforceable". This interpretation might base itself on the notion that the Edict's threat was never taken very seriously by those whom it targeted. Still, other modern historians claim that it was anything but vain: Tracy calculates that 1,300 Dutch were executed between 1523 and 1566 (1990, p 66). Thus, given Charles V's off-and-on resolve for following through with execution for treason, it seems doubtful that his contemporaries would ever dare take it upon themselves to guess whether their emperor was being serious or not. It would have been far safer first to assume his sincerity to punish.

Furthermore, the Edict of Worms was not Charles V's only instance of invoking draconian punishment. When quelling the Revolt of Ghent in 1539, Charles V personally marched into his birthplace and made an example of the traitors: he forced the town nobles to march behind him through town wearing representative nooses (i.e. the *Stroppendragers*) to advertise what the punishment might have been if the Emperor were not so magnanimous.

Some might see in this an unwillingness on Charles V's part to actually enforce capital punishment. Yet the situation of the revolt in Ghent was different from his opposition to the spread of Protestantism. The Revolt of Ghent occurred in response to what the locals perceived as unjust taxation—money that they saw was being used to fight foreign wars, i.e. the reconquest of Italian possessions. Yet, if the Emperor was unwilling to demand the execution of the traitors in Ghent, then to whom would the threats in the Edict of Worms apply? Charles V would have had plenty of justification to execute the Ghent nobles, since it was they who led the citizenry against their sovereign. Certainly, Charles V had prepared for such circumstances when dictating the Edict in 1521: "These laws will be applied regardless of person, degree, or privilege if anyone does not obey our edict in every manner." Was the treachery of the town leaders not exceptionally grave, since as the Emperor's "governors of kingdoms, lands, domains, and members of the council of [his] empire" they were deputies in defending the Empire? Those entrusted with government powers had led the burghers astray.

Still, as embarrassing and draconian (by implication) as Charles V's punishment was for the town leaders, it was far from actually matching the scope of his in the Edict of Worms. However, the incident in Ghent should not be seen as evidence of Charles V's unwillingness to follow through with his threats of capital punishment. Alternatively, it is possible that the Emperor considered the actions of the citizens of Ghent as something other than high treason, and therefore not deserving of the death penalty. This thesis is supported in part by a later event: Charles V's punishment of a leader of the Schmalkaldic War reveals that the act of heresy was a necessary element of actions worthy of the death penalty in the Emperor's mind (cf. 12.4.1). Clearly, the Revolt of Ghent had been started over issues of money and not over the promotion of anti-Catholic ideas.

12.3 Lead-up to the Schmalkaldic War

Prior to the Schmalkaldic War (1546–1547), several intriguing transfers of power brought about the situation in which Duke Maurice of Saxony found himself suddenly the wielder of a great deal of political power. Since the discovery of both MS L and *L occurred at an institution founded by Duke Maurice's decree, a brief look into his provenance is worthwhile. A discussion of his motives and measures will also reveal an interesting link that may suggest the origin of the Leipzig codex.

12.3.1 The Division of Leipzig

Maurice's paternal grandfather, Duke Albert (Albrecht) III of Saxony (1443–1500), and great-uncle Duke Ernest (Ernst) of Saxony (1441–1486) co-ruled Saxony as part of their inheritance. After acquiring the Margraviate of Thuringia in 1483, the two brothers signed the Treaty of Leipzig (1485) agreeing to divide their possessions into two realms: Albert III received the eastern portion, Meissen, as his residence, and the title of Margrave; Ernest received the western portion, Wittenberg as his residence, and the title of

Landgrave and Elector. From this date forward, the Saxon House of Wettin was divided into two branches—Ernestine and Albertine.

12.3.2 Ernestine Saxony

A year later, in 1486, Ernest died from injuries sustained from falling off a horse, and his title and lands were inherited by his son, Frederick (Friedrich) III (1463-1525), under whom the University of Wittenberg was founded in 1502. Sympathetic to Luther, Frederick III secured the Reformer's safe passage to the Diet of Worms in 1521. He also faked Luther's highway abduction on his way back to Wittenberg from Worms, hiding the Reformer thereafter in Wartburg Castle, where he completed his 1522 translation of the New Testament (the "Septembertestament").

Frederick III also succeeded in winning an exemption from Charles V's Edict of Worms for Saxony. His successors—his brother, John (Johann) (1468-1532), and John's son, John Frederick (Johann Friedrich) I (1503-1554)—were also both adherents of Luther, as well as Electors of Saxony who were instrumental in creating institutions that led up to the Schmalkaldic War. For example, in 1527 Elector John Frederick I officially founded the Lutheran Church, of which he was the *Landesbischof*, therewith establishing Protestantism as the Saxon state religion (Evangelisch-Lutherische Landeskirche Sachsens).

12.3.3 Albertine Saxony

In 1500 the Albertine dynasty's founder, Albert III, was succeeded by his son, George (Georg), who, in contrast to the men of the Ernestine line, was no friend of the Reformation. Despite harboring and expressing personal grievances with the Catholic Church, George was decidedly against what he saw as an apostate movement. In 1525, he and other German nobles established the League of Dessau in order to protect Catholic interests in the Empire. He attempted to persuade his cousin, Elector John, to join the league, but John refused and instead collaborated with Philip I of Hesse (1504-1567) in 1526 to create the pro-Protestant League of Torgau, predecessor of the Schmalkaldic League, which itself was founded in 1531 by Philip I of Hesse (again) and Elector John's successor-to-be (1532), John Frederick I of Saxony.

The Albertine Line might well have remained an anti-Protestant dynasty had one of Duke George's three sons survived to succeed him. Only one—Johann—survived childhood. He married but died childless in 1537. The next-in-line to Albertine Ducal Saxony (as compared to Ernestine Electoral Saxony) was George's pro-Protestant brother Henry IV of Saxony, who inherited the title upon George's death in 1539. George had tried to prevent this transfer by disowning Henry and bequeathing Ducal Saxony to Ferdinand I, but George died before succeeding. Had it not been for this horizontal transfer of the title, Maurice, son of Henry IV, would have never become Duke of Saxony.

12.4 Battle of Mühlberg

In 1545, Charles V called for Protestant involvement at the upcoming Council of Trent. In reality, the Emperor was already setting the stage for war against the Protestants—an option that became viable only after securing a détente with France and an armistice with the Ottoman Empire, both in 1544. As a result, the Emperor had the time and energy to re-focus on internal matters, and he was able to reallocate resources to deal with the religious rebels. By the end of 1545, the Emperor's forces began performing maneuvers just north of Leipzig. This development is reflected in Fabricius' 24 November 1545 letter to Meurer (cf. 6.2.4): "et ex iis, de quibus tu nunc scribis, dissensionibus ac periculis multis, quae quotidie intueor, plane exhorresco" (*"and because of what you describe now, I'm completely terrified by the dissensions and the many perils that I observe daily"*).

On 4 July 1546, Elector John Frederick I met with Landgrave Philip I of Hesse in Ichterhausen, just outside of Erfurt. There, the two decided on a pre-emptive strike, betting on their ability to mobilize the Schmalkaldic League forces before the Emperor could his. By the end of the month, League forces were marching southward with the intent of blocking Imperial and Papal forces from passing through the Alps. While Elector John Frederick I was in Württemberg, the nominally-neutral opportunist Albertine Duke Maurice marched on Ernestine Saxony and confiscated the Elector's territory. John Frederick I was able to return and regain much of his losses, but it took him until April 1547. Thus distracted from the initial goal, the Schmalkaldic League was unable to prevent the Emperor's troops from moving on Saxony. On 23 April 1547, the two sides met in the Battle of

Mühlberg. Fighting commenced on a meadow south of Annaberg between Leipzig and Wittenberg. That very day, Elector John Frederick I was captured near Falkenberg and was led before the Emperor.

12.4.1 Power Swap in Wittenberg

Though he was both pro-Protestant and a member of the Schmalkaldic League, Duke Maurice chose to remain neutral in the pre-war verbal conflict between the Schmalkaldic League and the Empire. This official neutrality masked what Maurice came to see on the eve of an impending war: the chance for gain. That is, Maurice hoped to benefit from the fallout by playing carefully between both sides. His ultimate goal was the long-term institutionalization of the Reformation on all levels of society in Saxony, a plan that had been coming to fruition since his 1543 "Neue Landordnung" (cf. 13.2). His plan was actually similar to that of the Schmalkaldic League—the protection of Protestant interests—but vastly different in method: Maurice sought to use education, not war, to secure Protestant stability (cf. Pernet, p. 33). Nevertheless, this method did not preclude battle: Maurice would eventually fall in 1553 during the Battle of Sievershausen, one of the continuing skirmishes in the wake of the Schmalkaldic War. Yet Duke Maurice's vision was deeper and broader than Elector John Frederick I's implausible goal of overtaking the Empire. Maurice's plan required securing his borders against the Empire to allow for the Protestant infrastructure to grow into a self-sustaining organism. This required political maneuvering to placate the Emperor while attempting to consolidate the Saxonies into a single and more contiguous entity than it had been: the result of the 1485 Division of Leipzig left the state divided in two generalized realms—east and west—yet also created a patchwork of enclaves between the two that weakened the integrity of the entire area.

Leading up to the Schmalkaldic War, Duke Maurice cleverly recognized the solution. This is what he saw: by 1546 the Schmalkaldic League was led primarily by Elector John Frederick I. This was due to Hessian Landgrave Philip I's having to tread softly with the Empire so as to not incur the direct wrath of the Emperor after engaging in bigamy in 1539. Thus, if the impending Schmalkaldic War was won by the Empire, Charles V would have but one man to punish as the leader of the revolutionary League. Once John Frederick I was removed from office, a vacuum would form in Ernestine

Saxony. If Duke Maurice were to make himself an ally of the Emperor, he would likely benefit from this power vacuum.

Truly, the Emperor saw in Elector John Frederick I both a traitor and a heretic (cf. 12.4.1). Though many princes and dukes had supported the Schmalkaldic League, John Frederick I stood out by virtue of his position as an Elector. After all, of the seven Prince-Electors (*Kurfürsten*)—the true power of the Empire—only he had engaged in revolution. Moreover, that attempt at revolution was made by an alliance sworn on the Augsburg Confession—the primary declaration of faith written in 1530 by the Protestant followers of Luther. The Schmalkaldic League was thus a Protestant militia and, therefore, an enemy of the "Catholic faith and the Holy Roman and Universal Church" for which Charles V had "appeal[ed] to the defense [...] and to the protection" in 1521. By such language, Charles V had more or less declared himself the defender of the faith. Moreover, his language reveals his belief that the Empire and the Church were two organs of the same "Holy Roman" body. As such, treason against the one and heresy against the other were equivalent. Moreover, the combination of both treason and heresy in the same person was the ultimate sin of all—*lèse majesté*. If Charles V had been unwilling to use execution against the tax-oriented revolutionaries in Ghent, he was certainly willing to fulfill his Edict of Worms threat when dealing with the doubly-treacherous Elector John Frederick I.

In the midst of the Battle of Mühlberg, Duke Maurice's calculation proved correct. Charles V's general, the future Emperor Ferdinand I, was crushing the opposition and managed to capture John Frederick I quickly. The Emperor immediately sentenced the Elector to execution. Before he could see out this decision, the Emperor's attention was diverted to an attack on Wittenberg. There, Schmalkaldic League forces under the direction of John Frederick I's wife, Sybille, were tormenting Imperial troops that were trying to capture the city. Preoccupied thus with battle, the Emperor stayed John Frederick I's death sentence until later. On 24 April 1547, i.e. the following day, John Frederick I negotiated for the safety of his family by surrendering the Electoral title to Duke Maurice and agreeing to exile in Worms.

Thus began a long-lasting animosity between the two branches of the Saxon House of Wettin, as the Ernestine line was bereft of its inherited role: Ernestine Saxony became Ducal Saxony; Albertine Saxony was raised to

Electoral Saxony. More still, Ernestine Saxony was forced to relinquish all but a small section of its lands east of the Saale to Maurice, including Wittenberg. Consequently, Maurice, now 26 years of age and having been born without any expectation of ruling at all, was suddenly highly influential: in six years he had gone from being a ceremonial noble to being a lesser prince and finally to being one of the Empire's seven most powerful princes. This position gave him increased sway at Imperial diets and a vote in the decision over the next Emperor. Moreover, the territories he gained solidified Saxony. As a result, Saxony was more secure both politically and territorially. An added bonus was the acquisition of Wittenberg and, with it, the university there. Suddenly now-Elector Maurice oversaw two of Europe's premier teaching institutions, both of which had played central roles in the Reformation and would continue to educate an upcoming generation of Protestant-minded humanists "[...] damit es an der Zeit mit Kirchdienern und anderen gelarten Leuten in unseren Landen nicht Mangel gewinne [...]" (Dorfmüller: 9). That is, Saxon society was already in need of learned men to fill the clerical, educational and bureaucratic posts that had gone empty when those that disagreed with the Reformation left for safer circumstances. The future of the Saxony thus relied on its ability to educate replacements. Elector Maurice needed only to ensure that university desks were being filled continuously each year. Luckily, using the advice at his disposal from the great Reformation fathers, Duke Maurice had already established the means to keep the universities full in 1543 through the "Neue Landesordnung" (cf. 13.2).

12.4.2 Continuing Wettin Influence

Returning to the now smaller territory of Ernestine Saxony with his newly-demoted title as Duke of Saxony, John Frederick I removed his capital to Jena. During his five-year exile in Worms, he developed a plan to establish the University of Jena as an alternative to the University of Wittenberg. Back in Jena, John Frederick I's three sons brought their father's plan to fruition in its first stage by building a high school (i.e. *Gymnasium*). In 1554, John Frederick I died. In 1558, Emperor Ferdinand I extended a charter to the high school, thereby formally establishing the University of Jena. After the Capitulation of Wittenberg, the authority of the Duke of Saxony was limited mostly to the governance of the high school/university in Jena.

John Frederick's three sons divided the remaining lands (mostly in modern-day Thuringia) into three new duchies. The Ernestine branch of the House of Wettin thus became three new royal houses: Saxe Eisenach and Saxe-Coburg; Saxe-Weimar; and Saxe-Gotha. Though the duchies remained insignificant to history, the family lines managed to produce individuals of influence. One descendant line in particular, the House of Saxe-Coburg and Gotha, produced kings (Belgium and Bulgaria) and consorts (Mexico, Portugal, and the United Kingdom). The current royal dynasty of Britain—the House of Windsor, headed by Queen Elizabeth II—has descended from Edward VII of England, who was surnamed Saxe-Coburg-Gotha. The name of the British royal family was changed to Windsor to avoid anti-German sentiment resulting from World War I. Thus, despite losing their electoral power within the Holy Roman Empire, the Protestant Ernestine dynasty has made its mark elsewhere in the World.

12.5 So-Called 'Peace' in Augsburg

Following the Schmalkaldic War, the Imperial Diet convened in Augsburg in 1547. The following year, on 15 May, the diet issued the Augsburg Interim—a decree calling for the Protestants to return to Catholicism in belief and in practice, but allowing for returning priests to marry. This attempt to placate the Protestants merely infuriated them all the more. Moreover, Catholic German princes and the Pope refused to support the document. Duke Maurice issued the Leipzig Interim as another compromise, but this too was generally rejected. Despite the lack of power behind either decree, one product of the attempts at reconciliation was the emigration of Martin Bucer (1491–1551) to England. Bucer was an associate of both Luther and Zwingli, as well as a collaborator with Melanchthon. In England, he influenced the English Reformation, already underway after Henry VIII's 1533 separation from Rome.

On the Continent, Charles V's "Dutch Inquisition" was still in effect. Technically speaking, the inquisition in the Netherlands is regarded as a sub-movement of the Spanish Inquisition (1478), due to the Netherlands' status as a territory of the Spanish Habsburgs. Nevertheless, Charles V's "Dutch Inquisition" began in earnest in 1521, as part of his actions to control the flow of Protestantism, and was justified by means of the Edict of Worms. This secularly initiated inquisition was ultimately matched by an official ecclesiastical one in 1542, when Pope Paul III initiated the Roman Inquisition as a Church-internal movement to defend the faith against Protestant heresy. With the Roman Inquisition underway, Charles V finally had what he saw as papal support for his activities.

While the Church's Roman Inquisition technically continues on to the present day (albeit under a thrice-altered title), Charles V's Imperial policy was repealed officially on 25 September 1555, when the Diet of Augsburg issued the Peace of Augsburg—remembered today by the motto "cuius regio, eius religio"—formally accepting Protestantism as equal to Catholicism for political purposes throughout the Holy Roman Empire. Despite allowing for this concession to be made, Charles V refused to be linked publicly to any compromise on religion. In spirit, he was still committed to his role as Defender of the Faith. Consequently, he was not present at Augsburg. Rather, he was represented at the diet by his brother and imperial successor, Ferdinand I. A year later, on 12 September 1556, Charles V abdicated. Thus, his direct influence ended on this date. Nevertheless, his actions against the Protestants continued, albeit in a much reduced way.

Charles V bucked both Salic tradition and papal desire by granting the title of Emperor to his brother rather than to his son. The effect of the anti-Protestant policy waned due to the more pragmatic approach of Ferdinand I (1503–1564), who sought less to destroy the Protestants and more to recuperate from the decades of battle. Despite this change in the Holy Roman Empire on the whole, Charles V's vision remained viable in that part of the Empire overlapped by the Seventeen Provinces. His successor as *Herr der Nederlanden* was his son, Philip II of Spain (1527–1598), who vehemently maintained the spirit of the Edict of Worms in the Netherlands.

12.5.1 Ferdinand I's New Approach

Ferdinand I was more tolerant of Protestantism than either his brother or his nephew. Therefore, he was seen by the Protestant electoral princes as the acceptable alternative to have as Emperor because, despite the obvious break with tradition, it went counter to the Pope's opinion. In reality, Ferdinand I's tolerance was merely a mask covering his doubt that any formal resolution could ever be made to bring the Protestants back into the fold (ADB). Instead, he sought to reign in the political powers of the Pope (something he accomplished only by the willing cooperation of Philip II, who convinced Pope Paul IV to accept Ferdinand I as Emperor)[1] and initiated therewith a Church-internal reformation, which was realized beginning in ca. 1560 as the Counter-Reformation. Through this, Ferdinand I hoped to regain territory from Protestant influence by mediating the doctrinal differences from the inside to make the Catholic Church more appealing to borderline Protestants.

12.5.2 Revival of Tactics by Philip II of Spain

Philip II was just as ardent a defender of the Catholic faith as his father. His repertoire of persuasive methods mimicked Charles V's, including at very least the threat of capital punishment for heresy. In 1559, Philip II attempted a gerrymander-like tactic in the Seventeen Provinces (Netherlands) by reorganizing (with Papal approval) the three extant dioceses into 14. The new bishops were charged with restoring the "Dutch Inquisition". For this, he borrowed a technique used by Charles V in the 1520s, when placards warning of the dire consequences of heresy were posted around the Netherlands. Philip II entrusted his new bishops to enforce the message of these placards. Heresy remained equivalent to treason, but the rationale behind the crime changed partially: now the treachery was committed against the King instead of the Emperor. All the same, anyone found guilty could still expect to lose his property if not also his life.

Ironically, Philip II's restructuring of the Catholic bureaucracy backfired. Besides being despised by his Protestant subjects—as might be suspected—the Catholic leadership of the three old dioceses unexpectedly began to resent the King, due to their having been forced to hand over rich abbeys to support his new bishops. The sentiment against Philip II was also influenced by his quitting the Netherlands for Spain in 1559, from where he insisted on ruling the Dutch from then on. Thus, by the 1560s there was once again resentment among the Dutch based on sentiments that they were being ruled by a foreign king who taxed them for foreign ventures. This hatred of Philip II culminated in the Dutch Revolt of 1568, beginning the Eighty Years' War from which the wholly independent (i.e. from the Holy Roman Empire as well as Habsburg rule) Dutch Republic emerged.

---

[1] After Paul IV's death in 1559, his successor Pius IV recognized Ferdinand I without reserve (ADB).

12.6 The *Heliand* as Response to Anti-Protestant Policies

Philip II's particularist policy was detested well-beyond the borders of the Netherlands. For example, a decade and a half after returning to Saxony from Strasbourg, Georg Fabricius, now rector of the *Fürstenschule* at Meissen, commented about Philip II's "Belgian Mandates", i.e. the anti-Protestant placards, in a letter to his brother Andreas, dated 24 March 1561 (emphasis mine):

> Mitto tibi ex antiquo libro Germanico praefationem, ex qua cognoscis opt(im)os Imperatores Germanorum vere Germanos non *interdixisse lectioni sacrae vulgo hominum, vt nostri nunc faciunt Belgicis mandatis et vt totus Papatus facit*: [...]
>
> I am sending you a preface from an ancient Germanic codex, from which you will learn that the best and truly German Emperors of the German people did not *prohibit the common folk from reading the Holy Word, as our leaders are now doing with the Belgian Mandates, and as the entire papacy does*: [...].

This same letter excerpt was introduced in 6.2.1 when Fabricius was identified as the source behind Illyricus' printing of the *Prefaces*. Fabricius' letter to his brother (sent from Meissen to Jena) proves useful on yet another plane: it shows the environment in which the *Prefaces* were published—namely, a revived assault on the Protestant cause.

Philip II's tactic was essentially identical to that of his father, as expressed in the Edict of Worms: Luther (dead since 1546) was a heretic; his writings were religiously and politically illegal; his Bible translation unjustified, unauthorized and therefore worthy of the fire; and furthermore, anyone supporting or sympathizing with the Lutheran message was guilty of treason against both God and the State, and was therefore to be dealt with using the strictest of means.

Fabricius might be seen as having released the *Praefatio*-and-*Versus* texts into the wild via Illyricus (a friend and notorious loose-cannon) as a deliberate play against Philip II's 'Belgium Mandates'. It has already been shown (6.2.1) that the letter cited above not only contained the *Prefaces* material (*Mitto tibi ex antiquo libro Germanico praefationem*: 'I am sending you a preface from an ancient Germanic codex'), but that Andreas was to pass this preface along to Illyricus. A year later, in March 1562, Illyricus printed the *Prefaces* in his second edition of *Catalogus testium veritatis*. The outcome for which Fabricius was hoping from this publication is now uncertain.

What is certain is that this surfacing of the materials from the Leipzig *Heliand* codex is the second instance during the Reformation period.

As discussed in Chapter 6, the first surfacing of the Leipzig codex can be traced to 1545. Its presence at the *Paulinum* was certainly known by at least three men by 7 January 1545—the date of Fabricius' first letter to Meurer on the subject (cf. 6.2.2). Still, because of the nature of that letter as a response, it can be assumed that Borner had the document in 1544 (cf. 6.2.4). The timing of both the Leipzig codex at the UBL and the founding of that library in 1543 are uncannily close to the establishment of another of Duke Maurice's pre-Schmalkaldic War educational innovations: the *Fürstenschulen*. Moreover, Borner and Meurer are known to have been involved in the establishment of, in particular, the first of the *Fürstenschulen*—one housed in a former monastery in Pforta, a village on the outskirts of Naumburg.

13. The Codex from Naumburg

13.1 Hypothesizing *Codex L

Fabricius' first letter to Meurer (7 January 1545) is the earliest mention of the Leipzig *Heliand* codex. Herein, Fabricius hints at the location from which Borner himself must have acquired the Old Saxon manuscript book (cf. 6.2.2, Appendix A.1, emphasis mine):

> Velim igitur cum Bornero agas, ut praefationem illam Latinam sui manuscripti, *quam ex Numburgensi bibliotheca habet*, mihi describendam curet cum una atque altera pagina veri operas Germanici; cupio enim de eo doctorum et inprimis B. Rhenani cognoscere judicium atque sententiam.

> So, I would like you to try to convince Borner to take care when transcribing the Latin preface of his doubtless Germanic manuscript for me, *which he has from the Naumburg library*, every page of it, because I am interested to know the assessment and opinion of learned men concerning it, including the foremost B. Rhenanus.

Regarding this very quotation, Hannemann, the discoverer of Fabricius' epistolary comments, remarks (1974, 31-32; cf. 1939, 11, emphasis mine):

> War der erste Versuch des G. Fabricius, durch Beatus Rhenanus den germanisch-lat. Praefatiokodex ins gelehrte Gespräch zu bringen, auch gescheitert — *an der höheren Gewalt der politischen Lage und an persönlich schwierigen Verhältnissen* —, so verdient doch der Hinweis auf die Naumburger « Praeexistenz » des *Leipziger Kodex, dessen Identität mit dem Ludwigs- und Luthermonotessaron hier behauptet oder postuliert wird*, volle Beachtung. Die Frage bleibt offen, ob der Kodex selbst den Naumburger Besitzvermerk auch noch im Leipziger Bestand besass, oder ob Fabricius die Kenntnis dieser Provenienz der mündlichen Belehrung durch K. Borner verdankte. Der « Lutherheliand » nähme sich in der Nachbarschaft der Naumburger Stifterfiguren nicht schlecht aus, *auch wenn er in Naumburg nur ein « Zugereister » gewesen wäre*.

Herein, Hannemann essentially offers points for discussion:

1. Fabricius' failure to transmit the contents of that codex to Rhenanus was due to the dangerous political situation and his own difficult circumstances;
2. Luther's rumored *Heliand*-codex (i.e. *L) can be identified as Borner & Fabricius' document (i.e. *F);

3. The possibility that the Leipzig codex did not actually originate from Naumburg *per se*, rather had only made a stop-over there prior to moving on to Leipzig

Point 1. speaks to Hannemann's gift for sleuthing. His conclusion here is supported by the discussion of the third (i.e. 24 November 1545) letter sent by Fabricius to Meurer (cf. 6.2.4). Though this letter seems to have been missed by Hannemann, his conjecture about how Fabricius' circumstances affected his ability to perform Borner's task was astutely on the mark.

Point 2. is far more important. Here, Hannemann, too, links the Fabricius-Borner codex at Leipzig with the rumored Luther codex. I have spent the past several chapters attempting to corroborate this connection by investigating the circumstantial evidence (timing, location, social network) surrounding the various references to the Old Saxon codex in Leipzig. Altogether, this evidence supports unifying *F, *Ch, and *L_m (cf. 13.1) into a single work. In short, Manlius' report about *L_m states that Luther had "had the book for a long time" (*Quem librum diu habuit apud se*; cf. Ch. 9). Therefore, it is easiest to assume that the Leipzig *monotessaron* traceable to the *Paulinum* to as early as October-November 1544 (cf. 6.3)—the codex that all three UBL founders (Borner, Camerarius, Melanchthon) discussed publicly and were recorded do so on three different occasions by three other men (Fabricius, Chemnitz, Manlius)—was the very same "book which at some point the Great Luther borrowed by permission of his very good friend Borner" (*qvo libro aliqvando Megalander Lutherus ex concessione amicissimi Borneri fuit usus*). It is also easiest to assume this was exactly the same codex described almost a century and a half later by the UBL librarian Feller: "I found a monotessaron—in other words, a one-from-four composed by order of Louis the Pious, i.e. a harmony of the four Evangelists" (*inveniebam Monatessaron, seu Unum de qvatuor jussi Ludovici Pii compositum h. e. Harmon. IV. Evangelistrum*; cf. Ch. 7). Therefore, *F = *Ch = *L_m = *L: a single codex present at the UBL's *Paulinum* for a period of at least 142 years (i.e. ca. 1544–1686). For this unitary codex, I propose the indicator **Codex L*, so as to prevent confusion with other scholastic theories that have not accounted for the similarities between the hypothesized rumor sources and the rumored Luther-*Heliand* as has been done here.

Point 3. entails a variety of possibilities. It is possible that the codex in question was housed in Naumburg for some time after its arrival from some other, still-unknown location. It may have even been part of the holdings of any of the Naumburg church edifices.[1] On the other hand, Hannemann also inquires whether the codex in question contained a bookplate, viz. mark of ownership, indicating to Fabricius that the book was from Naumburg, or if this piece of information was provided to him by Borner. Obviously, it is impossible to tell which was the source of Fabricius' knowledge of the codex's link to Naumburg; however, Hannemann's question introduces the idea that the codex had come to Leipzig *via* Naumburg, i.e., that Naumburg was merely a stop-off. Similarly, the codex might very well have come from the region *surrounding* Naumburg, and Fabricius' naming it was merely meant to serve as a point of reference for the general region. Indeed, when considering the region around Naumburg, the name of one village in particular stands out. This village was not only home to one of Saxony's recently-closed monasteries, but to the very one selected to be converted into Saxony's first *Fürstenschule* as part of Duke Maurice's "Neue Landesordnung": Pforta.[2]

13.1.1 Links between Leipzig and Naumburg

Concerning his attempts to find evidence of the Leipzig codex in Naumburg, Hannemann states (1974, 32–33, emphasis both his and mine):

> Leider hält die Naumburger Bibliothekgeschichte keinen Vergleich mit der überreichen Naumburger Kunstgeschichte aus. [...] Wenn H. Kramm [(1938, pp. 170ff.)] Borner nachrühmt, er habe « mit mehr als 4000 Büchern und Hss. das Beste des mitteldt. Bildungsgutes aus dem Mittelalter gerettet », so hatte doch Naumburg *nicht* zum Einzugsgebiet der zugunsten der Leipziger Paulinerbibliothek aufgelösten 10 Klosterbibliotheken des altertinischen Sachsen gehört, und die Domstiftsbibliotheken waren im wesentlichen erhalten geblieben.

Besides Heinrich Kramm, Hannemann cites Sibylle Harksen, in whose *Bibliographie zur Kunstgeschichte* are listed only three titles dealing with the Naumburg libraries—Juntke (1940), Mitzschke (1880), and Neumann

---

[1] It is important to note that Naumburg was the site of a bishopric and was thus spared from losing any of its local monastic churches to Duke Henry's closure-by-secularization.
[2] Known more now as Schulpforte, after the school still in operation there.

(1903)—and two dealing with the libraries of the Naumburg monasteries—Petzholdt (1875) and Schwenkes (1893). Despite his having found no mention of the former presence of the Leipzig *Heliand* codex in any of these works, Hannemann finds plenty of circumstantial reasons to consider a transfer of the document from Naumburg to Leipzig possible:

> Eine Verbindung zwischen dem Domstift in Naumburg und der Leipziger Universität bestand aber schon in vorreformatorischer Zeit durch die Zuweisung von Naumburger Stiftspfrüden an Leipziger Professoren, wie auch spätmittelalt. lat. Hss. des Naumburger Bischofs Dietrich von Boxdorf über das Leipziger Predigerkloster in den Besitz der Paulina gelangt waren.
>
> Es gab immer auch private Nebenwege, die von Naumburg nach der jungen Buchzentrale in Leipzig führen konnten. Praktischen Nutzwert hatte ein Heliandkodex als nicht mehr begriffene Buchreliquie der längst verklungenen Vorzeit auch für die Naumburger Stiftsgeistlichen nicht, die im 16. Jh. wie auch die Mönche der beiden 1543 aufgehobenen Naumburger Klöster ihren geistlichen Aufgaben nicht mehr gewachsen waren.

Hannemann doubts that either Fabricius or Melanchthon—or for that matter any number of unnamed "Reformatoren"—were responsible for the discovery of the document at Naumburg and its move to Leipzig. That he simply brushes aside any thought of Fabricius' being responsible seems odd considering he finds it probable that Fabricius was involved in moving a different, classical manuscript from Naumburg to Leipzig (33-34):

> Sicherlich hatte nicht etwa G. Fabricius selbst den Naumburger Kodex nach Leipzig und an Borner vermittelt, obwohl schon der junge Fabricius die Sallustarbeiten[3] seines Lehrers Joh. Rivius im J. 1535 durch die Übermittlung einer besonders alten Naumburger Hs. hätte fördern können.

Fabricius had been a pupil of Johannes Rivius (1500-1553) in Annaberg, Saxony (WBIS). Rivius had befriended Borner while studying in Leipzig prior to moving to Annaberg. Once established as a teacher in Annaberg, Rivius saw potential in Fabricius and sent the young man to Leipzig to study at the Thomasschule under Borner. As has been presented, Fabricius was indeed a gifted student: he quickly took over the teaching responsibilities of the overburdened Borner. Thus, despite his earlier resolution to the con-

---

[3] Gaius Sallustius Crispus (86-34 BC), who, coincidentally, was compared to Thucydides by Quintillian (1920, 59).

trary, Hannemann considers it a possibility that the Leipzig codex was included among materials sent to Borner by Rivius[4] via his student Fabricius.

Yet, when considering still other possibilities for the person responsible for the transfer of the Leipzig codex, Hannemann discounts all of the other major Reformation figures. As evidence for this, he cites not a lack of overall opportunity for one of them to have taken the document from its previous home, rather a conflict of interest that would have prevented such behavior (34, emphasis mine):

> Auch die Wittenberger konnten das « Monotessaron » Ludwigs des Frommen nicht aus Naumburg entführt haben, so eng ihre Beziehungen zu Naumburg, dessen Stadt und Land sich im Gegensatz zur Stiftsgeistlichkeit dem evangel. Bekenntnis angeschlossen hatten, auch gewesen waren. In der l. evangel. Kirchenordnung Naumburgs von 1537 war von den Bibliotheken keine Rede, und die problematische Einsetzung des evang. « Notbischofs » Nikolaus v. Amsdorf im J. 1542 in Naumburg war trotz der Teilnahme der Wittenberger Reformatoren nicht geeignet, etwa nebenher in den Naumburger Bibliotheken zu forschen. Melanchthon hatte sich zwar in Naumburg schon 1526, 1528, 1534, und 1536 aufgehalten, ohne das erst fast ein Menschenalter später von ihm erwähnte « Monotessaron » aufgespürt zu haben.

But Hannemann's doubt really only pertains to his assumption that the Leipzig codex must have come from Naumburg. Yet, through various searches of his own, he failed to discover any evidence of the document in the registers of the churches there.

13.1.2 Previous Search for Evidence in Naumburg

The Naumburger bishopric had previously been seated at Zeitz, from where it moved to Naumburg in 1028 (Heyer, 9). In 1266, the seat was moved back to Zeitz. As for the possibility that the codex in question was somehow misplaced in this relocation shuffle (perhaps to resurface later in Leipzig), Hannemann states the following (bolded emphasis mine):

> Ob von dem reichen Zeitzer Nachlass des letzten kathol. Naumburger Bischofs Julius v. Pflug, zu dem Melanchthon in humanistischer Verbundenheit fast freundnachbarliche Beziehungen unterhalten hatte, **Aufschlüsse für die Naumburger Heliandfrage zu erwarten sind, bleibt abzuwarten**, da die Erschliessung diese 1025 Bände umfassenden Nachlassgutes erst begonnen hat.

---

[4] Rivius was himself an expert commentator on Sallust.

> Das Fehlen eines Monotessaron im Katalog des Naumburger Moritzklosters aus dem 12. Jh. widerlegt die Naumburgthese so wenig wie die Nichterwähnung Naumburgs in den mittelniederdt. Hss. geltenden Reiseberichten C. Borchlings. Zu beachten bleibt, dass das Bistum Zeitz eine Gründung Ottos d. Gr. von 968 gewesen war, der Bischofssitz war 1030 nach Naumburg verlegt worden. Eine Heliandhs. war auch in dem lutherischen Wittenberg und überhaupt im 16. Jh. sprachlich keine *contradictio in adiecto*. Während die Bischöfe 1266 nach Zeitz zurückgekehrt waren, blieben Archiv, Bibliothek und Domschatz in Naumburg zurück.

The project of cataloguing the over 1000 volumes left behind during Naumburg's transition to Protestant hands (1542) had only just begun by the time of Hannemann's writing in 1974. Nevertheless, Hannemann had already prepared himself to find no evidence of the *Heliand* codex ever having been in Zeitz. Hannemann mentions in passing the ongoing status of the compilation of a catalogue of the 1025 volumes that constitute the Naumburg manuscript library. I have been unable to find anything on the status of this project, but one must assume that Hannemann finished it at some point between then and now. In reality, as Hannemann states, if no trace of the Leipzig *Heliand* codex can be found in this catalogue, this does not mean much. One can hardly expect to find in Naumburg that which has ostensibly been removed from there to Leipzig. Moreover, this lack of proof says nothing about whether the document in question was ever there at all. However, potentially fruitful evidence of the provenance of the Leipzig codex does exist elsewhere in the Naumburg region.

13.1.3 Alternative Hypothesis

The only indication that the Leipzig *monotessaron* was somehow tied to Naumburg stems from Fabricius' epistolary reference to something Borner had written him. A different conclusion can be made here: perhaps the *monotessaron* was never in the places (Moritzkloster and the *Domstift*) investigated by Hannemann. How, then, does one reconcile Fabricius'—and ultimately Borner's—claim that the codex had come from Naumburg?

The village of Pforta is located near enough (< 5 km) to Naumburg to be considered by modern definition to be a *Vorort* of the latter. In fact, the village has also been part of Naumburg's ecclesiastical jurisdiction at various times. This geographical and political proximity of Pforta to Naumburg might serve as an explanation for Fabricius' wording in his description of the Leipzig codex in his 7 January 1545 letter to Meurer.

Furthermore, the former Cistercian monastery at Pforta—abandoned in 1540 after its secularization in 1539 by Duke Henry IV of Saxony—was converted into a boys' school in 1543 as part of Duke Maurice of Saxony's "Neue Landesordnung". It is quite notable that this school was first operational in mid-November 1543 (Büchsenschütz, 10; Heyer) only a year prior to the working date (October-November 1544) proposed earlier for Fabricius' reception of Borner's task (cf. 4.3). During the intervening year, much happened at the fledgling school, including the hiring and subsequent resignation of several acting rectors and a dispute over the personal lives of those employed at the school. In fact, the confusion caused by this activity postponed the organization of the school's library for many years (Heyer). By the time the library there had been organized, it became evident that many of the materials left behind by the monks had disappeared. Could the Leipzig codex have been among the Cistercian monks' written materials?

Taken together, the proximity of Pforta to Naumburg, the timing of the establishment of the school there, and the school's many relationships to the UBL—in particular Borner and Meurer's role in the school's establishment—make it very likely that it was the immediate origin of the Leipzig codex. Thus, in contrast to Hannemann's doubt, I consider this to have been the Leipzig codex's most likely route to Leipzig, i.e. from Pforta via Borner himself. To build up a case supporting the hypothesis that the Leipzig codex was once located at Pforta, I will present the history of the school there, that of the Cistercian monastery that preceded it, and the role of this monastic order in the colonization of the lands won by the Saxon dukes during the Carolingian and Ottonian periods.

13.2 Saxony's *Fürstenschulen*

When Duke Maurice sought to increase his political power, he managed to win it in a rather adept and inventive way (Pernet, pp. 33-34):

> Der protestantische Fürstenstaat der Reformationszeit, in dem der regierende Fürst zusätzlich zu seiner weltlichen Herrschaft auch noch eine oberste geistliche Stellung erlangt hatte, kam in seiner Struktur dem Machtstreben des jungen Herzogs Moritz sehr entgegen, und im Laufe seiner Herrschaftszeit hat er sowohl die Politik wie auch die Religion sehr geschickt als 'instrumenta regni' zu nutzen gewusst.

Duke Maurice meant to maintain the social structure in Saxony while reforming the ecclesiastical instrument. This way, he was seen as a hero and not a tyrant by his subjects. The Duke used to his advantage his ability to install emergency bishops in the Saxon dioceses—men loyal to him and his agenda. This move mirrored the particularism of Charles V in the Seventeen Provinces; yet, though this government technique was unpopular in the Netherlands, it was greatly accepted by the Protestant majority in Saxony because there it suited the goals of the populace. Duke Maurice included with this plans for long-term revitalization through education (loc. cit.):

> Dass er den Gedanken des 'Notbischofs' energisch ausnützte, zeigt auch die Tatsache, dass er in seinem Ausschreiben vom 21. Mai 1543 an die Stände die Behandlung von kirchlichen Fragen mit hineingenommen hat, so neben dem Versuch, im Land eine Kirchenzucht durchzuführen [...] mit dem eingezogenen Kirchengut durchgeführte Stiftung der sächsischen Fürstenschulen. Diese waren dann auch „bessert dotiert und organisiert als irgendwo anders, sie sollten die grossen Pflanzstätten der neuen protestantischen Bildung wesen."

Maurice's plan had just as much an economic focus as a religious one. When the anti-Protestant Albertine Duke George died in 1539, his nearly-disowned pro-Reformation brother Henry IV (Maurice's father) inherited the Duchy and immediately issued the official conversion of Albertine Saxony to Protestantism.[5] Henry IV's first major act was the closure of countless monasteries and abbeys, with the excuse that the behavior of these institutions had lapsed (indeed, the Cistercian brethren at Pforta had become wealthy in the previous centuries and were facing censure from the Pope during the 1530s for failure to live according to monastic rules) (Arnhardt, 14, 16–17). The closure and subsequent confiscation of these (former) Catholic edifices was a potential economic boon for Protestant Saxony, so long as the leadership could decide what to do with the buildings and their contents. Duke Henry IV's first intention was to gather the monasteries' contents and sell them for a profit. Buildings were to be rented out as an additional source of income. Yet, before this real-estate vision occurred, many of the lesser nobility stepped in and took up some of the locations as their personal residences (Heyer, 11):

---

[5] Henry had succeeded in doing so for the districts under his immediate control (Freiburg and Volkenstein) in 1537 despite then-Duke George's opposition to the Reformation (Pernet, p. 30).

> Über die Verwendung der aufgehobenen Klöster und ihres Besitzes kam es zu langwierigen Verhandlungen zwischen dem Herzog und seinen Ständen, da beide die Nutzung für sich allein behalten. [...] Auch hatten die Stände offenkundige Mißwirtschaft getrieben. Moritz hielt ihnen vor: „Die Geistlichkeit sei unordentlicherweise hinweggedrungen in dem Namen und Schein, als täten sie es von wegen der Landschaft. Sie hätten ihre Freunde an deren Statt gesetzt und die Klostergüter und die Geistlickheit dermaßen versehen, daß er, der Herzog und die Landschaft, davon keinen Nutzen hätten, [...]. Es würde alles auf Unterhaltungskosten gerechnet, und die Güter würden doch immer schlechter gemacht, und die Gebäude fielen zusammen.

This was frowned upon seriously by many in Maurice's circle, including Luther, who saw it as an example of the "rich getting richer". Duke Henry IV died unexpectedly in 1541, and thus never solved the issue of what to do with his newly acquired property; that responsibility was inherited by his son, Maurice.

The purpose of Maurice's plan was twofold: (1) to make use of an otherwise crumbling infrastructure, the only use of which since his father's closures favored the upper class (and was therewith driving a social wedge into the new Duke's already uncertain attempt to break from the Empire); and (2) to provide places at which future generations of ecclesiastic and government bureaucrats could be educated, thereby institutionalizing them according to a pro-Protestant curriculum. To fulfill these goals, Duke Maurice introduced the "Neue Landesordnung" on 21 May 1543, calling for the creation of three *Fürstenschulen* to be built in Saxony. The school at Pforta was to be the pilot program—the litmus test for judging the possibility of opening at least two other similar institutions. Altogether, these three boys' schools were to be feeder institutions to the renewed University of Leipzig. On the following day, Duke Maurice announced the establishment of the UBL in the University's new building complex at the former St. Pauli monastery (cf. 5.1.4).

13.2.1 The Library at Pforta

Though the school at Pforta started operations in mid-November 1543, the organization of the school's library did not occur until 1570. Fritz Heyer relates the report of *Visitatoren*[6] to the school in 1569, wherein the materials of the old monks' library are critiqued (1543, 42):

> Dieweil für eine bibliothecam [...] in der alten Mönchsbibliothek unter denen Büchern so übrig, wenig vorhanden so ihnen dienstlich, so haben die Praeceptores gebeten, der Kurfürst wolle zum Anfang diese Bücher, so allhier verzeichnet, zu erkaufen von der Schulen einkommen gnedigst einhundert Gulden bewilligen [...]

The Elector mentioned here is Augustus I of Saxony, the younger brother of Maurice, who succeeded the latter after his death in 1551. Of interest here is the general feeling of those involved with establishing the *Fürstenschule* library regarding the nature of the materials left behind by the former monastic residents, the sole worth of which was to be gained by pawning them off. Specifically, the Duke was hoping to sell the monks' books *en masse* for 100 Guilders,[7] and to use this sum to purchase books that were more useful to the students. Additional moneys in support of the school and its students were to be collected through a perpetual tax on the yearly market at Leipzig. Thus, the economic support for the school was to be tied directly to the *Bücherstadt* itself—a relationship that might well have justified a transfer of certain materials from Pforta directly to the UBL.

The visitors' attitude toward the monastic materials is repeated the following year by the teachers: "[...] denn die Bibliotheca so von der alten Munchliberey übrig und vorhanden, wenig oder garnicht der Schulen nutz ist, diweil es alte Müncherey und Barbarey ist." In addition to suggesting that new books be financed through additional taxation, by 1573 the visitors hoped to follow suit after the UBL to acquire materials for the reorganized school library at Pforta (loc. cit.):

> [D]ie beiden Bibliotheken, so noch übrig und vorhanden, bei St. Peter zu Merseburg und im Kloster Bose bei Zeitz zu der Schulen Pforta zu transferieren, dieselbe angefangene Bibliothecam zu mehren und zu sterken, denn Bibliotheken bei Schule sein sollen, da man sie nützlich betrachtet.

---

[6] Not simply 'visitors', rather ecclesiastical (and therewith educational) or eleemosynary regulators who perform special visits (Germ: *Visitationen*) to ensure adherence to the institution's statutes.

[7] Equivalent to 100 florins—a considerable sum, especially when considering that the rector of the school at Pforta received a salary of 150 Guilders at the school's opening in 1543 (Arnhardt).

Thus, the libraries of the cathedral chapters in Naumburg and Merseburg were to relinquish to Pforta the materials consigned to them from the monastery at Posa ("Bosauer Kloster") near Zeitz (cf. 13.2). It is unlikely that the Leipzig *monotessaron* was among the archives originating from Posa, since these were moved to Pforta after 1573—a full three decades after Fabricius' first epistolary reference that places the *Heliand* codex in Leipzig.[8] Once at Pforta, these resources joined an indefinite number of materials original to the monastery-turned-boys' school. Nevertheless, much of the material from either source has been lost over time—a situation parallel to that of the Leipzig codex (loc. cit.):

> Heute lassen sich nur noch zwei Bücher nachweisen, die aus der alten Pförtner Klosterbibliothek stammen. Die übrigen sind spurlos verschwunden, es werden aber kaum viele gewesen sein, denn im Gegensatz zu den Bosauer Benediktinern hatten die Pförtner Zisterzienser wenig wissenschaftliche Interessen.

Though what remained of the monastic materials may have had little in the way of scientific interest at the time, that which had been removed from Pforta in the years between the monastery's closure in 1539 and the school library's reorganization in 1570 would have likely evoked a different opinion today. Indeed, even a catalogue of what the Cistercians had gathered at Pforta over four centuries would provide an interesting window into these monks' experiences.

13.3 The Cistercians at Pforta

The village of Pforta received its name from the monastery established there in 1137, when Cistercian monks originally from Walkenried Abbey were led by Bishop Udo I of Naumburg (ca. 1090–1148) after a failed attempt[9] at establishing a new branch well beyond the Saale River and into Slavic territory at Schmölln near Altenburg. In reflection of their mystic

---

[8] My attempts to find when these archives were transferred from Posa to Naumburg and Merseburg have been unsuccessful, though it must have been prior to 1587, since Heyer produces a list from that date. All the same, this detail seems to bear no importance whatsoever on the origins of the Leipzig *monotessaron*, since it has been determined that this codex could not have been part of the Posa archives.

[9] This first attempt took over an abandoned Benedictine cloister there in 1132 and failed due to pressure from the surrounding Slavs (Schütze, 8).

devotion to the Virgin Mother, the monks of the young Order[10] called their new home *Sanctae Mariae ad Portam* ('[the monastery] of Saint Mary at the Gate'). The *Porta* referred to therein was a doubtless still-standing transverse arch—a remnant of an unfinished crypt church begun some time between 985 and 1002 by Eckard I, Margrave of Meissen.[11] This once stood as a portal to the west of the Cistercians' first completed building, a Romanesque basilica finished by 1150. This original gate has long since been replaced with a gatehouse. Likewise, the swampy land was firmed up by four-centuries of monastic labor. What remains, however, is the original name by which the village has become known, which was nativized as *Pforta*.

13.3.1 Legacy of the Cistercians

What began under difficult circumstances soon flourished in its new location (Schütze, 8–9): "Durch eine zielstrebige, gelegentlich geradezu rücksichtslose Erwerbungs- und Arrondierungspolitik stieg sie im 12. und 13. Jahrhundert zu einem der reichsten Klöster Mitteldeutschlands auf." Within four decades of its own founding, Pforta became the mother abbey to the first in a row of daughter and granddaughter monasteries that stretched ever eastward into Silesia and, eventually, north-eastward along the Baltic: Leubus (1175, Polish: Lubiąż) and its daughters Heinrichau (1227, Polish: Henryków), Kamenz (1239, Polish: Kamieniec Ząbkowicki), Grüssau (1192, Polish; Krzeszów), Mogila (1222, Polish: Mogiła); Altzella bei Nossen (1175) and its daughter Neuzelle in Lower Lusatia (1281); Dünamünde (1208, Latvian: Daugavgrīva), Falkenau (1234; near Tartu, Estonia), and Stolpe in Pomerania (1305). Wealth and opportunity were created via these linear connections, as well as by the required yearly visits of the mother institution's Abbot to both his daughter monasteries and the Order's first abbey at

---

[10] *Ordo Cisterciensis* was founded in 1098 by Robert of Molesme at the Order's first abbey in Cîteaux, near Dijon, France, whence the Order took its name and grew swiftly throughout Europe. Pforta's mother abbey, Walkenried Abbey (1127), was the third Cistercian monastery in German-speaking territory after Morimond (1115) and Altenkamp am Niederrhein (1122).

[11] It was Eckard's sons, Eckard II and Herman I, who in 1010 erected a new fortress not far from the "Porta", which came to be called Naumburg (< *nawen burg*, 'neuen Burg'). In 1028, the bishopric was moved from Zeitz to Naumburg, whence Udo I established the Cistercian abbey in Pforta (Heyer, 9).

Cîteaux. Consequently, "Pforta stieg auf, es wurde ein geistlich bedeutendes Kloster, es wurde vermögend, sehr vermögend – und es verfiel in seinen Kräften" (9).

It was the Cistercians who first employed the waterwheel to accomplish their work—a technique that they helped spread throughout Europe. Furthermore, the Order was influential as agriculturalists and economists of the High Middle Ages: they turned successful profits as productive farmers and cattle-and-horse breeders by developing an organized method of selling produce and livestock, including the fostering of the cloth trade through the sale of wool (Thurston 1914). They have been noted also as millers, metallurgists (cf. Woods, p. 67) and architects. Indeed the rapid spread of Gothic architecture is attributed to the Cistercian Order (cf. Erlande-Brandenburg, p. 116). Consequently, the unsophisticated order of brethren was paradoxically quite wealthy.

Nevertheless, despite three fortunate centuries, the end was in some respects long foreseeable (9–10):

> Die gesellschaftlichen Veränderungen, insbesondere das Aufblühen der Städte, hatten zur Folge, dass der Zustrom der für die Eigenbewirtschaftung der ausgedehnten Güter unersetzlichen Laienbrüder schwächer wurde, schließlich ganz versiegte, und auch der Nachwuchs bei den Chormönchen wurde immer geringer. Man musste zur Pachtwirtschaft übergehen, die geistliche Zucht verfiel.

These societal changes created an atmosphere into which the Reformation came bursting. By 1540 the monastery at Pforta could no longer sustain itself properly (10): "Herzog Heinrich der Fromme[12] von Sachsen hob die Zisterzienserabtei Sankt Marien zur Pforte auf und zog den gesamten Klosterbesitz ein." Three years later, Henry IV's Albertine-Wettin heir and successor Maurice I of Saxony[13] determined the new use for the former abbey.

As for the Order itself, pressures eventually caused changes in organizational structure, ironically leading to its becoming centralized similar to the Benedictines. As a consequence, the Cistercians faced a period of reform during the seventeenth century, and an offshoot—the Trappists—was formed in 1637, once again with the goal of returning to their roots in simplicity. The failure and forced forfeiture of the monastery at Pforta came

---

[12] Henry IV, Duke of Saxony (1473–1541).
[13] Duke of Saxony (1541–1547), later Electoral Prince (1547–1553).

during the period of stagnation between that of wealth/expansion and that of reform. This stagnant period coincided with the larger Reformation already underway in the German lands.

13.3.2 Instruments of *Ostkolonisation*

Though the Cistercians eventually became wealthy and indolent—also very much like the Benedictine Order from which they had original separated themselves—they have continued to this day to maintain their uniqueness in their views on work ethic as was laid out in the original rule, the *Carta Caritatis*. Consequently, their belief in the mystical has never succeeded in overtaking their activities in such a way as to turn their interests inward. Consequently, the Cistercians have never developed an interest in philosophy.

Yet, if the scholastic and juristic (Heyer, 42) works common to the Benedictines have never been of interest nor value to the salt-of-the-earth Cistercians, then what could the monastic library at Pforta have possibly comprised? No doubt, there was practical literature on agriculture and architecture. The founders of the *Fürstenschule* would have no doubt found such writings useless for the needs of their students—a rising class of clerics and civil servants (cf. 13.2).

Still, albeit secondary to their pursuit of applied knowledge, the Order originated and grew with a missionary purpose. Especially for those monasteries established on the frontier of the Empire, the determination to Christianize the heathens was very real. This work was considered no less strenuous or fundamental than manual labor. That a proselytizing mission was included in the efforts of the monks at Pforta hardly seems deniable—their five-year stint at Schmölln prior to moving to Pforta was deemed unsuccessful due to the pressures exerted by the neighboring Slavs (Büchsenschütz/Kißling, 8), who were as equally reticent toward the Christianizing force of the Empire as the Saxons had been in the eighth century until Charlemagne finally enforced the Saxon conversions by the sword. Furthermore, as is evidenced by the rather late conversion of the Scandinavians, pockets of Germanic people resisted Christianization, if indeed this impetus for change did ever reach the more backwater locales during the centuries before the Reformation brought major upheaval to the landscape once again. The medieval frontier was a likely place to find such hold-outs.

Similarly, although a border between the Germanic and the Slavic worlds existed at the Elbe and Saale, this less-than-firm limit was hardly an impediment to people moving in either direction. Consequently, German settlement of the east had been occurring long before the Cistercians arrived in the eastern frontier. These two classes would have been the intended audience of the Order's proselytism. Indeed, they seem to have been reasonably successful in their proselytizing efforts (Arnhardt, 15):

> Durch Papst und Königtum geschützt und gefördert, entwickelte sich das Kloster zum Großgrundbesitz, der zur Zeit Friedrichs II. (1194–1250) seine größten Ausdehnung erreichte. Zuerst bewirtschafteten die Mönche, das heißt die Konversen, ihre Anwesen selbst. Die Zahl der Laienmönche wuchs mit dem Umfang des Besitztums. [...] Kaiser Otto IV. (1128–1218) erkannte darüber hinaus dem Kloster das Recht zu, Reichsgut frei zu erwerben. Neben der Abgabefreiheit erhielt es Zollfreiheit für die Mark Brandenburg, Mark Meißen, Thüringen und das Recht auf freie Saaleflößerei bis Halle. In dieser privilegierten juristischen Position erwarb das Kloster Eigentum von in Not geratenen oder abhängigen Bauern [...].

In contrast to Charlemagne and even the Inquisition[14] underway during their time, the Cistercians of the twelfth century were not set on forcing the heathen masses into the faith. Despite acquiring juristic control and free market access over much of the eastern territories, the Cistercians took a rather more peaceable approach to proselytism that included translation. This was part of their interpretation of *ora et labora*. Consequently, it is not wholly incredible that one of Pforta's daughter abbeys, Altzella[15] (1175) became "bedeutend [...] durch seine Schreibstube und [...] eine für ein Zisterzienserkloster ungewöhnlich große Bibliothek" (Büchsenschütz/Kißling, 9). Thus, through its four immediate descendents and eventual six granddaughter monasteries—all of which popped up east of the Elbe-Saale border—the abbey *St. Marien zur Pforta* was unquestionably a key participant in the Germanic *Ostkolonisation* (Heyer, 9):

> Denn nach der Völkerwanderung und der Zerstörung des Thüringer Reiches durch die Franken waren die Slawen bis zur Saale nachgerückt und hatten sie hier und da sogar überschritten. Noch heute lassen dies die Ortsnamen erkennen, die auf dem rechten Ufer überwiegend wendisch sind.

---

[14] The Medieval Inquisition (1184- ca. 1235).
[15] Located near Nossen, ca. 20 km south-west of Meissen.

That is, while the Carolingian dynasty had established the Saale as the eastern border, the Ottonian dynasty made it its goal to push beyond this into *Sclavania*—the territory that roughly comprises the modern-day Federal States of Brandenburg, Berlin, and Saxony. Medieval German military dukes[16] wished to protect and even profit from whatever territory they gained through war. A ready and willing group of settlers existed in the form of religious orders, to which the secular leadership extended prompt invitations. Both parties benefited from the deal: the leaders secured reliable and recognizable settlers, and the monks received land to live on and an audience of potential converts. Moreover, the mere presence of church officials in the territory was interpreted as even stronger justification for the leadership to protect their holdings— should anyone dare to attack the religious settlement, the Empire would feel justified in sending in the army in order to protect Christianity. Such an invitation was the impetus behind the Benedictine establishment (1122) at Schmölln—the failed monastery taken over by the Cistercians in 1132 before moving closer to but still east of the Saale. The Cistercians' predecessors at Schmölln—the Benedictines—had been invited to that location by Count Bruno of Pleissengau and his wife Willa (Heyer, 9): their avowed goal was to colonize his frontier lands.

13.3.3 Cistercian Proselytism: an Example

The Pforta Cistercians' daughter monastery at Altzella would be the colonizing guarantors in Lower Lusatia in the early thirteenth century, when a small group of monks was sent eastward to settle near the Oder, in the heart of the Sorbian nation on the Empire's new frontier border, which had steadily been pushed eastward. There, the Cistercians established a new daughter monastery at Neuzelle. It is of no concern that the timing of the establishment of either Pforta or Neuzelle came several centuries after the intervening territory had been conquered militarily. The process of guaranteeing this territory was ongoing, because so was the presence of non-Christian Slavs. This new monastery at Neuzelle serves as an example of

---

[16] ModE. *duke* < Lat. *dux* '(military) leader' < *ducere* 'to lead, pull'; cf. NHG *Herzog* 'army leader' (Goth. **harjatuga*; OHG *herizoho, herizogo*; OS *heritogo*) = *Heer* (Goth. *harjis*; OHG/OS *heri*) 'army' + *-zog* :: cf. *Zug* 'train' (OHG *zug* WGerm. **tuga-/*tugi-*) > NHG *ziehen* 'to lead, to pull' (OHG *ziohan*; OS *tiohan* < IE **deuk-* 'pull' > Lat. *ducere* 'to lead, pull) (Kluge).

Cistercian proselytism among the heathen Slavs, the particular focus of which was the local Sorbian population.

The success of the Cistercian missionary efforts at Neuzelle can be measured in part by the fact that by the early sixteenth century the Sorbs had long since been considered converted. This is noteworthy for the fact that, ironically, this "Wendish" folk gained the attention of Saxony's Reformation-focused leadership once again for religious reasons. Many Sorbs were deliberately circumventing the measures gained by the Protestants through Peace of Augsburg (*cuius regio, eius religio*) by returning to Catholicism—in spite of their Elector's proclamation that Saxony was to be a Protestant land.

To try to curb this shift in the Sorbian population, Elector Christian I sought to show that no rightful subject of the Kingdom of Saxony would be overlooked (though it is obvious that the non-Germanic Sorbs had been so for some time). As August I's heir and successor, he extended to the Sorbs something previously reserved solely for German-speaking residents in Saxony and Thuringia: he granted to the Sorbian community two *Gnadenstellen* at one of the three *Fürstenschulen*—a small gesture to indicate to the Sorbs that they belonged. Heyer cites an unpublished *Schulordnung* from Christian I (23):

> Nachdem wir auch berichtet, daß in unseren Landen der wendischen Prädikanten halben offt Mangell fürfallen, und das derentwegen die wendischen Kirchen mehrmals eine gute Zeit unbestellet bleiben mussen, daraus erfolget, daß sich dann unsere wendischen undertanen an die Päpstische kirchen wenden und daher mit irrig Lehr befleckt werden, So ordnen wir hirmit, daß auch in dieser Schulen wie in den anderen beyden zwene Knaben, so der wendischen Sprach kundig und woll erfahren, an Gnadenstellen genommen, dieselben auch nach Verlauffung ihrer Zeit, so sie in der Schulen sein, zu stipendiis bracht und dann fürder an die örter, da es von nöten, gesetzt werden sollen.

Of course, the true purpose behind Christian I's "mercy" had more to do with ensuring that a Sorbian revolt did not tip the precarious religiopolitical balance of Saxony back to the Catholics, and therewith invite the Holy Roman Empire to attack under the guise of protecting their "repentant" Catholic brethren.

This bit of Sorbian history shows not only the national and religious climate during the Reformation, but also proves that the original missionaries to the Sorbs—the Cistercians at Neuzelle—were not merely interested in agriculture and engineering. On the contrary, it seems that the Cistercians there had a profound effect on the Christianization of the Slavs. This, in turn, provides evidence that the Cistercian Order in general was not as reclusive as might otherwise be assumed—they did have a serious missionary drive. And this furthers the discussion of the *Heliand* codex at Leipzig, in that the Cistercians at Pforta were among the first to colonize the region east of the Saale. A question remains about how they prepared themselves prior to arriving in the East March. For if they were in need of scriptural materials with which to undertake their missionary work, but were not themselves translators of scripture, surely they must have used the works written in the scriptoria of other religious orders. A hint at where the Pforta Cistercians obtained certain of their literary materials comes from the history of the monks who lived there.

13.4 Before Pforta

As stated, prior to Pforta (1137), the Cistercians were at Schmölln (1132). Prior to Schmölln, they were part of a larger group at Walkenried[17] (1127), a now-ruined abbey on the southwestern edge of the Harz in Eastphalia—the region encompassing the eastern part of the Carolingian stem duchy, the Duchy of Saxony, which itself had been formed from the territory conquered from the Saxons. To aid in the slow conversion of the Saxons to Christianity, Charlemagne established two bishoprics in Eastphalia: one at Osterwiek (804; moved in 814 to Halberstadt by Louis the Pious), the other at Hildesheim (815). Both locations are located on the northern edge of the Harz Mountains.

13.4.1 Ottonian Homeland

It is notable that the region surrounding the Harz was the home of the Liudolfinger clan—the dynasty of Saxon nobles that would eventually come to rule the empire established by the Carolingians. That is, when the last of the direct male descendants of Louis the Pious (via Louis the German) died

---

[17] "Formerly one of the most celebrated Cistercian abbeys of Germany," Walkenried was "situated [...] between Lauterberg and Nordhausen. [...] The first monks came form the monastery of Altfeld or Camp in the Archdiocese of Cologne. [...] Walkenried grew rich and owned lands as far as the Rhine and Pomerania" (Löffler, "Walkenried.").

out in Louis IV (Louis the Child; 893-911),[18] the authority of the bloodline shifted to the descendants of Louis the Pious' daughter Gisela (820-874), whose granddaughter had married Otto I the Illustrious, Duke of Saxony (851-912). Otto the Illustrious was the son of the Saxon duke Liudolf, founder of the Liudolfinger dynasty. The importance of this dynasty is highlighted by Rotter and Schneidmüller (Widukind, Einleitung, 4):

> Die[se] Königsfamilie, wegen des früheren Leitnamens Liudolf auch Liudolfinger genannt, gelangte in der späten Karolingerzeit zu großen Besitzungen in Sachsen; führende Vertreter nahmen eine herzogsgleiche Stellung in Sachsen ein und können als Angehörige einer der mächtigsten Dynastien Ostfrankens um 900 gelten.

Although the Liudolfinger had become wealthy landowners in their own right, it was this marriage between Liudolf's son to the great-granddaughter of Louis the Pious (via his daughter and granddaughter)[19] that would turn family fortune into genuine power. For when Conrad I, King of Germany, died without issue in 918, and the bloodline shifted over to the remaining descendants of Charlemagne, it was Otto the Illustrious' son Henry I the Fowler who inherited the crown (4-5).

> Der Sachsenherzog Heinrich wurde als erster Nichtfranke nach dem Aussterben der ostfränkischen Karolinger 911 und nach dem Königtum des Frankenherzogs Konrad I. (911-918) im Jahr 919 König in Ostfranken und sicherte dieses Amt seiner Familie für etwa ein Jahrhundert. Dadurch verlagerte sich der politische Schwerpunkt des ostfränkischen Reiches, der sich bisher im fränkischen und bayerischen Gebiet befunden hatte, entscheidend nach Norden, da die liudolfingischen Herrscher seit Heinrich I. (919-936), von ihren sächsischen Besitzungen ausgehend, ihre Herrschaftsansprüche auch in Süddeutschland und in Franken durchsetzten. So trat der sächsische Raum, bisher an der Peripherie der Ereignisse gelegen, in den Brennpunkt europäischer Geschichte.

When Henry the Fowler married his second wife, Matilda of Ringelheim,[20] he married into the Immedinger family, another wealthy Saxon landholder family from the Eastphalian Harz region. As an Immedinger,

---

[18] Also after a short reign by Conrad I, Louis the Child's maternal second cousin, from 911-918.
[19] Hedwiga
[20] A.k.a. Saint Mathilda, i.e. Matilda.

Matilda was the great-great-great granddaughter[21] of Widukind—the very Saxon who had led the 30-year Saxon rebellion against Charlemagne only to lose in 785, thereafter submitting to baptism (Widukind von Corvey, 75). This marriage thus produced a scion who would inherit the holdings of the Immedinger clan, the title of Duke of Saxony from his Liudolfinger ancestors and, more importantly, the title *römisch-deutscher Herrscher*, i.e. King of the Germans and Romans. And so, ironically, in 936—a century-and-a-half after Charlemagne subjugated them—a Saxon nobleman was crowned Holy Roman Emperor: Otto I the Great.

Otto the Great's descent from two noble Saxon houses influenced a renewed interest in Saxon history that has come to be known as the Ottonian Renaissance. The writers during this movement were ecclesiastics who attempted to record Saxon genealogies and histories, justifying their secular writings as cultural duty (5–6):

> Hatte man als Mönch die Absicht, weltliche Geschichte zu schreiben (und nur Mönche waren in jener Zeit von den geistigen Voraussetzungen her hierzu in der Lage), mußte man dies zunächst ausführlich begründen. Widukind tat dies ähnlich, wie es Einhard formuliert hat. Nachdem er seinen gesitlichen Aufgaben nachgekommen sei, müsse er nun einer Verpflichtung enstprechen, die er als Angehöriger seines Standes und seines Stammes fühle, und darum eine bis dahin nicht vorhandene Geschichte des Sachsenstammes verfassen.

It has been speculated from Widukind von Corvey's writing that he himself was related to Matilda of Ringelheim: "Jene Königin [Matilda] aber war die Tochter Thiadrichs, dessen Brüder Widukind, Immed und Reginbern hießen" (75). To this, the modern editors add "[...] aus seinem seltenen Namen hat man eine Verwandschaft des Geschichtschreibers zum sächsischen Königshaus [...] gefolgert; dies ist zwar wahrscheinlich, keinesfalls aber sicher" (4). More certain is that Widukind von Corvey dedicates his history of the Saxon people to Matilda of Ringelheim. Moreover, later descendants and relatives of this queen show that the family was keenly aware of its heritage and interested in documenting it.

As stated, both Saxon dynasties to which Otto the Great belonged held the Harz to be their homeland. This tradition was maintained for generations even after the descendant lines had moved away from the region. The

---

[21] Whether this relationship was an invention of the Saxon nobility or not, the Immedinger clan was nevertheless noble, wealthy, and politically influential.

Hauskloster of the Immedinger clan—the place to which the descendants withdrew for special occasions, such as to honor their ancestors—was established by Queen Matilda at the center of the clan's land holdings, Ringelheim. The *Hauskloster* of the Liudolfinger was at Gandersheim. This abbey was established in 852 by Liudolf himself and therefore stems from a time just after that proposed for the creation of the *Heliand*. Furthermore, as an indication of the importance of the Harz to the Ottonians, it is important to note that Otto the Great was born at Wallhausen near Sangerhausen—on the southeastern edge of the Harz—and he died not far south of there at Memleben near Naumburg.

13.4.2 Quedlinburg, Gandersheim, Magdeburg

During the Ottonian period many abbeys and cloisters were founded throughout the region surrounding the Harz Mountains, mainly by the Emperor's relatives. For example, when Henry the Fowler died in 936, Matilda buried him in Quedlinburg and there founded an abbey, which she dedicated to him. She then retired there and served as abbess for 30 more years. Also of note is Matilda's relationship to the town of Nordhausen,[22] which Henry the Fowler had given to Matilda as a dower in 909. As a commemoration of this event he had a fortification built there (908–912). This was the location of the birth of their fourth child and second son, Henry I (919/922–955), later Duke of Bavaria. In 961, as yet another commemoration to her late husband, Matilda established an abbey near the fortification in Nordhausen. This became the Nordhausen Cathedral in ca. 1130.[23] Matilda of Ringelheim established three more religious sanctuaries in towns given to her as part of her dower. These three were all located southwest of the Harz: Pöhlde, Grone (Göttingen), and Duderstadt.

Succeeding his father as king in 936, Otto the Great had the edifices at Quedlinburg built up as his royal palace.[24] From there he ruled with his

---

[22] Nordhausen is located 35 km due west of Sangerhausen and 15 km southeast of where the Cistercians would eventually build Walkenried Abbey.
[23] From its founding in 1127, the Cistercian monastery at Walkenried seems to have had close ties with Matilda's convent in Nordhausen, eventually even maintaining a monastic yard there (*Walkenrieder Hof*) from 1292 on (Grabinski).
[24] The successors to the Ottonian throne maintained this palace as the location to which they would return to celebrate Easter.

queen, Edith[25] of Wessex (910–946), whom he married in 929. Edith was the half-sister of Æthelstan (895–939), King of England from 924/925 to his death. Æthelstan sought to maintain the close ties to mainland Europe that his father, Edward the Elder (871/872–925), and grandfather, Alfred the Great (849–899), had established. In 929, Henry the Fowler sent a delegation to England in order to find a bride for his son, Otto the Great. Æthelstan thus sent Edith and another half-sister to the bachelor Otto, who had evidently been made co-ruler by his father. As the customary *Morgengabe*, Otto gave the city of Magdeburg to his new bride. Edith loved the city, often residing there, and it thus became a center of action, as is proven by the royal assembly held there in 937. Ultimately, Edith was to rest in Magdeburg after her youthful death in 946. Her husband's body was laid beside hers after his death in 973. Prior to this, however, Otto and Edith had two children together, including a son, Liudolf (Duke of Swabia), who later became father to Matilda II, Abbess of Essen (949–1011).

In 951, seven years after Edith's death, Otto the Great remarried. He and his new bride, Adelaide of Italy, produced two children, namely his successor Otto II (955–983) and Matilda of Quedlinburg (954–999). In 966, Matilda of Quedlinburg was granted the responsibilities of Otto the Great's mother, Matilda of Ringelheim (after whom he named his daughter), as abbess of Quedlinburg Abbey. The elder Matilda died two years later; the younger lived to see her brother, Otto II, as well as her nephew Otto III, take the throne.

When Otto II died in 983, he left behind four children: Matilda (975–1025), Otto III (980–1002), Sophia (975–1039), and Adelaide (977–1045). As the only male heir, Otto III inherited the title King of Germany at age three. Consequently, the ruling responsibility was taken up by his regent mother, Theophanu, until the King came to majority in 996, at which point he was made Holy Roman Emperor. From 997–999, Otto III shared regency with his aunt, Matilda of Quedlinburg. Otto III's education was seen to by Bernward (later made bishop of Hildesheim) and by Gerbert of Aurillac, archbishop of Reims (later Pope Sylvester II). Similarly, Otto III's sister received an education from her half-cousin Mathilde II of Essen (daughter of Liudolf, Duke of Swabia, Otto II's half-brother by Edith). It was assumed that Matilda, daughter of Otto II, would replace her aunt, Matilda of Quedlinburg, as Ab-

---

[25] Also spelled *Eadgyth, Edgitha, Editha, Edgith*.

bess of Quedlinburg, but she married instead, making her ineligible for the post. Consequently, another daughter of Otto II, Adelheid of Quedlinburg (977-1044/45), became Abbess of Quedlinburg upon Matilda of Quedlinburg's death in 999. Together, Adelheid of Quedlinburg and her sister, Sophia of Gandersheim (975-1039), became the king-makers for the next generation of rulers by influencing the election of Henry II (973-1024) as King of the Romans in 1024, and Conrad II (990-1039) as Holy Roman Emperor in 1027, thus starting the Salian Dynasty of Emperors.

Of course, none of this recitation of Saxon royalty shows any evidence of the Old Saxon *Heliand*. However, it does serve to show that the members of two ancient noble Saxon families remained active in the Eastphalian region for many generations. If a copy of the *Heliand* ever existed in this area, it would be reasonable to think it resided in one of the many aforementioned locales. Moreover, at least one of these ancient Saxon families—the Liudolfinger—is traced by Widukind von Corvey back to 951.

13.4.3 Ottonian Links to the *Heliand* and Old Saxon Genesis

Eastphalia eventual became the center of the Carolingian Empire's successor institution, the Holy Roman Empire. Many religious buildings and monastic institutions were built there during this period. The first of these, Halberstadt (804/814) and Hildesheim (815), were erected by Charlemagne to encourage Saxon conversion to Christianity, to support those who had already converted, and especially to create much needed imperial infrastructure through which he could lead—most commonly by placing loyalists in power positions. These two colonial outposts became the first bishoprics of the region. Later, these were joined by Magdeburg (937) and Merseburg (968). During Ottonian rule, the building of monasteries continued to be used as a political vehicle, ensuring that influence remained in the hands of Ottonian loyalists. It is hardly any wonder that the Quedlinburg Abbesses were all related to the ruling German King for centuries. The same goes for the Abbesses of Gandersheim, itself an institution that reaches back to 852, when it was placed under the care of Hathumod (840-874) by her father Ludolf. In other words, by the time the Cistercians established Walkenried Abbey in 1127, they found themselves in the midst of many other abbeys built and run by long-standing Saxon nobility. If the Cistercians at Pforta did in fact have a *Heliand* codex, the swiftest conclusion assumes they got it during their stopover at Walkenried prior to migrating further eastward.

Still, this is not the only apparent link between the Ottonians and the *Heliand*. The calendar found with MS V reveals that manuscript fragment's link to Magdeburg (Baesecke, 56). Furthermore, as Mainz was the origin of MS V, the relationship between that city and Magdeburg is relevant. In 971, the daughter of Liudolf, Duke of Swabia—the firstborn son of Otto the Great and therefore half-brother of Otto II—was named Abbess of Essen. Mathilde II of Essen made numerous donations of memorials to Mainz with the blessing of the Emperor. Also, considering her familial relation to the abbesses of Quedlinburg and Gandersheim, and especially to their sister Matilda,[26] there are connections aplenty to suggest one of these as the pathway along which MS V came to Mainz. Also, Mathilde II of Essen undertook a trip to Mainz in 986 in order to bury her mother, Ida of Swabia. Besides having conducted this trip to Mainz, it is known that Mathilde II of Essen wrote to Anglo-Saxon *ealdorman* and historian Æthelweard[27] (?-ca. 998) regarding a history of the Saxon people. In return, he sent her a stiff Latin translation of the *Anglo-Saxon Chronicle*;[28] she sent him *De Re Militari*. Perhaps she also sent him another document—the *Heliand*. This timing of Mathilde II of Essen's correspondence with Æthelweard is intriguing: he was active between 973 and 998 in south-western shires of Wessex (Wojtek, 160), i.e. in southern England (cf. 2.3.1); however, his *Latin Chronicle*[29] ends at 975. This would mean that their exchange ca. 975 would stand as a second point at which

---

[26] Who is thought to have been raised and educated by Mathilde II of Essen (NDB).
[27] Wojtek: "as stated by Æthelweard, King Æthelwulf was their first common ancestor and the author was entitled to call Mathilda his *consobrina*" (160).
[28] In which he gives an account of Anglo-Saxon heritage called *adventus Saxonum* ('The arrival of the Saxons'). Wojtek: "it seems that Æthelweard was deeply interested in the geography both of the Saxons' land of origin and their distribution over Britain [...]"(163).
[29] Wojtek explains Mathilde II's interest (160):
"The Chronicon Æthelweardi must have been written after 975 as this is the date of King Edgar's death and the last event entered into the text. It appears that its origin is related to the connection between the ealdorman and the abbess. The circumstances of how this connection was established are vague, but it is likely that it took place after the year 982, when Mathilda's brother, Duke Otto of Suabia and Bavaria died in the course of Otto II's campaign against the Byzantines and Muslims in the south of Italy. The abbess, realizing that she was the last remaining member of the Anglo-Saxon line in the *Reich*, decided to turn to her English relatives for information on her family's genealogy and history."

the *Heliand* could have been transferred to England. Eckhard Freise settles upon the year 980 for this transfer (NDB):

> Der Ealdorman Aethelweard von Wessex stand in regem brieflichem Kontakt mit M. und widmete ihr 980 als seiner Verwandten – die Königstochter Edith war die erste Gemahlin Ottos d. Gr. gewesen – seine angelsächs. Chronik in lat. Sprache, in der an die gemeinsame Abstammung von Alfred dem Großen und an die Verwandtschaft von Sachsen und Angelsachsen erinnert wird.

That would have been the second clear opportunity for the *Heliand* to move to England. The first point was, of course, the 929 engagement of Edith to Otto the Great, at which time the emissaries to England could have transported the *Heliand* with them, or after which date Edith herself might have been responsible (until her death in 946).

A further notable fact about Æthelweard is that he was a second-cousin of King Æthelstan: Æthelweard's father was Æthelred of Wessex, brother of Alfred the Great. These relationships coming into contact with one another builds a case for an interest in genealogy that certainly grew on both sides of the English Channel. If the *Heliand* was somehow recognized by either party as having some historical import on the common ancestry of the insular and continental Saxons, then this would provide the motive for its transfer to England. Moreover, Mathilde II of Essen incorporates into one person the connections and possible explanation of the *Heliand*'s transfer to Mainz, as well as the supposed western, i.e. Frankish, influence argued for in the paleography and linguistics (particularly vowels) of MS C (cf. Brettschneider 1934). Furthermore, Æthelweard's activity in southern England makes him the first likely suspect when searching for the scribe of MS C (cf. 2.3.1).

In all, the connections between the Cistercians at Walkenried, the Ottonian abbesses in the Harz region, and the two relatives of Æthelstan lends a small degree of historical support for the claim put forth (cf. 2.2 ff.) that MSS L/P, V, and C stem from a common ancestral document (i.e. *A), as can be gleaned from the linguistic and paleographic features present on each. A corollary to this claim would thus hypothesize that common document to have been located likely somewhere in the Harz region, i.e. Quedlinburg, Gandersheim, Hildesheim, or perhaps even Magdeburg. Speaking to the reality of this final option, Mitzka says the following and also gives a nice summary of the various linguistic proposals for the *Heliand* homeland (134):

> Die Entdeckung der Genesis und der Vatikanischen Fragmente 1894 regte Jostes [...] an, die Heimat der Dichtung in Ostsachsen, mit nichtsprachlicher Argumentation genauer in Nordalbingen zu suchen. Die ostfälische Heimat (Friesenfeld und südl. Hassegau) vertritt Wrede [...], ohne Begründung durch Sprachbelege das südöstliche Ostfalen A. Lasch [...]. Das Fränkische sucht A. Brettschneider, Die Heliandheimat und ihre sprachgeschichtliche Entwicklung 1934 in der Heliandsprache und in der dortigen Landschaft auf. Doppelheit der Formen nimmt sie für das Original und für die gleichzeitige gesprochene Sprache an, als As. mit Fränkisch vermischt. Der hauptstädtische Sitz dieser Sprache, zugleich Heimat der Dichtung, ist für sie das karolingische Magdeburg.

Because of the national-socialist leanings, Brettschneider is often discredited for her *Heliand* proposals. Yet, in light of the present discussion—be it from reasons to doubt Fulda (cf. 4.2.1.3) or from historical evidence pointing to a more northerly and even easterly location as the place of composition—the discovery of MS L has only begun to show its potential effect on Old Saxon studies.

As for the Magdeburg proposal, several things speak to its credibility: the city's role as Otto I's imperial capital; its tie to his bride Edith and therefore to her English brother King Æthelstan (cf. MS C); its role as Otto I's ecclesiastical headquarters, and furthermore its ties to western bishoprics and abbeys, such as Mainz (cf. MS V); its location on the edge of the Empire, beyond which lay valuable land where heathens abounded; its position midway along the course of the Elbe—a major European waterway for which Prague's Vltava (cf. MS P) and Naumburg and Pforta's Saale (cf. MS L) are tributaries. Furthermore, Mainz's primary role in the Christianization of Europe and its proximity to the Main River link that city to both Würzburg and Bamberg (MS M, MS S?). This means that whatever was traded between Magdeburg and Mainz (in either direction) would have been relatively easily spread to all the locations at which *Heliand* manuscripts have been discovered. A major flaw in proposing Magdeburg as the writing location is that the Archbishopric there was first established in 968—more than a century after the ca. 840-date supposed for the penning of the *Heliand* Archetype (*A) (cf. 2.2.3). The current Magdeburg Cathedral stands on the site of the former St. Maurice Abbey, which was built in 937 by Otto I the Great. Yet the city of Magdeburg was established in 805 by Charlemagne[30]

---

[30] Mentioned 805 in the 'Diedenhofen Capitulary' (Gm. *Diedenhofener Kapitular*): "ad Magadoburg"(> OHG *magado*-'large' [cf. Goth. *mikils*, Eng. *much*] + OHG *burc* / OS *burg* 'fortification, stronghold' [Riese]).

as a frontier city in order to conduct business with the mostly-Slavic peoples to the east of the Elbe. It is Magdeburg's connection to the Ottonians that intrigues me, as it might provide a means by which the *Heliand* was transmitted, in most part because of the strong figures of Matilda of Ringelhiem, Matilda of Quedlinburg, Adelheid of Quedlinburg, Sophia of Gandersheim, and Mathilde II of Essen. Regarding this final figure, Wojtek argues (160–161, emphasis mine):

> The abbess [Mathilde II of Essen], realizing that she was the last remaining member of the Anglo-Saxon line in the Reich, decided to turn to her English relatives for information on her family's genealogy and history. This hypothesis is strengthened by the observation that high-ranking women were often responsible for the preservation of a family's past. In the tenth century this was very common in Ottonian Germany, and it is therefore not unlikely that Mathilda would have followed suit. In particular, those women who became abbesses were meant to fulfil the role of preserving the past. Because of their longevity (due to the favourable conditions in which they lived, and also because they did not face the dangers of childbirth), they were particularly suited to the transmission of memory of the family, its members, deeds, genealogy, and burial places. Abbesses were given necrologies, memorial books, and written genealogies of people for whom they were asked to pray. For instance, when only thirteen (968) Mathilda of Quedlinburg received on her grandmother's deathbed (Queen Mathilda I, King Henry I's widow), a roll with the names of people for whose souls she was expected to pray. Some similar necrologies and lists have survived in the form of books or codices, which were passed on in the female line for several generations to commemorate ancestors. Such a practice would have been familiar to Æthelweard since it also existed in Anglo-Saxon England. From the materials at their disposal, we can see what these abbesses were required to impart. First, families wanted them to have a precise genealogy and lineage as *these women were expected to pray for and remember the people of their stock*. Genealogies were often traced back to legendary pagan or Christian ancestors *in order to raise the importance of the house. Second, these abbesses wished to establish the burial places of their male kin, as memory and commemoration were less effectively linked to the abstract soul than to an actual grave in a particular abbey or church*. Sometimes this information can seem to read more like a graveyard catalogue or a tomb robber's shopping-list, than a religious and devout request for preservation from oblivion. Third, the families *desired an account of the deeds of these men*: their heroic (even if pagan) origins, their martial acts, their *dedication to God*, the miracles which happened to them and on their behalf, their connections with the saints.

The efforts of the Ottonian women in building and running abbeys—primarily in the Harz region—lead me to argue along Wojtek's line that they were focused on maintaining the memory of their dynastic house, linking it back to the devotion of their aristocratic Saxon forefathers in

Christianizing their heathen brothers. Whether named or not, the *Heliand* composer is described in the *Praefatio* with exactly these characteristics. Moreover, though his identity remains unknown to us today, these genealogically minded women may well have known precisely who of their ancestors was called by the Emperor Louis—whom they considered God's ordained representative on Earth—to bring the Holy Word to the very people who would one day rise up to lead the Empire.

One final notable link between the Ottonians and a discovery location of one of the extant manuscripts: as discussed in 6.1.1, MS M was rediscovered in 1794 at the Bamberg Cathedral library. James Thompson explains regarding the creation of the Bamberg bishopric in 1007 by Henry II, Otto III's successor (83, emphasis mine):

> Henry II, last of the Saxon emperors, having been destined in his youth to an ecclesiastical career, *naturally received a liberal education, first at Hildesheim*, and later under Bishop Wolfgang at Regensburg. There is abundant evidence to show that Henry II could read Latin with ease; and as a book collector he has a distinguished reputation. When he founded his favorite see, *the bishopric of Bamberg, he endowed the cathedral with a magnificent library. The nucleus of this collection was the books which he inherited from Otto III*, supplemented by the books which Henry had received from his teacher.

Otto III had similarly received a formidable education—"[i]n Otto III the inclination to studies was so strong that his duties as ruler suffered in consequence" (Thompson). He received this education at the side of Bernward of Hildesheim, who was made bishop there in 993. It is Bernward of Hildesheim that seems to be the linchpin in the transfer of the *Heliand* to the sites at which extant manuscripts have been found (Bodarwé, 3, bold emphasis mine):

> After a short period during which it was owned by the bishop of Hildesheim as an "Eigenkloster", **Essen** held the position of an Ottonian family convent and was one of the leading Saxon communities of female religious next to **Gandersheim** and **Quedlinburg**. [In the year 987 (MGH DOIII, Nr.32) the emperor Otto III. granted the women community Vilich, near Bonn, the status: *ad legem et ad regularem ordinem ceterorum monasteriorum in nostro regno degentium, scilicet Quidlingeburg, Ganderesheim, Asnithe*. Over and over again these three communities were mentioned at the time as a unity in connection with the Ottonian family.] How this monastery in Essen got in contact with the Liudolfingian family, is still unclear. But at the latest by the middle of the 10th century Essen was governed by members of the Ottonian family. When they were promoted to kingship, Essen was promoted from the family monastery of an important aristocratic family to a royal

community. The abbesses of the Ottonian family were now princesses, daughters and sisters of kings and emperors. The following three abbesses were the most important for the community of Essen [: Mathilde of Essen, Sophia of Gandersheim, and Theophanu of Essen].

Thus, we see that Hildesheim had a direct link to Essen via Bernward and Mathilde of Essen, allowing for an easy explanation of how the *Heliand* could have gotten to Essen, and thence to England (MS C). Further speaking to Bernward having access to the Old Saxon scripture is the conspicuous relationship between the bronze doors that he created for the Hildesheim Cathedral and images in the Junius MS, in which the Genesis B is found (Cohen & Derbes, 24, emphasis mine):

> William Tronzo, in his study of the Hildesheim doors, first suggested that certain iconographic features were drawn from the Anglo-Saxon tradition, as manifested specifically in the so-called Caedmon Genesis, more properly known as Junius 11 (Oxford, Bodleian Library, MS Junius 11). The manuscript, executed in the first quarter of the eleventh century, possibly in Canterbury, is a large collection of vernacular biblical poetry comprising Genesis, Exodus, Daniel, and Christ and Satan; the first ninety-six of the book's 229 pages contain illustrations. The Genesis portion of Junius 11, in fact, consists of two texts. Genesis A, the longer of the two, is essentially an Anglo-Saxon verse paraphrase of the Bible. Genesis B is a fragment of an older Saxon poem on Genesis that was translated and interpolated into Genesis A; it is a freer rendering of the Genesis story that offers a dramatic, psychological reading of the Fall of the Rebel Angels and the Fall of Humankind. *Tronzo plausibly connected the essentially contemporaneous Junius 11 drawings and Hildesheim doors, for the monuments have important thematic affinities.* Both focus to a remarkable degree on the role of Eve in the narrative of the Fall.

This would mean that Bernward of Hildesheim possessed a copy of the Old Saxon Genesis. His ties to Matilda II of Essen would imply that along with this Old Saxon Genesis, he also possessed a copy of the *Heliand*. As for the Junius MS, its "Lokalisierungen schwanken zwischen Winchester, Canterbury und neuerdings Malmesbury" (Taeger 1996, xxx). Interestingly, both Winchester and Malmesbury were active scriptoria in Wessex, over which Æthelweard ruled as ealdorman.

Hildesheim again comes into focus when considering how MS M might have ended up in Bamberg, i.e. via Henry II's donation to the library there. MS V, which can be linked back to Mainz, contains a calendar that stems from Magdeburg, linking that manuscript back to Ottonian territory. MSS L and P, which together represent the surviving elements of a single codex—*Codex L*—can be traced back to Pforta, the Cistercian monastery on the outskirts of Naumburg from where Fabricius reports *Codex L* had come before being at Leipzig. Prior to Pforta, the Cistercians had stayed for several years at Walkenried, one of several Imperial abbeys in the Harz region—the Ottonian homeland—including Quedlinburg and Gandersheim, both created by Liudoflinger leaders and directed by Ottonian princesses.

14. A More Easterly Provenance?

14.1 Great Contribution from a Small Fragment

The small number of original manuscripts limits the current state of Old Saxon Studies greatly. Researchers in a field that focuses such an ancient topic should probably expect little to remain in the way of primary source material. Still, this situation has been exacerbated for Old Saxon Studies by the numerous major wars that taken place in and near the historical Saxon homeland. It is, nevertheless, quite paradoxical how the story of loss of *Heliand* material repeats itself over the centuries. As an example of this, Hannemann recounts the resources lost in the twentieth century alone (1974, 104):

> Der Praefatioaufsatz in den Forschungen u. Fortschritten des J. 1939 sollte der Auftakt zu weiterreichenden Untersuchungen über den mitteldt. Heliandkreis um das Luthermonotessaron sein. Es kam der Krieg, die Einberufung zur Wehrmacht und am Ende mit dem Verlust der pommerschen Heimat auch der Totalverlust der umfangreichen Vorarbeiten und Materialsammlungen [...]. Gerettet wurde nur der Torso der 1939 in Greifswald eingereichten maschinenschriftlichen Dissertation über Die Lösung des Rätsels der Heliandpraefatio [...]. Der hier gebotene Rückblick auf die vielverschlungenen Wege der Heliandpraefatioforschung ist die späte Einbringung einer frühen, grossenteils vernichteten Ernte. Wenn er über die Förderung der Heliandforschung hinaus der Erschliessung des «Carmen ad Flavium Felicem» durch den Nachweis der unerkannt gebliebenen Reginbertüberlieferung dienen könnte, so wäre das ein tröstlicher Nebenertrag der im wesentlichen schon 1939 gewonnenen Erkenntnisse.

One can only surmise what must have existed up until modern times. Besides the materials that Hannemann reports were lost in the two World Wars, the original from which Illyricus took his *Prefaces* has been missing since some time before ca. 1820. That was the year that Eccard proposed the connection between the *Heliand* and the *Praefatio*-and-*Versus* piece. Nevertheless, a single word—*vitteas*—has allowed researchers to verify the authenticity of the *Prefaces* and, furthermore, to verify von Eccard's proposal. This single triumph exemplifies others, proving altogether that, despite the paucity of *Heliand* resources, there is still a wealth of data in what remains. These materials reveal startling details about the provenance of the Old Saxon epic. Then there is the new find, MS L, which despite providing only a single parchment leaf, is nonetheless monumental. It provides evidence that supports three quite revolutionary conclusions: (1) The Leipzig *Heliand* codex was well-known by many of Luther's closest allies—making the assumption that Luther also knew of it all the more believable; (2) the historical provenance of the *Heliand* coincides greatly with the activities of the Saxon nobility both preceding and corresponding to the Ottonian dynasty; and (3) the *Heliand* poet used as a resource some document that follows the Gospel of St. Mark. The last point is monumental; it causes researchers in the field of Old Saxon Studies to question what has become the status quo regarding when, where, and by whom the *Heliand* was authored.

14.2 Luther and the Leipzig *Heliand* Codex

Until recently, it appeared that the Leipzig *monotessaron* described by Joachim Feller in 1686 had been lost as well. Still, the discovery of MS L in the very institution that Feller once managed is only a small indication of what the University of Leipzig Library (UBL) once possessed. The rumor conveyed by Feller—that Luther once borrowed the Leipzig *monotessaron* codex—has long been taken as myth. Yet, the eventual sources of this rumor can be traced back before Luther's death to men who were very close to the Reformer—to Melanchthon, Borner, Camerarius, Fabricius, and Meurer. That these men all had a hand in the creation of the UBL, in the greater educational changes going on throughout Saxony, and in the Reformation Movement itself, serves as further indication that Luther was at least privy to the existence of the Leipzig codex. MS L thus corroborates physically that which previously could only be deduced (Hannemann):

> Fabricius und Flacius werden als «testes veritatis» für die Heliandpraefatio noch lange, wenn nicht für immer die verlässlichen und unersetzlichen Lückenbüsser bleiben müssen, da ein «Jahrhundertfund», wie er der Ulfilasforschung 1970 in Speyer beschieden war, für die «verlorene Hs.» des Lutherheliand kaum zu erwarten ist.

Hardly expected yet discovered nonetheless, MS L is the *Jahrhundertfund* that successfully replaces the "stopgap" formerly served by the *Praefatio* as evidence linking the *Heliand* to Luther.

Flacius' (i.e. Illyricus') tie to Fabricius represents only one connection that needs to be considered. There is also Manlius' printed statement, which declares outright that the Reformer did indeed have the Leipzig *Heliand* codex. Indeed, together Fabricius, Chemnitz, and Manlius show that all three founders of the UBL knew of the codex well within Luther's lifetime: as late as 1544, if not several years earlier. This is a conspicuous date, considering that the UBL was founded in 1543. Furthermore, the UBL's 1545 dedication by connects him directly to the codex's location, to the library founders, and to Borner and Camerarius as the institution's first two head librarians. Luther was involved with these men beyond the projects of Duke Maurice's educational reform—particularly with Melanchthon, whose sometimes-turbulent relationship with Luther is well documented in the correspondences between the two men. That they were in close contact is not in doubt—both were resident at Wittenberg for most of their adult lives. Thus, it is hardly a leap in logic to assume that, if all three UBL founders knew of it, Luther also knew of it.

Given the interest these men showed in determining the value of the Leipzig codex by appealing to Rhenanus, would they have not included Luther in their plans? It seems unlikely that they would exclude the Reformer from knowing about an ancient document that claimed its commission had come from the Emperor himself—an ancestor of the Holy Roman Title. This is especially true when one considers that it was precisely the issue of unauthorized Bible translation that the then-current emperor, Charles V, cited as Luther's crime. It was Charles V's basis for outlawing Luther in the Edict of Worms. Even more, one need not base an opinion of whether Luther knew of the codex based solely on his relationship to the UBL founders or any other historical character. After all, Manlius' report states explicitly that Luther possessed the codex at one time. One might argue that Manlius' report is hearsay, yet he is repeating what he heard from—in all likelihood—Camerarius (or Melanchthon). The constellation of evidence confirms the rumor: Luther knew of the *Heliand* codex. What he did with it is another matter.

14.3 Ottonian Connection to the *Heliand* Provenance

Thirty-plus years before MS L was discovered, Hannemann posited in his "Naumburger Hypothese" that the Luther-codex and the *Prefaces* can be linked back to the Ottonian dynasty (1974, 104):

> Die sich neu abzeichnende Möglichkeit der Herkunft des Heliandpraefatiokodex aus Naumburg führte wenigstens sekundär in die Nähe des südlichen Ostfalen, das von zahlreichen Forschern als Heimat des Helianddichters bezeichnet wird. Naumburg

läge im Bannkreis der ostfälischen Liudolfinger u. Ottonen. «Wenn man annimmt, dass der Heliand früh in den Kreis der ostfälischen Liudolfinger kam, erklärt sich seine Überlieferung am leichtesten» [...].

Indeed, it is tempting to take the historical information provided above to its logical ends by attempting to link the extant manuscripts back to historical characters and places. Such an involved analysis of the historical details and the implications, problems, and justifications they result in will have to wait. Until then, the discussion in Ch. 13 should give future researchers a head start.

14.3.1 MS M via Matilda of Ringelheim

In summary of Ch. 13, there exists reasonable historical information to link MS M back to Matilda of Ringelheim, who founded Quedlinburg Abbey in honor of her dead husband, Henry the Fowler. This hypothesis is based on the fact that MS M was discovered originally in Bamberg in 1720 (only to be lost again and rediscovered in Munich in 1792). The construction of Bamberg Cathedral (1004–1012) was commissioned by Emperor Henry II, who used that city as his religious headquarters. An avid book collector, Henry II created the library at the cathedral by donating books he had received from his predecessor Otto III (cf. 13.4.3), who was educated as a child under Bernward of Hildesheim. Moreover, while Otto III was still a minor, his sister, Matilda of Quedlinburg, acted as co-regent of the Empire. Matilda became the first abbess at Quedlinburg in 966, essentially inheriting her grandmother's role. Despite never holding the official title of abbess, Matilda of Ringelheim had performed all the perfunctory duties in leading Quedlinburg Abbey since its founding in 936. Matilda of Ringelheim was an Immedinger, and as such a sixth-generation descendant of the Saxon rebel leader Widukind. This fact links her back to the autochthonous Old Saxon aristocracy, whose allegiance was the Carolingians' goal. If the *Heliand* was handed down as part of a cultural tradition, this family alone links the Saxon homeland in the Harz Mountains to MS M.

14.3.2 MS C via Mathilde II of Essen and Matilda of Ringelheim

Similarly, if MS C does indeed descend from a copy of the *Heliand* that was transferred to Æthelweard by Mathilde II of Essen (cf. 13.4.3), then this would also link MS C to Matilda of Ringelheim. The original version of the *Heliand* that Mathilde II of Essen sent to southwestern England—*C for reference purposes—would have been copied as MS C (during which Anglo-Saxon linguistic and paleographic features were introduced). *C might then also be the source from which the Old English Genesis B author pulled his material. By recognizing that *C existed, one can hypothesize still one stage further, namely *C's matrix, *Essen. *Essen would have been the original that remained in the possession of Mathilde II of Essen, since one might safely surmise that she did not forfeit her copy by sending it away to England.

From where Mathilde II of Essen would have acquired *Essen is at present indeterminable. However, it is interesting to note that Mathilde II of Essen was the daughter of Liudolf, Duke of Swabia, who earned that title through his marriage to Ida, i.e. the descendant of another Old Saxon aristocratic line. As the oldest son of Otto I by his first wife, Edith of Wessex, Liudolf had originally been the presumptive heir to the throne. In fact, in 946 he even received "[...] durch einen feierlichen Eid der Großen des Reichs die Nachfolge in letzterem zugesichert" (NDB). However, years later his father's second marriage threatened to produce competition for the throne (the eventual son, Otto II). So, Liudolf, Duke of Swabia, revolted. In his youth, that Liudolf had received an education from Hrotsvitha of Gandersheim, the canoness-poet whose abbey was established by Liudolf's grandfather, the likewise-named Liudolf, Duke of Saxony (805–866), from whom Matilda of Ringelheim also descended.

When Matilda of Ringelheim's son, yet another 'Liudolf', died in 957, he left his property to his daughter, Mathilde, who had been raised in Essen since 953. Mathilde II of Essen's inheritance became the renowned *Essener Domschatz*. Thus, there is a reasonable possibility that Mathilde II of Essen's copy of the *Heliand*—namely the proposed *Essen—was handed down to her from her great-great-grandfather, Liudolf, Duke of Swabia, via her great-grandmother, Matilda of Ringelheim, and via her father Liudolf, Duke of Swabia. In other words, Mathilde II of Essen's copy of the *Heliand* might have stemmed from an original in Gandersheim, a city well within the Saxon's ancestral homeland.

14.3.3 MS C via Mathilde II of Essen and Bernward of Hildesheim

A second possibility for MS C can be seen through Essen Abbey's ties to the Bishopric of Hildesheim, which owned the Westphalian institution directly. Evidence for the *Heliand* at Hildesheim can be found in its bishop, Bernward. Recognized as both a man of letters and a master craftsman, Bishop Bernward created a set of metal doors for the Hildesheim Cathedral on which stories from Genesis are illustrated in frieze (cf. 13.4.3). Due to similarities in theme and visualization to the images accompanying the Old English Genesis B in the Junius Manuscript, the Hildesheim images have been linked back to the Old Saxon Genesis. Considering the aforementioned tie between MS M and Otto III, who received his education at Hildesheim from Bernward himself, it can be speculated that Bernward possessed a full codex of Old Saxon scripture, i.e., one containing both the *Heliand* and the Old Saxon Genesis.

It should also be noted that Hildesheim had historical importance for the Saxons. According to d'Alviella, "[a] stone column [was] dug up at Eresburg or Stadtbergen in Westphalia, under Louis the Débonnaire [i.e. Louis the Pious], and placed in the cathedral of Hildesheim, where it still serves as a candelabrum, [...]" (106–107). This column-turned-candelabrum is thought to have been the *Irminsul* (*Annales regni Francorum*, ch. 772): *Et inde perrexit partibus Saxoniae prima vice, Eresburgum castrum coepit, ad Ermensul usque pervenit et ipsum fanum destruxit et aurum vel argentum, quod ibi repperit, abstulit* ('He [Charlemagne] marched to that part of Saxony, captured the Eresburg fortification, went straightaway to the Irminsul, destroyed that idol, and carted off the gold or silver that he found there').

Charlemagne's destruction of the *Irminsul* was an attempt at converting an old, heathen symbol into a new, Christian one. Its relocation to Hildesheim, founded 815 after moving from Elze (established ca. 800 as a missionary diocese to aid in converting the Saxons) would have made Hildesheim Cathedral a symbolic center of the new religion. This process of converting the old rites into the new religion was similarly the impetus of the *Heliand* epic's creation. Given these circumstances, Bishop Bernward's possession of a *Heliand* codex at Hildesheim would seem rather appropriate.

14.4 The *Heliand*'s Eastern Genesis

Since five of the six extant *Heliand* manuscripts (i.e. minus MS C) predate Bernward of Hildesheim (960–1022) by a century or more and Matilda of Ringelheim (895–968) by at least half of century, it stands to reason that these five manuscripts were in transit before either of these historical figures came onto the scene. It appears that MS V had arrived in Mainz from Magdeburg quite early—ca. 850. This means that its predecessor manuscript, *V, must have been present in Magdeburg even earlier. Consequently, it seems fitting to hypothesize that the *Heliand* was very much present in the East from an early date.

Furthermore, MSS M and C, as well as the Old English Genesis B fragment, can be traced to three Liudolfing/Ottonian locations in the Eastphalian Harz—Hildesheim, Gandersheim, and Quedlinburg—within the century following 850. Given these various links to Eastphalia, I presume that the Saxon nobility had much to do with the epic's movement—perhaps even its creation. This hypothesis is strengthened by the discovery of MS L, which together with MS P can be traced back to the Harz region via the Cistercians at Pforta near Naumburg. This is the likeliest interpretation of what Fabricius meant when mentioning "Naumburg" in his 7 January 1545 letter to Meurer, especially given the educational reforms of Duke Maurice being furthered at the time. Though not conclusive, linking MSS L and P to the Cistercian monks, who arrived at Pforta in the twelfth century from Walkenried in the Harz, provides still more evidence to suggest Saxon *edhilingui* influence in the provenance of the *Heliand*.

14.5 Poet's Use of Something besides Tatian

Beyond the apparent link via Pforta back to the Ottonian home monasteries, MS L provides a new clue about the Heliand poet: that he followed something other than the Old High German Tatian and Rabanus Maurus' *Matthäuskommentar*. This conclusion comes from the presence of a single word—the naming of Peter explicitly—contained on MS L and shared by no other manuscript except for MS C. Given the proposal that MS L (along with MS P) represents the earliest extant manuscript, the presence of this word can be interpreted as being original to the *Heliand* epic, i.e. not a later emendation.

It has been generally accepted that the *Heliand* poet used as his primary resource the Old High German translation of Tatian's *monotessaron*, which was completed at Fulda ca. 832–834. This has been used as evidence for the timing of the *Heliand*'s creation. Furthermore, it has been assumed, in accordance with the Fulda hypothesis, that the *Heliand* poet had access to and made use of Fulda-resident Rabanus' *Matthäuskommentar*. Both assumptions are based on previous observations that the *Heliand* seems to follow the Gospel of St. Matthew, something Tatian's *monotessaron* does as well.

Yet, the *Heliand* names Peter specifically in fitt LXIX—parallel to St. Mark, not St. Matthew. Tatian does not name Peter in the parallel section. That is, Tatian follows Matthew, the Heliand here follows Mark. Where did the *Heliand* poet get this detail if it was not available in either Tatian or from Rabanus's writings?

This small detail, made available by the discovery of MS L and by the relatively recent (i.e. in the latter half of the twentieth century) development of computer-assisted text corpus analysis, has the potential to reveal information not known to the writers of the standard *Heliand* transcriptions. As much of the research performed in Old Saxon studies is based on these outdated transcriptions, a new transcription and, better still, new means of comparison via computer-assisted analysis stands to revolutionize current perspectives on the provenance of the *Heliand*, impacting therewith Germanic Studies as a whole.

Note, however, that this new evidence does not preclude his use of either Tatian or the *Matthäuskommentar* completely; rather the detail from the Gospel of St. Mark indicates that the poet had access to some other, still unidentified resource. What this other resource was will perhaps be discovered through future research, possibly also leading to a more definite identification of the poet's identity, his location, and the date of his work.

14.5 Remaining Questions

It is evident from Feller that the *Heliand* codex was present in Leipzig up until ca. 1686, for he mentions in his foreword to the catalogue published that year that he had found it. Yet he makes no explicit mention of it in the actual catalogue listing of materials. Assuming Feller wrote the foreword after compiling the catalogue list, is his mention of the codex in the foreword a tacit admission of its being lost and/or mutilated?

It is difficult to come to a conclusion on this question. We are left only to ponder this: an Old Saxon codex with a Latin preface (Fabricius) that was commissioned by Louis the Pious (Fabricius, Chemnitz, Manlius) was present at the *Paulinum* in Leipzig prior to 7 January 1545. In 1686, Feller mentions having found a similar sounding codex after cleaning up the *Paulinum*. In 2006 a leaf of the Old Saxon *Heliand*—which has been linked to Illyricus' Latin *Prefaces* and thereby to the codices mentioned in 1545 and 1686—was discovered in the UBL amongst a section of late-Reformation Period theological books that had been donated from the Leipzig Thomaskirche library.

Assuming all the mentions refer to the same document (in whole or in part), only a single, minor hole exists in the story of MS L's tenure in Leipzig: How did the Leipzig *Heliand* codex move the ca. 400-m distance from the *Paulinum* to the Thomaskirche? This might be explained easily: a theological student with access to library scrap materials later received a position at the Thomaskirche and donated his books to the library there. These combined characteristics ought to narrow down the list of candidates to a manageable number for further investigation.

Bibliography

AAV = Universität Wittenberg. *Album Academiae Vitebergensis ab a. Ch. MDII usque ad a. MDCII.* Ed. Carolus Eduardus Foerstemann. Halis: sumptibus M. Niemeyeri, 1841. *Album Academiae Vitebergensis: Ältere Reihe, Bd. 1: 1502-1560.* Eds. Karl Eduard Förstermann, Otto Hartweg, & Karl Gerhard. Aalen: Scientia, 1976.

Alonso, Jord, et al. "The severe gout of Holy Roman Emperor Charles V." New England Journal of Medicine 355, 5 (2006): 516-20.

ADB = *Allgemeine deutsche Biographie.* Leipzig, 1875-1912. 12 Feb 2009. <http://www.deutsche-biographie.de/>.

Anonymous. *Annales regni Francorum.* The Latin Library. 27 Feb 2010. <http://www.thelatinlibrary.com/annalesregnifrancorum.html>.

Arnhardt, Gerhard. *Schulpforte - eine Schule im Zeichen der humanistischen Bildungstradition.* In *Monumenta Paedagogica.* Reihe A: Geschichte der bürgerlichen Bildungspolitik und Pädagogik. Hrsg. von der Kommission für deutsche Erziehungs- und Schulgeschichte der Akademie de Pädagogischen Wissenschaften der Deutschen Demokratischen Republik. Berlin: Volk und Wissen Volkseigener Verlag, 1988.

"Aufsehen erregender Fund in der UB Leipzig: 'Heliand'-Fragment aus dem 9. Jahrhundert." 11 May 2006. *Pressemitteilung.* Ed. Volker Schulte. Universität Leipzig. 14 Nov 2007. <http://www.ub.uni-leipzig.de/service/aktuell/heliand.htm>.

Baerman, Matthew. "Deponency: definitions and morphological typology: to accompany the online Surrey Deponency Databases." Sep 2006. Surrey Morphology Group, University of Surrey. 13 Apr 2009 <http://www.smg.surrey.ac.uk/Deponency/Deponency_typology.pdf>.

Baesecke, Georg. "Fulda und die altsächsischen Bibelepen." *Neiderdeutsche Mitteilungen* 4 (1948): 5-43. Nachtrag (1972). In *Der Heliand.* Jürgen Eichhoff & Irmengard Rauch (eds.).

Bähring, Helmut, and Rüddiger, Kurt, eds. *Lexikon Buchstadt Leipzig.* Taucha: Tauchaer Verlag, 2008: 244-247.

Bartholin, Caspar. St. Thomas 1490. Leipzig, Universitätsbibliothek 'Bibliotheca Albertina'. Two books hand-bound as one: *Jacobi Martini Professoris Academici Logicæ Peripateticæ Per Dichotomias In Gratiam Ramistarvm Resolutæ Libri Duo.* Wittenberg, 1608; *Ianitores Logici bini.* Wittenberg, 1609.

Basler, Otto. *Altsächsisch: Heliand, Genesis und kleinere Denkmäler in erläuterten Textproben mit sprachlich-sachlicher Einführung.* Freiburg im Breisgau: Fr. Wagner, 1923.

Batcher, Dennis, ed. "The Edict of Worms (1521)." 07 Oct 2006. CRI/Voice Institute. 12 Dec 2009 <http://www.cresourcei.org/creededictworms.html>.

Bautz, Friedrich Wilhelm. *Biographisch-Bibliographisches Kirchenlexikon.* Nordhausen: Verlag Traugott Bautz, 1990. 31 Aug 2008 *Biographisch-Bibliographisches Kirchenlexikon (BBKL).* 09 Apr 2009 <www.bautz.de/bbkl>.

Bayerische Staatsbibliothek. *Verzeichnis der im deutschen Sprachbereich erschienenen Drucke des XVI. Jahrhunderts* = VD 16. Ausg. 1.2002 - 8.2005. München : BSB, 2002. Gateway Bayern. Bibliotheksverbund Bayern. 23 Mar 2009 <http://www.vd16.de/>.

Behaghel, Otto, ed. *Heliand.* Halle (Saale): Niemeyer, 1882.

———, ed. *Heliand und Genesis.* 2. Aufl. Altdeutsche Textbibliothek, 4. Halle (Saale): Niemeyer, 1903.

———, ed. *Heliand und Genesis*. 3. Aufl. Altdeutsche Textbibliothek, 4. Halle (Saale): Niemeyer, 1910.
———, ed. *Heliand und Genesis*. 4. Aufl. Altdeutsche Textbibliothek, 4. Halle (Saale): Niemeyer, 1922.
———, ed. *Heliand und Genesis*. 5. Aufl. Altdeutsche Textbibliothek, 4.Halle (Saale): Niemeyer, 1933.
———, ed. *Heliand und Genesis*. 6. Aufl. Altdeutsche Textbibliothek, 4. Halle (Saale): Niemeyer, 1948.
———, ed. *Der Heliand und die altsächsische Genesis*. Gießen: J. Ricker, 1902.
———, ed. *Heliand und Genesis*. Ed. Walther Mitzka. 7. Aufl. Altdeutsche Textbibliothek, 4. Tübingen: Niemeyer, 1958.
———, ed. *Heliand und Genesis*. Ed. Walther Mitzka. 8. Aufl. Altdeutsche Textbibliothek, 4. Tübingen: Niemeyer, 1965.
———, ed. *Heliand und Genesis*, 9. Aufl. Ed. Burkhard Taeger. Altdeutsche Textbibliothek, 4. Tübingen: Niemeyer, 1984. 10th ed., 1996.
Bennett, Charles E. *Latin grammar*. Boston: Allyn and Bacon, 1895. 20 Apr 2005. 15 Feb 2009 <http://www.gutenberg.org/etext/15665>.
Bischoff, Bernhard, and Burkhard Taeger, eds. *Die Straubinger Fragmente einer Heliand-Handschrift*. Tübingen: Niemeyer, 1979.
Boehme, Paul, ed. *Urkundenbuch des Klosters Pforte, 1. Halbbd. (1132 bis 1300)*. Hrsg. von der Historischen Commission der Provinz Sachsen. *Geschichte der Provinz Sachsen und angrenzender Gebiete*. Halle: Otto Hendel, 1893. *2. Halbbd.*, 1904.
Bodarwé, Katrinette. "Essen in Ottonian Times: A Woman's Convent as Symbol of Power and Proximity to the Royal Court." Kalamazoo, 2001. Katrinette Bodarwé. 23 Feb 2010. <http://www.bodarwe.de/kalame.html>.
Bolinger, D. *Aspects of Language*. New York: Harcourt Brace Jovanovich, 1975.
Borsa, Gedeon. "Der Drucker und Buchhändler Joannes Manlius im Dienste der Südslawen." *Studia Slavica Hungarica* 25 (1979). 63-69.
Brandenburg, Erich, ed. *Politische Korrespondenz des Herzogs und Kurfürsten Moritz von Sachsen, 1. Bd. (bis zum Ende des Jahres 1543)*. Leipzig: B. G. Teubner, 1900.
"Bretten." *Wikipedia, Die freie Enzyklopädie*. 10 Feb 2009, 11:36 UTC. 14 Feb 2009 <http://de.wikipedia.org/w/index.php?title=Bretten&oldid=56464270 >.
Brettschneider, Anneliese. *Die Heliandheimat und ihre sprachgeschichtliche Entwicklung*. Deutsche Dialektgeographie: Berichte und Studien über G. Wenkers Sprachatlas des Deutschen Reiches, Heft XXX Ferdinand Wrede (ed.). Marburg: N. G. Elwert'sche Verlagsbuchhandlung, 1934.
Büchsenschütz, Karl and Kißling, Eckart. "Einleitung." In Sigrid Schütze-Rodemann and Gert Schütze: *Pforta: das Zisterzienserkloster, die Landesschule*. Regensburg: Schnell und Steiner, 2001.
Burchhardt, Clemens. *Bistum Verden: 770 bis 1648*. **Strasbourg: Éd. du Signe, 2001.**
———, ed. *Heliand : die Verdener altsächsische Evangelium-Dichtung von 830 übertragen ins 21. Jahrhundert*. Verden: Wirtschaftsförderkreis des Domherrenhauses, 2007.
Camerarius, Joachim. *Thucydides cum scholiis et antiquis et utilibus, sine quibus autor intellectu multum est difficilis*. Basiliae: ex officina Hervagiana, 1540.
Chemnitz, Martin and Leyser, Polycarp. *Harmoniae evangelicae*. Francofurti ad Moenum: Excudebat Iohannes Spiess, 1593.
———, ———, and Gerhard, Johann. *Harmoniae evangelistarum Chemnitio-Lyserianae*. Jenae : Typis & sumtibus Tobiae Steinmanni, 1626-1627.

Cohen, Adam S. and Derbes, Anne. "Bernward and Eve at Hildesheim." *Gesta* 40/1 (2001): 19-38.

Collitz, Herman. "The Home of the Heliand." *PMLA* 16, 1 (1901): 123-140.

Cordesius, Johannes. *S. Hincmari Opuscula et epistolae*. Ed. by Jean Cordes. Lutetiae Parisiorum, 1615.

Cotton, Robert Bruce, Sir. *Catalogus librorum manuscriptorum Bibliothecæ Cottonianæ. Cui præmittuntur illustris viri, D. Roberti Cottoni, equitis aurati & baronetti, vita: et Bibliothecæ Cottonianæ historia & synopsis. Scriptore Thoma Smitho*. E Theatro Sheldoniano: Oxonii, 1696.

d'Alviella, Eugène Goblet. *The migration of symbols*. Westminster: Archibald Constable and Co., 1894.

"Das in der UB Leipzig neu aufgefundene 'Heliand' - Fragment aus dem 9. Jahrhundert." 18 May 2006. *UB Leipzig - Veranstaltungen*. Ed. Petra Löffler. 14 Nov 2007 <http://www.ub.uni-leipzig.de/service/aktuell/heliand1.htm>.

de Romilly, Jacquelin Worms. *Thucydide et l'impérialisme athénien, la pensée de l'historien et la genèse de l'œuvre*, Dissertation, 1947; Belles-Lettres, 1961

Dimitz, A. "Beiträge zur Reformationsgeschichte in Krain." *Jahrbuch der Gesellschaft für die Geschichte des Protestantismus in Österreich* 4 (1883). 49-66.

Dorfmüller, Petra. *Rectores portenses: Leben und Werke der Rektoren der Landesschule Pforta von 1543 bis 1935*. Sax-Verlag, 2006.

du Chesne (Quercetanus), Andreas. *Historiae Francorum Scriptores Coaetanei, ... Cum Epistolis Regum, Reginarum, Pontificum, Ducum, Comitum, Abbatum, et aliis veteribus Rerum Francicarum Monumentis*. Lutetiae Parisiorum [Paris], 1636.

Eccard, Johann Georg von. *Historia studii etymologici linguae germanicae hactenus impensi*. Hanoverae [Hanover]: Foerster, 1711.

Edgar, David and Sachs, Albie. *The jail diary of Albie Sachs*. Methuen: London, 1987. Literature Online. ProQuest: Cambridge, 2005. 15 Feb 2009. <http://gateway.proquest.com/openurl?ctx_ver=Z39.88-2003&xri:pqil:res_ver=0.2&res_id=xr i:lion-us&rft_id=xri:lion:ft:dr:Z0008 41789:0>.

Erlande-Brandenburg, Alain. *The cathedral builders of the Middle Ages*. London: Thames & Hudson, 1995.

Erler, Georg (Hg.). *Matr. Leipz. 1 (1909) - Die jüngere Matrikel der Universität Leipzig 1559-1809; Bd. 1 und 3*. Leipzig, 1909.

———, ed. *Die Matrikel der Universität Leipzig, I. Bd.: Die Immatrikulationen von 1409-1559*. In Otto Posse & Hubert Ermisch (Eds.). Codex Diplomaticus Saxoniae Regiae, XVI. Bd. Leipzig: Giesecke & Devrient, 1895. CDS II 16. 03 Apr 2009 <http://isgv.serveftp.org/Codex/>.

———, ed. *Die Matrikel der Universität Leipzig, II. Bd.: Die Promotionen von 1409-1559*. In Otto Posse & Hubert Ermisch (Eds.). Codex Diplomaticus Saxoniae Regiae, XVII. Bd. Leipzig: Giesecke & Devrient, 1897. CDS II 17. 03 Apr 2009 <http://isgv.serveftp.org/Codex/>.

———, ed. *Die Matrikel der Universität Leipzig, III. Bd.: Register*. In Otto Posse & Hubert Ermisch (Eds.). Codex Diplomaticus Saxoniae Regiae, XVIII. Bd. Leipzig: Giesecke & Devrient, 1902. CDS II 18. 03 Apr 2009 <http://isgv.serveftp.org/Codex/>.

——— and Joachim, E., eds. *Die Matrikel und die Promotionsverzeichnisse der Albertus-Universität zu Königsberg i. Pr., I. Bd.: Die Immatrikulationen von 1544-1656*. Leipzig: Duncker & Humblot, 1910.

Fabricius, Georg. *Saxoniae illustratae. Libri novem*. Lipsiae : Grosius, 1606. Universitäts- und Landesbibliothek Sachsen-Anhalt. 02 Jan 2008. Sammlung Ponickau. 18 May 2009. <http://nbn-resolving.de/urn:nbn:de:gbv:3:1-20503>.

Feller, Joachim. *Catalogus codicum MSSCtorum Bibliothecae Paulinae in Academia Lipsiensi*. Leipzig: Gleditsch, 1686.

Flacius (Illyricus), Matthias. *Catalogus testium veritatis*. Argentiniae [Strasbourg] sumptibus Oporinus (Basiliae): Machaeropoeus, 1562.

———. *Catalogus testium veritatis ... emendatior & auctior editus* Ed. 2: Basiliae: Oporinus, 1562. (The Prefaces occurs in the 2nd ed.).

———. *Catalogus testium veritatis qui ante nostrum aetatem Pontifici Romano atque Papismi erroribus Widukind von Corveyarunt ..., I-II*. Lugduni, 1597.

———. *Catalogus testium veritatis: qui, ante nostrum aetatem ... Nova hac ed. emendatior ... studio et cura Simon Goulart*. Geneva: Stoer, 1608.

———. *Catalogus testium veritatis ....* Frankfurt, 1667-1668.

———. *Catalogus testium veritatis cum auctario illustrante Joh. Cunr. Dietherico.* Frankfurtum, 1672.

Foerste, William. "Otfrids literarisches Verhältnis zum Heliand." *Niederdeutsches Jahrbuch: Jahrbuch des Vereins für Niederdeutsche Sprachforschung* 71/73 (1950): 40-67. Nachtrag (1972). In *Der Heliand*. Jürgen Eichhoff & Irmengard Rauch (eds.).

Friedberg, Emil. *Die Universität Leipzig in Vergangenheit und Gegenwart*. Leipzig: Veit, 1898.

Föstemann, Karl Eduard, ed. *Album Academiae Vitebergensis 1502 - 1560: Ältere Reihe*, Bd. 1-3. Magdeburg: Selbstverl. der Hist. Komm., 1976.

Frings, Theodor and Niessen, J. "Zur Geographie und Geschichte von *Ostern, Samstag, Mittwoch* im Westgermanischen." *Indogermanische Forschungen* 45 (1927): 276-306.

Goldberg, Eric Joseph. *Struggle for empire: kingship and conflict under Louis the German, 817-876*. Ithaca : Cornell University Press, 2006.

Google Finance. "US Currency: USDEURO." 22 March 2011. <http://www.google.com/finance?q=USDEUR>. Citing as its exchange rate source Citibank N.A. <http://www.google.com/intl/en-US/help/currency_disclaimer.html>.

Gößner, Andreas. "Die Studenten der Universität zu Wittenberg." *Studien zur Kulturgeschichte des studentischen Alltags und zum Stipendiumwesen in der zweiten Hälfte des 16. Jahrhunderts*. Leipzig, 2003.

Hawkins, John A. *A comparative typology of English and German: unifying the contrasts*. Austin: University of Texas, 1985.

Hannemann, Kurt. "Die Lösung des Rätsel der Heliandpraefatio." *Forschungen und Fortschritte* 15, 26 (1939): 327-329.

———. "Die Lösung des Rätsel der Herkunft der Heliandpraefatio." Nachtrag (1972). In *Der Heliand*. Jürgen Eichhoff & Irmengard Rauch (eds.).

———. "Der Humanist Georg Fabricius in Meissen, das Luthermonotessaron in Wittenberg und Leipzig und der Heliandpräfatiokodex aus Naumburg a. d. Saale." *Annali. Istituto Universitario Orientale di Napoli*, 1974. 7-109.

Harksen, Sibylle. *Bibliographie zur Kunstgeschichte von Sachsen-Anhalt*. Berlin, 1966.

Haubrichs, Wolfgang. "Die Praefatio des Heliand: ein Zeugnis der Religions- und Bildungspolitik Ludwigs des Deutschen." *Niederdeutsches Jahrbuch: Jahrbuch des Vereins für Niederdeutsche Sprachforschung* 89 (1966): 7-32. Nachtrag (1972). In *Der Heliand*. Jürgen Eichhoff & Irmengard Rauch (eds.).

"Heliand-Fragment (Einbandseite innen)." 26 Jun 2006. *UB Leipzig - Veranstaltungen*. Ed. Petra Löffler. Universität Leipzig. 14 Nov 2006. <http://www.ub.uni-leipzig.de/service/aktuell/heliand_innen.htm>.

"Heliand-Fragment (Einbandseite außen)." 26 Jun 2006. *UB Leipzig - Veranstaltungen*. Ed. Petra Löffler. Universität Leipzig. 14 Nov 2006 <http://www.ub.uni-leipzig.de/service/aktuell/heliand_aussen.htm>.

Henß, Walther. "Zur Quellenfrage im Heliand und ahd. Tatian." *Niederdeutsches Jahrbuch: Jahrbuch des Vereins für Niederdeutsche Sprachforschung* 77 (1954): 1–6. Nachtrag (1972). In *Der Heliand*. Jürgen Eichhoff & Irmengard Rauch (eds.).

Herzog, Johann Jakob. *Realenzyklopädie für protestantische Theologie und Kirche, Bd. 1-24*. Multiple publishers, 1854–1913. Links to digitalized versions of all volumes available at: <http://de.wikisource.org/wiki/Realenzyklopädie_für_protestantische_Theologie_und_Kirche>.

Heyer, Fritz. *Aus der Geschichte der Landesschule zur Pforte*. Darmstadt: Buske, [1943?].

Heyne, Moritz, ed. *Hêliand, mit ausführlichem Glossar*. Bibliothek der ältesten deutschen Litteratur-denkmäler, 2. Paderborn: Schöningh, 1866.

Hickes, George. *Linguarum veterum septentrionalium thesaurus*. Oxoniae [Oxford], 1705.

Hoffmann, Dietrich. "Die altsächsische Bibelepik ein Ableger der angelsächsischen"Index Auctorum Et Librorum Prohibitorum". *Index Auctorum, et Libroru qui ab Officio Sanctæ Rom. & Vniuersalis Inquisitionis caueri ab omnibus et singulis in uniuersa Christiana Republica mandantur sub censures contra legentes, uel tenentes libros prohibitos in Bulla, quæ lecta est in Cœna Dũi expreßis, et sub alijs pœnis in Decreto eiusdem Sacri officij conentis*. Romae [Rome]: Bladus, 1559. Münchener Digitalisierungszentrum. Bayerische Staatsbibliothek. 4 Nov 2005. Signatur: Rar. 1630. 23 Apr 2009. <http://www.digitale-sammlungen.de/>.

Howlett, D.R. "The Verse of Æthelweard's Chronicle." *Bulletin Du Cange* 58 (2000): 219–24.

IISH. "List of Datafiles of Historical Prices and Wages."22 Feb 2009. *International Institute of Social History*. 22 Mar 2011. <http://www.iisg.nl/hpw/>. Including spreadsheets and conversion calculator.

IISH: Calculator = "Value of the Guilder / Euro." 13 Jan 2011. *International Institute of Social History*. 22 Mar 2011. <http://www.iisg.nl/hpw/calculate.php>. For further details regarding the source of these conversion values, cf. "Source note for 'Value of the Guilder / Euro ?' <http://www.iisg.nl/hpw/cpi.php>.

IISH: Allen, Robert C. Consumer price indices, nominal / real wages and welfare ratios of building craftsmen and labourers, 1260-1913 Oxford Department of Economics, 2001. "List of Data Files." 11 Dec 2009 *International Institute of Social History*. 22 Mar 2011. <http://www.iisg.nl/hpw/data.php#europe>. Links to: "Prices and Wages in Augsburg, 1417-1830" <http://www.nuff.ox.ac.uk/users/allen/studer/augsburg.xls>. Excel Spreadsheet based on information from: Allen, Robert C. December 2001 Elsas, M.J. *Umriss einer Geschichte der Preise und Loehne in Deutschland, vol. II*. Leiden. Sijthoff, 1940.

IISH: Elsas, M.J. Frankfurt prices and wages, 1500-1800. Global Price and Income History Group. "List of Data Files." 11 Dec 2009 *International Institute of Social History*. 22 Mar 2011. <http://www.iisg.nl/ hpw/data.php#europe>. Links to: "Frankfurt: 1500-1800." <http://gpih.ucdavis.edu/files/Frankfurt_1500-1800.xls>.

"The Imaging of the Archimedes Palimpsest." *The Archimedes Palimpsest Project*. 23 Apr 2010. <http://www.archimedespalimpsest.org/imaging_initialtrials1.html>.

Grabinski, J. "Chronologie zur Kirchengeschichte Nordhausens." 4 Jun 2008. *Grabinski Online*. 3 Feb 2010. <http://www.grabinski-online.de/ndh/ndhchrono.html>.

Jones, Peter V. and Sidwell, Keith C. *Reading Latin: Grammar, Vocabulary and Exercises*. Cambridge: University Press, 1986 [2002].

Judasson, Hanss. "The Heliand Code." - *Frei Literarisch Orientierte Beiträge* 1 (2007). 2010. FLOB. 18 Apr 2008. <http://www.flob-die-zeitschrift.de/>.

Junius, Franciscus. *Academia : libellus hoc tempore iuventuti studiosae utilis et necessarius, in quo ex linguarum & priscae variaeque historiae monumentis, ortus Academiarum, genera, & partes, itemque studiorum & honorum gradus quos Academiae observant, & quae eo pertinent, exponuntur: ad calcem adiectus est Academiarum totius Europae seu orbis Christiana Catalogus.* 1587.

Juntke, F. *Die Wiegendrucke der Domstiftbibliotheken zu Merseburg u. Naumburg.* Halle, 1940.

Kluge, Friedrich, and Götze, Alfred. *Etymologisches Wörterbuch der deutschen Sprache.* 15. Aufl. Berlin: de Gruyter, 1951.

Kohnle, Armin. "Der Drucker und Buchhändler Johannes Manlius als Förderer der Reformation in Krain und Ungarn." Manuscript for forthcoming publication, 2009.

Kramm, Heinrich. *Deutsche Bibliotheken unter dem Einfluss von Humanismus und Reformation.* Leipzig: Harrassowitz, 1938.

Krapp, Philip, ed. *The Junius manuscript.* New York: Columbia University, 1931.

Krogmann, Willy. "Die Praefatio in librum antiquum lingua Saxonica conscriptum." *Niederdeutsches Jahrbuch: Jahrbuch des Vereins für Niederdeutsche Sprachforschung* 69–70 (1948): 141–163. Nachtrag (1972). In *Der Heliand.* Jürgen Eichhoff & Irmengard Rauch (eds.).

Krogh, Steffen. *Die Stellung des Altsächsischen im Rahmen der germanischen Sprachen.* Göttingen: Vandenhoeck & Ruprecht, 1996.

Lambek, J. "A Mathematician Looks at Latin Conjugation." *Theoretical Linguistics* 6 (1979), 221–234.

Lambel, Hans. "Ein neuentdecktes Blatt einer Heliandhandschrift." *Sitzungsberichte der kaiserlichen Akademie der Wissenschaften,* XXCVI. Bd, II. Hft. 1881: 613–624. 26 Apr 2010 <http://books.google.com>.

Le Gallois, Pierre. **Traitté des plus belles bibliotheques de l'Europe : des premiers livres qui ont été faits. De l'invention de l'imprimerie. Des imprimeurs. De plusiers livres qui ont été perdus & recouvrez par les soins des scavans. Avec une methode pour dresser une bibliotheque.** Paris: Chez Estienne Michallet, 1680. 2nd ed., 1685.

———. *A critical and historical account of all the celebrated libraries in foreign countries, as well ancient as modern : With General reflections upon the choice of books, and the method of furnishing libraries. A work of great use to all men of letters.* Transl. "By a gentleman of the Temple" (attributed to William Oldys). London: for J. Jolliffe, 1739. Digitized 18 Jun 2008 by Oxford Universisty. Google Book Search. 27 Apr 2009 <http://books.google.com/>.

Lewis, Charlton T. and Short, Charles. *A Latin Dictionary; Founded on Andrews' edition of Freund's Latin dictionary.* Trustees of Tufts University: Oxford, 1879.

Liddell, Henry George and Scott, Robert. *A Greek-English Lexicon.* 1940. Winter 2007. Perseus Digital Library. Tufts University. 7 Apr 2009 <http://www.lib.uchicago.edu/efts/perseus/reference/>.

Löffler, Klemens. "Walkenried." *Catholic Encyclopedia,* Vol. 15. New York: The Encyclopedia Press, 1913. 17 Mar 2007 <http://www.newadvent.org/cathen/15537a.htm>.

Lohr, Gerhard. *Geschichte der Universitätsbibliothek Leipzig von 1543 bis 1832: Ein Abriß.* Leipzig: VEB Bibliographisches Institut, 1987.

Luther, Martin, trans. *Das Newe Testament. Biblia : das ist : die gantze Heilige Schrifft Deudsch.* Wittenberg, 1522. Stiftung Weimarer Klassik/Herzogin Anna Amalia Bibliothek; shelf mark vol. 1: C1,I:58b; vol. 2:C1,I58c. Digitized by Göttinger DigitalisierungsZentrum.

———, trans. *Das Newe Testament. Biblia : das ist : die gantze Heilige Schrifft Deudsch.* Wittenberg, 1522. Vol. 2. Cologne: Taschen, 2003 (facsimile).

———, trans. *Das Newe Testament. Biblia : das ist : die gantze Heilige Schrifft Deudsch.* Wittenberg, 1522. "Lutherbibel." 13 Sep 2008, 23:42 UTC. *Wikisource. The Free Library.* Wikimedia Foundation, Inc. 13 Nov 2008 <http://de.wikisource.org/wiki/Lutherbibel>.

———, trans. *Das Newe Testament. Biblia : das ist : die gantze Heilige Schrifft Deudsch*. Wittemberg, 1546. "Lutherbibel." 13 Sep 2008, 23:42 UTC. *Wikisource. The Free Library*. Wikimedia Foundation, Inc. 13 Nov 2008 <http://de.wikisource.org/wiki/Lutherbibel>.

Manlius, Johannes Jacobus. *Luminare maius*. Ciuitate Venetiaru[m] de Giu[n]ta, 1517. 2008. OPAC. Bayerische Staatsbibliothek. 05 Mar 2009 <http://opacplus.bsb-muenchen.de/search?oclcno=165779774> = *Lvminare Maivs Lvmen Apothecariorvm, & Aromatariorvm Thesavrvs : Omnibus cum Mecidis, tum aromatariis pernecessaria ; Opera In Qvibvs Mvlta Clarissimorvm Medicorum Pharmaca, Nicolai Mvtoni Medici Mediolanensis, olim opera, & nunc aliorum plurium diligentissimorum medicorum addita ... Indices Dvo Insvnt*.... Venetiis: Bevilacqua, 1561. 2003. StaBiKat. Staatsbibliothek zu Berlin. 05 Mar 2009. <http://stabikat.sbb.spk-berlin.de/DB=1/SET=2/TTL=1/SHW?FRST=2>.

———. *Loci communi: Nicht allein den Theologen, ... sondern auch den Oberherrn ... sehr notwendig, dienstlich und kurtzweilig 2 Vielfeltige, ... Exempel, Gleichniß, ... und dergleichen viel andere ernste und schimpfliche reden, ... : sampt einem historische[n] nützlichen Calender*. Frankfurt/M.: Feyerabend, 1556. 2008. OPAC. Bayerische Staatsbibliothek. 05 Mar 2009 <http://opacplus.bsb-muenchen.de/search?oclcno=165376949 >.

———. *Locorum communium collectanea*. Basileae: Oporinus, 1562.

———. *Libellus medicus variorum experimentorum*. Basileae: Oporinus, 1563.

———. *Epistolarum Philippi Melanchthonis farrago*. Basileae: Queckus, 1565.

———. *Loci communes Manlii*. Johann Huldreich Ragor, trans. Frankfort: Reffeler for Feyerabend, 1574.

"Manlius, Johann". *Deutsches biographisches Archiv*. Fiche Location: I 800, 395-396. Saur Document Number: D462-1307-1. Source Citation: Allgemeines Gelehrten Lexicon: Fortsetzung und Ergänzung zu Christian Gottlieb Jöchers allgemeinem Gelehrten-Lexicon, worin die Schriftsteller aller Stände nach ihren vornehmsten Lebensumständen und Schriften beschrieben werden / von Johann Christoph Adelung [Bd. 3-6] von Heinrich Wilhelm Rotermund. [Bd. 7] von Otto Günther, - Leipzig [et al.]: Gleiditsch [et al.], 1784-1897. - 7 Bde.

Manns, Sophia. *Zwischen Denkmalschutz und Nutzeranspruch: Wiederaufbau und Erweiterung der Bibliotheca Albertina in Leipzig*. Berliner Handreichung zur Bibliothekswissenschaft, 151. Berlin: Institut für Bibliothekswissenschaft der Humboldt-Universität zu Berlin. 2005. 24 Feb 2009 <http://www.ib.hu-berlin.de/~kumlau/handreichungen/h151/>.

Melanchthon, Philipp. *Loci Commvnes Rervm Theologicarvm Sev Hypotyposes Theologicae*. Basileae: Petri, 1521.

Mitzschke, P. *Die Bibliotheken Naumburgs*. Naumburg/Saale, 1880.

MS C = Cottoniani. Cotton Caligula A. VII sign. 3-11. London, British Museum.

MS L = [Lipsiensis]. St. Thomas 4073 (Ms). Leipzig, Universitätsbibliothek 'Bibliotheca Albertina'.

MS M= Monacensis. Cgm. 25. Munich, Bayerische Staatsbibliothek.

MS P= Pragensis. R 56/2537 (PA). Berlin, Deutsches Historisches Museum.

MS S = Straubingensis. Cgm. 8840. Munich, Bayerische Staatsbibliothek.

MS V = [Vaticani], also 'Fragmenta Palatina'. Palatini Latini 1447. Rome, Biblioteca Apostolica Vaticana.

Meyers Konversationslexikon, Vierte Auflage. Verlag des Bibliographischen Instituts: Leipzig, Wien, 1885-1892. retro|bib. 2001-2009. 13 Mar 2009 <http://www.retrobibliothek.de/retrobib/stoebern.html?werkid=100149>.

Mitzka, Walther. "Die Sprache des Heliand und die altsächsische Stammesverfassung." *Niederdeutsches Jahrbuch: Jahrbuch des Vereins für Niederdeutsche Sprachforschung* 71/72 (1950): 32-39. Nachtrag (1972). In *Der Heliand*. Jürgen Eichhoff & Irmengard Rauch (eds.).

Mohn, Claudia. *Mittelalterliche Klosteranlagen der Zisterzienserinnen: Architektur der Frauenklöster im mitteldeutschen Raum*. In Berliner Beiträge zur Bauforschung und Denkmalpflege 4. [Dissertation der TU Berlin, 2003]. Petersburg: Michael Imhof, 2006.

NOAA. "Autumn". *National Weather Service Glossary*. 12 Jan 2008. National Weather Service. 20 May 2009. <http://www.crh.noaa.gov/glossary.php>.

NDB = *Neue Deutsche Biographie*. Berlin, 1953- . 12 Feb 2009. <http://www.deutsche-biographie.de/>.

Neumann, O. *Katalog der Bibliothek der Wenzelskirche zu Naumburg*. Naumburg/Saale, 1903.

Nyerup, Rasmus, and Petrus Fridericus Suhm, eds. *Symbolae ad literaturam Teutonicam antiquiorem: Ex codicibus manu exaratis, qui Havniae asservantur. Ed. sumtibus Petri Friderici Suhm*. Havniae [Copenhagen], 1787.

Otfrid von Weißenburg. *Evangelienbuch: Auswahl Althochdeutsch/Neuhochdeutsch*. Hrsg., Hrsg., überstzt., kommentiert von Gisela Vollmann-Profe. Althochdeutsche Literatur III. Stuttgart: Widukind von Corvey, 1987.

Oxford Englisch Dictionary, 2nd ed. 1989. 15 Feb 2009. <http://dictionary.oed.com/>.

Peter, Hermann, ed. *Georgii Fabricii ad Andream fratrem epistolae ex autographis primum*. Meissen: C. E. Klinkicht, 1892.

Pernet, Martin. Religion und Bildung: eine Untersuchung zur Geschichte von Schulpforta. In Gottfried Adam & Rainer Lachmann (eds.) *Studien zur Theologie, Bd. 21*. Würzburg: Stephans-Buchhandlung Matthias Mittelstädt, 2000.

Petzholdt, Julius. *Adressbuch der Bibliotheken Deutschlands*. Dresden, 1875.

Quintillian. *Institutio Oratoria*. Loeb Classical Library, IV. Cambridge, Mass.: Harvard Press, 1920. Lacus Curtius. 22 Jan 2009. Bill Thayer. University of Chicago. 18 May 2009. <http://penelope.uchicago.edu/Thayer/E/Roman/Texts/Quintilian/Institutio_Oratoria/10A*.html>

Rauch, Irmengard. *The Old Saxon Language: grammar, narrative epic, linguistic interference*. Berkeley Models of Grammar, vol. 1. New York: Peter Lang, 1992.

Riedel, Horst. *Stadtlexikon Leipzig von A bis Z*, 1. Auflage. Leipzig: ProLeipzig, 2005: 613–614.

Riemsdijk, Henk van. "On Pied-Piped Infinitives in German Relative Clauses." In Jindřich Toman (ed.), *Studies in German grammar*. Dordrecht: Foris (1985): 165–192.

Riese, Christian. "Magdeburg: Jungfrau oder Groß? Der Name erklärt." *Onomastik: Namen und Mehr*. Thomas Liebecke. 21 Feb 2010. <http://www.onomastik.com/on_geschichte_magdeburg.php>.

Rohdenburg, Günter. "Aspekte einer vergleichenden Typologie des Englischen und Deutschen. Kritische Anmerkungen zu einem Buch von John A. Hawkins." Claus Gnutzmann (ed.), *Kontrastive Linguistik*, 133–152. Frankfurt: Lang, 1990.

Rooth, Erik. "Über die Heliandsprache." In Th. Frings *Fragen und Forschungen im Bereich und Umkreis der Germanischen Philologie*. Berlin: Akademie-Verlag, 1956: 40–79. Nachtrag (1972). In *Der Heliand*. Jürgen Eichhoff & Irmengard Rauch (eds.).

Rüegg, Walter. *Geschichte der Universität in Europa*, 2. Bd. München: Beck Verlag, 1993.

Sahm, Heike. "Neues Licht auf alte Fragen: die Stellung des Leipziger Fragments in der Überlieferungsgeschichte des 'Heliand'." *Zeitschrift für deutsche Philologie* 126, 1 (2007): 81–98.

Scherer, Wilhelm. *Zur Geschichte der deutschen Sprache*, 2nd ed. Berlin: Weidmann, 1878.

Schmeller, Johann Andreas. *Heliand. Poema saxonicum seculi noni. Accurate expressum ad exemplar Monacense insertis e Cottoniano Londinensi supplementis nec non adiecta lectionum varietate nunc primum edidit J. Andreas Schmeller*. Sometimes cited as *Heliand oder die altsächsische Evangelienharmonie*. Monachii [Munich]: Cotta, 1830.

———. *Glossarium Saxonicum e poemate Heliand inscripto et minoribus quibusdam priscae linguae monumentis collectum, cum vocabulario latino-saxonico et synopsi grammatica*. Monachii [Munich], 1840.

Schmid, Hans Ulrich. "Ein neues 'Heliand'-Fragment aus der Universitätsbibliothek Leipzig." *Zeitschrift für deutsches Altertum und deutsche Literatur* 135 (2006): 309-323.

Schwenke, Paul. *Adressbuch der deutschen Bibliotheken*. Leipzig, 1893.

Sehrt, Eduard. *Vollständiges Wörterbuch zum Heliand und zur altsächsischen Genesis*. Baltimore: The Johns Hopkins Press, 1925.

Semmelweis, Karl. *Der Buchdruck auf dem Gebiete des Burgenlandes bis zu Beginn des 19. Jahrhunderts (1582-1823)*. Burgenländische Forschungen Sonderheft 4. Eisenstadt, 1972.

Seyfert, Sebastian. *Sprachliche Varianzen in Martin Luthers Bibelsetzungen von 1522-1546: : eine lexikalisch-syntaktische Untersuchung des Römerbriefs*. Stuttgart : Deutsche Bibelgesellschaft, 2003.

Sievers, Eduard, ed. *Der Heliand und die angelsächsische Genesis*. Halle: Max Niemeyer, 1875.

———, ed. *Heliand*. In *Germanistische Handbibliothek, 4*. Halle (Saale): Buchhandlung des Waisenhauses, 1878. Google Book Search. 15 Jul 2006 <http://books.google.com>.

———. *Altgermanische Metrik*. Halle: Niemeyer, 1893.

———, ed. *Heliand: Titelauflage vermehrt um das Prager Fragment des Heliand und die Vaticanischen Fragmente von Heliand und Genesis*. Ed. Edward Schröder. Rev. ed. Germanistische Handbibliothek, 4. Halle (Saale): Buchhandlung des Waisenhauses, 1935.

Simon, Matthias. "Johann Manlius, der erste Herausgeber von Melanchthonbriefen." *Zeitschrift für bayerische Kirchengeschichte* 24 (1955). 141-149.

Simons, Olaf, ed. "Holy Roman Empire: Money." 17 Mar 2008. *A Platform of Research in Economic History*. 5 Apr 2008. Pierre Marteau, Cologne: Virtual Publisher for over 340 Years. 25 Apr 2009. <http://pierre-marteau.com/wiki/index.php?title=Holy_Roman_Empire:Money>.

Smith, Thomas, and Robert Cotton. *Catalogus librorum manuscriptorum Bibliothecæ Cottonianæ cui præmittuntur illustris viri, D. Roberti Cottoni, equitis aurati & baronetti, vita: et Bibliothecæ Cottonianæ historia & synopsis*. Oxonii [Oxford]: E Theatro Sheldoniano, MDCXCVI [1696]

Spangenberg, Johannes. *Postilla slovenska, to ie: Karhauske evangeliske predige (etc.): Die Postille Slovenisch das ist christliche evangelische Predigten ueber die Sonntagsevangelien*. (Übers. von Seb. Krellius.). P. 1. Ratisbonae [Regensburg]: Joh. Burger, 1567.

Spangenberg, Johann. *Postila, to je Krščanske evangeljske pridige*. V Liublani: skosi Ioannesa Mandelza, 1578.

Thompson, James Westfall. *The Literacy of the laity in the Middle Ages*. New York: B. Franklin, 1960.

Thurston, Herbert. "Cistercians in the British Isles." *The Catholic Encyclopedia*. Vol. 16 (Index). New York: The Encyclopedia Press, 1914. 19 May 2009 <http://www.newadvent.org/cathen/16025b.htm>.

Tagungsbericht *Die Sächsischen Fürsten- und Landesschulen. Interaktion von lutherisch-humanistischem Erziehungsideal und Eliten-Bildung*. 01.04.2003-03.04.2003, Evangelische Akademie Meißen. In: H-Soz-u-Kult, 02.06.2003, <http://hsozkult.geschichte.hu-berlin.de/tagungsberichte/id=229>.

Tracy, James D. *Holland under Habsburg rule, 1506-1566: the formation of a body politic*. Berkeley: University of California Press, 1990.

———. *The founding of the Dutch Republic: war, finance, and politics in Holland 1572-1588*. Oxford: University Press, 2008.

"Universitätsbibliothek Leipzig." 2009. *Leipzig-Lexikon*. André Loh-Kliesch. 24 Feb 2009 <http://www.leipzig-lexikon.de>.

Universität Wittenberg. *Album Academiae Vitebergensis ab a. Ch. MDII usque ad a. MDCII, volumen secundum.* Ed. Otto Hartwig. Halis: sumptibus M. Niemeyeri, 1894. Album Academiae Vitebergensis: Ältere Reihe, Bd. 2: 1560-1602. Eds. Karl Eduard Förstermann, Otto Hartweg, & Karl Gerhard. Aalen: Scientia, 1976.

Universität Wittenberg. *Album Academiae Vitebergensis ab a. Ch. MDII usque ad a. MDCII, volumen tertium.* Eds. G. Naetebus & Karl Gerhard. Halis: sumptibus M. Niemeyeri, 1905. Album Academiae Vitebergensis: Ältere Reihe, Bd. 3: Indices. Eds. Karl Eduard Förstermann, Otto Hartweg, & Karl Gerhard. Aalen: Scientia, 1976.

"Value of the Guilder / Euro." 9 Feb 2009. International Institute of Social History. 25 Apr 2009. <http://www.iisg.nl/hpw/calculate.php>.

Vogtherr, Thomas (trans.). *Chronicon episcoporum Verdensium: Die Chronik der Verdener Bischöfe.* Stade: Landschaftsverband der ehemaligen Herzogtümer Bremen und Verden e.V., 1998.

Wackernagel, Hans Georg, ed. *Die Matrikel der Universität Basel, I. Bd.: 1460-1529.* Basel: Universitätsbibliothek, 1951.

———, Sieber, Marc and Sutter, Hans, eds. *Die Matrikel der Universität Basel, II. Bd.: 1532/33-1600/01.* Basel: Universitätsbibliothek, 1956.

WBIS = Walter de Gruyter GmbH Co. KG. *World Biographical Information System.* K. G. Saur. 03 Apr 2009 <http://db.saur.de/WBIS/>.

Wells, C. J. *German: a linguistic history to 1945.* Oxford: Clarendon, 1985.

Widukind von Corvey. *Res gestae Saxonicae / Die Sachsengeschichte.* Ekkehart Rotter and Bernd Schneidmüller, trans. Stuttgart: Widukind von Corvey, 2006.

Wolf, Johannes. *Handbuch der Notationskunde.* Leipzig: Breitkopf & Härtel, 1913.

Woods, Thomas. *How the Catholic Church Built Western Civilization.* Washington: Regnery, 2005.

Wortschke, Theodor. "Markgräflich ansbachische Stipendiaten in Wittenberg." In *Zeitschrift für Bayerische Kirchengeschichte* 2 (1927), pp. 197-207.

Jezierski, Wojtek. "Æthelweardus redivivus." *Early Medieval Europe* 13.2 (2005): 159-78.

Wulfila Project. Ed. Tom De Herdt. 2004. University of Antwerp, Belgium. 26 Oct 2008 <http://www.wulfila.be>.

Zangemeister, Karl, and Wilhelm Braune, eds. *Bruchstücke der altsächsischen Bibeldichtung, aus der Bibliotheca palatina.* Heidelberg: G. Koester, 1894.

Zedler großen Universallexikon Online. 08 Mar 2009 < http://www.zedler-lexikon.de/>.

Appendix A

A.1: Letter to Meurer: 7 January 1545 (17–18)

1545.

XV.
S. Vereor, Volfgange, ne tibi gravis sim multitudine mandatorum; nullas enim post discessum meum ad te dedi literas quae non haberent aliquid laboris atque molestiae. Sed me consolatur amor et humanitas tua, neque dubito tibi imponere, quod tua caussa ipse quoque facturus sim cum libenter tum diligentissime. mihi enim certe officium, quod dignis fit, parit delectationem. Velim igitur cum Bornero agas, ut praefationem illam Latinam sui manuscripti, quam ex Numburgensi bibliotheca habet, mihi describendam curet cum una atque altera pagina veri operis Germanici; cupio enim de eo doctorum et inprimis Beati Rhenani cognoscere judicium atque sententiam.[1] Huic adjunge ex peregrinationibus Italicis Jureconsultorum epitaphia, iis tamen omnibus exceptis, quae Patavii, Bononiae, Pisis sunt. nam ea mecum habeo. Petit a me quidam, quem puto aut ipsum scripturum eorum vitas, aut alicui qui id moliatur communicaturum*). Sturmius nostro rogatu auspicatus est suas partitiones dialecticas, easque aliqua accessione singulis lectionibus auget, efficitque et ratione interpretandi et verborum genere, ut ipse etiam Aristoteles, quem sequitur, facilis et apertus videatur. Utinam ne vis aliqua subiti morbi aut bellum inopinatos nos hinc extrudat, aut machinationes eorum, qui hanc urbem evangelii caussa oderunt, timeo enim quadam animi mei divinatione. Si Vvetteri ita pergent, constituent nobilitati exemplum virtutis et doctrinae, id faxit ad ecclesiae suae et Reip. utilitatem Deus. Litteras hic adjunctas ad Agricolam mitte, ex quibus ille cognoscet, quibus se rationibus ἀνταγωνιστὴς Alciatus tueatur, quod ad ponderum et mensurarum tractationem attinet. Reservat sibi aliquid ille, et ut homines, qui quod respondent (l. respondeant) non habent, id in occupationes rejicit, sed tamen ad extremum manus videtur dare. Si quid novorum librorum apud vos, mihi significa et de Badehorno meo aliquid laeti adde. Vale et me ama. DD. Camerario et Bornero salutem. Argentorati VII. Idus Februarii MDXLV.
Tuus Fabricius.
Doctissimo viro Volfgango Meurero, Philosophiae professori, amico suo. Lipsiae im großen Collegio. postridie Reminiscere. 1545.

---

*) *Sturmius*. Refert haec verba usque ad *apertus videatur* Schreber. vit. Fabric. p. 301

---

[1] "So, I would like you to try to convince Borner to take care when transcribing the Latin preface of his doubtless Germanic manuscript for me, which he has from the Naumburg library, every page of it, because I am interested to know the assessment and opinion of learned men concerning it, including the foremost B. Rhenanus."

A.2: Letter to Meurer: 16 September 1545 (21-22)

Ad ep. XIX. Haec est in apogr. bibl. Paul., in autogr. non servata. Verba Ego Terentium usque ad satisfactum erit labori meo reddidit etiam Schreber. vit. Fabric. p. 214

XIX^a.
S. Superioribus literis scriptis et obsignatis, puer qui ad te iturus erat in morbum incidit; neque ego interim inveni quemquam qui ad vos iret, neque nunc magnopere habebam, quod ad illas adderem, nisi illud scire vis, Sturmium alterum quoque jam mensem abfuisse, neque adhuc, quando lectiones auspicaturus sit, certi sumus, quod sane nobis molestum est. Ego Terentium ex libro illo, quem Romae in Pintificis bibliotheca*) contuli, emendatum intra mensem Vuendelino typographo nostro excudendum dabo. Eum inscripsi Augusto Principi; argumenti illus (epistolae v. praefationis) summa est, Terentium puerili propter res ipsas inutilem et propter sermonis genus intempestivum (esse)†). Explicationem castigationum addere necesse est. ea Rivio inscribetur. Explicabo in iis multorum locorum obscuritatem et veterum imitationem in quibusdam ostendam. Quod si assecutus fuero, ut et quarundam scholarum communis error tollatur, et optimus auctor intelligatur melius, satisfactum erit labori meo. De Odis nihil adhuc accepi a Stigelio, et vellem ipsum ad me eas remisisse. D. Badehorno scripsissem, sed fui occupatissimus, et in fasciculo, quem Hallim misi, etiam ad ipsum adjunctae erant, et maxime de eo sermone scribebam, quem ille tibi retulerat. Vestrum erit, hominis amicissimi et conjunctissimi caussam non deserere. Audivi ei desponsam esse filiam doctoris cujusdam ex aula Principis nostri: quod si ita est, Deum precor ut illi cedat ex sententia matrimonium; puto autem socerum illi futurum aut Cummerstadium aut Pistorium. is tamen qui retulit, nihil certi affirmavit. Novi apud nos nihil est, nisi de novis comitiis Ratisbonae. Hic tributim delectus fiunt, timetur enim Caesar, qui creditur apud Metense hybernaturus. Aurifex, quem tu Venetiis noveras, hic apud me fuit; is Caesaris et Galli legatos ad Turcam profectos dicebat. Strozza Maranum oppidum Venetis vendidit; talibus artibus sibi quaerunt imperium, quod mihi non videtur esse posse diuturnum. De novo quodam societatis foedere inter nostros duces inito hic rumor est. Sed a te plura et certiora expecto. D. Bornerum mone de eo quod rogavi. Vale. Ex Argentina. XVI. Cal. Sept. MDXLV.²
G. F a b r i c i u s.
Doctissimo viro Volfgango Meurero, philosophiae professori, amico bene merito Lipsiae in collegio Principis. IX. Sept. 1545.

---

*) Schreber in Bibliotheca Pontificis.
†) Apogr. Lips. et Schreber. uno tenore sed communi vitio: et propter sermonis genus intemestivum Explicationem Castigationum addere necesse est seq.

---

² "Remind Dr. Borner about what I requested. Greetings. From Straßburg. 16 September 1545."

A.3: Letter to Meurer: 24 November 1545 (22-24)

XIX[b].
Ad hunc locum pertinet epistola ad Meurerum Argentorato XI. Cal. Decembr. a. MDXLV. scripta, quam Schreberus habuit, nunc amissa vel aliquo loco abscondita, cujus hanc partem ille exscripsit vitae Fabric. p. 71.[3]

„Vocas me ad munus scholasticum: sed labor scholarum qualis sit ipse nosti, et ego, cum lego Borneri epistolam ea de re scriptam ad me anno superiore, quoquo modo illud onus fugere cupio; et ex iis, de quibus tu nunc scribis, dissensionibus ac periculis multis, quae quotidie intueor, plane exhorresco. Neque mihi desunt, quae me alio trahant: nam ut praesentem statum omittam, in quo studiorum meorum gratia acquiesco, hoc ipso mense Fuggerorum[4] nomine in singulos annos LL. (fort. CL. v. CC) coronati cum victu, libris, vestibus oblati sunt, adjuncto etiam copioso honorario, si triennium cum Hulderico, quem tu Patavii vidisti, vivere velim. Judicium igitur Borneri, res ipsa, spes amplissimi praemii me facile deterrent ab eo munere, ad quod nemo nisi vi coactus aut impulsus inopia accedit. Verum causas tui consilii affers magnas, caritatem patriae et studia juventutis, quae quidem apud bonorum animos non solum istis quae dixi praemiis, verum ipsi etiam vitae sunt anteponenda. Atqui non una ratio est demerendae patriae et consulendi studiis aliorum, quarum etiam aliquot continet Borneri epistola. Quid igitur facies? inquis. Ego, mi Volfgange, laborem scholasticum neque fugio neque detrecto, imo hunc mihi a puero proposui et in eadem nunc quoque maneo sententia, quem etiamsi non uno aut altero etiam anno subeam et intra breve annorum spatium, non puto me idcirco patriae defuturum aut officio meo, et dum illa mihi comparo argumenta (scr. adjumenta), quae ad tale negotium munusque necessario pertinent, et patria mihi ignoscet et amici viri boni atque aequi concedent. Tamen ad epistolae tuae partem praecipuam."[5]

---

[3] "At one point there was a letter belonging to Meurer written from Strasbourg 24 Nov 1545. Schreberus had it, but it has since been lost or misplaced. He copied the following part in Vitae Fabricii, p. 71.

[4] The Fuggers: a wealthy Swabian family headquartered in Augsburg, known in the 15th and 16th centuries for their public generosity, e.g. scholarships. Similarly, the oldest continuously-operating social housing project—the *Fuggerei* in Augsburg—carries their name.

[5] "'You're calling me to do scholarly favor, yet you know as well as I do how much work this task is. Especially now, as I read the letter about the matter that Borner wrote to me during the past year, I just want to run away from the burden; and because of what you describe now, I'm completely terrified by the dissensions and the many perils that I observe daily. I do not miss the things that would take me elsewhere, since I would [have to] give up [my] present situation, where I gladly give in to my endeavors [and] for this reason: every year during this month 100 (sometimes 150 or 200) awards are offered in the name of the Fuggers5 for living expenses, books, and clothes. This generous award would be of great help to me, considering I want to spend the next three years staying with Ulrich5 (whom you visited in Padua). So, this is what is keeping me from [performing] that favor (which nobody [else] will even come close to unless forcibly bound and compelled out of necessity):

A.4: Letter to Meurer: 18 December 1545 (23-24)

XX.
S. Cum Gregorio Jordano agas, ut, si illi aliquid offeratur Vuerterorum nomine vel nostro, id ne gravetur Francofurdiae Vendelino Rihelio typographo ad nundinas vernas redere: precium vecturae (nam fortasse mittentur libri quidam ex bibliothecis mihi) illi solvetur Lipsiae a Vuerterianis praefectis, si erunt (l. fuerint) admoniti. Nuper Philippus noster Selestadium animi caussa morbo liberatus ivit, et convenit ibi Rhenanum, qui de te, de studiis tuis, de loco ubi esses, de precio quo doceres, omnia interrogavit, cum singulari praedicatione humanitatis tuae. Obsecro te, impetra nobis illam praefationem a D. Bornero, et illi adjunge literas tuas ad Rhenanum: nam cum primum accepero, ego reddam. Versiculos etiam Dantis Lipsiae in collegio Paulino, de quibus, ni fallor, in aliis literis egi, mitte.[6] Scripsi enim ad te subito, et singulis diebus, nam quatuor nuncios (l. nuncius) est hic moratus, aliquid attexui. Vale igitur, mi Meurere, et me ama, et Celerem, Naevium, amicos alios saluta. Arg. IX. Cal. Decembr.
G. F a b r i c i u s.
Doctissimo viro D. Volfgango Meurero, philosophiae professori, amico suo in Leipzig uff dem Fürsten Collegio. XVIII. Decembr. 1545.

Borner's decision, the matter of business itself, [and] the hope of [receiving] the ample prize. You bring up valid reasons in your advice, I'll grant you that: yes, in the minds of good men, the prizes of which I speak are not what should be put first in life only, but also the love of one's country and of the passions of youth. Regardless, there is no one reason for lying under obligation of one's country and for considering pursuing other things, only some of which are contained in Borner's letter. 'What are you going to do?' you ask? Well, Wolfgang, I'm not going to run away from my scholarly work, nor will I shrink from it. Since I was a young lad, I have resolved myself to this, and I'm sticking to that same determination still—even if I do not succeed in one or even two years, and I am unable on account of my country or my office within the short space of the years to come, as long as I provide that evidence that applies inevitably to such business and service, and my country excuses me and my peers allow me—at least toward that particular part of your letter.'"

[6] "I beg you, get me that preface from Dr. Borner, and attach your letter to Rhenanus to it. I will give it to him as soon as I receive it. As for you, send the passages that were donated to the *Paulinum* collection in Leipzig—you know: the ones I keep bugging you about!"

A.5: Letter to Andreas Fabricius: 24 March 1561 (16–17)

[24. Mart. 1561] **78.**
S. D. Gallia nunc est quietior, quam fuit, et Nauarrae rex a religione non est alienus, et puerum regem aiunt recte institui. Iacobi profectio iam instituitur cui literis sum bene precatus, quas dedi M. Schirnero ciui nostro,*) qui propter patrem defunctum iam domi adhuc est et post dies Paschales rursus abbit. Eblebium[†]) autem circa id tempus veniet, cui potes tuas quoque literas mittere et illi prospera optare. D. Neandri opus impediri iniuria hominum malorum doleo, quod iam sub praelo esse vellem: nescio quae sit illi instituta euulgandi ratio, vt partem eius ederet, reliquam interea adornaret[‡]) Literas eius legi, vel potius non legi, quia legere non potui: id ei ne velim signifíces. Cui cum aulis negotium est, non potest grauius habere; cui cum contemptoribus literarum, non potest habere molestius. Sunt tamen eius experientiae etiam vtilitates. Hortare, quantum potes, nostrum Neandrum, ne deponat pus praeclarum suum et fatiget auditores, donec in aliquam formam redigatur. Mitto tibi ex antiquo libro Germanico praefationem, ex qua cognoscis opt(im)os Imperatores Germanorum vere Germanos non interdixisse lectioni sacrae vulgo hominum, vt nostri nunc faciunt Belgicis mandatis et vt totus Papatus facit: eam potes Ienensibus,[§]) qui historiam colligunt, communicare. Habet D. Illyricus Lotharii Saxonis Imp. genealogiam, quam si mihi impetrabis, facies rem omnium gratissimam.[7] Christum tibi remitto, quem descriptum trado Strasburgo, vt curet excudendum, non sumptu tuo, quem petunt typographi, sed eius, qui inde captat lucrum. Si tibi videtur aliter, tuae etiam acquiesco sententiae. Literas Alesii non habeo alias, nisi ad Menium,[‖]) eas si non legisti, mittam proxime. De Trepta cognosces ex literis ipsius; nam mihi ad scribendum non est otium. Filii mei iam bene valent, Dei beneficio: capitis dolores, qui me cruciarunt, diminuti sunt; bene etiam habet vxor. Tibi tuisque etiam precor optata omnia. Vale feliciter. Misena IX. Cal. April. MDLXI. Georgius Fabricius.
Andreae Fabricio Chemnicensi fratri suo carissimo. (Cod. ep. 197.)

---

*) *Fort. Henrico, cui et Iudithae Dasipodiae G. F. carmen nuptiale inscripsit Poem. sacr. I p. 789 sq.*
[†]) *in principatu Sondershusano, domicilium Ebelebiorum.*
[‡]) *V. ad ep. 72, 2.*
[§]) *Alexander A. Scotus [1500–1565] a. 1532 in Germaniam migrauerat ibique fulem euangelicam amplexus maximam uitae partem degerat [A. D. B. I p. 336]; Iustus Menius Fuldensis [1499–1558], 'reformator Thurigniae' [A. D. B. XXI p. 354–356]. Scripta utriusque multa sunt; nam multis contentionibus interfuerung, post Lutheri mortem et Melanthonis et Georgii Maioris doctrinam defendentes.*
[‖]) *Flacio, Musaeo, Wigando, Iudici, uid. ad 72, 1.*

---

[7] "I am sending you a preface from an ancient Germanic codex, from which you will learn that the best and truly German Emperor of the German [people] did not prohibit the common folk from reading the Holy Word, as our leaders are now doing with the Belgian Mandates, and as the entire papacy does: you can pass this on to those who are compiling the history [i.e. the Magdeburg Centuries] in Jena. Dr. Illyricus has a genealogy of Lothar [i.e. Lothair I.], Emperor of the Saxons. If you can procure this for me, you will be doing me the greatest favor of all."

A.6: Letter from Christoph von Carlowitz to Georg Fabricius: 19 October 1556 (418)

Doctrinâ virtute & pietate præstanti viro D. Georgio Fabricio, Ludi Misnensis Rectori, amico suo plurimum deamando.

S. Quod ex libri Syriaci inspectione nullam te vtilitatem cepisse scribis, equidem facile credo: sed de eo dubito, assentiaris ne Lucretio affirmanti, hancipsam & non Hebraicam linguam esse, quâ Christus in terris dum versatus est, vti sit solitus. Quod autem non Saxones solùm, & Dalmatæ, quos nominas; sed etiam multæ aliæ gentes, sacras literas iam inde à multis seculis in sua lingua legerint: id non modo verum esse credo; sed valdè vtile atq; adeò necessarium etiã esse statuo. Quale verò sit factum Heluetiorum, quos nuper translationem Germanicam concremasse scribis; in vrbibus, quoq; consilio id susceptum fuerit: de eo me abs te certiorem fieri cupio. Ac interim dißimulare apud te non possum, mihi nec factum ipsum, nec exemplum probari. Quod ad Genealogiam Saxonicam attinet, est ita, vt scribis: quòd cognatus meus in ijs, quæ meo nomine ad te perferre debuìt, memoriæ lapsus sit.[8] Nam mandata, quæ ad te dedeam eò pertinebant; cùm & à Sabaudiæ, & à ferrariæ Ducibus toties tamq; benignè rogatus essem: vt coniunctionem Domus Saxonicæ cum domibus ipsorum, alterius quidem à Geroldo quodam Saxone, qui filiâ Othonis (si rectè memini) Secundi, clàm patre raptâ, in Allobrogibus consedit; alterius verò filiâ postremi Guelphi, quæ Azoni Estensi nupsit, descendente; ab Agricolâ nostro, me potißimum authore, describi cœptum, ad ipsos transmitterem: cumq; Agricolâ mortuo tibi operus ab illo inchoati absolutio imposita esset, me abs te petere, vt quæ tibi de eâ coniunctione hactenus comperta essent, ea mihi pro amicitiâ nostrâ communicatre velles: nam me viciβim tibi non soùm ea, quæ ab Ernesto Brousfio ijsdem de rebus notata haberem, quæq; tibi ad absoluenda cætera fortasse non omniò nulli vsui essepossent, communicaturũ. verùm etiam honorariũ nõ contemnendum hoc nomine impetraturum esse. Quæ cùm ille minùs rectè ad te detulerit, hisce literis repetenda duxi: teq; magnoperè rogo, vt si quid fide dignum his de rebus notatum habueris, sicuti haud dubiè habes, id mihi per ocium significes. Nã vbi primùm mihi à reliquis negocijs tantum vacui temporis concessum fuerit: cogito tibi currum aut equos isthuc mittere, quibus ad me in Hermannianum meum, quod non pluribus, quàm Dreda miliaribus à Misenâ distat,

---

[8] "Greetings. Surely I find it easy to believe when you write that you have gained nothing useful from your investigation of the Syrian book; but I doubt it that you will agree with Lucretius, that it is that very language [i.e. Syrian] and not Hebrew, in which Christ thought while on earth whenever he was alone. Moreover, I not only believe it to be true, rather I strongly consider it to be correct and therefore even necessary, that not only the Saxons and Dalmatians that you have named, but also many other peoples read the holy scriptures as well as from many secular [writings] in their own language. "In fact," you say concerning the Swiss, "by whom not long ago a German translation was defended in towns and by council": certainly, I myself wish from you for this to be done. But meanwhile, I can not keep you secret, nor approve of either what you are doing or what you possess. As far as the Saxon genealogy is concerned, it is just like you say: that my relative is mistaken in memory of those who ought to permit you."

excurrere; & chartas tuas huc pertinentes tecum ferre poßis. Libros autem, quos significas, omninò te habere oportet: nec dissuaserim, vt præter eos, quos tibi Princeps emendos curare debet, illos etiam, quos Agricola habuit, & haud dubiè alicubi notis peculiaribus insigniuit, tibi commodato dari roges. Vale, & me tibi amicißimum esse, tibi persuade. Dresdæ 19. die Octobris Anno 1556.
Christophorus à Carolobitz.

Appendix B

B.1: Extract from Feller's *Catalogus codicum manuscriptorum Bibliothecae Paulinae, Dedicatio*

DEDICATIO
Munere itaqve Bibliothecarii substituti ante decennium vix obtento, temperare mihi, ut thesauri id patefacerem, haud qvibam, qvin ex Catalogis librorum Paulinorum Anno CIƆ IƆCI confectis (neqve enim recentiores suppetebant) solos Manuscriptos excerperem hinc inde, utpote impressis intermixtos, atq; una cum Oratione, qvam de ortu & incrementis Bibliothecæ Paulinæ in solenni XIX. Baccalaureorum Philosophiæ promotione habueram, in publicum evulgarem.[1]
[...]
[...] Promittebam itaqve novum, eumq; pleniorem & accuratiorem cum impressorũ, tum Manuscriptorum maxime Catalogum, constituebamqve pennes animum firmissime, cum pulvisculo excutere omnia, & qvic. qvid tractatuum in voluminibus Manuscriptis reperissem, bona fide annotare,[2] inqve meliorem pariter ordinem redigere. Nam præter alia beneficia non parce olim in me effusa, & illud Daumio jam laudato, cujus ex disciplina ante XXX. admodum annos prodii; referre habeo acceptum, qvod Manuscripta, qualia describenda mihi subinde dabat; felicius faciliusqve aliis possim legere.
[...]
[...] Prius autem, qvam ad novum Catalogum concinnandum accingerer, unum præter cætera perqvam erat necessarium, Paulinæ videlicet ipsius μεταμόρφωςισ, & nova librorum dispositio; qvod utrumqve etiam unanimis Procerum Academicorum suffragiis decretum tum fuerat [...]
[...] Vindobonensem Cæsaream repererunt talem & ego Paulinum Lipsiensem reperi, confusam nempe ac pulverulentam, non æqve tamen male habitantem, cum Paulina nostra in loco illustri, amplo, pulcherrimisqve fornicibus exornato, non obscuro, angusto & lignis tabulato, qualem ibi Lambecius[3] invenit, sit reposita.

---

[1] "To the officers and substitute librarians on the verge of the tenth anniversary, I was by no means able to restrain myself from disclosing the treasures from the Catalogue of the *Paulinum*'s books created in the year 1601 (not even the more recent were at hand)—and why not?—I should henceforth pick out only manuscripts from there, seeing that printed works are mixed in with them, and ones with the speech, which I had held in the open public for the stimulation and growth of the *Paulinum* Library at the 19th advancement ceremony of the Bachelors of Philosophy."

[2] "Furthermore, I released a new catalogue—even fuller of the great manuscripts, and more accurate, along with that of the printed works—when, in going to shake the fine dust off everything, and having touched something among this, I discovered volumes of manuscripts, I set the pens of the soul most firmly to comment in earnest, [...]"

[3] Peter Lambeck (1628-1680).

Novum itaqve Augiæ stabulum[4] ut repurgarem, pulpita initio, qvæ pro libris supportandis una cum scamnis interpositis D. Caspar Bornerus SS. Theol. PP. & Primus Bibliothecarius An. CIƆ IƆ XLVII. exstrui fecerat, ex Academiæ decreto removi omnia; libros etiam catensis ferreis, qvibus alligati ab illo tempore in pulpitis jacuerunt liberavi, eosqve vice plus simplici propria excussi manu, & à pulvere aliisqve sordibus defecavi.[5]

Labore Herculeo isthoc functus nova in vetere Paulina (nam Bornerus jam olim Paulinam in veterem distinxit & novam, qvarum illa fornicata & columis XIV. suffulta est, hæc superne tabulata habet lignea) Repositoria, adhibitis scriniariis, erexi numero XXVIII, cum loculamentis qvodq; qvinis, qvorum tria inferiora libros in folio, duo superiora libros in IV. & VIII. vel etiam in XII. forma reciperet; cumqve in eadem Paulina vetere XIV. lapidæ stent columnæ, qvibus fornices innituntur, eam in conclavia XIV. eaq; occlusissima, sed clathrata, viridiqve & albo forinsecus coloribus superducta, distribui; Conclavi etiam cuilibet & mensam & sellas duas pro libris respondendis evolvendisqve intuli, qvemadmodum & qvodvis Conclace sive Cavædium lumen à duabus fenestris majoribus (utinam recentioribus etiam, & magis pellucidis!) accipit.[6]

[...]

Scrib. Lipsiæ in Bibliotheca Paulina pr. Non. Mart. An. ær. Chr. CIƆ IƆC LXXXVI.[7]

---

[4] Referring to the Greek demigod who in 30 years had never cleaned his stable full of 3000 cattle, until Hercules came and, in his might, cleaned it in one day (Lewis/Short).

[5] "They found Vienna like that and I found the Leipzig *Paulinum* in total disarray and covered in dust: a poor, uninviting use of the space, whereas the halls of our *Paulinum* could be restored to a distinguished position, spacious and furnished with the most beautiful vaulted ceilings; not how Lambeck found it: dark, cramped, and with its floors covered in wood. And so, I cleared out Augeas' Stable anew: at first the lecterns—ones with stools pushed in under them—that Dr. Caspar Bornerus (D.Th. and first librarian in 1547) had erected to pile up and store books on—I removed everything according to the University's decision. I also unleashed the books from the iron chains, which lay bound to the lecterns since Borner's time; I removed them from the dust and other filth, and spread them out by hand in turn on their own."

[6] "Once I had accomplished this Herculean effort, I set up 28 new cabinets in Old *Paulinum* (for Borner already divided the *Paulinum* in his day into old and new areas: the latter is the room with the vaulted ceiling supported by 14 pillars; the upper story has a wooden one). The cabinets have shelves inserted, five each, of which the three lower ones received the books in folio, and the two upper ones received the books in quarto and octavo, or otherwise those in duodecimo format. Since there are 14 stone columns in Old *Paulinum* upon which the arches rest, I divided it into 14 spaces, each mostly enclosed, but also furnished with grating that has been covered on the outside with green and white paint. Furthermore, I brought both a table and two chairs into the spaces for anyone for placing and unrolling books on. The manner by which the room, i.e. the empty space, receives whatever light it does, is from two very large windows receives (as of late, however, I wish they were more transparent!)."

[7] "Written in Leipzig in the *Paulinum* Library on the day before the Nones of March in the year A. D. M DC LXXXVI" (i.e. 6 March 1686)."

B.2: Extract from Feller's *Catalogus codicum manuscriptorum Bibliothecae Paulinae, Praefatio*

PRÆFATIO
AD LECTOREM BENEVOLUM
[...]
[...] Nec inter latinos non reperiebam raros oppido, ac memoratu omnino dignos. Nam præter illos, qvos inter Theologicos codices MSStos signo manus cum exerto digito feci notabiles, inveniebam *Monatessaron, seu Unum de qvatuor* jussi Ludovici Pii compositum h. e. Harmon. IV. Evangelistrum, qvo libro aliqvando Megalander Lutherus ex concessione amicissimi Borneri fuit usus, & cujus a Polycarpo Lysero in Harmoniæ part. I. p. 13. non fallax fit mentio: expressissima autem in *Traite des plus belles Biblioteqves de L'Europe par le Sieur Le Gallois* pag. 77. 78. qvi Tractatus Gallicus Parisiis A. 1685.[1] denuo prodiit. Inter Juridicos autem *Ivonis Carnotensis Compilationem veterem ac primam Decretorum* in XVI. partes divisam. MSStum certe rarissimum, & juris Canonici veluut archetypum, unde & D. Andreas Rivinus, Medicus, Poeta, & Criticus hujus olim Academiæ clarissimc, qvi illud sumptibus publicis AO 1639. eo reposuerat, illud distinchonei adidit: *Ultima non laus est, Pandectas si qvis Hetruscas Viderit, haud minor est quisquis Ivonis opus*; duos item membraneos Codices *Speculi Saxonici Germanici*, qvi vetustatem Vidobonensi Cæsari, qvem 400. præter propter annorum esse. Lambecius lib. II. c. 8. p. 831. censet, non tam æqvant, qvam suerant, uti non obscure ex orthographia & Dialecto Saxonica magis antiqva. (sunt enim **vetustior a pleraq̃**₃ MSStæ fine die, qvod æjunt, & Consule exarata) licet colligere.

---

[1] "Among the Latin [manuscripts] I did not find the exceptionally rare (not to mention entirely priceless) ones. In contrast to these (which I have made noticeable among the theological codices by a sign of a hand with a stretched out a finger), I found a *monotessaron*—in other words, a *one-from-four* composed by order of Louis the Pious, i.e. a harmony of the four Evangelists—a book which the Megalander Luther borrowed at some point by permission of his very good friend Borner, and of which a mention made by Polycarp Leyser in Harmoniae part. I. p. 13 is rendered true: printed also by Mr. Le Gallois in *Traitté des plus belles bibliotheques de l'Europe* (pp. 77-78), a French treatise that came out again in Paris in 1685."

Appendix C

C.1: Extract from Chemnitz' *Harmoniae evangelicae* (Part I, Prolegomenon, Caput 2, 4-8)

CAPVT SECVNDVM.
De præcipuis Scriptoribus, qui ad inuestigandam & constituendam Harmoniam historiæ Euangelicæ utiliter aliquid contulerunt, & quam quisque rationem contexenda Harmoniæ secutus sit.
DE Euangelistis, quomodo in monstratione ordinis mutuas inter se operas tradiderint, in præcedenti capite aliquid dictum est. Iam de Ecclesiasticis Scriptoribus, qui in illustranda Harmonia historię Euangelicæ operæ aliquid posuereunt, quædam annotabimus.
Lib. 2.
Timot. I.
Har. 51.
In hoc verò argumento illustrando Epiphanius etiam circa annum Domini 280. aliquid operæ posuit. Scribens enim contra Hæreticos Alògos dicit, & hos & Porphyrium, item Celium, & Philosabbatinum ex Iudæis oriundum, accusasse Euangelistas, quod in descriptione historiæ Euangelicæ inter se non consentirent. Ostendit igitur, Epiphanius, in historia Euangelica, si diligens & accurata instituatur collatio, inueniri & distributionem annorum, & ordinem aliquem historiarum. Ex festis enim, ad quæ apus Iohan. nem Christus scribitur Hierosolyman ascendisse, colligit tres annos prædicationis Christi, de qua supputatione in sequenti capite dicemus.
Exempli verò gratia (cum argumētum illud ex professo explicandum non suscepisset) ostendit, quomodo ex quatuo Euangelistarum descriptionibus inuestigari possit historia, à Baptismo Christi vsque ad capturam piscium, Luc. 5. De quo ordine postea in ipsa Harmonia quædam dicemus. Illam autem distributionem annorum, & notationem ordinis historiarum, elegantissimis vocabulis Epiphanius appellat ἀκρίβειαν, hoc est, exactam rationem Euangeliorum: συμφωνίαν hoc est, Harmoniam, consonantiam, concordiam seu consensionem: ἀκολυθίαν hoc est, Ordinem, seriem, seu consequentiam historiarum, qua antecedentia & consequentia inter se cohærent aut coniuncta sunt, & historiæ se consequuntur, sicut Victor Capuanus loquitur. Dicit enim Epiphanius, Euangelica continere εμέωθαπροσαλληλα, hoc est, sicut in Harmonia Musica vocum & sonorum concors ratio & proportio, licet diuersitas quædam videatur. Atque inde sumptum est vocabulum Harmoniæ Euangelicæ.
Post hos omnes Augustinus, videns à multis quidem contexi Harmonias Euangelicas, neminem verò illorum vel ostendere vel exponere rationes ordinis & consequentiæ.
Ipse igitur ex diligenti consideratione & collatione circumstantiarum ita cœpit inquirere ordinem temporum & rerum gestarum in historia Euangelica, hoc est, sicut ipse loquitur, ante quid & post quid præcipuæ historiæ & accidessent & collocandæ essent, vt fundamenta & rationes ordinis, vbi ostendi poterant,

exponeret. Vbi verò nulla manigesta ratio ordinis poterat inueniri, vel quæstionem in medio reliquit, vel quid verisimile videretur, indicauit. Quæstiones etiam de circumstantiis, vbi in descriptione historiarum vel eædem sunt vel diuersæ, licèt similes videantur, ibi etiam variare & quasi speciem diffonantiæ præbere videbantur, eruditè soluit & diligenter explicat, ostendens narrationes quatuor Euangelistarum inter se pulcherrima quasi Harmonia consonare, cõtra illos, qui calumniabantur, Euangelistas sibi non constare in narrationibus, sed inter se dissentire, multa dissonantia, quædam etiam repugnantia scribere. Et libros illos Augustinus inscripsit, *De Consensu Euangelistarum*, in quibus multa, quæ ad illustrandum hoc argumentum pertinent, continentur. Extant illi in Tomo quarto operũ ipsius, p. 371.

Post Augustinum etiam quosdam hoc argumentum tractasse, historia Scholastica, quæ circa annum Domini 1160. composita est, testatur. In illa enim aliquoties mentio fit quorundam, qui post veteres illos vnum ex quatuor scripserunt, & quem ordinem secuti sint, ostenditur, sicut postea in ipsa Harmonia suo loco monebimus.[1]

Rhenanus etiam de rebus Germanicis scribens, Historiam Euangelicam rhythmis Germanicis olim populis Francicis fuisse expositam, videtur significare, tali ratione, de qua iam agimus, ex quatuor Euangelistis decerptas esse historias, sicut ex illis, quæ inde citat, colligitur. Et memini D. Philippum dicere, se vidisse Monotessaron, sumptibus Ludouici Pij compositum, quod existimet in bibliotheca Lipsica haberi.[2]

---

[1] "Furthermore, Historia Scholastica, which was composed around the year 1160, demonstrates that some men treated this subject after Augustine. In it, in fact, it makes mention of certain men after the Church Fathers who composed one [harmony] out of the four [Gospels], and what order they followed. This is apparent, as we point out hereafter in this Harmonia by their respective location."

[2] "Additionally, when writing about Germanic accounts that the Gospel story had been distributed to the Frankish people of old in Germanic rhythms, Rhenanus seems to mean – according to the kind of reasoning with which we proceed in our day – that the stories are plucked from the four Evangelists, as if that which refers to them is drawn directly from them. I also remember Dr. Philipp say he had seen a monotessaron, composed at the expense of Louis the Pious, which he reckons is being held in the Leipzig library."

Appendix D

D.1: Deutsches Biographisches Archiv entry for Ioannes Manlius

Deutsches Biographisches Archiv (DBA)
Fiche Location: I 800, 395-396
Saur Document Number: D462-1307-1
Source Citation: Allgemeines Gelehrten Lexicon: Fortsetzung und Ergänzung zu Christian Gottlieb Jöchers allgemeinem Gelehrten-Lexicon, worin die Schriftsteller aller Stände nach ihren vornehmsten Lebensumständen und Schriften beschrieben werden / von Johann Christoph Adelung [Bd. 3-6] von Heinrich Wilhelm Rotermund. [Bd. 7] von Otto Günther, - Leipzig [et al.]: Gleiditsch [et al.], 1784-1897. - 7 Bde

Manlius (Johann), ein seinen Lebensumständen nach weing bekannter Gelehrter, von dem G. Th. Strokel in Hummels Bibliothek von seltenen Büchern Band II. p. 310 f. einiges anführt. Er war ohne Zweifel aus dem Marggrafthum Anspach gebürtig, studierte zu Wittenberg und war ein großer Verehrer Melachthons, dessen Reden und Gespräche er fleißig aufzeichnete, 1562 hielt er sich zu Basel auf, und nahm zu Wittenberg 1563 die Magisterwürde an. Darauf reisete er durch Teutschland und in einige ans gränzende Oerter, Briefe von Melanchthon aufzusuchen, die er hernach auch wirklich herausgab. Wann und wo Manlius zu einer Bedienung beföder wor-den sey, weiß ich nicht. 1570 bekleidete ein Bruder von ihm ein geistliches Amt zu Kitzingen. Er gab heraus:
Epistolarum D. Philippi Melanchthonis Far-rago, in partes tres distributa, quorum prima varies materias theologicas continent. Secuda familiars epistolas habet quibus plures cum doemesticae, tum publicae res exponunture. Tertia ex diversis doctorum ec praestantium virorum epistolis constat, quibus non solum private sed etiam eccle-siastica et politica negotia tractanture. Basil, per Paulum Queckum. 1565 8. 560 Seiten.

Sind weitläufig angezeigt, in G. Th. Strobels literar. Nachr. von Melanchthons sämtlichen Briefen. Nürnb. und Altdorf 1784. p. 1 folgg. und in dessen Beyträgen zur Literat. besonders des XVI. Jahrh. I. B. 1. St. p. 1 fgg.
Locorum communium collectanea a Jo. Manlio per multos annos, pleraque tum ex lectionibus D. Philippi Melanchthonis, tum ex aliorum doctissimorum virorum relationibus excerpta, et nuper in ordinem ab eodem redacta etc. Basil. per Jo. Oporinum (1563) in 8. 176, 418 und 287 Sei-ten, ohne 96 Seiten Vorbericht und Register. Vergl. Baumgarten Nachr. von merkwürdigen Büchern. VI. Band p 149 f. Hommels Bibl. von seltenen Büchern II. Band p. 302. folgg. Nachgedruckt Basel 1565. 8. per Jo. Wolrah, 801 Seiten, ohne 63 Seiten Vorder. und Reg. Vergl. Baumgarten, l. c. pag. 431. Teutsch übers. Jo. Manlii, herrliche schöne Historien, an vielen Orten gemehrt durch Joh. Huldreich Ragor. Frankf. 1574. Fol.

Libellus medicus variorum experimentorum, quae nunquam in lucem prodierunt. A. Jo. Manlio ex plurimis D. Philippi Melanchthonis et quorundam aliorum clarissimorum virorum praelectionibus collectus ac ab eodem in ordinem distributus etc. Basil. 1563. 8. 82 Seiten und 5 S. Register. S. Baumgarten l. c. pag. 151. Francf. 1566.

Jöcher, Christian Gottlieb: Allgemeines Gelehrten-Lexicon. Fortsetzung und Ergänzung von J. C. Adelung. Bd. 4. 1813.
396

D.2: Excerpt from Manlius' *Locorum communium collectanea* (Tomus III, 99–102)

E N V M E R A T I O   Q V O R V N dam præstantissimorum uirorum, cùm ex magnatum, tum ex alijs familijs ortorũ, qui uel ipsi literarũ cognitione studioq́; indefesso, uel liberalitate & alijs beneficijs de Ecclesia benemeriti sunt, & adhuc in id incumbunt.[1]

COLL.
Philippus rex Macedoniæ cùm aliquando animaduertisset in filio Alexãdro, nõ sane prauã, sed tamẽ asperiorẽ & impatientẽ in imperãdo naturã esse, uideretq́; cum nõ pati domitorẽ asperũ: cepit consiliũ, doctrina & philosophia flectẽdi eum ad suauitatẽ & comitatẽ. Hac ratione adeò correxit & excoluit illã naturã, ut in ipso cursu uictoriarũ uix quisquã fuerit unq̃, humanior ac moderatior.[2]
Ludouicus Pius curauit fieri Monotessaron, id est, concordantias quatuor Euangelistarum, magno sumptu. Quem librum diu habuit apud se Lutherus, & hodie est in Lipsica bibliotheca. Præfatio est partim Latinis uersibus, q̃ ualde boni sunt, partim prosa oratione, etiã bene et Latinè scripta.[3]
Memini, uiuo pio & optimo duce Eberardo Vuirtenbergensi, illam consuetudinem cõtinenter cum obseruasse, ut audiret nobiles adolescentes in cubiculo reitantes Catechismum: & cum alicuius negligentiam animaduerteret, cæsus est in conspectu ipsius & reliquorum nobilium. Carolus Magnus est educatus in Collegio monastico, & habuit principes, qui coacti sunt legere singulis diebus horas matutinas. Et ipse hoc pulchrè obseruauit, ut si quando animaduerteret aliquem ebriosum aut adulterum, iusserit eum legere aliqua capita in Biblijs ab ipso monstrata, contrã ebriosos aut adulteros: ut sic ipsos de disciplina cõmonefaceret. Otto Secundus est educatus in Ecclesia Hildesheimensi.[4]

---

[1] "AN ACCOUNT OF SOME of the most outstanding men (while they stood out from great men, they do so all the more now from those of other peoples) who either were aware of their own literacy and worked tirelessly at it, or have benefited greatly from other services of the Church and devote themselves to it still to this day."
[2] "DISC[ourse](cf. 11.1.2, Footnote 4) Philip the King of Macedonia once noticed an unhealthy defect in his son Alexander, though despite his ruthless and merciless nature when it came to giving orders, he perceived that this situation would not permit a impatient approach: he called together a council to train him in the principles and methods of kindness and gentleness. By this reasoning, he corrected and improved his nature, such that there has hardly been anyone fairer or more humane throughout the history of conquest."
[3] "Louis the Pious saw to it, at great cost, that a monotessaron was made, i.e. a harmony of the four Evangelists. Luther had this book had with him for a long time, and which today is in the Leipzig library. The preface is partly in Latin verses, which are very good, and partly in prose language, also good and written in Latin."
[4] "Concerning the devout and great Duke Eberhard of Württemberg, I remember the way he continually saw to it that the noble children recite the Catechism before bed, and how he turned his attention to the negligence of others [and] was struck down because of this and other renowned deeds. Charlemagne was brought up among the fraternity of monks and

Audiui ab Appiano[5] & Hūmelio,[6] amicis notris, se miratos esse, nostrum Imperatorem Carolum V. uirū occupatum tanta gubernatione Imperij, tamen domi & militiæ contemplationibus & meditationibus in doctrina Astronomiæ adeò deditum esse, ut etiam disputet multa quæ ignorant docti in schola.[7]

Audiui dici à sapiente uiro, nec auditum nec lectum esse, ullum principem tam studiosum fuisse literarum, atq; Carolvm V. Imperatorem, præcipuè cum sit obnoxius multis calamitatibus seu morbis.[8]

Ille plurimùm legit Thucydidem, qui admodū difficilis est intellectu: bene etiam nouit paternam historiam suam: & est consuetudo cubiculariorum suorum, ut postquam manè, iuxta consuetudinem, dixerunt precationes, postea singuli aliquid legāt, donec Imperator surgat: alius Thucydidem, alius Herodotum, alius Liuium, alius Gallicam historiā, alius aliud.[9]

Postquam Imperator surrexerit, recitatis precibus, interrogat, quid singuli legerint, ut sic imperatorem ad hilaritatem excitent. Imperator etiam ipse legit Thucydidem, lectisq́; aliquot pagellis, sumit sibi spacium de ijs rebus meditandi.[10]

Thucydides lingua Gallica est bene uersus, & interpres eius adiutus est à Iano Lascare,[11] qui fuit præses studiorum Lutetiæ.[12]

Granuelus[13] adferens imperatori Thucydidē primò Gallicè uersum, dixit: Hunc librum dono Tuæ Maiestati, sed ea cōditione, ut ea promittat mihi, quòd uelit illum

---

had leaders who were brought in to read passages in the morning. And he kept this practice consistently, so that when he noticed some drunkard or adulterer, he would tell them to read a specific chapter in the Bible pertaining to the very lesson against drunkenness or adultery: so that in this way he might impress discipline upon these people. Otto II was raised in the church at Hildesheim."

[5] Peter Bienewitz (1495-1552), a.k.a. Apian, Apianus.
[6] Johann Hommel (1518-1562), a.k.a. Hummel, Homelius, Humelius.
[7] "I have heard from our friends, Apian and Hommel, that they marvel at our Emperor Charles V, a man occupied entirely by the management of the Empire, yet at home and at war is still given to studying and contemplating Astronomy so much, that he considers many things that the learned ignore in school."
[8] "I have heard it said by a knowledgeable man, that it is neither heard nor read that any ruler was ever so studious in the letters as Emperor Charles V, especially when one considers that he is subject to great misfortune, that is to say, bad health."
[9] "The same man [who told me] has read a lot of Thucydides, who is difficult to understand correctly; nevertheless, he has come to known well the history of his fathers and the traditions of the women's chamber-servants: that in the morning after they have said their prayers (as is the practice), they then read a few passages until the Emperor arises from bed – one [reads] Thucydides, another Herodotus, another Livy, another the history of France, [and] another something else."
[10] "After the Emperor has arisen, [and] prayers uttered, he asks who is reading, in order to inspire the Emperor with cheerfulness. For the Emperor himself reads Thucydides, and while reading a few pages, he take upon himself to consider the nature of their meaning."
[11] A.k.a. Rhyndacenus (ca. 1445-1535).
[12] "Thucydides has been translated well into the French language, and a helpful interpretation of him is by Janus Lascaris who was the head of studies at Lutetia [i.e. Paris]."
[13] Nicolaus Perrenot de Granvelle (1484-1550).

perlegere. Euolutis uerò in eo libro ab imperatore aliquot pagellis, ita placuit, ut tertià perlegeret.[14]

Noster Imperator Carolus Quintus non libeneter multum pecuniæ profundere dicitur: sed tamẽ ualde est liberalis erga doctos. Cuidam Poetæ carmen lingua Italica de nauigatione Africana componenti, donauit mille coronatos. Alius quidam in Gallia uertit Psalterium uersibus in linguam Gallicam, quod ob facundiam ipsius insignem celebratur. Oblato hoc Psalterio Imperatori, dixit Imperator: Non dabo tibi multum. dedit tamen quadraginta coronator.[15]

---

[14] "When Granvelle first recommended Thucydides' poems in French to the Emperor, he said: 'I present this book to Your Majesty, but on the condition that he promises me that he will read it.' Truly, the Emperor's reading of several passages in that book has so pleased him that he is reading it for the third time."

[15] "It is said that our Emperor Charles the Fifth willingly spends much of his wealth, and is all the more generous toward the learned. When some poets were composing a song about an African voyage in the Italian language, he contributed a thousand crowns. In France, another [poet] translated a song into the French language, which is praised because of its extraordinary eloquence. When this song was offered to the Emperor, the Emperor said: 'I will not give you much.' Even so, he gave forty crowns."

D.3: Excerpt from Manlius' *Locorum communium collectanea* (Tomus II, 283–285)

IVDICIA ET MONVMEta uarijs rebus.¹
Rex Danicus legit multos libros Sibyllinos, & dixit eos continere multa mirabilia: sed non esse bonum eos uenire in manus hominum.²
Valla magnum mouit tumultũ, siputans: symbolum Apostolorũ primùm esse traditũ & excogitatum in concilio Nicæno. nam non facit discrimen inter symbolũ Apostolorum & Nicænum. Allegabat dicta ex Iure canonico: & in quibus contra Grammaticam aliquid erratum erat, reprehendebat. Erat enim bonus Grammaticus.
Erasmus unà in conuiuio, D. Martinus, D. Hieronymus Schurpf, & ego: cùm hîc fortè esset alius doctus uir. ubi cùm de uarijs rebus, tum etiam de studijs colloqueremur, ille doctus uir dicit: Recēs perlegi Odyßeam Homeri, quæ erat Germanicè edita: quo libro non quicquã legi ineptius. Certè bellũ illud gestũ esse, & fuisse etiam ibi præstantes Principes in utraq; parte, non dubiũ est. inde aliquæ mutationes secutæ sunt.
Oda septima Pindarica tantæ fuit admirationis apud Rhodios, ut fuerit scripta in templo aureis literis, siue id in pariete, siue in membrana factum sit.
Ratisbonæ in monasterio est Testamentũ nouum, scriptũ aureis literis in mẽbrana: quod uidi.³
Basiliæ fuit etiam nouum Testamentum græcum, aureis literis scriptum: quo ego usus sum adolescens. Erasmus eius etiam facit mentionem, quia eo est usus in emendatione noui Testamenti.⁴
Albertus Durerus, pictor Norinbergensis, sapiens uir, dixit: hoc interesse inter Lutheri & aliorum Theologorum scripta, quòd ipse legens in prima pagina tres uel quatuor periodos scriptorum Lutheri, scire posset, quid esset expectandum in toto opere. Et hanc esse laudem scriptorum Lutheri, uidelicet illam perspicuitatẽ & postquam perlegisset totum librum, oporteret attentè cogitare quid uoluisset author dicere, uel de qua re disserat.⁵

---

¹ "JUDGMENT OF AND TESTA ment to various facts."
² "The Danish King has read many Sibylline books and says they contain many wonderful things, but that it is not good for them to come into the hands of common men."
³ "In a Regensburg monastery there is a New Testament, written in gold letters on parchment, which I have seen."
⁴ "There was also a Greek New Testament at Basel, written in gold letters, which I used as a young man. Erasmus makes mention of it because he makes use of it in [his] revision of the New Testament."
⁵ "Albrecht Dürer, the artist from Nuremburg, an intelligent man, said: The Scriptures differ between Luther and the other theologians to the extent that, within three or four sentences on the first page of Luther's Scriptures, the reader can know what to expect from the whole work. Indeed this is what is good about Luther's Scriptures, namely this clearness and inasmuch as one finishes reading the whole book, it is necessary to reflect carefully upon what the author was wanting to say, specifically, what he was arguing about."

Imperator Carolus V. interrogauit legatum Brunsuicensem, dicens: Audiui in curia uestræ urbis multa esse monumenta ueterum Imperatorũ. Est´ ne hoc ita? Respondit Legatus: Sic esse. & quædam monumenta recitauit. Bene, inquit Imperator: ipse ueniam aliquando, ut ea inspiciam. Vidi ibi monumentum Henrici Aucupis, & coniugis eius, quæ fuit comitissa Northeimensis.

D.4: Names resembling 'Manlius' in *Album Academicae Vitebergensis*

Surname	Origin	Given name	Attended
Mandlinus			
	Halle	Michael	1588–89
Manica			
	Stargard	Johann	1537–38
Manicke, Manecke, Manick, Manike			
	Anklam	Joachim	1566–67
	Herzberg	Andreas	1592–93
	Jessen	Andreas	1559–60
	Wusterhausen	Georg	1582–83
	Wusterhausen	Thomas	1559–60
Manlius			
	Ansbach	Nicolaus	1584–85
	Arzberg	Michael	1597–98
	Brieg	Jacob	1590–91
	Langenzenn	Wolfgang	1572–73
	-- s. a.Maul (Auerbach), Menlin		
Mann, Man, Mannus			
	Arnstad	Johann	1529–30
	Augsburg	Georg	1578–79
	Baldersheim i. Unterfranken	Wolfgang	1582–83
	Bayreuth	Friedrich	1546–48
	Bayreuth	Lorenz	1523–24
	Eilenburg	David	1568–69
	Marienberg od. Marienburg	Christian	1585–86
	Regensburg	Nicolaus	1540–41
Manne			
	Lauingen	Johann Jacob	1597–98
Mantel, Mantelius, Mantell			
		Johann	1502–03
	Aschersbeben	Andreas	
	Aschersbeben	Andreas	

Ochsenfurt	Georg	
Wittenberg	Johann (alias Sacellanus)	1526–28
Wittenberg	Jonas	1540–41
Wittenberg	Zacharias	1539–41

Maul, Maulius

Amberg	Martin	1568–69
Auerbach i. Oberpfalz	Johann (=Manlius?)	1586–88
Bamberg, Diöc.	Sixtus	1515–16
Dietz	Wilhelm	1578–79

Mende, Mendius

Erfurt	Nicolaus	1534–35
Goldberg	Kaspar	1563–64
Hirschberg i. Schlesien	Georg	1599–1600

Mendel v. Steinfels, Mendel a Steinfels, a Steinfels

	Johann Simon (oder Johann Simon aus Steinfels?)	1569–70
	Sebastian	1569–70

Mendel

Auerbach i. Voigtland	Jacob	1518–19
Auerbach i. Voigtland	Wolfgang	1586–87
Neumarkt	Simon	1549–50

Menden *s. Menten*

Mendius *s. Mende*

Mendle

Philocensis	Georg	1536–37

Mendlen

Rosburgk	Nicolaus	1509–10

Mener

Amberg	Georg	1593–94
Köstendorf od. Kestendorf i. Salzb.	Leonhard	1521–22

Menlin
    Ansbach   Johann   1546–48
    -- s. a. Manlius

Mentz, Mencius, Mens, Mencz, Menzius

Döbeln	Johann	1502–03
Eckmannsdorf	Johann	1563–64
Niemegk	Balthasar	1564–65
Niemegk	Balthasar	1528–29
Quedlinburg	Albert	1562–64
Stargard i. Pommern	Joachim	1522–23
Wittenberg	Balthasar	1601–02
Wittenberg	Constantin	1601–02
Wittenberg	Tiburtius	1569–70
Wittenberg	Tiburtius	1531–32

Mentzel, Mencelius, Menczel, Mentzelius, Menczell, Menzelius, Mintzelius

(ordinis diui Augustini)	Cleophas	1511–12
Amberg	Johann	1572–73
Amberg	Thomas	1584–85
Bitterfeld	Peter	1572–73
Döllstädt	Johann	1545–46
Dresden	Johann	1587–88
Eger	Clemens	1550–51
Ellersleben	Heinrich	1579–80
Freistadt i. Schlesien	Balthasar	1572–73
Freistadt i. Schlesien	Johann	1574–75
Glatz	Adam	1572–73
Hof	David	1550–51
Hof	Simson	1576–78
Jauer	Daniel	1601–02
Lanzendorf i. Oberfranken	Georg	1514–15
Lanzendorf i. Oberfranken	Heinrich	1519–20
Lauban	Johann	1577–78
Leipzig	Johann	1570–71
Löwenberg i. Schlesien	Nicolaus	1560–61
Neumarkt i. Oberpfalz	Stephen	1520–21
Schweidnitz	Hieronymus	1539–40
Schweidnitz	Matthias	1572–73
Weissenstadt	Wolfgang	1594–95

Zittau	David	1592–93

Ment
Augsburg	Johann	1586–87
Augsburg	Ulrich	1551–53

Mente
Braunschweig	Henrich	1567–68
-- *s. a. Mende, Menten*		

Menten, Menden, Mentenius
Braunschweig	Johann	1563–64
Braunschweig	Marcus	1587–88
Gandersheim	Georg	1563–64

D.5: 'Johannes Manlius' in *Die Matrikel der Universität Basel* (II. Bd., pp. 130–135, 623–625)

> Rektorat von Basilius Amerbach
> 1. Mai 1561 – 30. April 1562
> BASILIUS AMERBACHIUS, Bonifacii iurisconsulti flius, Academiae Basiliensis rector calendis Maii annno 1561 electus, subsequentes in album studiosorum retulit.
> [...]
> [p. 135 ...]
> 62. magister Johannes Manlius, Onoltspachiensis – 6 ß [= solidus (Schilling)] 1548 I. Wittenberg (Jo. Menlin Onoltzbachensis).
>   Alb. Viteberg. 1, 237b. – s. Anhang.
> [... (62 of 69 matriculants)]
>
> Anhang: Nachträge zu Band 2
> Seite   Nummer
> [...]
> [p. 624 ...]
> 135 62 = Jo. Manlius (Männlein, Mendlein), der erste Herausgeber von Melanchthonbriefen. – * zu Ansbach. – 1558 4. VIII. m[agister] a[rtium] Wittenberg. – 1564 S[ommer] Leipzig. – Pfarrer: 1565 Langenzenn ; 1569 Wiesentheid. – In Basel veröffentlichte Manlius folgende Werke: «Locorum communium collectanea : a Johanne Manlio per multos annos, pleraque tum ex Lectionibus D. Philippi Melanchthonis, tum ex aliorum doctissimorum virorum relationibus excerpta, et nuper in ordinem ab eodem redacta» (1562, bei Jo. Oporin); «Libellus medicus variorum experimentorum, quae nunquam in lucem prodierunt. A Joanne Manlio ex plurimis D. Philippi Melanchthonis, et quorundam aliorum clarissimorum virorum praelectionibus collectus...» (1563, bei Jo. Oporin).
>   «Epistolarum D. Philippi Melanchthonis farrago... A Ioanne Manlio passim collecta, ...nunc primum publicata» (1565, bei Paul Queck).
>   Matr. Leipzig 1 (1909) 279. – Mathias Simon, Ansbachisches Pfarrerbuch, 2. Lieferung (1956) 309.
> [...]

Index

Adelaide of Italy, Saint, 13.4
Adiaphoristic Controversy, 8.3
Æthelstan, King of England 13.4
Æthelweard, ealdorman and historian, 13.4, 14.3
Albert, Duke of Saxony, 8.1, 12.3
Alexander V, antipope, 5.1
Alfred the Great, King of Wessex, 13.4
Altzella Monastery, 13.3
Anglo-Saxon Chronicle, 13.4
Ansbach, 8.1, 9.2, 11.2; see 'Onoltzbachensis'.
Anskar, Saint, 3.3
Apian, Peter, 11.2; see 'Bienewitz'.
Augsburg, Diet of, 9.2, 12.1, 13.5; Peace of Augsburg, 9.2, 13.3
Autbertus, Missonary to the Saxons, 3.3

Baesecke, Georg, 1.4, 2.2, 3.3, 4.2, 6.1, 6.2, 13.4
Bamberg, 5.2, 6.1, 6.2, 13.4, 14.3
Basel, 9.2, 11.1
Behaghel, Otto, 1.4, 2.1, 2.2, 4.1, 4.2
Belgian Mandates, 6.2, 12.6
Benedictine, Order of Saint, 13.3
Bernward, Bishop of Hildesheim, 13.4, 14.3, 14.4
Bienewitz, Peter; see 'Apian'
Bischoff, Bernard, 2.2, 3.3, 4.1
Bollandists, 3.3
Boniface, Saint (Wynfrith), 3.2
Borner, Caspar, 1.4, 5.1, 5.2, 6.2, 6.3, 7.1, 7.2, 10.3, 11.2, 12.6, 13.1, 13.2, 14.2
Braunschweig, 8.1, 8.3, 10.3
Bruno, Count of Pleissengau, 13.3
Burchhardt, Clemens, 3.3

Caedmon, Anglo-Saxon poet, 1.4, 2.2, 13.4
Camerarius, Joachim, the Elder, 1.4, 5.1, 5.2, 6.2, 6.3, 7.1, 10.3, 11.2, 13.1, 14.2, 14.3
Catalogus codicum manuscriptorum, 2.3, 7.2
Charlemagne, 1.4, 3.2, 3.3, 5.2, 6.1, 6.2, 7.2, 11.2, 13.3, 13.4, 14.4
Charles II, Archduke of Austria, 9.3
Charles IV, Holy Roman Emperor, 5.1

Charles the Bald, Holy Roman Emperor, 3.2
Charles V, Holy Roman Emperor, 6.2, 7.1, 8.1, 8.4, 8.4, 9.2, 11.2, 12.1, 12.2, 12.3, 12.4, 12.5, 13.2, 14.2
Chemnitz, Martin, 1.4, 5.1, 6.2, 7.2, 7.3, 7.4, 8.1, 8.2, 8.3, 8.4, 9.1, 9.2, 9.3, 10.1, 10.2, 10.3, 11.1, 11.2, 13.1, 14.2, 14.6
Christian I, Elector of Saxony, 13.3
Cistercians, Order of the, 13.2, 13.3, 13.4, 14.5
Cologne, Archdiocese of, 3.3, 6.1, 13.4
Conrad II, Holy Roman Emperor, 13.4
Corvey, Imperial Abbey of, 3.2, 3.3, 6.2, 13.4
Cotton Manuscript, 4.1
"cuius regio, eius religio," 12.5, 13.3

Dalmatin, Jurij, 9.3
Döring, Thomas, 2.1
Duderstadt, Sanctuary at, 13.4
Dürer, Albrecht, 11.2
Dutch Inquisition, 12.5

Eastphalia, 13.4, 14.5
Eckard I, Margrave of Meissen 13.3
Edith of England (Eadgyth), Holy Roman Empress, 13.4, 14.3
Edward the Elder, Anglo-Saxon king, 13.4
Egidiengymnasium, 11.2; see 'Fürstenschule'.
Eichhoff, Jürgen, 2.2, 3.1, 6.1, 6.2, 8.2, 9.1, 11.1
Eighty Years' War, 8.4, 12.1, 12.6
Elbe River, 3.3, 13.3, 13.4
Ernest, Duke of Saxony, 12.3
Essen Abbey 1.4, 13.4, 14.3
Evangelienbuch (by Otfrid), 6.2, 7.1

Fabricius, Georg, 1.4, 2.2, 5.1, 6.2, 6.3, 7.1, 7.2, 7.3, 7.4, 9.1, 9.3, 10.3, 11.1, 11.2, 12.4, 12.6, 13.1, 13.2, 13.4, 14.2, 14.5, 14.6
Fabricius, Andreas, 4.1, 6.1, 6.2, 7.2, 8.1, 12.6
Feller, Joachim, 1.4, 2.2, 2.3, 5.2, 7.1, 7.2, 8.2, 13.1, 14.2, 14.6
Ferdinand I, Holy Roman Emperor, 12.5
fitt, 2.1, 4.1, 4.1, 6.1, 6.2, 14.5
Francis I, King of France, 11.2

Frankfurt (Oder), 8.1, 8.3
Friedrich IV, Margrave of Meissen, 5.1
Frings, Thomas, 3.3
Fulda Abbey, 1.4, 3.3, 4.2, 6.2, 13.4, 14.5
Fürstenschulen, 6.2, 6.3, 12.6, 13.1, 13.2, 13.3

Gandersheim Abbey, 13.4, 14.3, 14.5
Genesis (OS), 1.4, 2.2, 2.3, 13.4, 299; Genesis B (OE), 1.4, 2.2, 13.4, 14.3, 14.4, 14.5
George, Duke of Albertine Saxony, 13.2
germanicus, 3.3
Ghent, Revolt of, 8.4, 12.2, 12.3
Gisela, daughter of Louis the Pious and Judith of Bavaria, 13.4
Gnesio-Lutheran Controversy, 8.3
de Granvelle, Nicolas Perrenot, 11.2
Gregory XII, Pope, 5.1
Grone, Sanctuary at, 13.4

Hannemann, Kurt, 6.2, 7.1, 8.4, 9.1, 9.3, 10.3, 11.1, 11.2, 13.1, 14.1, 14.3
Harmonia quatuor Evangelistarum, 7.2, 8.2, 8.4, 10.1
Harmoniae evangelicae, 7.2, 8.2, 8.4, 9.3, 10.1, 11.1, 11.2
Harz Mountains, 13.4, 13.4, 13.4, 14.3, 14.5
Hathumod, Abbess of Gandersheim, 13.4
Haubrichs, Wolfgang 3.2, 3.3
Heligandus, Bishop of Verden, 3.3
Henry I "the Fowler," King of East Francia, 13.4
Henry II, Holy Roman Emperor, 11.2, 13.4, 14.3
Henry IV, Duke of Albertine Saxony, 12.3, 13.2
Heyne, Moritz, 4.1
Hickes, George, 4.1, 6.1
Hildesheim, Bishopric of, 3.3, 13.4, 14.3, 14.4, 14.5
Holy Roman Empire, 1.4, 5.1, 6.2, 9.2, 12.2, 12.5, 12.6, 13.3
homeland of the *Heliand* poet, 3.3, 6.2, 13.4, 14.1, 14.3
Hommel, Johannes, 11.2
Hummelius; see 'Hommel'
Hus, Jan, 5.1, 12.2

"Illyricus," *cognomen of* Matthias Flacius (Matija Vlačić), 2.2, 5.2, 6.1, 6.2, 7.2, 9.1, 10.3, 12.6, 14.1, 14.6
Immedinger Dynasty, 13.4, 14.3
Irminsul, 14.4

Jena, University of, 12.5
John Frederick I, Duke of Ernestine Saxony, 12.3, 12.4
John III "the Pious," King of Portugal, 11.2
Junius Manuscript, 13.4

Königsberg, 8.1, 8.4
Krogmann, Willy, 3.3, 4.2, 9.1

Lambel, Hans, 2.2, 2.3
lapidem, 3.3
Le Gallois, Pierre, 7.2
League of Torgau, 12.3
leia, 3.3
Leipzig, 1.1, 1.2, 1.4, 2.1, 2.2, 2.3, 4.2, 5.1, 5.2, 6.1, 6.2, 6.3, 7.1, 7.2, 7.3, 7.4, 8.1, 8.2, 8.4, 9.1, 9.3, 10.1, 10.2, 10.3, 11.1, 11.2, 12.3, 12.4, 12.5, 12.6, 13.1, 13.2, 13.4, 14.2, 14.6
lèse majesté, 8.4, 8.4, 12.2, 12.4
Lex Frisionum, 3.3
Leyser, Polycarp, 7.2, 8.2, 8.4, 11.1
Liudolf, Duke of Swabia, 13.4, 14.3
Liudolf, Duke of Saxony, 14.3
Liudolfinger, 13.4, 14.3
Loci communes, 8.1, 8.3
Locorum communium collectanea, 7.2, 9.2, 9.3, 11.1, 11.2
London, 1.1, 4.1, 6.1; *see* 'MS C'.
Lothar I, Emperor of the Romans, 3.2
Lothar II, King of Lotharingia, 3.2
Louis "the Child," *a.k.a.* Louis IV *or* Louis III, King of East Francia, 13.4
Louis the German, King of Eastern Francia, 3.2, 3.3, 4.2, 6.1, 6.2, 13.4
Ludger, Saint, 3.3
Ludouicus pijssimus Augustus, 3.2, 6.1, 6.2, 7.1, 9.1, 11.1, 11.2; *see* 'Louis the Pious', *cf.* 'Louis the German'.
Lupus Servatus, Abbot of Ferrières, 3.3

Luther, Martin, 1.1, 1.2, 1.3, 1.4, 4.2, 5.1, 5.2, 6.2, 7.1, 7.2, 7.3, 7.4, 8.1, 8.3, 8.4, 9.1, 9.2, 9.3, 10.1, 11.1, 11.2, 12.1, 12.2, 12.3, 12.4, 12.5, 12.6, 13.1, 13.2, 14.2, 14.3

Magdeburg, 1.4, 6.2, 8.1, 8.2, 8.4, 13.4, 14.5
Mainz, 1.4, 2.2, 3.3, 13.4, 14.5
Manlius, Ioannes, 1.4, 7.2, 7.3, 7.4, 9.1, 9.2, 9.2, 9.3, 10.2, 10.3, 11.1, 11.2, 13.1, 14.2, 14.3, 14.6; *as* "Mandl, Hans," 9.2, 9.3, 11.3; *as* "Menlin, Johannes," 9.2, 9.3, 11.2
Maraula, Leonhard (Maravlja), 9.2
Mathilde II, Abbess of Essen, 13.4
Matilda, Princess-Abbess of Quedlinburg, 13.4, 14.3
Matilda of Ringelheim, Saint, 13.4, 14.3, 14.5
Maurice, Duke/Elector of Albertine Saxony 5.1, 5.2, 6.2, 6.3, 7.2, 11.2, 12.3, 12.4, 12.5, 12.6, 13.1, 13.2, 13.3, 13.4, 14.2, 14.5
Maximilian I, Holy Roman Emperor 7.1, 9.2, 9.2
Melanchthon, Philipp, 1.4, 4.2, 5.1, 5.2, 6.2, 6.3, 7.1, 7.2, 8.1, 8.2, 8.3, 8.4, 9.1, 9.2, 9.3, 10.1, 10.2, 10.3, 11.1, 11.2, 12.5, 13.1, 14.2, 14.3
Merseburg, 5.1, 13.2, 13.4
Meurer, Wolfgang, 6.2, 6.3, 7.1, 7.2, 12.4, 12.6, 13.1, 13.2, 14.2, 14.5
Mitzka, Walther, 2.2, 4.1, 13.4
monotessaron, 1.4, 5.2, 6.1, 7.2, 7.3, 7.4, 8.1, 8.2, 8.3, 8.4, 9.1, 9.2, 9.3, 10.1, 10.2, 10.3, 11.1, 11.2, 13.1, 13.2, 14.2, 14.5
Mörlin, Joachim, 8.3
MS C, 2.1, 2.2, 3.3, 4.1, 4.2, 6.1, 13.4, 14.3, 14.4, 14.5
MS L, 1.1, 1.2, 1.3, 1.4, 2.1, 2.1, 2.2, 2.3, 4.1, 4.2, 5.2, 7.1, 7.3, 7.4, 9.1, 11.1, 12.3, 13.4, 14.2, 14.3, 14.5
MS M, 1.4, 2.1, 2.2, 3.2, 4.1, 4.2, 5.2, 6.1, 9.1, 13.4, 14.3, 14.5
MS P, 1.4, 2.1, 2.2, 2.3, 4.1, 4.2, 6.1, 9.1, 13.4, 14.5
MS S, 2.2, 4.2, 13.4
MS V, 1.1, 2.2, 3.3, 4.2, 13.4, 14.5
Mühlberg, Battle of, 12.4
Munich, 1.1, 4.1, 4.1, 4.1, 5.2, 9.2, 14.3

Naumburg, 6.2, 6.3, 9.1, 11.2, 12.6, 13.1, 13.2, 13.3, 13.4, 14.3, 14.5
Netherlands, the, 11.2, 12.1, 12.5, 12.6, 13.2
Neue Landesordnung, 12.4, 13.1, 13.2
Neuzelle Monastery, 13.3
Nordhausen Abbey, 13.4

Onoltzbachensis, 9.2; see 'Ansbach'.
Osiander, Andreas, 8.2
ōstara, 3.3
Osterwiek, Bishopric of, 13.4
Ostkolonisation, 13.3
Otto I the Great, Holy Roman Emperor, 13.2, 13.4
Otto I the Illustrious, Duke of Saxony, 13.4
Otto II, Holy Roman Emperor, 13.4
Otto III, Holy Roman Emperor, 13.4, 14.3
Otto the Great, Holy Roman Emperor, 1.4, 13.4, 13.4

pāscha, 3.3
Paulinerkirche, i.e. eventual home of the Leipzig University Library, 9.1, 11.1, 11.2; *see 'Paulinum'*, 'Universitätsbibliothek Leipzig'.
Paulinum, 2.3, 5.1, 5.2, 6.2, 6.3, 7.1, 7.2, 10.3, 12.6, 13.1, 14.6; *see* 'Universitätsbibliothek Leipzig'.
Pforta Monastery, later made into a *Fürstenschule*, 6.2, 6.3, 12.6, 13.1, 13.2, 13.3, 13.4, 14.5
Philip I, Landgrave of Hesse, 12.3, 12.4, 12.5, 12.6
Philip II, King of Spain, 11.2, 12.5, 12.6
poet, identity of the *Heliand* author, 1.4, 2.1, 2.2, 3.1, 3.2, 3.3, 4.1, 4.2, 6.1, 6.2, 7.1, 14.2, 14.3, 14.5
Pöhlde, Sanctuary at, 13.4
Posa Monastery, 13.2
Praefatio and *Versus*, 1.4, 2.2, 2.3, 3.2, 3.3, 4.2, 6.1, 6.2, 7.1, 9.1, 12.6, 13.4, 14.1, 14.2; *see Prefaces*.
Prague, 4.1, 5.1, 5.2, 9.1, 13.4
Prefaces, 2.2, 3.2, 3.3, 5.2, 6.1, 6.2, 7.1, 7.2, 9.1, 10.3, 11.1, 12.6, 14.1, 14.3, 14.6; *see* '*Praefatio* and *Versus*'.

Quedlinburg Abbey, 13.4, 14.3, 14.5
"Quercetanus" *cognomen of* Andreas du Chesne, 6.1, 7.2

Rabanus Maurus, Archbishop of Mainz, 1.4, 3.3, 14.5
Rauch, Irmengard, 2.2, 2.3, 3.1, 4.1, 6.1, 6.2, 8.2, 9.1, 9.3, 11.1
RE (Reporting Event), 8.2, 8.4, 9.3, 10.1, 10.3, 10.3, 11.1, 11.3
Regensburg, 11.2, 13.4
Reinhold, Erasmus, 11.2
Rhenanus, Beatus, 6.2, 7.1, 13.1, 14.2
Rooth, Erik, 2.2
rumors of Luther's possession of an Old Saxon *monotessaron* in Leipzig, 1.1, 1.2, 1.4, 4.2, 5.2, 7.1, 7.2, 7.3, 7.4, 8.2, 8.4, 9.1, 9.2, 9.3, 10.3, 11.2, 13.1, 14.2, 14.3

Saalfeld, 8.1
Sahm, Heike, 2.1, 2.2, 2.3
Sanctae Mariae ad Portam, 13.3
Saxony, Albertine, 12.3, 12.4, 13.2; Ernestine, 12.3, 12.4
Schmalkaldic War, 6.2, 7.1, 8.1, 8.4, 12.3, 12.3, 12.4, 12.5, 12.6
Schmeller, J. A., 1.3, 1.4, 3.3, 4.1, 5.2, 6.1, 7.1
Schmid, Hans Ulrich, 2.1, 2.3, 9.1, 11.1
Schmölln Abbey, 13.3, 13.4
Seventeen Provinces, 8.4, 12.2, 12.5, 13.2
Sievers, Eduard, 1.4, 2.1, 3.3, 4.1, 4.2
Slovenia, 9.2
Smith, Thomas, 6.1
Sophia I, Princess-Abbess of Gandersheim, 13.4, 13.4
Sorbian population in Saxony, 13.3
Spangenbergische Chronik, 3.3
St. Mark, 14.2, 14.6
St. Pauli, 6.2, 13.2
Stellinga Revolt, 3.2
Strasbourg Oaths, 3.2
Straubing, 2.2
Styria, 9.2, 11.2
Suleiman "the Magnificent," Sultan, 11.2
Sylvester II, Pope, 13.4

Tacitus, Publius Cornelius, 3.3
Taeger, Burkhard, 2.1, 2.2, 2.3, 3.3, 3.3, 4.1, 4.2, 13.4
Tatian, metonym for Tatian the Assyrian's *Diatesssaron*, 1.4, 2.2, 3.3, 4.2, 14.5, 14.6
TE (Transfer Event), 8.2, 8.3, 9.3, 10.1, 10.2, 10.3, 11.1
theodiscus, 3.3
thitt, 2.3, 4.1, 4.2
Thucydides, 11.2, 13.1
Treaty of Verdun, 3.2, 3.3
Tübingen, 9.2

Universitätsbibliothek Leipzig (UBL), 2.2, 5.1, 5.2, 6.2, 7.2, 9.1, 9.2, 10.3, 11.1, 11.2, 12.6, 13.1, 13.2, 14.2, 14.3, 14.6
Udo I, Bishop of Naumburg, 13.3
Ungnad, Hans, Freiherr von Sonneck, 9.2, 9.3

Vatican, 1.1, 3.3, 8.4
Verden, Bishopric of, 1.4, 3.3
Vltava River, 13.4
von Eccard, Johann Georg, 3.2, 5.2, 6.1, 6.2, 7.1, 14.2
Vreden Abbey, 1.4

Walkenried Abbey, 13.3, 13.4, 14.5
Wenceslas, King of the Romans, 5.1
Werden Abbey, 1.4, 3.3
Wessex, 13.4, 14.3
Wettin, House of, 12.3, 12.4, 12.5, 13.3
Widukind, Saxon leader, 3.3, 13.4
Widukind of Corvey, monk-scribe, 3.2, 6.2, 13.4, 14.3
Wilhelm II, Margrave of Meissen, 5.1
Wittenberg, 1.2, 2.2, 6.1, 6.2, 7.2, 7.3, 8.1, 8.2, 8.3, 8.4, 9.1, 9.2, 9.3, 10.3, 11.1, 11.2, 12.3, 12.4, 12.5, 13.1, 14.2
Worms, 8.3, 12.1, 12.3, 12.4, 12.5; Edict of Worms, 6.2, 8.4, 12.1, 12.2, 12.3, 12.4, 12.5, 12.6, 14.3
Wrede, Fredinand, 3.3, 13.4
Würzburg, 3.2, 52, 6.1, 13.4

Zeitz, Bishopric of, 13.1, 13.2, 13.3

BERKELEY INSIGHTS IN LINGUISTICS AND SEMIOTICS

Irmengard Rauch
General Editor

Through the publication of groundbreaking scholarly research, this series deals with language and the multiple and varied paradigms through which it is studied. Language as viewed by linguists represents micrometa-approaches that intersect with macrometa-approaches of semiotists who understand language as an inlay to all experience. This data-based series bridges study of the sciences with that of the humanities.

To order other books in this series, please contact our Customer Service Department at:

800-770-LANG (within the U.S.)
212-647-7706 (outside the U.S.)
212-647-7707 FAX
CustomerService@plang.com

Or browse online by series at:
www.peterlang.com